International
Political Economy
in the 21st Century

International Political Economy in the 21st Century

Contemporary Issues and Analyses

Roy Smith, Imad El-Anis and Christopher Farrands

Longman
is an imprint of

Harlow, England • London • New York • Boston • San Francisco • Toronto
Sydney • Tokyo • Singapore • Hong Kong • Seoul • Taipei • New Delhi
Cape Town • Madrid • Mexico City • Amsterdam • Munich • Paris • Milan

Pearson Education Limited
Edinburgh Gate
Harlow
Essex CM20 2JE
England

and Associated Companies throughout the world

Visit us on the World Wide Web at:
www.pearsoned.co.uk

First published 2011

ISBN 978-0-582-47368-3

British Library Cataloguing-in-Publication Data
A catalogue record for this book is available from the British Library

Library of Congress Cataloging-in-Publication Data
Smith, Roy H.
   International political economy in the 21st century : contemporary issues and analyses / Roy Smith, Imad El-Anis, and Christopher Farrands.
      p. cm.
   Includes index.
   ISBN 978-0-582-47368-3 (pbk.)
   1. International relations—History—21st century. 2. Globalization. 3. International economic relations. I. El-Anis, Imad. II. Farrands, Chris. III. Title.
   JZ1318.S625 2011
   337—dc22

                                                                                            2010044451

10 9 8 7 6 5 4 3 2 1
14 13 12 11 10

Typeset in 10/12 Times by 3
Printed by Ashford Colour Press Ltd., Gosport

Brief contents

Contents

Introduction   1

1 The theoretical foundations of IPE   7

2 Mainstream contemporary approaches of IPE   23

3 Alternative contemporary approaches of IPE   41

4 Globalisation and IPE   63

5 National, international, regional and global governance   83

6 Trade   99

7 Global finance   115

8 Development   131

List of figures and tables

Figures

Tables

Contributors

Dr Roy Smith is Principal Lecturer in International Relations at Nottingham Trent University, and received his PhD from Southampton University and specialises in the IR and IPE of Australasia and the Pacific Islands.

Dr Imad El-Anis is Lecturer in International Relations at Nottingham Trent University, and received his PhD from Nottingham Trent University and specialises in the IR and IPE of the Middle East and North Africa.

Dr Christopher Farrands is Principal Lecturer in International Relations at Nottingham Trent University, and received his PhD from Nottingham Trent University and specialises in IR and IPE theory and philosophy and the European Union.

Preface

This textbook is intended as an aid to study for those looking at IPE as a discrete discipline, or as a part of a broader Politics, International Relations or Global Studies degree programme. It can be read as an introductory text, or as a supplement to prior reading in related fields. For example, most universities offer IPE as a second-year optional module which will build on first-year foundations that introduce concepts of power, wealth distribution and the respective roles of governments, non-governmental organisations and market forces.

IPE is a field of study that has increasing significance in relation to 'everyday' life. Processes of globalisation are both widening and deepening and are impacted upon by a range of events and related processes which are beyond the control of most individuals and even their national governments.

The manner in which this book is structured is designed to enable students to gain an initial understanding of the historical and philosophical foundations of various approaches to the study of IPE. This is then followed by a closer look at what might be described as the mainstream approaches. However, one of the appealing aspects of this discipline is the diversity of approaches that it encompasses, and we then go on to look at a number of alternative approaches. It is not suggested that this is a fully exhaustive list of such approaches but it does include a representative range.

Between the theory section and the issues section there is a linking chapter that discusses processes of globalisation and how these are represented and analysed by various schools of thought. There is quite a broad spectrum of attitudes towards the scale and importance of globalisation. For some authors these processes are at the heart of IPE and cannot be underestimated in terms of their impacts in shaping the contemporary world. They apply at the political, cultural and socio-economic levels, and also have huge environmental impacts. Others have a more sceptical approach and refer back to international trading patterns that have developed over several centuries. Although the scale and speed of transport and communication systems may have advanced significantly over time, the fundamental trade and other international relationships have not changed that dramatically. It remains a largely state-centric and competitive world. Finally, there are those who inhabit the middle ground between these two extreme positions. They recognise the importance of new technologies and that issues of scale and speed do have an impact on relationships, but they also note the ongoing relevance of the state as a political unit and the lack of meaningful global governance.

The final section looks at a number of issue areas identified as relevant to the study of IPE. By definition there is a certain element of selectivity taking place here in determining which issues are deemed 'worthy' of a chapter. Health is clearly a major issue but rather than having its own chapter, health issues are raised in other parts of the book, such as in the chapter on development. Similarly, the role of the media plays a crucial part in how processes of globalisation are understood. Indeed, media organisations are active players and key drivers in many aspects of these processes. This point is referred to in the chapter on technology and elsewhere in the book. Hopefully the reader should see that the issue areas intersect with each other and are only a sample of the myriad examples that could have been included. If you notice a particular 'gap' it would be worthwhile reflecting on why it is that you feel that a particular issue area has not received due attention. That may also indicate what type of theoretical approach you may feel most at ease with. We all have preferences in terms of how we view the world. One of the purposes of this book is to draw attention to both the range of issues that IPE is concerned with studying and the fact that there are many differing ways in which to study them.

Roy Smith
Imad El-Anis
Christopher Farrands

Acknowledgements

The authors would like to recognise the contributions made by those involved with this project in its initial stages. These include Chris White, Jilly Walden and Stephen Hurt. We would also like to thank the several editors at Pearson Education who have been involved during the preparation of this manuscript.

Roy Smith
Imad El-Anis
Christopher Farrands

Publisher's acknowledgements

We are grateful to the following for permission to reproduce copyright material:

Figures
Figure 9.1: Adapted from the original data published in 'Attitudes of European citizens towards the environment', *Special Eurobarometer*, 295, p. 11 (European Commission, 2008). Copyright © European Union 2008, responsibility for the adaption lies entirely with Pearson Education Ltd; Figure 11.1: From Andy Singer, The Funny Times (www.funnytimes.com/cartoons.php?cartoon_id= 19981202); Figure 12.1: From Food and Agriculture Organization of the United Nations, Aquastat, global map: Total actual renewable water resources per inhabitant, http://www.fao.org/nr/water/aquastat/globalmaps/index.stm

Tables
Table 9.2: Adapted from *State of the World's Forests 2009* (Food and Agriculture Organization of the United Nations, 2009)

Every effort has been made to trace the copyright holders and we apologise in advance for any unintentional omissions. We would be pleased to insert the appropriate acknowledgement in any subsequent edition of this publication.

List of abbreviations

ACP	African, Caribbean and Pacific
AOSIS	Alliance of Small Island States
APEC	Asia-Pacific Economic Council
ASEAN	Association of South East Asian Nations
BIS	Bank for International Settlements
CDOs	collateralised debt obligations
CFA	Chartered Financial Analyst
CRAs	Credit Rating Agencies
CSR	Corporate Social Responsibility
ERTMS	The European Rail Traffic Management System
EU	European Union
FDI	Foreign Direct Investment
FTA	Free Trade Agreement
GAFTA	Greater Arab Free Trade Area
GATS	General Agreement on Trade in Services
GATT	General Agreement on Tariffs and Trade
GCC	Gulf Cooperation Council
GDP	gross domestic product
GNI	gross national income
GNP	gross national product
G7	Group of Seven
G20	Group of Twenty
HST	Hegemonic stability theory
ICBMs	intercontinental ballistic missiles
ICC	International Criminal Court
IGF	Internet Governance Forum
IGOs	intergovernmental organisations
IMC	Independent Media Centre
IMF	International Monetary Fund
INGO	International non-governmental organisations
INSTRAW	International Research and Training Institute for the Advancement of Women
IPCC	Intergovernmental Panel on Climate Change
IPE	International Political Economy
IPRs	intellectual property rights
IR	International Relations
ITU	International Telecommunications Union
IUCN	International Union for Conservation of Nature

KBI	knowledge-based industry
LDCs	least/lesser developed countries
LLR	lender of last resort
LoN	League of Nations
M&As	mergers and acquisitions
MAD	mutually assured destruction
MBA	Masters in Business Administration
MDGs	Millennium Development Goals
MFN	most favoured nation
MNCs	multinational corporations
NAFTA	North American Free Trade Area
NATO	North Atlantic Treaty Organisation
NGOs	non-governmental organisations
NPT	Nuclear Non-Proliferation Treaty
OECD	Organisation for Economic Cooperation and Development
OPEC	Organisation of Petroleum Exporting Countries
R&D	research and development
RMA	revolution in military affairs
SAPs	Structural Adjustment Programmes
START	Strategic Arms Reduction Treaty
TRIPs	trade-related aspects of intellectual property rights
UN	United Nations
UNESCO	UN Educational, Scientific and Cultural Organisation
UNICEF	United Nations Children's Fund
UNIFEM	UN Development Fund for Women
WB	World Bank
WBCSD	World Business Council for Sustainable Development
WEF	World Economic Forum
WHO	World Health Organisation
WIPO	World Intellectual Property Organisation
WMD	weapons of mass destruction
WSF	World Social Forum
WSIS	World Summit on the Information Society
WTO	World Trade Organization

Introduction

One of the key characteristics of life in the twenty-first century is the importance of political and economic relationships both within and between states. Governments and citizens are increasingly affected by structures and processes beyond their immediate locality and control. These changes in the nature of world politics can initially appear overwhelmingly incomprehensible. Such phenomena are at the heart of contemporary debates within the discipline of international political economy (IPE).

The first part of the book is designed to introduce you to the evolution of IPE as a distinct discipline. We also provide a summary of the theoretical tools that have emerged to help make sense of the increasingly complex contemporary world. The second part of the book considers a range of issues and trends pertinent to the study of IPE. Reference will be made to challenges to state sovereignty, the increased interconnectedness between national economies and the growing number of issues that are most appropriately understood within the context of either sub-national or international/global frameworks of analysis. You will be guided through the key concepts and issues in a structured manner using reflective exercises. The book is designed with boxes highlighting key authors, concepts and issues and at the end of each chapter further reading is indicated. A companion website is also available to support this text and offer additional related materials.

So what is IPE?

The relationship between the political and economic spheres can be traced back to the earliest times of human interaction. Social anthropologists would recognise the questions of 'who gets what, when, where and how?' as having relevance to all societies at all times. Political decision-making is influenced by what is economically viable. This may seem an obvious point. A more subtle observation is the recognition that the economic values assigned to all manner of goods, services and general resources are politically determined.

What is notable about the contemporary world is the growing complexity of the relationships and processes that relate to these questions. In particular it is increasingly problematic to answer such questions purely in terms of local interactions. Over time we have witnessed the spread and dominance of cash-based economies, as opposed to subsistence-based. Linked to an international system of exchange of goods and services, this means that a greater degree of contextual understanding and analysis is required to fully grasp what is happening. In part this can be seen as the impetus for the emergence of IPE as a distinct discipline. Neither political studies nor simply economics-focused approaches offer a complete picture.

The discipline of International Relations (IR) originated post-First World War with a focus on issues of war and peace, commonly known as 'high politics'. During the 1960s and 1970s there were those who thought that international relations were being not just under-theorised but fundamentally misunderstood. For example, the increasing significance of MNCs and natural commodities (especially oil), previously thought of as 'low politics', moved towards centre stage both within the practice and analysis of IR. This shift in focus led to an emerging school of thought that would become known as IPE. Susan Strange's work is widely recognised as being at the forefront of this new approach. She was controversial in her argument that rather than IPE emerging as a sub-discipline within the subject of IR the reverse was the case. Strange's view was that the discipline of IR, particularly those approaches that continued to highlight the centrality of the nation state, was misguided if it failed to take into account both macro and micro issues, processes and trends that resulted from the intertwining of the political and economic spheres. Moreover, Strange and a growing number of other writers argued that it was impossible to usefully separate these two areas.

One of the key elements of IPE is the relationship between the political and the economic. This informs all theoretical approaches, although some more than others, such as structuralism. It is also one of the defining characteristics of how a government operates in terms of the level of intervention it attempts to implement in relation to the operations of the so-called free market. As such, the relationship between state governments and the market economy is central to the study of IPE.

Recent decades have seen what has been termed the 'triumph of liberalism'. Historically this refers to the end of the Cold War period and the collapse of the Soviet Union. More broadly it is an assessment of the expansion of neo-liberal economics and a relative withdrawal of government intervention policies. China is probably the best example of the move away from a command economy, while still maintaining a communist political regime. Beyond this example though there is a more general sense of all governments finding it increasingly difficult to maintain political control over economic issues. This is not such a recent phenomenon as interdependence between economies is something that has evolved over an extended period. What is of increasing significance though is that the free flow of capital and, in some cases, unequal exchange and terms of trade can seriously threaten a state's fiscal policies and financial stability.

The relationship between governments and the free market was severely tested by the mortgage lending and subsequent banking crisis of 2009. Despite the dominant ethos of neo-liberalism the governments of the United States and Western Europe found themselves in a position of having to intervene on a massive scale to 'bail out' failing banks and other companies. The implications of not doing so could have led to an even more severe crisis and economic downturn to the point of recession and mass unemployment. This example demonstrates that despite the rhetoric of neo-liberal policies there remains a close connection between the operations of the market and a degree of government oversight, at both the national and international level.

Analyses of political economy reflect an attempt to make sense of a matrix of actors, issues and processes. As mentioned above, this complexity is evolving over time and greater emphasis on interconnections on a global scale adds to the need to check and reassess one's view of the world. The apparent rise of a global civil society, the ongoing power plays between nation states and the increased significance of free-market liberal economic policies, both in terms of the role of MNCs and the aim of sustainable development, are all factors that feed into the multi-faceted contemporary world. The following chapters will look at how various theoretical approaches have attempted to order the world and make sense of it. This will also involve our own review of what we believe to be the most relevant and significant trends in the world with regard to processes of globalisation. This will recognise that there will be disagreements among analysts not only over what is happening, but also what various identifiable trends might mean, or if they should be welcomed or actively resisted. It is acknowledged that such disagreements are inherent within any exploration of social trends. Differing analysts will have varied worldviews or moral frameworks. Political ideology permeates all aspects of academic study and it would be wrong to suggest that pure objectivity can be found in any of the approaches under review here, including our own. Similarly, you will also form your own opinions on the issues under consideration here.

In addition, this book provides a sense of how the discipline of IPE has developed over time and how relevant some of the antecedents of the discipline remain today. For example, do the writings of Adam Smith, David Ricardo, Karl Marx, Antonio Gramsci or John Maynard Keynes offer useful insights into the politics and economics of the twenty-first century? Or are they simply historical figures that went some way towards developing our understanding of the evolution and diversity of political and economic thought, yet provide little in the way of insightfulness with regard to contemporary affairs? Has the world changed so much in relation to technological innovation and social transformations that newer, more relevant approaches are required? If so, of what might these approaches comprise, which actors are seen as key and how are their interactions best represented and understood? Piecing together the 'jigsaw' is a common analogy for gaining an insight into how complex mechanisms operate. As an introduction to how this book is structured it is useful to spend some time looking at how such an analogy might be applied in relation to IPE.

The global jigsaw

All theoretical approaches can be seen as trying to create a 'picture' from an array of initial beliefs, apparently supported by empirical evidence. However, the basic principle of creating a worldview from a range of evidence-based pieces to form a coherent and understandable whole is a broadly common theme in both the social and physical sciences. How then might this be applied to our understanding of a rapidly changing and complex international political economy?

First of all, do we have a picture on our box of jigsaw pieces to act as a guide that we can follow? For normative theorists, who talk of how the world should be rather than how it is, there can be a sense of a picture of a world to which they aspire. Unfortunately they may not be able to find the pieces with the correct patterns or shapes to fit together to create such a world-picture. The more optimistic of such theorists may still cling to the belief that all the pieces are there but some are face down and not recognised or there are reasons why the piecing together is not progressing as well or as quickly as they would hope. Perhaps some of the pieces are being withheld or there is some form of breakdown in the communication between the various players responsible for fitting the pieces together. The added complication of a changing world means that the picture on the box itself may need to alter as different shapes and patterns of pieces evolve as the puzzle is still being put together. If there is a single theme that reflects the character of globalisation it is that of change. A second theme would be adaptation and the levels of speed and success with which actors and environments can accommodate various changes.

The jigsaw analogy has within it several common assumptions that any theorist or scholar needs to reflect upon. How can we be sure that we have a correct set of the necessary pieces required to arrive at a complete picture? In terms of competing analysis this may be thought of in terms of two different puzzles being mixed together. Both may make coherent pictures but a certain level of skill and discernment is necessary to separate them out, or see how they relate to each other. Marx and Smith were creating pictures with similar actors and similar issues and processes. However, the style and emphasis of both pictures was significantly different, as we will see. Note here that despite having different views both writers were able to piece together coherent pictures using similar pieces. To take this analogy a step further this can be thought of as a puzzle where the pieces have images on both sides. Depending on which side one views a different picture emerges. Imagine a discipline where the pieces are not flat with only two distinct planes. Rather they are cubes, or many-more-sided geometric shapes, with each plane representing a competing worldview. This gives some sense of the enormity of the task involved in determining how the kaleidoscope of pieces that make up the contemporary world are best ordered and understood.

Despite the scale of the undertaking to order, analyse and explain the world in relation to varying IPE theories we need to begin somewhere. If we continue our jigsaw analogy for a little longer let us assume that we are dealing with a traditional rectangular shape. Therefore, we can deduce that this will have four corner pieces from which we can arrive at a framework within which our remaining pieces should fit together to provide a coherent picture. No doubt from the potential problems alluded to above it is clear that what is being described is an 'ideal' jigsaw and that what we have here is a rather loose analogy that should be seen as a guiding strategy to map our way through the review of the historical development of IPE as a distinct discipline. Now imagine that this rectangle has what we will call a political axis running up the left-hand side and an economic axis running along the bottom. From this would it be possible to begin to map where and how certain writers or issues relate to each other? For example, one would imagine that the free-market school of thought would be well to the right on the economic axis but relatively low on the political axis. In contrast those advocating command economies would score higher on the political axis than on the economic axis. As a simple graph this could tell us something in very general terms about where the emphasis is placed by various writers in relation to the politics/economics spectrum.

Yet before such plotting can take place one needs to consider what factors are in play to pull the subject under consideration towards the political or economic poles. Strange and other writers that will be discussed below would baulk at the idea that these poles can be so easily disaggregated. A defining characteristic of many IPE writers of more recent times has been their desire to highlight the connections between economics and politics. Rather than a mechanistic plotting of a single point on a graph they would create a more complex picture. Here the jigsaw analogy becomes insufficient, as what is being described now is more akin to a moving picture. Shades of colour could become important, representing the emphasis on particular issues. A familiar example could be the depth of green associated with various environmental groups or red for socialist-type policies. The movement in the picture would be a reflection of the dynamics of the processes that see a continual shift in the dominance of certain ideas and capabilities over time. So, although the jigsaw analogy remains a useful starting point, we need to move beyond this to help us order and understand a world most aptly characterised by change.

At the risk of taking our use of analogies too far we suggest that rather than a jigsaw what we are now looking at is a picture more closely related to that of a television screen. In order to receive a clear picture one needs to be 'tuned in' to the relevant signals. Of course, there are myriad signals to pick up and viewers have a range of channels that they may receive. This channel selection or preference can be seen as relying on one's dominant beliefs and prejudices. The signals may be the same, but various viewers may see and understand things differently. Numerous signals and receivers are in operation around the world. This is not a simple one-way broadcasting process. In this book you will see that there have been a wide range of views formed and promoted. In looking at how such views are formed we will also be asking questions regarding what element of various schools of thought retain contemporary relevance.

Structure of the book

The book is structured in line with the above analogies in that the first part introduces various theoretical positions and the 'pieces' that they identify and put together. After identifying these foundations the second part of the book looks at an array of actors, and the third part considers relevant issues and trends that reflect the main aspects of the contemporary world.

Chapter 1 introduces the reader to the theoretical foundations that underpin the study of IPE: realism, liberalism and Marxism. The emphasis here is on the key distinctions between these approaches and their historical evolution. Key historical figures are highlighted by the use of author boxes and although the major focus of the chapter is the development of theoretical approaches, you will be prompted to consider the relevance of each approach to the real world.

Having established the theoretical foundations of the discipline, Chapter 2 assesses the impact of IPE scholars since the early 1970s when many turned their attention to what had been perceived as 'low politics'. It focuses on the growth of different strands of thought within the neo-realist, neo-liberal and structural approaches.

Chapter 3 introduces the most significant alternative theoretical approaches that have developed in response to the 'orthodoxy' described in Chapter 2. You will be introduced here to feminist, green and postmodern approaches.

Having introduced a broad range of theoretical perspectives, Chapter 4 begins to develop an understanding of how these relate to 'real world' experiences. The degree and significance of processes of globalisation (itself a contested concept within IPE) is the subject of varying interpretations. Here we ask you to consider the salient points of the globalisation debate. This chapter links the perspectives discussed earlier in the book to the more specialised issue-based chapters.

The second part of the book focuses on actors and issues within IPE. We begin with Chapter 5 which considers governance at the national, international, regional and global levels. After an overview of the origins and development of the Bretton Woods Institutions the attention shifts to more contemporary debates. The number of international organisations at the end of the 1990s was over 2500, as compared with around 30 that existed at the start of the twentieth century. Their role has become more complicated as the transnational flows that these institutions are attempting to regulate become larger and harder to control. The role and significance of the major 'private' political economy actor will also be described. Here, issues as to how and in what ways MNCs are seen as both the drivers and victims of global changes are highlighted. In what ways and forms are they reflectors of a political–economic ethos, and by which routes and methods do they lobby for a political environment that reflects the current dominance of neo-liberalism? How and to what extent do they interface with both states and civil society? Finally, the role of civil society in increasing the representative nature of global governance institutions is focused upon in more detail.

Chapter 6 considers world trade and the development of the international trade system after 1945. Particular attention is paid to the management of this system. Pertinent issues in world trade are discussed, including the position of developing countries and the 'free trade versus fair trade' debate.

Chapter 7 analyses the development of a global financial system and the impact this has had on actors within the world economy. The demise of the post-war system of fixed exchange rates, the wave of market-oriented reform in domestic financial markets and the rapid integration of many once-national capital markets across political and regulatory boundaries provide the focus of the discussion. The chapter concludes with a focus on the impact of financial crises and the stability of the contemporary financial system.

Chapter 8 considers the position of development issues and strategies in the world economy. The contested nature of the term is highlighted and the historical understandings are outlined in the first section. The shift towards a neo-liberal orthodoxy in development is discussed and the impact of salient issues such as foreign aid and the debt crisis are highlighted.

Chapter 9 addresses the diversity of opinion and debate in relation to environmental ramifications of current and proposed future practices of production. At one end of the debate 'deep ecologists' question the wisdom of exclusively human-centred development policies; whilst other commentators ('environmentalists' in varying shades of 'green') prefer to emphasise conservationism and the utilisation of natural resources. Climate change, potential rises in sea levels, acid rain, deforestation and loss of other habitats resulting in decreasing biodiversity are among the issues that will be discussed. The range of responses from the various parties, both private and public, will be illustrated and explained.

Chapter 10 considers the paradoxical role technological developments have in many aspects of IPE. On the one hand, they may be seen as the means by which the neo-liberal project has been advanced and come to dominate much of the world. On the other, they offer potential solutions to many pressing global problems, both in logistical and coordinating capacities. Debates over access to technology and the significance of English as the leading medium of international discourse will be considered. Comparative advantages within the international trading system and the entrenchment of divisions of wealth are a direct result of the ownership of relevant resources and application of technical expertise.

Chapter 11 looks at cultural issues as another significant factor in relation to globalisation. It has even been suggested that the seeds of a global monoculture have already been sown. This chapter considers this proposition in the light of the issue areas discussed above and related theoretical debates. The potential impact of the spread of a dominant system of production, and the possibility that a common set of intrinsic values necessarily follows, will be critically presented. The emphasis here will be on the promotion of certain types of 'knowledge', values, norms and 'rights'. Huntington's 'Clash of Civilisations' thesis has attracted renewed attention with regard to competing value systems. The ongoing debate surrounding cultural relativism and/or universality will be reviewed. In particular this chapter discusses the possible relationship between a near-universal trading system and a concomitant system of assumptions and values.

Chapter 12 is designed to relate to all of the above issues and trends in the context of a dynamic, contentious and evolving set of security agendas. Whereas many IR textbooks will focus on state- and military-centric security, the distinctive nature of IPE approaches, as opposed to IR, tend to adopt a broader interpretation and analysis of security issues.

The conclusion reviews salient aspects of processes of globalisation and the relative values and explanatory powers of the competing analytical perspectives. These aspects include: which ones are actors focussed upon, what are the constraints within which they operate, and how do they relate to each other?

This book does not claim to offer a full explanation for all contemporary phenomena. However, it does provide you with an introduction to the various IPE schools of thought and their relevance to a number of selected issues. In doing so, insights into how the world is evolving in response to aspects of globalisation will be demonstrated. It will become clear that in reading this book students of IPE will gain not only enhanced knowledge of the discipline, but also of the world around them and their place within it.

1 The theoretical foundations of IPE

Chapter learning outcomes

After reading this chapter students should be able to:

- Understand and summarise the historical foundations of the three main theoretical approaches considered in this chapter.
- Cite the work of one or more key authors associated with each approach.
- Recognise how each approach explains 'real world' events.
- Explain how 'real world' events have shaped the development of these core theoretical approaches.
- Demonstrate a critical awareness of the broad strengths and weaknesses of each approach.
- Understand how debates between associated theorists influenced the development of these approaches.

Introduction

This chapter outlines the key arguments of the three dominant orthodox theoretical perspectives in IPE and their historical evolution. It should be emphasised from the beginning that these perspectives are to be understood as broad schools of thought that are used as a means of simplifying the situation. The division of this chapter into three sections is intended only as a useful starting point. Over time the boundaries between these three approaches have often become blurred. Within each perspective there are also a number of distinctive ideas. Given the diversity within each perspective and the cross-fertilisation between them, it should be understood that it is a mistake to think that all thought in IPE can be neatly packaged into one of three theoretical boxes. Adopting the 'three perspectives' approach often results in a rigid and stale explanation of theory. It could be argued that some of the issues discussed in the second half of this book, such as technology, the environment and culture, cannot be adequately understood by recourse to these orthodox approaches. It is for this reason that more recent theoretical developments in IPE will be discussed in detail in Chapters 2, 3 and 4, and this chapter needs to be read in conjunction with the following three chapters in order to gain a more rounded understanding of theory within IPE.

Realism

The term 'realism' is used to describe this broad approach to understanding IPE. Others use mercantilism and economic nationalism; however, here these terms will be employed to outline the historical development within the realist perspective.

Central arguments

Despite the variety of views that are held within realism, there are a number of core values that define these thinkers as distinctive from others. The four most central of these are as follows:

■ The most important actor in the international system is the state.
■ Human nature is seen as inherently selfish and bad.
■ International economic relations between states are competitive.
■ There is a direct relationship between the pursuit of political power and economic wealth.

In very simple terms, realism advocates the primacy of politics over economics. It is a doctrine of state building and proposes that the market should be subordinate to state interests. The organisation of the national economy and its external relations should, at all times, remain consistent with national security concerns. National economic interests, especially those that are directly related to the security and survival of the state (for example, the defence industry and energy resources), should be maintained to avoid dependence on other states. This may result in the discouragement of foreign ownership of firms and the adoption of protectionist measures in trade policy.

The starting point for the realist perspective is that the international system is anarchical. This means that in the absence of a world government, states are the highest form of political power and the main actors in international relations. It is natural for states to pursue power in such a system and they aim to shape the economy to this self-interested end. The implication here is that the domestic and international spheres of the economy are viewed as distinct and separate. What is crucial for realists is the relative position of a state vis-à-vis other states, and for this reason their view of the world is often described as a zero-sum game. In other words, one state's gain is viewed as another state's loss. Realist thinking is mostly concerned with how changes in the distribution of power in the international state system affect the workings of the international economy. It is the relative power resources between states that are the ultimate arbiter in the outcome of international economic relations.

Historical evolution

The development of the realist perspective in IPE can be directly traced back to ideas and practices that emerged during the creation of an international system of states, which occurred in the period from the sixteenth to the eighteenth century. Medieval business practices gave way to the emergence of what were to become the basic structures of the modern commercial world. The dominant view during this period is known as mercantilism. This was a significant break with the past because the nation state was the new focus of economic thinking. The central concern of mercantilism, as with many realist scholars in IPE today, was the security of the state. The security of a state was seen as directly related to its power in relation to other states in the system. It was believed by the mercantilists that this security could be enhanced, not just by the creation of a large and well-equipped army, but also by the acquisition of wealth. At the domestic level this led to policies designed to maximise tax revenues. The logical consequence of this belief, for the nature of economic relations between states, was that a state should aim to export more and import less. By doing so it would increase its holdings of gold and silver, thus gaining an advantage over other states in the system. These precious metals could then be easily converted into money, which could in turn be used to fund national armies and stimulate the economy.

Therefore, the aim of any state in such a competitive system was to achieve a surplus in its trade balance. Of course, it is impossible for all states in an international economic system to achieve this, as one state's surplus is another state's deficit. Mercantilists did acknowledge that the result of such a policy approach was a system of economic relations that would be likely to lead to conflict. This very simple logic had a significant impact, not just in the realm of ideas, but also in the actual policies adopted by states. Many absolutist monarchs fully embraced the mercantilist view. Such a theoretical position dovetailed with the era of state building in Europe and the creation of what we now understand as the 'modern state'. Hence the term mercantilism is also often used to describe this period in the history of the international economy.

In the eighteenth century the early liberal writers significantly and successfully challenged this fairly simple theoretical position. They criticised the military conflict that appeared to result, and the threat that state control of the economy posed to the freedom of the individual. Led by Adam Smith, the liberal view suggested that, contrary to mercantilist thought, policies of intervention and protectionism would not maximise the interests of the state. These arguments are discussed in more detail in the next section of this chapter. A more robust defence of the mercantilist position was developed in response to this liberal critique. The focus shifted from the prioritisation of achieving a trade surplus to the need for more direct support of the national economy. The term economic nationalism is used here to distinguish this from the classical mercantilist position. The origins of economic nationalism can be traced back to the work of Alexander Hamilton and Friedrich List (see author boxes).

AUTHOR BOX

Alexander Hamilton (1755–1804)

Alexander Hamilton was born on the Caribbean island of Nevis and spent his formative years outside the American colonies. It is often suggested that this allowed him to remain untainted by internal political rivalries, and contributed to his view of the United States as a single nation. He fought in the revolutionary army against the British in the American War of Independence.

Hamilton became the first US Secretary of the Treasury. His major concern was with economic development at the level of the nation state. His report to the US Congress in 1791, known as the *Report on Manufactures*, argued that the US government needed to help promote the national manufacturing sector. This required an interventionist approach, both in providing support to overcome shortages in capital and trade protectionism to shelter the fledgling manufacturing sector from external competition. This was seen as central to the strengthening of the state and the economic development of the United States.

Hamilton made the direct link between the need for an increase in economic self-reliance and issues of national security. He argued that by becoming more self-sufficient in manufactured goods the United States would also increase its security. Hamilton was concerned that a reliance on imports served to weaken the military strength of the US. His life came to a premature end when he was killed during a duel with Aaron Burr, who was a political rival.

The economic nationalist approach that developed during the nineteenth century could be viewed as a critique of the practicalities of liberal ideas, rather than a sustained attack on the theories themselves. Both Hamilton and List emphasised the importance of developing a strong manufacturing sector. Only by achieving this could other states hope to compete with Britain in the economic, political and military senses. However, List's 'infant industry' approach failed to challenge the central logic of liberalism and in particular the justifications for free trade. This was demonstrated by List's campaign for the removal of internal duties on trade between the various German states that existed at the time. The argument was that liberal ideas of free trade, while perfectly justified, were not applicable to the reality of a world of nation states. Rather than being in the interest of all individuals, in reality a free trade system would favour the most advanced manufacturing states. Moreover, List in particular highlighted how Britain had achieved its dominance by adopting protectionist measures, rather than the laws of free trade. In this sense, it was a significant compromise of early mercantilist views of international trade. The main impact it had was in refocusing attention at the level of the nation state and away from the individual and the world as a whole.

AUTHOR BOX

Friedrich List (1789–1846)

Friedrich List published arguably the most convincing realist attack on liberal thought during the nineteenth century. In his book *The National System of Political Economy*, published in 1841, List criticised liberals for failing to recognise the importance of national rivalries and conflict. He distinguished between what he called 'cosmopolitical economy', which is concerned with the benefits of economic activity for all human beings, regardless of nationality, and 'political economy', where the concern is how a nation can maximise its wealth and power.

List was born in the German state of Würtemburg and in his working life he quickly became a senior figure in the civil service. Contrary to the official view held at the time, he was a strong advocate of the removal of internal trade tariffs and for an economic union between Germany's many states. He was eventually imprisoned by the King of Würtemburg for these views, and was forced to relinquish his citizenship. Imprisonment did not change his views and the years he spent abroad convinced him of how a liberal approach of free trade would result in Britain's dominance in the Industrial Revolution being maintained. Applying the law of comparative advantage to the situation in this period of history, List argued, would result in Britain exporting manufactured goods to other states such as Germany. List argued that such a situation would result in Germany's perpetual dependence on Britain. His solution was to use economic protection to allow the development of a manufacturing sector, which would enable other states to challenge Britain. This is often called the 'infant industry' approach, where local firms are protected in their early years to give them time to adjust to the rigours of foreign competition.

His 1841 publication continued to bring him into conflict with the authorities. It was only a combination of widespread public support and criticism by the British press that eventually convinced the King that List deserved a formal apology for his previous treatment. He visited Britain in 1846, as the repeal of the Corn Laws was implemented, and returned convinced that this was part of an attempt to maintain British supremacy as the 'workshop of the world'. By this point, however, his health had deteriorated and it is claimed that he eventually took his own life in November that year.

Economic nationalism has taken on many different guises over the decades since Hamilton and List put forward their arguments. However, it is possible to discern some common themes and attitudes. The central contention of this position is that the goal of building state power should be prioritised over economic activities. The distribution of power between states will determine the pattern of what are inherently conflictual relations. Hence, the struggle between states is also about economic resources. This leads to the view that the economic prosperity of a state is not enough in itself. It is the relative economic power of the state, in direct comparison with other states, that is most important. The nationalist emphasis of this approach has meant that it has remained influential due to its political appeal. It is possible to point to numerous examples throughout history where states have implemented policies designed to promote the development of domestic industry and technological advancement (see the example box, on the next page).

EXAMPLE BOX

Realism in action: the Japanese developmental state

The idea that government support of the manufacturing sector is crucial to economic development was reflected in the approach adopted by the Japanese government in the period after the Second World War. In 1949 they created the Ministry of International Trade and Industry (MITI), which became a powerful force during the economic recovery of this period. MITI was given total control over both imports and exports and directed investment into the sectors of the economy, such as coal and steel, which were seen as central to industrial growth. By the mid 1960s foreign criticism grew of MITI's activities, but although it began to allow liberalisation of some areas of Japanese trade, it continued to play a role in guiding the direction of economic activity in Japan. During the 1970s it shifted its attention to the support of Japanese firms operating in high-tech industries. This approach has led to the term 'developmental state' being applied to Japan. See Chapter 8 for a more detailed discussion of this issue.

Criticisms of realism

- One perceived weakness of the realist perspective is that international economic relations are always viewed as a competitive exercise. Liberals insist that mutual gains can result from economic cooperation between states. This debate was advanced in the 1970s when liberal scholars argued that the existence of regimes facilitated cooperation between states.
- As with realist theory in IR, there is an assumption, especially within economic nationalism, that it is possible to have a comprehensive and objective national interest. Many critics have highlighted that policies designed to advance the interests of the nation state as a whole can actually represent the particular interests of certain groups that are able to influence policy-makers. A realist approach needs to explain how economic interests are translated into the politics of the state.
- The active role of the state may not guarantee economic development as some realist thinkers may suggest. Liberals argue that, in most cases, such intervention in the free operation of the market may actually hinder, rather than help the promotion of economic growth.
- Realism portrays the state as the central actor within IPE. However, more recent critics have questioned this assumption, by focusing on what they argue is the increasingly significant role played by non-state actors, such as firms, international organisations and non-governmental organisations. It is suggested that structural changes taking place in the world economy are gradually eroding the importance of the state.
- The realist approach is ambivalent about questions of equality and 'who gets what'. Marxists would argue that the state, rather than reflecting the 'national interest', is reflective of the interests of the dominant economic class.

Liberalism

The roots of liberalism can be traced back to the eighteenth and nineteenth centuries. Its ideas have become embodied in orthodox economics and it is the most influential perspective in the world today, with most key states and international economic organisations operating broadly along liberal lines.

Central arguments

■ It is beneficial in the long run if markets are allowed to operate freely.
■ States should be able to trade openly with each other.
■ The role of the state in economic affairs should be kept to a minimum.

Liberalism assumes that, at least ideally, politics and economics exist in separate spheres. Markets should be free from political interference for the sake of efficiency and growth. Liberalism assumes rationality in economic behaviour. It is argued that human beings are able to maximise their own utility; in other words, they possess the ability to assess the potential costs and benefits of any individual decision or action. There are clear links here to liberal political theory, which is committed to individual equality and liberty.

The harmony of interests, which liberals argue exists within states, is also said to exist between states. Contrary to the realist position, trade between states is viewed as a mutually beneficial exercise and this is often described as a positive-sum game. International economic relations between states are also judged by liberals to be a major source of peaceful relations among nations. By expanding the interdependence of national economies through free trade relations, more cooperative and less hostile relationships become more likely. The greater the degree of economic interdependence that exists, the less likely states will be to enter into military conflict.

The degree to which the state should be involved in the economy is one of the key debates between various liberal thinkers, and differences of opinion do exist. In general, we can say that from a liberal perspective the state should only concern itself with the provision of the legal framework and infrastructure that is necessary for the market to operate smoothly. Governments should only intervene when imperfections in the market mechanism exist, or in order to provide public goods. These imperfections could be the result of negative externalities, by which we mean spillover effects of the production process that are not included in the costs incurred. For example, there may be social costs to society that result from pollution that is produced by a firm, which the state needs to account for. The market could also 'fail' if there are a limited number of producers (oligopoly) or even one single producer (monopoly), where the pressures of competition do not exist. Public goods are specific goods and services that cannot be provided by a free market. At the domestic level, national defence or street lighting are good examples. The consumption of these goods could not be limited under a free market to those who had paid for them. Therefore, they have to be funded by the state through the collection of taxes. At the international level, public goods such as an open international economy and a stable monetary regime are more problematic as there is no 'world state' to collect taxes to provide them.

Historical evolution

David Hume laid the first foundation of liberal thinking by demonstrating a central problem with the mercantilist position. Prior to the First World War almost all currencies were convertible into gold, and this was how international economic transactions were resolved. Hume, in one of a series of nine essays published in 1752, showed how changes in price levels would *naturally* correct the inflows and outflows of gold that resulted from international trade. Before this the mercantilist view was that states should aim for a permanent balance of payments surplus. Hume demonstrated that such a policy would be unsustainable as a continual inflow of gold would raise domestic prices and cause economic activity to move abroad, therefore reversing the flow of gold.

Although there is a tradition of liberal thought that can be traced back to Jeremy Bentham, John Stuart Mill, John Locke and Thomas Jefferson, who all made political arguments for the freedom of the individual, the central figure in the birth of liberal political economy is Adam Smith (see author box). Smith provided a critique of the mercantilist view, that the pursuit of power and wealth by a nation can only be achieved at the expense of other nations. He also sought to demonstrate how the free market is the most beneficial way of organising the economy, and in doing so aimed to show how this required a minimum of state involvement.

David Ricardo shared Adam Smith's belief in the benefits of free trade, although he arrived at this position for slightly different reasons. Rather than being focused on the protectionist polices supporting businessmen, Ricardo was critical of the landowners. He argued that their desire to protect the agricultural sector would lead to rising food prices, which would in turn be reflected in the need for higher wages, ultimately hindering economic development. He became a member of parliament in Britain, and demonstrated these views on a practical level with his opposition to the Corn Laws. Ricardo also developed a theoretical defence of his belief in free trade. It seems easy to see why two countries should trade if Country A produces different goods from Country B and they are efficient in the production of different goods. But if you want to endorse free trade as a general principle, you will also have to advocate trade between two countries where both countries produce the same goods and where Country A is more efficient than Country B at producing both goods. Ricardo demonstrated this by arguing that although individual countries may not always have an *absolute* advantage over another country, they will almost always have a *comparative* advantage in the production of certain goods or services. What type of economic activity this comparative advantage is achieved in depends on a number of factors. These may include the availability of natural resources, climate, and the composition and skills of your workforce. This resulted in a belief that trade had positive benefits for all, although these benefits would not necessarily be equally distributed. It also meant that the international division of labour should become more specialised. Ricardo also talked about how trade would bind nations together and therefore he provided an early example of the view that free trade could contribute to more peaceful international relations.

There was a key difference in the approach adopted by Ricardo in comparison with Smith. His approach was more abstract, and less narrative, and he was not as concerned with the practical difficulties resulting from the implementation of liberal ideas as Smith had been.

AUTHOR BOX

Adam Smith (1723–1790)

The legacies of the work of Adam Smith are twofold. First, he developed a convincing critique of mercantilism, which at the time still dominated the economic policies of states. Second, he was instrumental in developing a distinctly new approach to thinking about political economy.

Smith was born in Kircaldy, a small Scottish port, in 1723. He was an amazingly clever youngster and he took up a university place aged just fourteen. His work forms part of what is commonly called the Scottish Enlightenment. This was centred in the universities and Smith held an academic post at Glasgow University from 1748 to 1764. All the thinkers attached to this 'project' were committed to taking a secular and scientific approach to the study of human society. They also shared a belief in progress.

In his most famous work, *The Wealth of Nations*, published in 1776, Smith's attack on mercantilist thinking focused on the understanding of how we understand the 'wealth of a nation'. Contrary to the mercantilist view that this was measured by how much gold and silver a state held, Smith sought to demonstrate how production and economic growth were the determinants of wealth. He then explained how this economic growth would be best achieved by the operation of free markets with a minimum of political interference. Central to Smith's argument was the belief that human nature, which he understood as a desire for self-betterment guided by the faculties of reason, was what drives social change. He famously coined the term the 'invisible hand' to describe how the market converts the individual pursuit of self-interest into benefits for society as a whole.

Smith also argued that if his ideas were best for the wealth of *one* nation, then they should also apply to the wealth of *all* nations. His call for the free market was translated to the international level in an argument for free trade. However, we should not interpret him as a mere idealist. Smith was mindful of the dominance of mercantilist thinking at the time, and aware of the ability of vested political interests to gain control of the economy. He did provide certain qualifications to his call for free trade. Interestingly one of these was that tariffs could be used, as a temporary retaliatory measure, against states engaged in trade protectionism to convince them of the error of their ways. This is an idea that is reflected in the rules of the World Trade Organization today.

It appears that Smith's ideas are still influential today. In the celebrations that followed the election of Ronald Reagan as president of the United States in 1980, it is claimed that many of his supporters wore the same necktie, which featured a profile of Adam Smith. In the United Kingdom a pro-market think-tank, 'The Adam Smith Institute', exists in his name.

After successfully challenging the ideas of mercantilism, and in particular developing the idea of free trade resulting in mutual gain, liberal thinking became the dominant theoretical approach in political economy. One early political triumph was the repeal of the Corn Laws in Britain in 1846. This marked the removal of tariffs that had previously been imposed on imported grain.

Subsequently, a significant shift occurred in liberal thought in the period after the First World War and in particular after the Great Depression of the 1930s. The idea that minimal state involvement would result in benefits for all was questioned. At the international level, international institutions were now viewed as necessary to ensure that a system of free trade would be mutually beneficial. Up until this point, the classical liberals had demonstrated a faith in the strength of the interdependence that results from trade. They did not foresee the need for institutions to guarantee world peace. John Maynard Keynes, who was one of the architects of the post-Second World War global economy, led these significant changes in the liberal approach (see author box).

AUTHOR BOX

John Maynard Keynes (1883–1946)

Keynes was part of the English elite and attended Eton and then King's College, Cambridge. He had a significant impact on liberal thought at both a theoretical and practical level. He spent part of his career working for the civil service and was the head of the British delegation at the Bretton Woods Conference which took place at the end of the Second World War. Keynes differed from many liberal thinkers in emphasising the importance of imperfections in the market. He argued that the existence of producer groups, labour unions and so on meant that the liberal interpretation of markets as self-regulating was not matched by reality. In his opinion, to avoid the negative consequences of economic recession, full employment should be the major goal of macroeconomic policy and this required state intervention at the domestic level. At the international level, to avoid the desire to pursue protectionist policies to achieve full employment, he advocated cooperation. He believed that the world economy could be managed.

Nevertheless, Keynes was still a liberal. His experience of the Soviet Union convinced him of the failings of Marxism, and the First World War, the Great Depression and the Second World War had alerted him to the dangers of mercantilist policies. He still believed in the efficiency of the market and his calls for state intervention were designed to complement the workings of the market, rather than replace it.

During the 1920s there had been a steady growth of protectionism, partly as a result of the settlement made after the First World War. The international recession of the 1930s heightened the appeal of economic nationalism. At the Bretton Woods Conference in 1944 there was a liberal consensus among the delegates concerning the causes of the Second World War. The rise in economic nationalism in the 1930s was viewed as a direct cause of economic decline. This was thought to have led to the rise in popularity of fascism, which in turn was seen by the post-war economic planners as the main cause of the war.

The Bretton Woods System was created in an attempt to prevent states pursuing protectionist measures during times of economic hardship. A framework of institutions was created to enable management of the world economy. These institutions were the International Bank for Reconstruction and Development, more commonly known as the World Bank, the International Monetary Fund, and the General Agreement on Tariffs and Trade. The Bretton Woods System reflected many of Keynes' ideas and has famously been described as being based on 'embedded liberalism'. The aim was to encourage a stable but open world economy at the international level, while allowing individual states the independence to pursue domestic policies designed to provide employment and social welfare. In other words, it can be described as a system of strong states embedded in a liberal market-based world economy.

CONCEPT BOX

Laissez-faire economics

Laissez-faire is a French term meaning 'to let be' or 'to allow'; this idea is synonymous with free trade policies. The laissez-faire school of thought holds a pure capitalist or free market view that capitalism is best left to its own devices, as capitalism alone will progress and it will advance faster and become more efficient without involvement from any legislative body. The basic idea is that less governmental interference in private economic matters, such as pricing, production and distribution, makes for a better system. Laissez-faire economics emerged throughout the eighteenth and early nineteenth centuries in the wealthier states in Europe and North America. It is possible to argue that despite its many critics laissez-faire is still dominant and drives economic policies in many contemporary states.

It is clear that there have been many different strands of thought within the liberal perspective. However, there are some enduring ideas that remain at the heart of this approach. One of these is the belief that the most efficient way of organising international economic relations is by allowing the free market to operate. The emphasis on free trade, which can be traced back to the work of Smith and Ricardo, is still pertinent today. As a general idea this has informed the organisation of world trade since the Second World War (see the example box, below).

EXAMPLE BOX

Liberalism in action: GATT and the international trade regime

The central liberal contention that restrictions on trade should be removed has had a direct impact on the practice of international relations. The General Agreement on Tariffs and Trade (GATT) that was created after the Second World War was designed to promote and protect this principle. GATT was not a formal institution but a framework for negotiations with the idea being to reduce barriers to trade; initially these were chiefly tariffs and quotas. Different rounds of negotiation focused on increasingly complex issues. In 1995 a new organisation was created as a result of the Uruguay Round of GATT talks. The World Trade Organization (WTO) now has the main purposes of promoting free trade and settling disputes between member states. If you were unaware of the WTO, you probably noticed it after its third Ministerial Conference in Seattle in November 1999, which attracted a large number of protestors. See Chapter 6 for a more detailed discussion of world trade.

Criticisms of liberalism

- One of the major criticisms of liberalism is that markets are not a natural phenomenon.
- Economic liberalism is criticised for not looking at the political and social context. It is suggested that this is needed if we are to understand how economic actors operate. In the liberal world, individuals are seen as rational actors operating in a system free from political boundaries and social constraints.
- Liberalism is also charged with being ahistorical. It is charged with being a reflection of the values and ideas associated with a successful minority. This makes the analysis rather static and the virtues of the status quo are assumed.
- One clear Marxist critique of economic liberalism is that the justice and equality of economic outcomes are disregarded. The argument is that liberalism is merely an attempt to manage a market-based economy as efficiently as possible. At the international level, the asymmetry between North and South has led to the charge that liberalism only serves the interests of the strong.
- Liberal thinking has been criticised for underplaying the importance of the state in the international political economy. Although differences exist within the liberal perspective, in general the market is central and the state is given the limited role of only delivering those things that the market is unable to provide. Over recent years fierce debate has taken place over whether the state's importance is declining or not, and how central it is to our understanding of the international political economy.

Marxism

This perspective is extremely broad and wide-ranging. Others may use 'structuralism' but this term is employed here to describe one particular strand of thinking within the broader Marxist tradition.

Central arguments

Despite the different forms of Marxist thinking it is possible to identify common elements:

- Historical change is ultimately a reflection of the economic development of society.
- Capitalism is the main driving force of world economic relations.
- In a capitalist society there is class conflict between the bourgeoisie and the proletariat.

The general view of Marxist approaches is that we should analyse the social world in its totality. In Volume 1 of *Capital*, Karl Marx (see author box) decided to begin by studying the simplest form of social relations, on which he could then build. Social change is explained by alterations in what Marx called the 'means of production'. These are the various elements necessary to the process of production. These would include knowledge, labour, tools and technology. As these change, the 'relations of production' change. These are the institutional relationships (for example, wage labour) that are also necessary for production. Together these two elements create the economic base of society. Marxist approaches tend to argue that changes in this economic base are then reflected in the superstructure (the legal, political and cultural institutions). This approach is known as historical materialism.

Marx was not an impartial commentator but hoped that by increasing our understanding of capitalism it would be easier ultimately to overthrow the system. In Marx's analysis capitalism was built on a logic that would ultimately result in contradiction and crises that would inevitably lead to collapse. More contemporary Marxists are, in general, less keen to emphasise that capitalism sows the seeds of its own destruction. Marx spent most of his time analysing in great detail the nature of capitalism. In contrast to the liberal approach that emphasises the harmony of interests that exists between social groups, Marxism highlights the central role that class conflict plays in capitalist society. The main clash is between the bourgeoisie (the owners of capital) and the proletariat (the workers). Capitalism is built upon the two key principles of the pursuit of profit and the protection of private property. These principles allow the bourgeoisie to exploit the proletariat by paying them a wage that is less than the market value of the goods and services that they produce.

Historical evolution

The major strength of this approach, in contrast to the other two perspectives discussed in this chapter, is that the analysis is focused directly on the link between the social and economic structure of the economic system (what Marx called the mode of production), and the operation of political power and influence. It also provides students of IPE with a toolkit for the systematic critique of the current international order.

Quite clearly the development of the Marxist perspective begins from the work of Karl Marx. Although Marx did devote a very limited amount of his time to the effects of capitalism on parts of the world outside Europe, his analysis of capitalism was chiefly at the national level. He did not develop an organised account of international economic or political relations. Since his death, others have used his ideas and applied them to many of the issues central to the study of IPE.

Central to Marx's thought was a critique of the liberal view that had become dominant during the nineteenth century. As discussed earlier in this chapter, this approach suggested a harmony of interests could be possible under capitalism and that economic exchange could lead to mutual gain. For Marx, in a capitalist society there can be no inherent social harmony. On the contrary, he argued that there were three laws governing its operation, which together explain both the evolution and eventual demise of this mode of production. He saw capitalism as composed of internal contradictions that would cause frequent crises and the eventual downfall of the system as a whole.

The first of these objective laws is known as the falling rate of profit. Capitalism is a system based on the private ownership of the means of production and the existence of a wage labour system. In other words, workers 'sell' their own skills at a price determined by the market. Marx highlighted how the rate at which workers are paid is less than the value of the goods and services that they produce. He called the difference between the two the 'surplus value', which is now more commonly known as 'profit'. The driving force of capitalism is the accumulation of as much profit as possible. One of the ways to do this is to increase the efficiency of the production process by introducing better technology and labour-saving techniques. As competition increases it becomes increasingly difficult to maintain the same rate of profit. We should maybe describe this as a tendency, rather than a law, as Marx acknowledged that there were a number of factors that could halt such a decline. Second is the law of disproportionality. This denies the liberal perception that capitalism has a tendency towards equilibrium. Marx suggested that in reality it is subject to the overproduction and underconsumption of goods and services. Periodically there are periods of boom and slump as the amount of goods produced outstrips the demand by consumers. Over time he predicted that these crises would become increasingly severe and would create the conditions for the proletariat to revolt against the system. Third is the law of the concentration (or accumulation) of capital. The drive for profits makes it necessary for the bourgeoisie to accumulate capital and to invest this in order to maintain their competitive edge. As the system evolves, this leads to the increasing concentration of wealth in the hands of the successful capitalists, at the expense of an increasing number of impoverished masses. This increases the pool of unemployed workers, which puts a downward pressure on wages, and again this makes the capitalist system ripe for revolution.

Marx did develop a critique of why the capitalist system can be maintained for so long even though these inherent contradictions were so obvious to those who examined the system from a critical perspective. This is based on two factors and is referred to as false consciousness: the production and maintenance of tautological values such as the pursuit of material possessions as a 'natural' objective of humans and the importance of spiritual belief and religious observance. Together these things help to reinforce class relations and reduce the chance of manifestations of the 'hidden' class conflict. In effect, the proletariat are kept in a state of non-action against the existing order by the satisfaction of *some* 'perceived' desires and by the control and distractions inherent within religious belief systems. The Catholic Church in Italy, for example, often professed support for the government of Mussolini and professed that social disobedience was sinful (this included disobedience against the capitalist system). Marx also held a very different opinion of the role of the state. Unlike the realist view that sees the state as directing economic affairs in the national interest, or the liberal view that the state should be kept out of economic matters wherever possible, Marx saw the state as intimately linked to the economic base. He argued that the state was wholly reflective of the interests of the bourgeoisie and that it created a political and legal framework to these ends.

AUTHOR BOX

Karl Marx (1818–1883)

Karl Marx was born in Prussia. The son of a lawyer, he studied law at university before becoming interested in philosophy during his PhD. He began his career as an editor of a radical newspaper in the Rhineland, but this was soon censored. After brief spells in Paris and Brussels, he moved to London in 1849. There he lived in poverty and spent much of his time in the reading room of the British Museum.

The sheer quantity of Marx's work makes it hard to make generalisations and there is often dispute about precisely what Marx said. A common approach is to divide his work into two distinct eras: the earlier writings that set out his philosophical approach and outline the concept of historical materialism. Then, the later work, known as the 'economics', which begins with the *Grundrisse* (unpublished at the time). This was followed by *Capital*, the first volume of which was published in 1867.

The aim of Marx's economics was to devise a radical critique of the classical liberal political economy of Smith and Ricardo, which his longstanding friend and colleague, Friedrich Engels, had introduced him to. It is a vast understatement to say that the aim of this project was ambitious. He had hoped to complete six volumes in total, covering capital, landed property, wage labour, the state, international trade, and the world market. *Capital* eventually grew to three volumes, and only the first of these was published in his lifetime.

Marx was also a political activist. The *Communist Manifesto* (1848) was published with the direct intention of helping to trigger social revolution. He witnessed first hand the Industrial Revolution in Great Britain and expressed moral indignation at the working and living conditions of the men, women and children who were employed in the mills and factories at the centre of this economic transformation. He was one of the founders of the International Workingmen's Association in 1864 and his ideas and reputation steadily grew. Marxist thought has had a significant influence on the world over the last century and a half. This influence would not have been predicted at the time. Only eleven mourners are thought to have attended his funeral at Highgate cemetery.

After Marx's death it became increasingly apparent that the revolution that Marx had predicted was not occurring. Almost every Marxist thinker since has been concerned with the continued vitality of capitalism. The logical interpretation of his arguments was that change should have taken place in those countries that were in the most advanced stages of capitalist development (at the time this was within Western Europe). However, in the years after Marx's death capitalism had expanded to other areas of the world.

Lenin (see author box) significantly extended Marx's ideas. He sought to explain how both imperialism and conflict were also endemic to capitalism. Lenin argued that as capitalism decayed in the most advanced states, the drive for profit and new markets would lead capitalists to export capital abroad. Governments, through colonisation and the extension of empire, would protect these overseas interests. This, in turn, would result in rivalry between states and conflict over potential colonial territories. Hence, Lenin agreed with Marx that capitalism had inherent contradictions, but that imperialism was another stage of historical development necessary before its downfall.

AUTHOR BOX

Vladimir Illyich Lenin (1870–1924)

Lenin was born in Russia and was engaged in revolutionary activities, for which he spent both time in prison and in exile in Siberia. He spent over a decade abroad before returning in 1917 to lead the first Soviet government after the Bolshevik Revolution.

He made a major contribution to the debate over the role of imperialism. As an active revolutionary Lenin sought to assess how the capitalist mode of production had remained resilient to the crises predicted by Marx. In *Imperialism: The Highest Stage of Capitalism*, which was written while Lenin was in exile in Switzerland in 1916, he argued that the nature of capitalism had changed since the time of Marx. Lenin suggested that colonies provided the advanced industrial economies with a market for unwanted goods and cheap natural resources. Most importantly, they also halted the potential for revolution, by providing additional profits that could be used to placate their own proletariats with higher wages.

Some Marxist thinkers have since argued that, despite the demise of the colonial era after the Second World War, the era of imperialism has continued via the operation of multinational corporations.

The idea that imperialism was contributing to the global spread and eventual demise of capitalism was challenged by dependency theory during the 1950s and 1960s. This approach shares some of the concerns of earlier Marxist thought; however, the structure of the world economy and the nature of the trade relations between states is central. This led to fierce criticism from other Marxist thinkers.

Raúl Prebisch was one of the pioneers of this approach. He was an economist from Argentina who became the inaugural director of the United Nations Economic Commission for Latin America (ECLA). His analysis of the world economy rested on a division between the advanced industrial countries ('the core') and the global South ('the periphery'). Prebisch argued that capitalist development in the core was not leading to industrialisation in the periphery and the conditions for socialist revolution, but rather to the perpetual underdevelopment of the latter. His analysis rested on the nature of the trade between the two. He noted that the core tended to trade manufactured goods (for example, televisions) in exchange for primary commodities (such as bananas) from the periphery. Prebisch argued that this situation was undesirable as in the long-run the tendency is for the terms of trade to work against those economies based on primary commodities. His reasons for this belief were that the application of technology to primary products, to increase efficiency, was far more difficult than in the production of manufactured goods, such as in the example of televisions. Second, demand for primary commodities tends to remain relatively fixed compared to the demand for manufactured goods. To take the example of bananas, demand for this good is unlikely to change drastically over time.

This concern with the structural importance of capitalism was then explored by Immanuel Wallerstein to develop what is commonly referred to as world-system theory. This furthers the view that there is polarisation between countries in the world economy. The essence of world-system theory is that every domestic political struggle or economic difficulty should be viewed as part of the system as a whole. Wallerstein introduced a new group of countries, the semi-periphery, which he argued were vital to the consolidation of the capitalist world economy. The semi-periphery acts as a buffer between the core and periphery. These states are relatively less dependent on the core and they tend to have both some level of industrialisation and more organised administrative structures relative to the periphery.

It is evident from this section that there have been a number of different approaches within the Marxist perspective. With the collapse of the Soviet Union, many scholars of IPE sought to write off the potential use of this approach. This rather simplistic view fails to distinguish between the application of Marxism–Leninism in the former communist states and the ideas of Marx and his followers. Many of these still appear pertinent to the current situation. One key theme that continues to unite scholars within this perspective is the continued existence of oppression and inequality in the era of globalisation (see the example box on the next page).

> **EXAMPLE BOX**
>
> ## Marxism in action: underdevelopment
>
> Marxist approaches continue to highlight how the world economy is extremely unequal. A number of measures of global inequality can be used to describe the current situation. A brief sample includes the following:
>
> - More than 1.2 billion people (about 15 per cent of the world's population) are living on less than US$1 per day.
> - More than 1 billion people in developing countries do not have access to clean water.
> - In 2008 inflows of foreign direct investment (FDI) to Africa totalled approximately US$11 billion, which represents only around 1.7 per cent of global FDI inflows.
>
> This situation led to the world's heads of state adopting a UN Declaration in 2000. This set out the Millennium Development Goals, which were designed in an attempt to tackle such indicators of inequality. However, many Marxist writers would highlight the inevitability of such gross inequality within a capitalist system. See Chapter 8 for a more detailed discussion of development.

Criticisms of Marxism

- The classical Marxist view of the state as a tool for the promotion of the interests of the bourgeoisie is often criticised as being overly simplistic. Realist scholars, for example, view the state as an independent actor that is able to promote the 'national interest' rather than the interests of the capitalist class. Other theorists have undertaken a comparative historical analysis to demonstrate how the policies adopted by states do not always reflect the interests of the capitalist class.
- Marx's view of history as a dialectical process, whereby capitalism would eventually be replaced by communism is now generally viewed, with hindsight, as optimistic at best. Moreover, with the end of the Cold War and the adoption of free market economics in many former communist states, the alternatives to capitalism appear problematic.
- Many critics view the explanation of all issues within the framework of class struggle as an oversimplification. Other radical theorists have highlighted how oppression based on different divisions, for example inequality based on gender, are masked by a purely class-based analysis.
- The importance attached to economic factors in explaining relations between states is perceived as a major weakness. Strategic and political issues are also deemed to be essential in understanding the behaviour of states within IPE. Lenin's view of imperialism as being of purely economic importance to the colonial powers is deemed highly questionable from such a perspective.

Summary

This chapter has provided a simplified account of the historical development of theoretical approaches to the study of IPE. By adopting an approach based on three perspectives it has been possible to summarise some of the major developments over the last few centuries. We have seen that the realist perspective puts states at the centre of its analysis. The pursuit of wealth within a competitive state system is viewed as the most important aspect of IPE. The liberal perspective, in contrast, wishes to minimise the role of the state so that markets can be allowed to function freely. This is seen as the most efficient way of organising the world economy. Finally, the Marxist perspective provides us with a critical approach to analysing IPE. Here it is class conflict that is vital to our understanding.

What this chapter has also demonstrated is the relationship between real world events and the development of theory. Social realities have been shown to influence the individual experiences of some of the leading figures in the development of theory. It is therefore important to appreciate that theoretical development does not take place in a vacuum, and that an appreciation of historical context is important. With this in mind, the following chapter considers 'mainstream' approaches to IPE in a contemporary setting.

Reflective questions

1   What features distinguish the above approaches from each other?
2   Do writings from the eighteenth and nineteenth centuries still have contemporary relevance?
3   How might the concepts of 'core' and 'periphery' be applied to contemporary IPE?
4   What historical examples can you give of 'real world' events helping to shape theoretical approaches?
5   How significant was critique between the main proponents of each approach in refining their relative positions?

Suggestions for further reading

Backhouse, R. (2002) *The Penguin History of Economics*, London: Penguin.
Bucholz, T. (1999) *New Ideas From Dead Economists: An Introduction to Modern Economic Thought*, London: Penguin.
Crane, G. and Amawi, A. (eds) (1997) *The Theoretical Evolution of International Political Economy: A Reader*, Oxford: Oxford University Press.
Hamilton, A. (1791) *Report on Manufactures*, Washington, D.C.: US Congress.
Hume, D. (2009) [1752] *Political Discourses*, Whitefish: Kessinger Publishing.
Lenin, V. (1997) [1916] *Imperialism: The Highest Stage of Capitalism*, New York: International Publishers.
List, F. (1977) [1841] *The National System of Political Economy*, Fairfield: Augustus M. Kelley.
Marx, K. (2008) [1867] *Capital*, Oxford: Oxford University Press.
Marx, K. and Engels, F. (2002) [1848] *The Communist Manifesto*, London: Penguin.
Mill, J.S. (1998) *On Liberty and Other Essays*, Oxford: Oxford University Press.
Ricardo, D. (1996) [1817] *Principles of Political Economy and Taxation*, New York: Prometheus Books.
Smith, A. (1999) [1776] *The Wealth of Nations*, London: Penguin.
Wheen, F. (1999) *Karl Marx*, London: Fourth Estate.

2 Mainstream contemporary approaches of IPE

Chapter learning outcomes

After reading this chapter students should be able to:

- Understand and summarise the assumptions and theories of the three core approaches considered in this chapter.
- Cite the work of one or more key author(s) associated with each approach.
- Recognise how debates between scholars have shaped each approach.
- Explain how changes in the 'real world' since the mid 1900s have shaped the development of these core theoretical approaches.
- Demonstrate a critical awareness of the broad strengths and weaknesses of each approach.
- Understand the criticisms of each approach.
- Be able to use these approaches in the study of international political economy.

Introduction

Having established the theoretical foundations of the discipline, this chapter will develop the discussion in Chapter 1. Here we look at what we identify as the three 'core' paradigms/approaches to IPE. While not an arbitrary choice, we recognise that some scholars may feel that what we have termed as 'alternative' paradigms, to be discussed in Chapter 3, are in fact 'mainstream'. Our selection is based upon the underlying assumptions and theoretical lineage of the literature under discussion. Furthermore, the majority of IPE literature utilises – rightly or wrongly – one of the three paradigms we discuss here.

The aim here is to introduce new approaches and concepts while encouraging the reader to make correlations with the historical approaches discussed in Chapter 1. Also, the reader will be prompted to consider the relevance and importance of each contemporary approach and how these make up the different pieces of the global jigsaw, which ultimately fit together in interpreting events in the globalising world.

The main focus of the discussion which follows in this chapter will be on the contemporary neo-realist, neo-liberal and structural approaches. We will outline the emergence of sub-paradigms, the evolution of some of the basic principles, or more precisely the evolution of how these aims and objectives are best understood and met. Whereas the main principles of the classical approaches may not have changed entirely, the utility of these in understanding and explaining an increasingly complex set of international/global interactions has been questioned. Therefore, as the world has changed, the manner in which it is analysed has had to adapt. This applies to all the paradigms discussed in Chapter 1. Here we will consider how these approaches have attempted to maintain their core analytical principles but in a modified form in order to address contemporary issues and concerns.

In distinguishing between 'mainstream' and 'alternative' approaches to the study of IPE, one of the criteria we refer to is the difference between those approaches which are positivist and those which are normative. By positivist we mean a scientific approach which seeks to understand and explain phenomena using empirical observation and rational analysis and deduction. In contrast, normative approaches rely more upon subjective interpretation in the study of phenomena in a manner which seeks to understand and explain how the world could and, crucially, *should* be. The 'mainstream' approaches we are focusing on here are all positivist.

Neo-realism

Central arguments

- Human nature is seen as inherently selfish and bad (Waltz, 1959).
- The state remains the primary actor but there is recognition of the significance of non-state actors, particularly MNCs (Krasner, 1982).
- Power relations also remain central, but can take many forms.
- State security can be influenced by physical, economic and environmental factors (Krasner, 1982).
- The international system remains anarchic; however, there are instances of issue-specific inter-state collaboration and governance.
- The most important ways in which events and outcomes can be explained is at the international system level. The structure of the system shapes – or maybe even determines – the behaviour of the 'units', whether they are states or other actors, and it is not the case that individual unit behaviour determines the way the system works, although over time they may affect its structure (Waltz, 1979).

Neo-realists adopt the same founding principles of classical realism, but recognise that in the contemporary system economics influences state behaviour. For neo-realists states are in conflict in the anarchical international arena over issues including security, foreign policy and economics, especially international trade and monetary relations. For example, one state's increase in military expenditure is presumed to threaten the security of other states. In precisely the same way, one state's policy to increase its trade surplus leads to other states' trade deficits. This is a zero-sum situation, in other words; where there is any redistribution of resources (military power or economic) in favour of one state this will necessarily be at the expense of another.

Security and economic issues are closely related, although the latter is determined by factors relating to security issues. Security for neo-realists, however, is not limited to the military aspect of world affairs. It also includes resource security, food security, energy security and the capacity to secure capital. Since the international system is deemed to be anarchical, states aim to attain autonomy to avoid the influence of other economies. Neo-realism has emerged to address the economic changes in the international system but concepts such as anarchy, security and power are still very much in vogue in neo-realism. A key advocate of neo-realist thought is Kenneth Waltz (see author box). Waltz's contribution to realist thought has modernised the realist paradigm, and incorporated realist positivism into the discipline of IPE.

AUTHOR BOX

Kenneth Waltz

Kenneth Waltz's seminal text *Man, the State and War* can be seen as the neo-realist starting point for analysing the causes of war. His *Theory of International Politics* represents a divergence from classical realism. He argues that international relations can be analysed by applying a systemic framework; although he still gives primacy to the state, anarchy and security, he recognises the existence of structures. For Waltz the international system operates on three levels:

System	Hierarchical vs Anarchical
Unit	States/Non-state actors
Individual	People

The international system, in Waltz's view, is rigid and defined. This has forced states and economic institutions to act as units in the system. It is the system which defines the actions of all the units within the given system. Waltz argues that there are two kinds of system:

- A hierarchical system where all units are organised under a clear structure of authority.
- An anarchical system where all units interact with one another without a clear structure of authority.

This differentiation of the system is crucial in Waltz's thought as he argues that the international system is anarchic. Contrary to what liberals believe, there is no clear line of hierarchy and no established legitimate world government. Waltz also identifies the anarchical system as being characterised by self-help, where each state regards other states as potential threats. Each state must change their stance in the system by assessing the power of others.

Waltz also agrees with the classical realist conception of the balance of power; however, for Waltz economics plays a significant part. Inter-state cooperation is sought in terms of 'relative gains', thus states will only cooperate when the gains outweigh or at least equal the gains of all other actors.

By incorporating structural analyses into realism, Waltz was able to address changes in the international system and answer questions that classical realism found problematic.

By concentrating on the nature of the system-level structure, Waltz avoided the need to make assumptions about human nature, morality, power and interest. Neo-realists were thus able to see power in a different way. For classical realists power was both a means and an end, and rational state behaviour was simply accumulating the most power. Neo-realists found a better channel was provided by assuming that the ultimate state interest was in security. The balance of power is central to neo-realism but takes into consideration non-state actors such as corporations and regional power blocs. However, states are still the most important actors; states only join international organisations or institutions to maximise and pursue their own interests; and agreements can easily be broken or suspended when this membership conflicts with a state's national interest. Again, this captures the risk and uncertainty of the international arena, for example economic changes in the international system such as the emergence of the Organisation of Petroleum Exporting Countries (OPEC) as a powerful world actor. The increased competitiveness between the United States, European Union (EU) and Japanese economies, and economic (in)stability in the post-Cold War era forced realism to consider what had previously been referred to as low politics.

ISSUE BOX

Agents of the state

A key element of neo-realist thought deals with the relationship between states and MNCs. By examining this relationship, neo-realism provides a more in-depth and sophisticated analysis of international patterns of power and influence. Neo-realists highlight the roles played by MNCs in relation to both their home and host states. Patterns of wealth creation and accumulation within state economies are increasingly tied to the operations of MNCs. The extent to which these operations are actively directed by states is open to debate. However, a clear correlation can be identified with regard to the interests of the home state and the activities of 'its' MNCs. The degree to which MNCs are seen as acting as independent actors in the global system is a key point in distinguishing between various approaches to the study of IPE, as will be seen when we consider neo-liberal approaches.

Superficially, US MNCs such as MacDonald's and Coca-Cola can be viewed as simply profit-orientated business ventures. However, neo-realists claim that their influence extends beyond the purely financial to socio-cultural realms. The attractiveness of American products is, arguably, related to the potential attractiveness of American cultural values. Classical realists would be sceptical of making such connections between issues.

Within the discipline of IPE, neo-realist theory has developed to analyse the complex economic governance of the global economy, economic institutions, foreign debt crisis, and issues surrounding regional interdependence. The neo-realist approach to IPE posed direct challenges to both structural and liberal approaches. Neo-realists accused liberal and structural IPE theories of focusing on economics and underestimating the importance of state power. For neo-realists it is the distribution of state power which determines how economic interaction will operate, and not the growth of interlinked economies as liberal theory would argue. Neo-realism believes that the major factor when analysing power distribution within the international system is whether or not there exists a dominant power.

Hegemonic stability theory

Hegemonic stability theory (HST) is one of the most highly developed forms of neo-realism, but hegemonic stability theory is a hybrid theory which relates to neo-liberalism and structuralism. Both neo-realist and neo-liberal scholars encompass the idea of hegemonic stability in their theoretical horizons, but there are significant differences. The most distinctive difference is that while neo-liberals analyse hegemonic stability in terms of the supply of public goods in a free trade economy, neo-realists use it to justify protectionist policies.

A key principle of the nation state system is sovereignty and the maxim that there is no authority higher than the state. This does not mean that the international system is completely without order or hierarchy. Over time it is possible to identify several states that have held the position of the dominant state for a period of years. Such a state is known by the term 'hegemonic'. Hegemonic stability theory, most famously developed and articulated by Charles Kindleberger in *The World in Depression: 1929–1939* (1986), argues that a dominant power is needed to enforce rules of interaction between states in order to avoid the security dilemmas associated with a system that lacks the oversight of such a power. These ideas also have their roots in Albert O. Hirschmann's *National Power and the Structure of Foreign Trade* (1980), a book published in the 1940s and neglected until it was republished by a group of neo-realist scholars who found in it a sharply drawn justification for their attack on liberal trade theories.

Different states have ascended and descended from hegemonic status throughout history. Paul Kennedy charts such patterns in his book *The Rise and Fall of the Great Powers 1500 to 2000* (1989). During the fifteenth century Portugal and Spain vied for hegemonic position as they dominated the early years of European exploration and expansion. The sixteenth century saw the ascendancy of Holland with Dutch control of international finance and credit. Following this Britain became particularly successful in relation to its textile trade and dominance of the high seas. This position was later reinforced by its leading role in the Industrial Revolution and development of steamships and railway networks. Despite challenges from other European powers *Pax Britannica* remained in place until the ascendancy of the *Pax Americana*. Britain's decline began following the tremendous drain on resources inflicted by the First World War. However, it was not until after the Second World War that the US rose to prominence, as both an actor in its own right and, crucially, as a key player in the global institutions set up after the war. Britain's decline was marked by the point in spring 1916 when it became a net importer of capital for the first time for two centuries or more, and when the US became the world's primary exporter of capital. But the 1920s and 1930s were a period when, at least according to HST, the absence of a clear hegemonic structure contributed much to the instability and chaos of the period in political and social terms as well as in the world economy.

The dynamic of a stable hegemonic system has three basic requirements. First, there has to be a state with the capability to lay down and enforce the rules of a given system. Second, such a state has to have the political will to actually utilise this capability. Third, the other major states in such a system must see that there are mutual benefits to be had from engagement, even if the main benefits accrue in disproportionate measures to the hegemonic state. The underlying principle is one of consent rather than coercion. Clearly the hegemonic state would have the resources to impose its will on other players, at least in the shorter term. Yet such a policy would ultimately be counter-productive, as it would lead to resentment from other states and reluctance to engage in the hegemony-controlled order. The hegemonic power can afford to provide incentives for cooperation to other states to engage with the system, as it will ultimately reap benefits from such engagement (see also Strange, 1987).

By now it should be clear that longer-term stability cannot necessarily be guaranteed. As we have seen, 'great' powers come and go. The cycle of transition is based on the rise of rival states. Hegemonic states can endure for many years but, to date, they always peak and then enter a period of relative decline. In part this is due to increased difficulty in maintaining their domestic order while simultaneously concentrating on upholding international stability. At the same time other powers rise in their positions of power within the system. Once this train of events is in motion there can be a regression towards a greater risk of conflict as the challenging powers vie for supremacy in the reordering of the system. Such manoeuvres have previously been associated with open warfare. This does not, though, have to be the case and transitions of power can equally be played out in terms of economic dominance or more abstract elements such as respect for the authority of the hegemonic state. In contemporary terms there is a sense that it is this latter point that is the current challenge for the US in maintaining its position of authority.

Both neo-liberalism and neo-realism agree that a hegemonic state must be willing and able to lead but they have differing views on the leadership methods and motives (liberal views are discussed later in this chapter). Kindleberger saw the global system and viewed the hegemonic state as ensuring the stability of the economic system for the greater good. Neo-realism directed the attention away from this idea to the idea of a dominant state structuring economic international relations in the pursuit of power, wealth and security. Furthermore, neo-realism portrays the hegemonic state as pursuing and maximising its own national self-interest, and is also interested in relative gains. The hegemonic state would also act coercively in the pursuit of such gains, for example it is capable of cutting off trade investment and aid in order to force other states in the system to accept its hierarchical position. The dominant state also has the power to impose a standard and a regime and this situation is beneficial to economic relations, the free market international economy, which is protected. Neo-realism uses the idea of hegemonic stability to show how war is avoided and national interest is maximised through the protection of economic policies.

The United States was seen as the state that most championed, and gained from, such a global framework. In contrast to this view, there were arguments that although remaining powerful the United States was in decline relative to the rise of an expanding European Union trading bloc and other growing economies, notably China. While it is true that the US 'market share' of the global economy may have declined relative to other states, it should be noted that the underlying principles of the system continue to favour the United States. The opening of China's economy has yet to lead to an equally liberal political system. However, for the United States the increasing engagement of China with the global economy remains an advantage. Although in some respects a competitor, China's burgeoning economy currently stimulates international trade to the advantage of the United States.

Criticisms of neo-realism

■ Neo-realist theory in IR makes an assumption, especially within economic nationalism, that it is possible to have a comprehensive and objective national interest. Many critics have highlighted that policies designed to advance the interests of the state as a whole can actually represent the particular interests of certain groups that are able to influence policy-makers.

■ The neo-realist conception of rational action is an assumption and not always a reality. Also, there is no way of deciphering if decisions are rational in adhering to national interest or rational for the administration in power. Rational actor models do not take into account the implementation of a decision, or lack of it, through organisational processes and procedures.

■ Neo-realism can be accused of underestimating economics. Hegemonic stability theory, and its emphasis on relative gains and security, marginalises economics. This causes critics to be doubtful of the influence of economic organisations in promoting peace. Also, this restricts realists and places limitations on their understanding of globalisation.

■ Neo-realism strives to maintain the structural status quo, by reducing history to recurring patterns. Neo-realists do not envisage any structural change within the international system. The balance of power may alternate but the basic rules of the system are fixed and rigid.

■ Neo-realist conceptions of power are too simplistic. Neo-realism does not take into account broader non-state-centric power relations, for example gender or class.

■ Neo-realism is incapable of giving an account of the complexity of inter-institutional behaviour at either the international or domestic level on issues such as trade and monetary policies where core ideas are embedded in institutional practices and procedures and reflected in outcomes and behaviours (the criticism most strongly made by neo-liberal institutionalists such as Goldstein – see below).

Neo-liberalism

Central arguments

■ Human nature is inherently good, or at least strongly inclined towards good.
■ Conflict is avoidable through cooperation for mutual gains.
■ Global governance is attainable and desirable.
■ Plurality of actors with no single type of actor maintaining universal primacy.
■ Free market economics is the preferred system of exchange, bringing benefits to all even if they are not evenly distributed across the global system.
■ Power can be manifested in many forms and is not purely state- and military-centric.

Liberalism is the most influential perspective in IPE. Liberal approaches to IPE are difficult to summarise as they are pluralist in nature and seek to analyse a wide range of issues and actors within IPE.

Neo-liberals share the Enlightenment scholars' optimistic view, reflected in nineteenth-century British political economy, that human nature is inherently good and capable of achieving peace through cooperative actions. The emphasis on trade in liberal thought highlights interactions that move away from self-sufficiency but remain self-interested in overall aims and objectives. So, from this viewpoint the 'rational' policy is one where there is an increased reliance on the actions of others. This is the basis of interdependence theories which are discussed further below.

The orthodoxy of liberal economics can be seen as a combination of self-interest and, with varying degrees of rhetoric, the promotion of the interests of others. For example, in terms of international aid from the more prosperous to the less economically advanced parts of the world. In rational terms there is a self-interest in the more developed states to prevent others 'failing' and becoming destabilised, with a risk of conflicts disrupting trade flows and, possibly, extending conflict beyond their borders. Such a scenario brings together the free market economics of classical liberal thought with the more state-centric realist position. However, the role of the state in neo-liberal theory differs significantly from realist perceptions; the state according to neo-liberals is sovereign but it is not an autonomous actor. Before the First World War, Norman Angell (1911) predicted that there would be no war because any conflict would irreparably damage the structure of international trade and payments and cause long-term financial problems too irrational to be bearable. He was wrong, in the sense that of course the war did come in 1914; but he was also right in that it was enormously destructive to the shared interests of the European powers, and brought about not only the eventual collapse of their empires but also an economic instability that was not restored until 1949.

Although viewed differently by varying approaches, the concept of sovereignty remains central to the study of both IPE and IR. In terms of autonomy of action, states are, in principle, free to act as they choose. Of course such autonomy is constrained by a range of impediments such as access to resources, geographical position, demography, technological expertise and so forth. Within a neo-liberal analysis, all states benefit from cooperation rather than conflict, regardless of their relative capabilities. Governance is a key issue and is relevant to the political, economic, socio-cultural, environmental and security spheres (later chapters provide examples of aspects of governance in all of these areas). The neo-liberal position is that national interests are better pursued and maximised in a cooperative and collaborative environment, including state and non-state actors, rather than the realist scenario of a war of all against all. The issue of governance has moved beyond state-centrism with an exotic kaleidoscope of various actors and issues.

While recognising the ongoing importance of the state, neo-liberals distinguish the relative power of states at certain times and in relation to particular issue areas. For example, the United States might be seen as the world's only superpower. This is accurate with regards to some criteria such as military capabilities and in some areas of technological expertise. However, in certain circumstances the United States may appear to be relatively weak. In economic terms the United States has the world's largest trade deficit and its per capita rates of consumption are non-sustainable over the longer term. In contrast a successful MNC could be viewed as having greater financial autonomy and influence. MNCs also have an advantage in not being territorially bound; therefore, in this mixed-actor analysis certain actors are in a more advantageous position relative to others depending on the political, economic and social environment. This situation can also change dramatically over time as events unfold. Other non-state actors such as NGOs are increasingly a part of this dynamic set of relationships.

Neo-liberalism accepts notions of hierarchies of power, albeit interpreted differently to the power politics model of classical realism *and* the structural realist model of neo-realism. Power relationships can be identified in all of the sectors referred to above. Forms of power can be categorised either as physical/military power, productive power, financial power or knowledge as power. For neo-liberals, all of these forms of power can have a significant impact on the relative status and influence of various actors. Furthermore, all the types of actors may possess one or more of these forms of power. Physical/military power remains a key component of state power but there are many examples of civil wars, insurgency movements, terrorist organisations and what are effectively 'military' personnel in the private sector. Productive power will vary relative to the strength of an economy in particular sectors, for example primary resources, manufacturing, finance and service industries. Financial power can be seen in the context of a state's overall economy, the performance of associated MNCs and particularly wealthy individuals. The power of knowledge and technological expertise has always been important in the evolution of human history especially with regards to the development of certain types of weaponry. In the contemporary world this is particularly pertinent in the fields of information and communication technologies.

Neo-liberals are also critical of the idea that national interest is defined in terms of territorial or military security. Instead there is no fixed or consistent 'national interest' as it changes and reflects the positions of groups both inside and outside the state. Furthermore, where neo-realists assert that state interaction is carried out on the basis of relative gains, neo-liberals argue that interaction in the international system is about securing absolute gains. In this view cooperation is possible and intensified by interdependent relationships, so the role of the state is to ensure that the various interests of governments and society are represented in the international system. Economic neo-liberal thought is not solely concerned with the promotion of state interests but, rather, entrepreneurs and business communities. Entrepreneurial communities are seen as profit-maximisers; their goals are simple, to sell more products and to accumulate more capital without political intervention.

Interdependence

Interdependence theories are a strand of neo-liberal thought. They provide a critique of neo-realist positions of power politics, highlighting the inability of neo-realism in interpreting certain areas or events which happen in contemporary relations. However, this perspective does share similarities with the neo-realist conception of the international system in that both schools of thought recognise the anarchic nature of the system. Furthermore, interdependence approaches are fundamentally different, in that they uphold and adhere to neo-liberal traditions.

As mentioned above, a key feature of interdependence approaches is a recognition of the plurality of actors and issues. In terms of interdependence, while power relationships remain important they cannot be as easily understood and explained as in classical realist zero-sum games. In part this is because of the complex set of intertwined issues and relationships that represent contemporary political, economic and socio-cultural interactions. For example, China's increased engagement with the rest of the world illustrates this point well. On the one hand, China's trading partners welcome the growth of the Chinese economy and the market opportunities that this provides. On the other hand, there is growing international concern as China's economic growth has led to a huge demand for energy which, at present, is largely fuelled by the burning of coal which results in a massive amount of greenhouse gas emissions. This example represents the increasingly fluid and dynamic nature of international relations. Depending on a combination of circumstances at a particular time, individual actors will enjoy greater or lesser power and influence in relation to other actors. This is in contrast to generally more fixed attributes of power associated with classical realism. While classical realists acknowledge fluctuations in power relationships, the diversity of power relationships across the political, economic and socio-cultural sectors make this approach somewhat limited.

There are two variants of interdependence that can be described and explained, the first being asymmetric or uneven interdependence and the second being a mutually beneficial or mutually disadvantaging level of interconnectedness. In a situation of asymmetric interdependence two or more actors are dependent on each other but to varying degrees. This is best explained using a two-state model. In this scenario, state X is highly dependent on state Y for raising revenues through exports to the consumer market of the latter while state Y is only marginally dependent on state X for imports. The disparity in levels of interdependence results in an asymmetry of power potential where power is the ability of one actor to compel another to act in a certain way that it would otherwise not.

The second variant of interdependence that can be described is one that is an ideal type of world system and is known as complex interdependence. This system is characterised by peace and stability through necessary cooperation due to extremely high levels of interdependence. In this system, the use of military force or other forms of violent confrontation will be counter-productive and irrational due to the reliance of actors on each other. Quite simply put, by violently confronting other actors in the international political economy you will be 'shooting yourself in the foot'.

In their book *Power and Interdependence*, Robert Keohane and Joseph Nye (2000) argue that classical realism is inadequate in explaining the contemporary international system. They depict an international system where states and non-state actors interact at varying levels. They developed the notion of a complex and interdependent system. Their cobweb model demonstrates how different actors interact within the system. These include states but, importantly, Keohane and Nye stress the distinction between state governments and the societies they claim to represent. There is also an emphasis at the level of the individual and their ability to form relationships and communities that can be cross-border in nature. For example, MNCs, by definition, operate across borders. Although differing perspectives vary in how they view the relationship between governments and MNCs, from a complex interdependence viewpoint the emphasis is on both the end result of MNC activities and also the process by which relations are formed and maintained between MNCs and their home and host governments. The role of new social movements is also highlighted. Relationships are formed which are non-governmental in nature. The existence of a common cause or set of interests has created a plethora of global networks. Some of these may be focused on lobbying governments but their essential character is one that is drawn from civil society.

The cobweb model refers to the range of actors involved. It depicts the multiple interactions which occur between different actors, such as states, MNCs, IGOs and NGOs. These actors are all representative of changes in the evolution of relations between states and non-state actors. This model demonstrates the complex nature of the international system. In contrast to the rather simplistic nature of the system presented by realism, the above model shows that there are interactions between multiple actors, and at various levels. Pluralism, within the context of neo-liberalism, is about more than recognising the role and position of non-state actors. It also extends the range of issues which are theorised, for example gender, sexual politics, indigenous rights, migration and diasporas issues and other aspects of identity politics.

EXAMPLE BOX

Examples of interdependent relationships

State-to-state relations – can be bilateral or multilateral. It is important to note that these may be symmetrical or asymmetrical in nature. For example France, Germany and the UK are generally comparable powers within the context of the EU. In contrast, relations between the US and some of the smaller Central American or Caribbean states are of a different order.

State-to-MNC – again asymmetrical relations exist whereby differing states will be in a greater or lesser position of influence in relation to MNCs operating in their territory. For example, Coca-Cola has operations in various states. However, the relationship between Coca-Cola and the US government and the governments of India, Columbia and Ireland are markedly different.

State-to-NGO – this can operate as either a domestic or international relationship. Friends of the Earth and Greenpeace both have national branches that lobby their respective governments. In addition they operate an international office that coordinates environmental campaigns (civil society-to-civil society).

MNC-to-civil society – many non-governmental pressure groups and trade unions have called for consumer boycotts of MNC-produced goods.

Individual-to-individual – this would include various types of cross-border and domestic relationships. These can include networks, such as academics, health sector and media professionals. Personal relationships can be extended and internationalised by way of migration, inter-marriages and study abroad.

In addition to the relationship examples given above there are also examples of broader systemic change. The foremost among these has been described as the 'triumph' of neo-liberalism. This refers to both political and economic sectors. This position argues that following the collapse of the former Soviet Union there has been a global trend towards adopting more democratic political systems. Similarly, there has been a wide adoption of neo-liberal economic models.

Neo-liberal triumphalism

One of the main characteristics of globalisation has been the spread of neo-liberal political and economic ideas and practices. Political autonomy remains a core principle of the international system, whereas economic autonomy has been transformed by the growth of interdependence and the increased role and influence of private sector actors. Michael Doyle is associated with democratic peace theory and the so-called 'zone of peace'. He argues that the empirical record suggests that stable liberal democracies are highly unlikely to engage in armed conflict with each other. The argument here is that liberal democracies are more representative of their citizens who, from a neo-liberal perspective, are fundamentally peaceful and prefer cooperation to conflict. It therefore follows that the spread of liberal democratic forms of governance should be encouraged. There is a suggestion within neo-liberalism that in order to achieve this, one should encourage liberal economic policies.

With the fall of the Soviet Union, authors such as Francis Fukuyama (see author box) in his *End of History* thesis, claim that capitalism and liberal democracy have triumphed and that it is difficult to imagine a world order that would overturn the current economic and political landscape. It is important to highlight that Fukuyama's argument refers to the principles of political and economic neo-liberalism rather than referring to a particular state or economy. Liberal triumphalism argues that human history has been a single evolutionary process from one condition to a final and ideal form of human organisation. This final 'destination' has been reached with the attainment of capitalism and liberal democracy. Of course this position can be critiqued as certain individuals are actively disadvantaged under capitalism. Similarly, liberal democracies can include disadvantages for certain minority groups.

AUTHOR BOX

Francis Fukuyama: *The End of History and the Last Man* (1992)

This book was published shortly after the Cold War. In his book Fukuyama formulated an explanation and provided an analysis of the collapse of the Soviet Union. According to Fukuyama, the Soviet Union collapsed because people in the Eastern bloc wanted material wealth and consumerism; the command economies and authoritarian political systems of communism were resisted and eventually rejected. Fukuyama hailed this as a triumph for both political and economic liberal thought and practice. The title of this book is significant as the 'end of history' denotes the arrival of a liberal political and economic system that is unlikely to face serious challenges from a competing ideology. This apparent victory led to the US having a renewed confidence in liberal policies. Since the end of the Cold War the US has become more assertive and widened their foreign policy agenda. This more proactive position, coupled with Fukuyama's thesis, led scholars and politicians to present an idea of a 'new world order,' one in which the US dominates politics and economics promoting their ideas to states which have not previously subscribed to liberal ideas. This new order is based on the principles of liberal democratic politics and 'free' market economics. Fukuyama's ideas have to some extent been appropriated by US neo-conservatives as justification for increasing US hegemony. This is why Fukuyama's work has been so controversial. His ideas can be associated with both historical and neo-liberal perspectives. His work has also received much criticism from Marxist-inspired approaches as well as other critical approaches.

Triumphalism has been identified largely in the historical context of the end of the Cold War. However, the processes leading towards this so-called triumph had been taking place for decades. Significantly these processes have taken place within emerging political and economic structures, particularly those created post-Second World War. In particular, the creation of international organisations such as the World Bank, the United Nations and the International Monetary Fund signalled a new world order that reflected the decline of European empires and the emergence of the United States in particular as the leading world power. In terms of ideology the liberal democratic model adopted and to some extent promoted by the United States was countered by the communist bloc led by the former Soviet Union and China. As important as this political divide was, it is arguable that the real driver for change and development was in the sphere of economics. The example of China's greater willingness to embrace the principles of free market economics rather than democracy also illustrates this point further.

Criticisms of neo-liberalism

- Overestimation of the ability of the free market to provide for the basic needs of all and the assumption that 'developing' states will achieve economic 'take-off' with a resulting 'trickle down' effect benefiting all of society.
- Neo-liberalism does not critique the hierarchical nature of the international system. Interdependence may be assumed to reflect a fairly equal relationship that can involve active power relations of dominance, coercion and submission.
- They have misinterpreted fundamental aspects of human nature – i.e. that it is inherently passive and cooperative as opposed to aggressive and prone to conflict.
- Neo-liberalism fails to acknowledge structural contexts, such as inequalities within so-called 'free trade agreements' or patriarchal social structures. Without an understanding of such structural constraints this results in a partial and misleading understanding and analysis of relationships.
- The *End of History* thesis assumes a 'triumph' of capitalism and liberal democracy without giving sufficient consideration to alternative futures. The long-heralded 'crisis of capitalism' has, arguably, already arrived – albeit focused on particularly marginalised social groups and environments.
- 'Complex interdependence' may be a condition which we can *describe* in the global political economy, especially in relations between advanced industrialised economies; but neo-realists and structuralist Marxists would join together for once in agreeing that that does not therefore *explain* anything at all – Waltz (1979) is especially insistent on this point.

Structuralism

Central arguments

- Political, social and economic structures develop over time.
- The global system can be subdivided into core, periphery and semi-periphery components.
- Understanding and analysis is based upon class divisions.
- Processes create and then reinforce structures.
- A central focus is on inequalities within the global economic system, and how to promote greater equality and justice.

Structuralism within IPE provides an important critique of neo-realist and neo-liberal explanations of international political economy. Structural analysis originated from the ideas and workings of Karl Marx (discussed in Chapter 1). This is not to say that each theorist working under the rubric of structuralism has been influenced by Marx in the same way. Each scholar has developed different theoretical strands within the workings of Marx. It is also important to note that structuralism within IPE also has distinct strands such as dependency theory and world-system theory.

Structuralism is concerned with the hierarchical systemic nature of international political economy as opposed to states acting as autonomous units. For structuralism events in international relations such as war, the signing of treaties, the transfer of aid and the operations of MNCs all occur within one identifiable structure which is the global capitalist system. This structure places limits and constraints which in turn affects the outcome of world events.

Structuralism can be identified as a 'bottom-up' approach, in that it prioritises and sides with the world's poor and disadvantaged. Specifically, the structural approach highlights both the tiered hierarchical structure in which industrially advanced states dominate and exploit less developed states and the differentiation between classes within states. Structuralist theories, unlike neo-realism and neo-liberalism, aim to expose the underlying or hidden truths of the workings of global capitalism. By concentrating on the nature of the hierarchical system, structuralism aims to show how global capitalism ensures that the powerful and wealthy (states, individuals and corporations) continue to prosper at the expense of the world's powerless.

Attempts by advocates of Marxism to radically change the structure of the international system can be identified in the examples of Russia, Cuba and China. These domestic revolutions had their own idiosyncrasies. Each had determining factors specific to their situations. The stated aims of these revolutions were a combination of overthrowing the existing domestic ruling elite, while also locating this within a broader international class struggle. What these revolutions had in common was an objective to unite revolutionary forces across state boundaries. It is the international dimension that more accurately reflects the attempt to instigate structural change. Change did occur, but the major structural changes happened inside the states in terms of reordering the class system and ownership of the means of production via collectivisation. Structural change in the international stage occurred in the form of a shift from a multi-polar system, which can be traced back to the European imperial era, to a post-Second World War bi-polar system. Arguably this might be seen as tri-polar following the Sino-Soviet split during the 1960s. But the fundamental divide was an ideological one between capitalist-based societies and those following a Marxist/Leninist-inspired approach. This divide was, of course, also overlain with the nuclear division and competition between the US and USSR.

The failure of these revolutions to create a domino effect and radically overthrow the world economic system led opponents of Marxism to render it insufficient, both in theory and practice. Due to the collapse of Eastern European communism, Marxist popularity diminished and the world moved in to what has been termed a new world order, an order which is dominated by liberal ideologies and free market capitalism. Political, economic and technological changes through the latter part of the twentieth century have all contributed to increased disparities, inequalities and marginalisation of certain economies and people. These growing disparities within the global economic system prompted the further development of Marxist-inspired theory.

Processes of globalisation have increasingly integrated national economies, especially with regards to methods of production, distribution and consumption. Advocates of the structural perspective would view and interpret globalisation as an extension and entrenchment of the capitalist process (see Chapter 4). Capitalist processes have worked to marginalise, subjugate and disadvantage some people and states, yet empower others. Crucially for structuralists these processes develop over time. As they do so they reinforce and embed power relationships and capabilities.

Neo-realism focuses on states and tends to be hierarchical in terms of various forms of power. Neo-liberalism, on the other hand, has a more implicit sense of power relationships with the emphasis being more on highlighting the number and diversity of actors under consideration. For structuralism the range of actors is important but the crucial and distinctive aspect of this school of thought is the channels and flows of economic and cultural processes leading to and underpinning power relationships. Neo-realism and neo-liberalism can account for changes in the structure of the international system. For example, albeit within an enduring state-centric paradigm, system change can occur as in shifts between uni-polar, bi-polar and multi-polar structures. Change for neo-liberalism is incremental as more states and non-state actors emerge and evolve. The overall structure of the international system therefore becomes more complex. Structuralists, however, demand a radical change to occur. This is the main distinction between a reformist and revolutionary approach.

World-system theory

Immanuel Wallerstein is the main advocate of world-system theory. In his influential book *The Modern World System: Capitalist Agriculture and the Origins of the Modern World System* (1981), Wallerstein develops a theoretical framework to understand and explain historical changes brought about by the creation of the modern Westphalian states system. For Wallerstein the changes brought about by the modern states system explain the supremacy of Western Europe during the nineteenth century. According to Wallerstein, his theory provides a comprehensible framework in which to analyse and understand external and internal facets of the modernisation process. World-system theory allows for a comparative analysis of different parts of the contemporary world system. For Wallerstein history has witnessed two types of world system, world empires and world economies. The difference between world empires and world economies can be seen in terms of how power and resources are distributed.

CONCEPT BOX

World empires and world economies

The Roman Empire is a good example of how 'world empires' operate. Political power was centralised into a strong bureaucracy. The extent of the empire was also well defined, although had clearly expanded over time. This territory was governed by a central seat of power and the rule of law was maintained by way of a standing army. There was an obvious class division in the form of slavery and the rights of Roman citizens. Flows of wealth from the conquered territories were directed towards the central point of administration and power, as in 'all roads lead to Rome'.

In a world economy there is no single centre of political authority; instead there are competing centres of power. Resources and wealth within world economies are redistributed and managed through a market. The era of world empires has been surpassed by the evolution of a world economy: this was achieved by the establishment of a capitalist world system. The world economy does not have a standing army in the same way that empires had. Similarly, the geographical dimension is transformed and encompasses global rather than regional limits.

The world economy with which Wallerstein associates his theory emerged in Europe during the sixteenth century. This system has expanded and evolved into the contemporary global economic system within which no state or economy is wholly independent.

How, then, does Wallerstein conceptualise the contemporary economic system? As with the majority of structuralists, Wallerstein highlights the importance of the international division of labour. It must be noted that this division of labour is a functional division characterised by relationships of exploitation. For Wallerstein the techniques of modern capitalism enabled the world economy to extend beyond the political boundaries of any one state empire; the entire globe has been merged into divisions of labour.

Wallerstein argues that the contemporary world system can be divided into three distinct categories: the core, periphery and semi-periphery. These categories describe each region's relative position within the world economy as well as certain internal political and economic characteristics. Wallerstein established his world-system perspective in the 1970s when the world could also be divided into regional ideological categories. He did recognise the different characteristics of communist states, but in the world-system model all states are located somewhere within the core, periphery or semi-periphery. It is the division of labour which reinforced the polarisation of states within the world system and enabled the core to develop at the expense of the periphery through unequal exchange on the world market. The division of labour, then, determines different relationships between geographical regions, as well as types of production and labour conditions within each region.

By core he is referring to centres of power associated with capitalism. Core states have successfully developed complex economic activities, such as mass market industries, advanced agriculture, international and local commerce, which are in the hands of the bourgeoisie. States in the core are strong both internally and vis-à-vis other states. The creation of a strong state coupled with a national identity/culture enabled core nations to protect their wealth and widen the disparities that had arisen in the world system, and this is managed through diplomacy, war or subversion. A core state is then able to dominate and extract wealth/surplus from peripheral regions.

Similarly, the periphery can be seen as referring to the less developed or marginalised areas of the world, or domestic divisions. States within the peripheral regions are all socially and politically diverse; they are also thought of as having a relatively low degree of autonomy within the world system. However, one similarity is that they continue to trail behind core and semi-peripheral areas in their level of economic growth. States in this region are largely specialised in producing raw materials, low-technology goods and agricultural produce. This relatively low level of economic growth is also reflected in the labour market, with a low level of wages.

The semi-periphery, as one might expect, describes a mid-point between core and periphery. It is also important to note that some aspects of the embedded core and marginalised periphery are relatively well established in their positions, and therefore difficult to transcend. This model also has an element of dynamism and the opportunity to move along the spectrum from core to periphery or vice versa. This is most readily apparent in the semi-periphery where there is greater opportunity for movement. Of course, those in the core are unlikely to want to advocate and implement change as they are already in a position of power and advantage. In contrast, those in the periphery, and therefore most likely to want to affect change, are least able to achieve such structural change.

The semi-periphery is worthy of particular attention. The dynamic of key decision-makers in this area has a tendency towards emulating the norms and values of the dominant core, even though this might mean adopting policies that are fundamentally non-sustainable and draw still further on the environment and social resources of the periphery, both domestically and internationally. For example, the so-called 'tiger economies' of South East Asia can be seen as inhabiting the semi-periphery. They have achieved significant growth in GDP per capita, but the dynamics of core/periphery/semi-periphery can also be seen within these states. As with all states, they have an elite social stratum of government officials and within the private sector. Yet the growth and advancement achieved at this level is made possible by further exploitation of workers and resources. Such growth might also be enhanced by drawing upon migrant labour from more peripheral states. This reinforces the drain on peripheral resources to benefit the semi-periphery and subsequently the core states and economies. For Wallerstein and other structuralists, the structure of the global economic system is, by definition, fundamental to their approach.

However, of similar if not equal importance is the flow of wealth and related resources within this structure. The semi-periphery is especially useful as an indicator of how it both draws upon the periphery and also feeds in to the core.

Within a world economy the dynamics of resource distribution are fundamentally different to that of empires. However, the effects of both systems remain synonymous, in that wealth and resources are directed from the periphery to the core.

Dependency theory

The concept of dependency was first formulated by Raul Prebisch in *The Economic Development of Latin America and Its Principal Problems* (1950) and was later expanded upon in the 1960s and 1970s. This theory was developed with particular reference to development issues in Latin America. It has since been more widely applied and utilised in more general analysis of the global economic system and issues of development worldwide. Dependency theory emphasises the relationship between the core and peripheral economies. The engagement of the core with the periphery via foreign direct investment leads to a flow of wealth that Andre Gunder Frank (1966) described as a 'sucking out' effect. This unequal exchange of goods and services is also characterised by biased trade agreements, debt repayments and the exchange of relatively low-priced raw materials for higher-priced manufactured goods.

Once a peripheral economy is tied into a trading relationship it becomes extremely difficult for them to break away and establish economic autonomy, as they become dependent on the core for aspects of security, technology transfer and markets for their goods. Even though they may recognise that they are in a disadvantaged position there is a sense that this is better than the alternative of not engaging with the core. For example, many peripheral economies are quite narrow in the range of goods which they export. The market for raw materials and various cash crops tends to be dominated and controlled outside the country of origin of these goods. Therefore, core economies, usually via 'their' MNCs, have an advantage in terms of being able to choose which country to buy goods from and are able to keep prices low. In contrast, the producing states must sell their goods for the best price they are able to negotiate. The notable exception to this is the Organisation of Petroleum Exporting Countries (OPEC) which has managed to develop a cartel that reverses this process. Oil is a seller's market as opposed to the buyer's market demonstrated throughout the majority of the developing world.

Dependency relationships are characterised by inequality. The intent of dominance by the core powers cannot necessarily be proven. What is clear is the effect of these unequal relationships. Patterns of wealth and relative consumption demonstrate inequalities both within and between states, as seen in the example below.

EXAMPLE BOX

Dependency in action: Kenya

As with many post-colonial economies, Kenya remains tied to reliance upon the export of primary and agricultural commodities, many of which have low and/or variable market values. For example, Kenya's main exports are tea, horticultural products, coffee, crude petroleum products, fish and cement. In addition, the imports tend to have a much higher market value, thereby creating a trade deficit. Kenya's main imports are machinery, transport equipment, refined petroleum products, motor vehicles, iron and steel, resins and plastics. Furthermore, pressure to liberalise Kenya's economy, in the form of IMF-required structural adjustment programmes, further disadvantages Kenyan manufacturing and capital-intensive industries and welfare provision.

> Kenya's continuing dependency is reinforced by economic structures which prevent Kenya realising the full value of its material and human resources. Although there is economic activity and capital generated, the bulk of the profits tend to return to the external actors that have provided foreign direct investment. Until such time as Kenya can maintain ownership and control of the income generated via its resources, and develop internationally competitive high-value-added commodities itself, it will continue to be dependent on unequal trading patterns and international aid.

Criticisms of structuralism

■ Many advocates of neo-realism and neo-liberalism argue that structuralism downplays the role of individual actors and their level of agency.

■ It can be claimed that structuralism is overly pessimistic and tends to focus on highlighting problems within the international system rather than generating problem-solving analysis.

■ This approach tends to reduce all issues and phenomena to a class-based analysis related to capitalism, thereby potentially overlooking other significant aspects and factors.

■ For neo-liberals in particular, structuralism misinterprets and dismisses the potential benefits of capitalist 'economic spread' and the 'trickle-down' effects of industrialisation.

■ The concept of underdevelopment denies the opportunity for developing states to enjoy the benefits of economic growth and modernisation.

Summary

This chapter has considered neo-realism, neo-liberalism and structuralism as the mainstream contemporary approaches within IPE. Each approach identifies key actors and processes within international political economy. Neo-realism remains state-centric but identifies non-state actors, particularly MNCs, whose actions can have a direct impact on the relative success or failure of state economies. Neo-liberals also recognise the importance of MNCs; however, this is a more pluralistic approach which also encompasses the role of other, non-state actors ranging from individuals through to IGOs and INGOs. Structuralism draws upon earlier Marxist perspectives emphasising class-based divisions and analysis.

The following chapter concludes the first part of this book by considering a number of alternative contemporary approaches in IPE. These are feminism, green thought and postmodernism.

Reflective questions

Neo-realism

1 How do neo-realists define the nature of the international system? How do they view the role of the state?

2 What conceptual tools do neo-realists employ to explain events within the international system?

3 What are the differentiating features of neo-realism from classical approaches?

4 What evidence or examples can you think of which reflect ideas about the concept of 'agents of the state'?

Neo-liberalism

1   How do neo-liberals define the nature of the international system? How do they view the role of the state?
2   What conceptual tools do neo-liberals employ to explain events within the international system?
3   What are the differentiating arguments of neo-liberalism from classical liberalism?
4   Do you agree with Fukuyama's *End of History* thesis? What evidence would you cite to support or contest his argument?

Structuralism

1   How are international economic structures created?
2   What is the relationship between structure and agency in the global economic system?
3   What are the main characteristics of the core, periphery and semi-periphery and how do they relate to each other?
4   In what ways can the periphery of the international economic system be dependent upon the core?

Suggestions for further reading

Neo-realism

Keohane, R. (ed.) (1986) *Neorealism and its Critics*, New York: Columbia University Press.
Gilpin, R. (1987) *The Political Economy of International Relations*, Princeton: Princeton University Press.
Hirschmann, A.O. (1981) *National Power and the Structure of Foreign Trade: The Politics of the International Economy*, Berkley: University of California Press.
Kennedy, P. (1989) *The Rise and Fall of the Great Powers 1500 to 2000*, London: Fontana Press.
Kindleberger, C. (1986) *The World in Depression: 1929–1939*, 2nd edn, Berkley: University of California Press.
Kindleberger, C. (1996) *World Economic Primacy: 1500–1900*, Oxford: Oxford University Press.
Strange, S. (1987) 'The persistent myth of lost hegemony', *International Organization*, 41, 551–74.
Waltz, K. (1979) *Theory of International Politics*, Columbus: McGraw Hill.

Neo-liberalism

Angell, N. (1911) *The Great Illusion*, London: Heinemann.
Doyle, M. (1986) 'Liberalism and world politics', *American Political Science Review*, 80 (December), 1151–69.
Fukuyama, F. (1992) *The End of History and the Last Man*, New York: Free Press.
Keohane, R. (1984) *After Hegemony: Cooperation and Discord in the World Political Economy*, Princeton, NJ: Princeton University Press.
Keohane, R. and Goldstein, J. (eds) (1993) *Ideas and Foreign Policy: Beliefs Institutions and Political Change*, Ithaca, NY: Cornell University Press.
Keohane, R. and Nye. J. (2000) *Power and Interdependence*, 3rd edn, London: Longman.
Krasner, S. (ed.) (1983) *International Regimes*, London: Cornell University Press.

Structuralism

Amir, S. (1992) *Empire of Chaos*, New York: Monthly Review Press.

Arrighi, G. (2009) *The Long Twentieth Century: Money, Power and the Origin of Our Time*, 2nd edn, London: Verso.

Frank, A.G. (1966) 'The development of underdevelopment', *Monthly Review*, 18(4) (September), 17–31.

George, S. (1988) *A Fate Worse Than Debt*, London: Penguin Books.

Prebisch, R. (1950) *The Economic Development of Latin America and Its Principal Problems*, New York: UN.

Wallerstein, I. (1979) *The Capitalist World Economy*, New York: Cambridge University Press.

Wallerstein, I. (1981) *The Modern World System: Capitalist Agriculture and the Origins of the Modern World System*, London: Academic Press.

3 Alternative contemporary approaches of IPE

Chapter learning outcomes

After reading this chapter students should be able to:

- Understand and summarise the assumptions and theories of the five alternative approaches considered in this chapter.
- Cite the work of one or more key author(s) associated with each approach.
- Recognise how these approaches emerge out of a broad critique of traditional approaches.
- Explain how changes in the 'real world' since the late twentieth century and early twenty-first century have shaped the development of these theoretical approaches.
- Demonstrate a critical awareness of the broad strengths and weaknesses of each approach.
- Understand the criticisms of each approach.
- Be able to use these approaches in the study of international political economy.

Introduction

This chapter introduces the most significant alternative theoretical approaches that have developed in response to the 'orthodoxy' described in the previous chapter. Here you are introduced to constructivism, feminism, postmodern approaches, Critical Theory and green thought. Each of these approaches have drawn on a range of disciplines not traditionally associated with mainstream IR and IPE theory. For example, feminism has close associations with both sociology and cultural anthropology in terms of concepts and the issues addressed. Below we highlight the historical development of each of these approaches and the manner in which they are currently being applied.

As we consider the following alternative approaches you should see how each of them, albeit in markedly different ways, relates to the study of IPE. As with all theoretical approaches, the underlying assumptions have a significant impact upon the focus of any analysis and subsequent conclusions drawn. Constructivists focus on social structures and dynamics and the way in which they are interpreted, and potentially misinterpreted by the actors involved. Therefore, a constructivist approach could be applied to analysing issues such as trade relations between certain states. For example, why does the United States have a free trade agreement with Jordan but not Syria? Feminist theory has its focus at the level of the individual. As such, this immediately sets this approach apart from many other theories. Issues of equality, distributive justice and emancipation are all key concerns of this approach. Feminists tend to focus on analysing issues such as human trafficking, prostitution, modern-day slave labour, child soldiers, maternal healthcare and women in governance.

Postmodern approaches question truth claims and argue that all positions and arguments are necessarily subjective. Arguably then, this is the most encompassing of all approaches. Although it applies to all IPE issues, disputes over truth claims are more apparent in some areas than in others. The dynamics of religious disputes, claims for human rights and other aspects of cultural relativism all involve competing world views. Specific examples include the discourse on 'the war on terror', what constitutes sustainable development, and what strategies and policies should be applied in dealing with these issues. Green theorists would also see all aspects of IPE through the lens of environmental issues. This can include protection of the world's biodiversity, the manner and level of resource exploitation and how the international trading system operates. With regard to international trade, green theorists would highlight the fact that the majority of this trade undervalues environmental protection. Critical Theory highlights inequalities between people at both national and international levels and it calls for these inequalities to be addressed. It also highlights the structural dimensions of the global system in perpetuating these inequalities, for example unequal terms of trade.

As you read the following pages you should be able to see how each of the approaches outlined has its own discrete world view. That said, you should also notice that there are some elements of overlap between both the approaches and the issues which they consider.

Constructivism

Historical development

The majority of theoretical approaches in IPE offer varying and often contradictory assumptions and explanations for social phenomena. Constructivism also offers different positions on international political economy and international relations from, say, liberalism and realism. However, constructivism can also be set apart to an extent as unique in IPE theory as a school of thought which allows for the synthesis of elements of other approaches. Constructivism has emerged as one of the more recent theoretical approaches in IPE and seems in many ways to side-step some of the key theoretical debates. While realism and liberalism seem endlessly engaged in critique of each other, constructivism has developed in a manner which allows for the rebuttal of common critiques because it has an inclusive nature. So while advocates of realism and liberalism debate the suitability of state-centrism and pluralism, constructivism offers an approach which can adopt either state-centricism or pluralism at varying times. This is because questions such as this one, as well as others like debates regarding the nature of the international system (in other words, is it anarchic or not?), are not central to constructivism's primary assumptions. These assumptions have developed over the latter half of the twentieth century and include issues of subjectivity, identity, perceptions and metaphysical considerations.

Through the 1990s constructivism as an approach to understanding international relations was developed by a range of scholars; but Nicholas Onuf (1997) is often cited as key in its emergence. In many ways this approach developed as a response to what was seen as a common flaw on both realist and liberal perspectives. This was that international relations were being studied in a manner which was only concerned with the tangible and material elements of the social world. Scholars like John Ruggie (1998) and Richard Ashley (1988) shared Onuf's ideas that intangible features of human relations such as beliefs, perceptions and understanding are also important. The constructivist approach gained in influence and theoretical complexity through the 1990s and is now a major alternative approach within the study of international political economy.

Central arguments

- Subjectivity is the key to understanding agency and actor behaviour at the domestic and international levels.
- Identity is an important element in the creation of coherent actors and helps to determine how other actors are perceived.
- Perceptions of other actors, issues and processes are more important than structures, institutions and regimes in determining international relations.
- All types of state and non-state actors can be important and worthy of study in varying situations.
- All types of issues including, among others, war, cooperation, trade, development, labour rights, financial flows and environmental change are important and worthy of study in IPE.

Specific theories

At the heart of constructivism are assumptions about the importance of subjectivity and inter-subjectivity in all domestic and international relations. For constructivists, phenomena in both the human and natural worlds do not have any relevance until we ascribe some form of meaning to them. Furthermore, the meaning and interpretations of phenomena will determine how they impact on us and our relations with each other. Metaphysical debates are thus of prime importance to the constructivist. How a given phenomena is observed and interpreted can and will vary from one person to another and from one collective group of people to another. The differences in the ways in which events, issues, processes, actors and so on are viewed and interpreted are the determining factors in actor behaviour. For example, constructivists agree with realists (and some liberals) that the global system is one of domestic governance but international anarchy. However, the relevance of the lack of existence of a global governing authority and the existence of anarchy in the international arena do not necessarily mean conflict is inevitable – which is exactly what the liberal counter-argument to the realist assumption of the effects of anarchy claims.

AUTHOR BOX

Alexander Wendt

Born in 1958 in Mainz, West Germany, Wendt is one of the leading scholars in the field of social constructivism. He has held positions in several US universities including Yale, Chicago and Ohio State, where he is the Ralph D. Mershon Professor of International Security.

Wendt claims that 'anarchy is what states make of it' (1999), denoting different possible outcomes of the existence of anarchy. A group of teenage friends may exist in an anarchic environment (in other words they may have no authoritative figure watching over them) yet they remain friends. A group of rival teenagers may exist in an anarchic environment and engage in hostilities. The key for constructivists is not whether or not there is anarchy but how actors perceive this anarchy and each other.

Constructivists claim that cooperation is possible between states or peoples in the international arena (and indeed between people in the domestic arena), but not simply because institutions and regimes are created to control actor behaviour, as liberals claim. Instead, the perception of international institutions and regimes as being beneficial and perceptions of other actors as friends, partners or even collaborators leads to cooperation. If a state, for example, sees an international institution, such as the World Intellectual Property Organisation (WIPO), as actually infringing on its sovereignty and damaging its economic interests then it may not cooperate with other states via this organisation. On the other hand, if a state perceives an organisation or other external actor as good and useful to work with then it probably will cooperate. The very fact that institutions and regimes exist does not guarantee cooperation.

While Marxian analysis focuses on economic materialism as a key factor in driving world history and international relations, constructivism also sees social relationships as key drivers. The existence of economic materialism and material capabilities are acknowledged by constructivists as being important. But social relationships between individuals or groups of individuals are seen as playing very significant roles in determining international relations. When we discuss 'international relations', constructivists say we must remember that we are discussing human relationships as acted out by individual humans and so the personalities, characteristics, beliefs, values and relationships of individuals must be seen as important. For example, the personal friendship between the late King Hussein of Jordan and the late former Prime Minister of Israel, Yitzhak Rabin, was pivotal in the signing of a treaty of peace between the former enemies in 1994. Israel and Jordan had been in a state of war since 1948 and conventional understandings of the international relations of the Middle East at the time suggested peace and a normalisation of relations between the two states would not be likely. The long friendship and mutual respect the two leaders had for each other allowed an agreement to be made. Constructivism claims we should examine this factor.

In order to possess a measure of agency in international relations an actor usually has to have a relatively large and capable number of members. The state, for example, is a collective of individuals who are grouped together politically, economically and socio-culturally. Constructivism argues that even this type of actor is not natural and no state exists prior to the creation of a subjective perception of the collective group. In other words, states are not really real, there is no such thing as a 'nation' until people 'create' a sense of communal belonging. National anthems, certain versions of historical stories, patron saints and other religious figures, national sports teams, religious beliefs, languages and so on are all socially constructed phenomena which allow for the creation of a shared identity.

EXAMPLE BOX

English–French relations

England and France were engaged in a bitter rivalry during the nineteenth century not because that was the natural relationship between the two actors but because their created identities were opposed to each other. Englishmen saw Frenchmen as their enemies and vice versa because of the subjective interpretation of the 'other' as different and hostile. It could be argued that they could just as simply have seen each other as friends and hence had a fruitful and cooperative relationship. Using this theoretical assumption we could say that Germany and France have not engaged in another war with each other since the Second World War because the social structure has been altered and they now perceive each other as friends, not enemies. Their respective national interests and subsequent policies have been adjusted to fit this new perception.

Criticisms

For many theorists and scholars of IPE, the constructivist approach has some weaknesses in terms of its explanatory power and coherency. A common criticism of constructivist analysis is simply that it lacks applicability in the realm of IPE and IR. Realists, for example, claim that in order to understand and explain social phenomena and international relations we need to be able to set firm theoretical parameters and outline solid assumptions. Constructivism can be said to be too encompassing in terms of its assumptions of which actors are important and possess significant agency as well as which issues are influential in shaping international interactions. The focus on subjective perceptions and interpretations as well as the emphasis on identity as key determining features of international relations is criticised as being inappropriate. Here, realists argue that there is little value in considering how a person's opinions are formed and how they may perceive others. Ultimately the anarchic world system and the self-interested decision making of states determine interactions. Individuals have little input and issues such as identity are simply said to be unimportant.

The liberal critique, on the other hand, is based on the assumptions that rules and rational interests govern relations between actors at the international level. The constructivist suggestion that regardless of what rules, institutions and regimes may exist, actors cannot always be considered to be rational maximisers is seen as counter-productive to sound analysis. Furthermore, this view of actor behaviour is seen as incorrect because even though individuals do vary in terms of their respective identities they always remain rational and are driven by specific goals. Even though liberals share the constructivist's concern with the human condition, the latter's focus on subjective experiences can be seen by the former as a hindrance to analysis which considers the roles played by international organisations and regimes. A weakness of assuming that perceptions and values and so on determine behaviour is that as scholars of IPE we cannot necessarily expect to achieve an analysis which considers all the relevant individuals. Put in other words, there are too many individuals to study and if we cannot study all of the individuals and their perceptions then we cannot claim to offer a complete analysis.

A broader critique of constructivism which is often levelled by advocates of most other approaches is that constructivism borrows too much from other schools of thought to the extent that it can sometimes be incoherent. For example, constructivism accepts that the non-state actors are often significant in international relations. However, at other times constructivists express a much more state-centric approach. Another example is the position that anarchy does exist in the international arena yet either conflict or cooperation can prevail. As explained above, constructivists argue that how anarchy is perceived is more important than whether it exists or not. Nevertheless, the view that constructivism sometimes does not offer solid assumptions which remain constant has led to the opinion that it simply avoids inter-paradigm debate.

Feminism

Historical development

An area of human relations which has traditionally been ignored in both IR and IPE is the role of women in domestic and international relations as well as in economic and political processes. The existent structures of human societies have often led to the marginalisation, subjugation, exploitation and even exclusion of some elements of society. Women have, throughout history and still largely in the contemporary world, found themselves in this position of being dominated. While there are examples of societies where women's issues, rights and roles in society have been equal with those of men or even primary over men, this is the exception to the norm. However, at various stages in the modern era attention has been paid to the position of women in society and processes of change have been witnessed. The eighteenth and nineteenth centuries, for example, saw much more attention being paid to the political and economic rights of women in Europe and North America, with thinkers such as Mary Wollstonecraft (1996) commenting widely on discrimination. It is important to note that feminism as a school of thought emerged in sociopolitical realms outside academia but soon was integrated into fields such as sociology, anthropology and politics. Feminism was integrated in earnest into IPE and IR in the second half of the twentieth century.

There are three general historical phases of the emergence and development of feminism as a perspective on human relations. These phases tend to be referred to as 'waves'. The first wave of feminism took place in the nineteenth and twentieth centuries and centred on the women's suffrage movements of Europe and North America. This phase of feminism was encouraged by demands for equal economic and marital rights for men and women but soon expanded to encompass a range of issues pertinent to women's rights, including the right to partake in political processes. The second wave of feminism evolved during the 1960s and is said to have lasted until the late 1980s. Here, 'feminists' built on the earlier efforts and successes of the first wave of feminism and expanded the issue areas of concern as well as the societal scope of feminism. While a range of political and many economic rights had been won for women in Europe and North America as well as (albeit less convincingly) in other regions, the 1960s saw feminists focusing on issues of equality in a broader sense.

AUTHOR BOX

Cynthia Enloe

Born in 1938, Cynthia Enloe has been at the forefront of the development of feminist theory. She has placed a particular emphasis on military issues and the impacts these have on women's lives. This relates to both the experience of female military personnel and women who live close to military bases. She has also developed these ideas further in considering how the labour of women is used both to prepare for and to support military operations.

Cynthia Enloe (1989) began to discuss issues such as ending discrimination against women in the workplace or in public office as well as in education and these became central to the feminist remit. Sexual liberation and equality also became key issues. This phase of the development of feminism also saw the spread of the feminist project to many other societies and countries around the world.

The third wave of feminism can be said to have emerged in the early 1990s as a response to the failures of the second wave. This most recent era of feminism has been the most critical as it seeks to incorporate metaphysics into the discussion of equality and emancipation. Earlier forms of feminism are seen by many contemporary feminists as having adopted patriarchal definitions and assumptions of what it is to be female and what is good for women. Third-wave feminists such as Gloria Anzaldua (2010) suggest that how we understand gender needs to be re-evaluated and the goals of feminists need to be re-examined. In short, we need to consider whether equality with men, or masculinity, is what women should be seeking, or should feminists focus more on broader senses of equality and liberty for both men and women to pursue. In this sense feminism as a meta-narrative in IPE offers broader analytical tools which allow us to consider equality and liberty in a more critical manner. Also, we can use feminism to examine not only women's rights but the rights and experiences of all exploited or marginalised people. It should be noted that throughout the development of feminism men as well as women have been involved in both practical and academic/intellectual ways – you do not have to be a woman to be a feminist.

Central arguments

- Women are equal to men and so should be seen as, and treated as, equal to men in all areas of human society and relations.
- Domestic and international relations are characterised largely by the exploitation of weak, poor and marginalised actors by dominant ones.
- The individual is an important actor in international relations and the agency as well as experiences of individuals should be considered as very important in international political economy.
- Change in contemporary structures and processes is necessary to achieve equality of all people, the emancipation of those who have been exploited as well as a more egalitarian and prosperous world. This requires change in the structure of patriarchy as well as a critique of male-dominated knowledge.

Specific theories

Feminism is a very broad school of thought with many differing assumptions and specific theories. This is partly a result of the relatively long history of feminist ideology and the adoption of feminist thought in many different academic disciplines as well as the varied range of feminists and the intellectual products they have given rise to. A number of specific theories of feminism (or branches of feminism) deserve attention here with regards to their use in IPE. Socialist feminism, often called Marxist or Marxian feminism, is founded on the core assumption of exploitation in human relations. Here, the exploitation of women is connected to Marxist explanations of injustice as resulting from capitalist economic structures. In order to achieve equality and emancipation for women the capitalist system, which maintains patriarchy through economic competition, must first be overthrown. This can be done through social and military revolution and requires all societies in the world to be engaged in revolutionary action. Socialist/Marxist feminism is therefore a global theory and not restricted to a small number of states or societies.

Liberal feminism advocates the pursuit of equality between men and women through legal and institutional means. The inherent good nature of humans is a key assumption here, as is the ability of humans for rational calculation and peaceful cooperation, issues which Betty Friedan (1982) commented on at the start of the second wave of feminism. Inequality and exploitation of women is seen as a result of historical processes which were shaped by a more anarchic and competitive global system. In the contemporary era of globalisation, where institutions and regimes are increasingly leading to integration and cooperation between states and peoples, the environment is being created for egalitarian relations between men and women. Unlike socialist feminism, liberal feminism sees dialogue and the collaborative creation of institutions, norms and rules as the way to ensure equality between men and women. In a similar manner to socialist feminism, liberal feminism can also be global in scope.

EXAMPLE BOX

Human trafficking

The issue of human trafficking is a global problem. The US State Department estimates that between 600,000 and 800,000 people are trafficked across international borders every year, although the nature of this illegal operation makes it difficult to obtain accurate figures. The majority of those trafficked are women and children, many of whom are likely to become part of the international sex trade.

Several feminist writers have focused their work on aspects of prostitution. The political economy of the sex trade deals with issues such as health, wealth, power, control and emancipation. It not only looks at gendered power relations but also deals with the interface between the personal experiences of the sex trade, for prostitute, pimp and punter. Beyond that it considers the factors that may lead to an increase in trafficking, which may be as a result of a 'push' factor to escape conflict zones and other disadvantaged areas. There can also be 'pull' factors, such as the increased demand for prostitution services during major international sporting events such as the World Cup or the Olympics.

The recent historical experience of imperialism and colonialism is seen by some feminists as the cause of inequality and exploitation in developing states. This includes exploitation by one class over another and the subsequent inequality. However, post-colonial feminists also claim that relations between men and women have also been affected by this historical experience in many places. While women from developing regions are not seen to be inherently and timelessly obedient, marginalised and passive they are seen to be exploited and marginalised in more recent times. Post-colonial feminists claim this is because the societal, political and economic structures put in place in former colonies during the era of imperial domination mirrored patriarchal structures from the former imperial powers. In effect patriarchy was exported to the colonies following subjugation as part of the process of imperial domination. In order to achieve equality and full rights for women, therefore, neo-imperial relationships such as economic dependency must be removed and full national independence achieved.

Christian and Islamic feminism share a number of key assumptions with other forms of feminism but differ in others. The historical experience of both Christianity and Islam often suggest that these religious belief systems have inherent structures which encourage patriarchy. Nobel Peace Prize winner Shirin Ebadi (2003) has often argued that Islam, for example, does not prohibit women's rights. Instead Islam can be used to guarantee such rights and it is varying (patriarchal) interpretations of Islam that have led to discrimination in some Islamic societies. However, both Christian feminism and Islamic feminism highlight the religious grounds of equality before God of all men and women and the role of women in both religions' histories to argue for divinely ordained rights for women. For the former, the role of women in establishing and maintaining the early Christian communities is highlighted to demonstrate how men and women had equal roles and rights. For Islamic feminists a similar focus on women as key parts of the early Islamic community and passages of the Quran which are dedicated to outlining the importance of women's rights are highlighted. In the contemporary era, religious feminists call for a return to earlier forms of their respective religions as a way to liberate women from patriarchal systems on a global scale.

Criticisms

Feminists have been the target of many criticisms levelled by practically all schools of thought in IPE as well as by anti- or post-feminists in sociology, anthropology and politics. In terms of the traditional theoretical approaches discussed in Chapter 2 there are two main strands of critique. The first is centred on questions of agency and actor behaviour. The second strand is concerned with theories of processes at the international and global levels. Realism, for example, does not share the feminist belief in the agency of the individual in international relations. Even neo-realist theories do not offer any significant consideration of the individual. In fact realist theories reject outright the relevance of individuals as important actors. Instead, the primary units of importance are the state and, in neo-realism, also MNCs, IGOs and perhaps civil society groups (although most realists would also disregard these latter actors). Individuals are seen as simply lacking in agency or the ability to significantly act in international relations on their own and so are not seen as worthy of consideration. Furthermore, the equality of women with men is not seen as a significant issue as it is claimed to have little influence on relationships of power between states in the global arena.

While liberals place more emphasis on the agency of individuals, they too suggest that focusing too much on individuals as opposed to states or international institutions is counter-productive. Some of the key assumptions of liberalism do deal with the human condition, or in other words the experience and well-being of human individuals (indeed, some of the core premises of classical liberalism revolve around the emancipation of humans as they pursue liberty and happiness). However, this concern is secondary to the neo-liberal focus on enhancing international cooperation, stability and prosperity. Even though individuals are seen as important in terms of their inherent worth, they are not seen as possessing enough agency on their own to influence international relations in a significant manner. The feminist concern with and focus on individuals is therefore not suitable for the study of the world in IPE.

Marxists and structuralists share many of the concerns of equality and freedom from exploitation that feminists hold as primary. In Marxism the main goal of Marxian thought is change of the global system and structure of modern human society to allow for the equality of all and the eradication of marginalisation and exploitation of poorer and weaker segments of society. This mirrors some of the concerns of feminism. On the other hand, however, Marxist and structuralist analysis focuses on the impact of economic materialism and the capitalist system as the causes of inequality and exploitation. This is in contrast to the argument in most strands of feminism that patriarchy and historical socio-cultural processes lead to inequality and exploitation. Furthermore, Marxists and structuralists do not focus on any perceived distinction between men and women as opposed to the bourgeoisie and proletariat. In other words, these schools of thought claim exploitation and inequality are perpetrated by one socio-economic class against another as opposed to the feminist claim that the divide is between genders.

Postmodernism

Historical development

The history of postmodernism can be linked to the earliest examples of philosophical thinking and attempts to justify knowledge or truth claims. More accurately postmodernism should be seen in relation to, and in a critical position with regard to, all such claims. The essence of postmodernism is to highlight that there is no wholly objective 'truth' and that all knowledge claims must be seen as subjective, originating from a particular perspective and for it to be recognised that such perspectives are formulated and framed within a set of power relationships and structures. The nature of postmodernism makes it difficult to determine when it emerged or even how it has evolved. An initial assumption may be that it emerged after the 'modern' era. There is some 'truth' in this but this is more obviously associated with emerging movements in the fields or art, poetry, literature, architecture and music from the early decades of the twentieth century. For IR and IPE there was a greater emphasis on social change and the questioning of established norms and values in the 1960s. This, in turn, led to a more clearly defined branch of IR and IPE postmodern thought being developed, albeit with numerous facets, in the 1980s.

Ontology

Inquiry into, or theory of, being. In twentieth-century IPE usage, ontology is the general theory of what there is. For instance, questions about the mode of existence of abstract entities such as numbers, imagined entities (which underpin different perspectives) and impossible entities such as square circles and so on.

Epistemology

Theory of knowledge: the branch of philosophy that inquires into the nature and possibility of knowledge. In other words, 'how we know what we know'. In IPE epistemological questions derive from the methodologies used by the leading perspectives because each orthodox approach has a different epistemological framework, for example (and in general terms) idealists are normative and realists are positivists. You should also be aware of the term 'epistemic communities' which is sometimes used to designate a certain perspective and its approach to epistemology.

Postmodernist writing can include reference to ancient philosophers such as Socrates and Plato. Martin Heidegger (1991) placed particular emphasis on the nature of 'being' and, crucially, how 'being' is understood. This immediately places individuals, institutions and events in the realm of the social and the subjective. Each become subject to interpretation with each interpretation, by definition, being formulated from a socially constructed position and open to critique. With this in mind it is unsurprising that various strands of postmodernism have emerged at particular times in relation to dominant values and social structures. Revolutionary ideologies clearly pre-dated the 'counter-culture' movement of the 1960s. However, this was a period of particularly creative output from leading postmodern thinkers, especially in France. Notably, they were not 'traditional' social or political revolutionaries who wished to overthrow one system and replace it with another. Rather, they questioned the concepts of all systems. They highlighted aspects of power to be found in the use of language and the framing of discourses. In his 1597 essay *The Meditationes Sacrae* Francis Bacon said 'Knowledge is power'. Postmodernists expose the basis for such knowledge claims and challenge the power relations that follow from them.

Central arguments

■ All 'truth' claims are subjective and based on prejudiced interpretations of events.
■ Claims that are made are self-serving with regard to certain socio-economic and political agendas.
■ No alternative claims are being made to replace the 'truth' claims being challenged.

Specific theories

As indicated above, there is a vast array of thought and criticism that can come under the broad heading of postmodernism. In its most inclusive meaning it can refer to anything that challenges widely accepted principles of style and order that emerged in the so-called 'modern' era of the early twentieth century. The years immediately following the First World War saw a burgeoning of literary and artistic movements that attempted to challenge and reshape the existing establishment forms and endeavours in these areas. Narrative styles changed, as did the use and representation of space and even time. This was in line with changes in the modern world that were even more far-reaching than those of the Industrial Revolution. The inter-war years were times of upheaval in terms of rebuilding war-torn societies and also facing the economic downturn of the Depression era. Political and cultural theorists reflected this change by turning their attention to far-reaching questions about the underlying premises and assumptions that were used to either justify change or retain the status quo.

James Der Derian and Michael Shapiro (1989) have written about how power politics are driven by the interplay of different texts, referring to not only the written and verbal meaning given to certain terms and phrases but also the implications of these meanings and their usage in social settings that necessarily involve power relationships. For example, the attacks on the World Trade Center on 11 September 2001 have been subject to a bewildering array of interpretations. Postmodernists question the meaning of these attacks and how what 'happened' on that day is interpreted. How should these events be understood? This is far more complex than determining who the perpetrators of these attacks were and what their motivations were. What factors need to be taken into account to explain, understand and react to this event? It is inevitable that differing explanations and interpretations will lead to differing understandings and reactions; for postmodernists this demonstrates that nothing can ever be established as undeniable truth. The whole project of the 'war against terror' is fraught with misunderstanding and open to deliberate misrepresentations of issues and events.

AUTHOR BOX

Jean Baudrillard

Jean Baudrillard's collection of three essays entitled *The Gulf War Did Not Take Place*, written in 1991 (and later collected into a short book (2004)), is a deliberately controversial analysis of the Gulf War, intended to highlight the use of language and the different meanings that can arise from various interpretations. The underlying point being made was that the engagement between US and Iraqi forces was so unequally in favour of the United States, and that the technology and methods available to the far superior military might of the United States meant that this conflict could not be considered and understood in the same way that previous wars have been. Moreover, the visual representation and overall reporting of the war in the Western media could be seen as something more akin to the imagery associated with computer games rather than the 'reality' of bloody warfare. As with the attack on the twin towers, Baudrillard does not deny that a conflict occurred. What he does argue is that the way in which this conflict was generally reported was so far removed from the 'reality' of events that its meaning had been lost on the majority of those listening to or watching media reports. This is a characteristic postmodern approach where the actual event is seen as almost less important than the interpretation, or very often misinterpretation, of the event.

Although not particularly regarded as postmodern authors it is appropriate to refer to the work of Edward Herman and Noam Chomsky here. Their text *Manufacturing Consent* (1988) looks at the way in which the media, often in conjunction with government press offices, can frame certain issues to suit political agendas. Notably this may be by excluding the reporting of some issues altogether. Alternatively the use of language can be employed to create a particular tone or attitude towards the 'facts' that are subsequently presented. This is straying into the field of discourse analysis but this is a fundamental aspect of postmodern approaches. Any approach that is reliant on interpretation must acknowledge the ways in which language is used to project a particular meaning, and that this meaning has an aspect of power associated with it. In the post-9/11 world anything that has the word 'terror' associated with it has gained a deeper meaning. One only has to look at national legislation brought in by a large number of states to enhance police power in the name of counter-terrorist policies. The definition of who might be regarded as a 'terrorist' or what might constitute activities that could bring these new powers into play has been expanded significantly. Again this highlights the power relationships that are in play surrounding these issues.

Aspects of power are also dealt with in the works of IPE writer Susan Strange. Again, this is someone who would not normally be 'pigeonholed' as a particularly postmodern writer but certain aspects of her work lend themselves well to this discussion. In her seminal text *States and Markets* she describes four key structures. These are security, finance, production and knowledge. The knowledge structure includes the advantage of being more advanced in research and development in all aspects of science for military, economic or any other competitive endeavour. Importantly it can also refer to what is considered to be 'known' or true. This clearly relates to the postmodern aspect of understanding or meaning. Strange develops this point with particular reference to how power relationships are developed, enforced and maintained. In the context of IR and IPE this can be in terms of the way in which terms such as 'progress' or 'development' are understood and promoted. These may appear to be self-evident in their meaning but on closer inspection they are profoundly subjective and open to manipulation. Policies described as 'progressive' may have highly negative impacts on various individuals and communities.

Chomsky and Strange both deal with issues that are also of interest to postmodern writers but their approach is qualitatively different. Both highlight inequalities but they also suggest ways in which these inequalities might be addressed and rectified. This is in complete contrast to postmodern writers who will criticise the knowledge claims presented in various positions taken, but who do not offer alternative claims. Far from it, as their whole point is to show that *all* positions and arguments should be open to be challenged and discredited. They explicitly do not offer alternative standpoints as this would, by definition, undermine their own approach of universal scepticism. This, however, has led some critics to doubt the usefulness of postmodernism as an approach.

Criticisms

Although there is much to be said in favour of adopting an openly sceptical approach when assessing various arguments, positions and schools of thought, there may be a problem in taking this to extremes. Critics of postmodern thought argue that if everything is open to questioning and disbelief then what hope can there be for even beginning a field of inquiry? James Rosenau (2007) has identified several aspects of postmodern thought that he argues are contradictory. First, he argues that even an anti-theoretical stance is, in essence, a theory in itself. Second, postmodernists stress the irrational, yet employ rationality and reason to further their own arguments. Third, although they stress the importance of intertextuality they often consider certain texts in isolation. Fourth, postmodernists decry inconsistencies in other approaches, yet fail to remain consistent themselves. Finally, by rejecting the truth claims of other approaches postmodernists are making judgements, thereby undermining their claims to avoid the subjective and judgemental.

Postmodern thought plays an important role in highlighting the underlying agendas that may lie behind certain arguments and positions. This is particularly the case when looking at the terms that are used and the way in which arguments are framed and presented in such a way that what may be seen as 'common sense' prevails. For postmodernists, though, there is no 'common' sense. All knowledge is subjective and potentially open to manipulation and even abuse. In the latter case this can be a direct contributing factor to how power relations are created and reinforced. This can be applied at all levels of interaction, be it between states, civil society organisations or individuals. Even this analysis can be criticised for being anthropocentric and failing to take into account other species and the wider eco-system. In essence, postmodern thought is generally negative in tone in that its emphasis is on being critical of all claims to knowledge and truth. This does not mean that it does not have a useful role to play in the overall panoply of IR/IPE approaches. In some respect it is a healthy position to take to require falsification of statements and to require arguments to be adequately justified. Unfortunately for many postmodern writers there can be no justification as they are unwilling to accept claims that they see as inherently subjective and, therefore, suspect.

Green thought

Historical development

Human awareness of interaction with our physical surroundings is as old as recorded history. It has played a part in our survival as a species from the successes of the earliest hunter-gatherer communities, through settled cultivation of land and animal husbandry to more recent developments with regard to our understanding of the physical consequences of resource exploitation. That said, it is only the last few decades that environmental concerns have been formulated into a range of theoretical approaches that put these concerns at the centre of an understanding and analysis of IR/IPE.

Rachel Carson's seminal text *Silent Spring* (1962) is widely regarded as one of the first pieces of writing to highlight the serious consequences of human impact on the natural environment. In this book she explained how the introduction of the pesticide DDT resulted in unintended consequences as this poisonous substance entered the food chain. The 'silence' in the title refers to the lack of birdsong following the spraying of this product on farmland. The initial impact had been positive, as the pesticide had indeed killed the insects that were damaging the crops. However, these insects were then easy prey for birds that ingested the harmful chemicals as they ate the insects. Subsequently this led to a softening of the shells of the eggs laid by these birds, to the point that they broke before they were fully hatched. This had a devastating impact on the following generation of birds. By making these connections Carson opened a whole field of inquiry regarding human impact on the environment.

The 1970s saw a burgeoning of interest in, and writing on, environmental issues. Governments were beginning to recognise that growing interdependence was not simply restricted to economic ties. All domestic and international interactions take place within the confines of our finite planet. The notable exception of course is extra-terrestrial activities, such as space flights. The first manned flight to leave the Earth's orbit was the Apollo 8 mission in 1968. It was from this spacecraft that the classic image of a small, blue planet was photographed. This is argued to have had a profound impact on popular, and political, consciousness in terms of how the world is perceived. There are no political boundaries or ideologies visible from space. Land and water masses and weather systems dominate. More recent satellite images have highlighted issues such as deforestation and advancing areas of desert. Such technological capabilities have been fundamental in demonstrating the scale of the problems faced due to environmental degradation. Green thought has evolved with different writers emphasising various aspects of the relationship between humans and the physical environment. Some 'deep' green theorists argue that it is unhelpful to think of this as a 'relationship' and that it is preferable to take a more eco-centric view which, rather then separating human's from their environment, sees humans as being an inextricably linked part of a single environmental whole.

Central arguments

- Both 'light' and 'deep' green theorists agree that humans have the capacity to have a disproportionate impact on other species and their habitats.
- The planet is viewed as a finite resource and the majority of human activities are seen as depleting the 'capital' of Earth's resources in a non-sustainable manner.
- Human activities cannot be separated out from the consequences they have on the natural environment.

Specific theories

Green thought can be roughly divided into two main camps, those taking an environmental or anthropocentric approach and those that are eco-centric. The former sees humans as somehow separated from the natural environment, often at odds with it and trying to overcome difficulties. This approach, therefore, has some similarities with power politics, as it appears to think in terms of conflict and zero-sum games. On the other hand, eco-centric approaches are much more holistic, placing humans alongside other species as part of a complex web of interconnected habitats and biodiversity. The latter is most famously associated with James Lovelock's Gaia thesis (2000).

AUTHOR BOX

James Lovelock

The Gaia thesis was named after a Greek goddess associated with fertility and creation. Lovelock's emphasis was on a series of connected 'feedback' systems which keep the Earth's biosphere in balance. For example, the atmospheric cycle of the conversion of carbon dioxide into oxygen via plant photosynthesis. Human activities that generate excessive amounts of carbon dioxide risk unsettling this balance. With deforestation reducing the area of what are known as carbon 'sinks' this adds to the imbalance in this particular feedback system. There are many such systems in the natural world and Lovelock highlights how they interconnect and that it is impossible, even actively dangerous, to assume that actions in one area of the biosphere will not have consequences elsewhere within what is a closed system. Unfortunately the political system of sovereign states can also be seen as a 'closed' system, albeit a socially constructed one. Regardless of the legitimacy of Lovelock's analysis human organisation is dominated by the nation state system and the concept of sovereignty. As such it remains problematic to manage the feedback systems which have no regard for political boundaries.

The concept of managing eco-systems is more closely related with anthropocentric approaches, although one may assume that Lovelock would also argue in favour of first recognising and then managing, or at least working in balance with, these feedback systems. Environmental approaches tend to focus more on finding a balance between humans being able to exploit natural resources and minimising the impact this has, both in terms of the rate at which resources are depleted and also the potential negative impacts of pollution and other factors associated with resource extraction, transport and manufacturing processes. This can either be at the level of national government or, increasingly, via international bodies such as the Intergovernmental Panel on Climate Change (IPCC). Here green thought intersects with other theories, such as neo-liberal institutionalism, which deals with the conflicts and cooperative actions of governments in institutional settings. As environmental issues have come to the fore in both domestic and international political agendas this has been reflected in how what might be thought of as 'non-green' theories have dealt with these issues.

Resource scarcity and competition

Thomas Homer-Dixon (1994) has written about environmental issues, but in a manner that classical realists could easily comprehend and relate to. His emphasis is on the reduction in resources and, therefore, increased competition for access to dwindling supplies. Although this is a form of green thought, as it places natural resources at the centre of the analysis, the way in which this is done highlights traditional power politics concerns of competition and potential conflict. Access to oil and gas reserves has long been a contributing factor to a number of the world's protracted conflicts. A similar analysis can be made of access to water supplies, although there is also an argument that, because the parties involved all need access to water, then this could be seen as the issue that might bring them together in a more cooperative conflict resolution-based scenario. For example, riparianism in the Jordan River system has led to intense competition between rival states (in particular Israel and Syria). During the 1967 Six Day War a strategic objective of the Israelis was the capture of the head waters of the Jordan River in the Golan Heights and complete control of Lake Tiberias. Almost by definition, environmental issues are so all-encompassing that they lend themselves to all manner of interpretations by the various stakeholders involved, including a growing number of politically active non-state actors.

The range of actors involved in environmental issues is in line with liberal pluralist approaches, which highlight the diversity of international actors. Green thought is divided over the extent to which multi-stakeholder negotiations are beneficial. Some environmental pressure groups are in favour of sharing platforms with governments and multinational corporations in order to find common ground and possible solutions to environmental degradation. Others take a much harder line and prefer to stay at some distance from the actors they are critical of, fearing engagement may lead to co-option and the hijacking of the debate in favour of corporate interests. The whole issue of corporate social responsibility in particular has been labelled as 'greenwash' by certain groups who highlight that while some MNCs may promote what green credentials they have, these usually represent only a small fraction of their overall business, which continues to cause enormous environmental damage.

Criticisms

As demonstrated above, green thought is a very diverse array of approaches and, therefore, the criticisms of the various schools of thought differ accordingly. One of the most high-profile debates on environmental issues is the credibility of the science behind the claims and counter-claims involved in the prediction of trends. This has been a particularly bitter dispute with regard to climate change and alleged global warming. For example, if you were to view Davis Guggenheim's Oscar-winning documentary film *An Inconvenient Truth* (2006), featuring Al Gore, followed by the television programme *The Great Global Warming Swindle* (2007) you would hear two wildly differing arguments on this issue. Both sides accuse the other of presenting dubious scientific analyses in misleading ways. There is even an accusation that predictions of climate change have been exaggerated to support the vested interests of a 'climate change industry' made up of scientists, journalists and academics who have self-serving agendas associated with presenting climate change as more of a problem than it actually is.

The producer and director of *The Great Global Warming Swindle*, Martin Durkin, has also made documentaries arguing in favour of genetically modified crops and a particularly notorious programme entitled *Against Nature* (1997), which suggested that some environmental activists were actually holding back development strategies. One of the examples used was the opposition to a large hydroelectric dam project being built in India. Durkin suggests that without this dam thousands of poor Indian villages will be denied access to electricity. This, in turn, means they will be reliant on the burning of cow dung for their heating and cooking and that this causes ill-health and shortened lifespan due to inhalation of toxic fumes. While there is some truth in his claims about respiratory illnesses, the manner in which the overall criticism of the environmental groups referred to, including Friends of the Earth, was questionable. Numerous complaints about this programme were made to the Independent Television Commission, some of which were upheld. Environmental issues are clearly emotive and there is a lively debate among green theorists and activists themselves, as well as criticisms of the environmental movement as a whole.

Against Nature also featured an academic who questioned the validity of the argument for maintaining the Earth's current range of biodiversity. One might imagine that the 'default' position would be that the extinction of a species should be avoided, hence the protection afforded to endangered species. However, the position taken here is that species come and go and that the world is no worse off for no longer having either the dodo or any number of dinosaurs still roaming the Earth. This appears to fly in the face of the logic of the Convention on Biological Diversity adopted at the Rio Earth Summit. That said, it is an interesting position to take and one that goes to the heart of humanity's position as part of, or in relation to, the natural world. The academic who took this position, Professor Becker, appears to be saying that individual species do not necessarily have a value in and of themselves. Rather, they should be seen in terms of how they add to, or perhaps detract from, human experience and well-being. They are simply to be seen as a resource to be exploited or as something that plays a part in ensuring we have a healthy bio-environment.

Critical Theory

Historical development

Critical Theory is largely seen to have its roots in early Marxist thought and as such reflects some of the theoretical traits found in Marxism/Structuralism. Like other theoretical approaches, Critical Theory is not an exclusively IPE approach. Instead it has developed as part of the broader social sciences and humanities. During the 1920s and 1930s a group of scholars based at the University of Frankfurt in Germany formed what came to be known as the Frankfurt School. This school focused on critical analysis of the contemporary world system and international relations. Karl Marx, Friedrich Engels, Immanuel Kant, Georg Hegel and Max Weber were all key influences on the Frankfurt School, as can be seen by the attention paid to critiques of capitalism, positivist methodologies and materialism.

AUTHOR BOX

Max Horkheimer

Horkheimer was born in Stuttgart, Germany in 1895. In 1930 he was appointed Director of the Institute of Social Research, which was the base for the so-called Frankfurt School. With the rise of the Nazi Party in Germany, Horkheimer emigrated initially to Switzerland and then on to the United States. For many years he was a close collaborator with Thomas Adorno. He died in 1973.

Max Horkheimer (1982) was one of the leading early Critical Theorists. He was interested in the historical transition from feudalism to limited capitalism to the emergence of the global capitalist system. The experiences of urbanisation, industrialisation and mechanisation combined with enduring poverty, inequality and widening divisions of wealth between rich and poor across Europe led Critical Theorists to study the structural causes of human suffering.

Building on the work of Antonio Gramsci (1998) on the nature of knowledge and the creation and evolution of hegemonic forms of knowledge, Critical Theorists began to consider the value of dominant methodologies. Theodor Adorno (1997), for example, argued that there are knowledge structures which are created by social and political processes. This phase of Critical Theory's development saw a broader critique of not only capitalism or social science methodologies but also of Western civilisation as a whole and the move towards supposed scientific, rational and triumphant knowledge production. In this way, this approach shares some of the core theoretical arguments or assumptions of postmodernism in its critique of modernity. Following the end of the Cold War and the 'triumph' of liberal capitalism as a world system and ideology, Critical Theorists have developed their critique of capitalism and modernity to include broad criticism of inequality and injustice in the world. In many ways, Critical Theory has increasingly been informed by a desire not only to understand the world but also to change it – again, a reference to the early Marxist thought which influenced the early Frankfurt School.

Central arguments

- The contemporary world system is characterised by inequalities between people.
- There are global structures in place which rely upon and perpetuate inequalities between people.
- Change is necessary in the global system in order to remove structural impediments to equality.
- There is no real distinction between relations in the national and international realms.
- Knowledge is always subjective and linked to human interests and interpretations.

Specific theories

Robert Cox (1987) has claimed that all 'theory is *for* someone and *for* some purpose'. Critical Theory agues that there are processes of theory-creation in the social sciences which are all influenced by subjective values. This is a direct critique of the positivism of realism which claims that the social world can be observed in an objective and empirical manner, allowing for the creation of 'scientific' theories. This position relies on the assumption of the existence of objective facts which cannot be interpreted in different ways and so are not influenced by any subjective agendas. Critical Theorists, on the other hand, suggest that knowledge is never entirely objective and we cannot observe the social world in an empirical manner without interpreting what we observe and its meaning in different ways. The reflexivity of human minds along with the variance in values, beliefs, perceptions and so on mean that the same social phenomena can be observed and interpreted in different ways. At the same time both 'knowledge' and theories are created by people, and so are inherently subjective and vary from other forms created by other people. This leads Critical Theorists to question how knowledge has been constructed and received. Questions about the origin, purpose and value of different forms of theoretical approaches are also raised.

Many other approaches such as realism, liberalism and structuralism look at structure in the global system as an important element in determining international relations. Critical Theory also looks at a structural determinant in the form of capitalism. Here, Critical Theorists argue that capitalism is inherently founded on competition and accumulation and this has led to global divisions of labour, wealth, resources, power and control between the two classes: the bourgeoisie and the proletariat. In order for industrial development, economic growth and prosperity the bourgeoisie must exploit the mass of workers and accumulate profits. This structure is seen as very negative and damaging to the vast majority of the global population. Furthermore, capitalism and its structures of exploitation and competition is the primary cause of both domestic and international conflict. While liberals would point to the value of international institutions in preventing conflict and aiding the development of the poor, Critical Theory argues that these institutions are established and controlled by powerful elites and therefore serve the purpose of the bourgeoisie. Instead of relying on contemporary international institutions, Critical Theorists suggest that peace and stability can only be achieved on a global scale when the proletariat are no longer exploited.

EXAMPLE BOX

Unequal exchange and terms of trade

Exploitation is a fundamental aspect of the contemporary capitalist global economy. It is the basis by which the core economies, and rich elite classes, both maintain their position of dominance and prevent the dominated from significantly improving their own position. Critical theorists emphasise the negative factors associated with an international trading system whereby one party to an exchange benefits a great deal more than the other. This can be represented in many sectors across the global economy.

Many examples of unequal exchange have their roots in imperial history. Even post-independence, the economic structures that characterised the colonial era can remain very similar. Often this involves the developing countries continuing to exploit its primary resources, such as minerals or timber, for a relatively low market value. The value of such commodities are often determined by world markets rather than by the exporters. There can be a stark contrast between these low-value exports and the often high value of imported, manufactured goods, especially when local purchasing power is taken into account. Another dimension of inequality, despite the rhetoric of free-marketeering, is the disadvantages faced by the exporters of agricultural produce from the developing world when many developed states, notably those in the EU, create an unfair advantage for their own farmers by heavily subsidising this sector.

While in the modern era we have known the 'state' as the main unit of societal organisation in international relations, 'states' are in fact a relatively new form of unit. Furthermore, the idea that every geographical territory and every people are divided up into specific states is also a new concept. Many states have existed as modern states in their current form for only a few decades. Others still have existed for only a year or two. Even the oldest states do not go back very far in terms of the entirety of human history. Critical Theory claims that the state as a unit or political and economic entity in which people are grouped and 'belong to' is a result of the capitalist system and the need to organise and control the masses. State creation is done much the same way as knowledge creation, as discussed above. States are created and maintained through knowledge which is created and perpetuated to generate timeless 'truths' about the state – or what can be seen in a critical sense as national myths. Critical Theorists, therefore, acknowledge the importance in studying states as actors in international relations but in the sense of how they maintain the capitalist system and how they perpetuate the class division. At the same time, however, states are seen as rarely being 'real' as opposed to being constructed to serve some purpose – which usually has led to inequality, injustice and exploitation of the masses. A re-orientation of how the 'state' is seen and maintained is necessary if change and emancipation are to be achieved.

Criticisms

Critical Theorists argue that there is much inequality and injustice in the world and that this needs to be changed in order to attain a fairer system. However, critics argue that Critical Theory's own critique of dominant forms of knowledge as being subjective and as privileging some over others can be used against its own call for a universalistic human condition. As highlighted above, and especially in the case of Gramscian forms of Critical Theory, hegemonic forms of knowledge and theory as well as overarching universal claims are invalid and undesirable. It does seem somewhat strange, then, that Critical Theorists themselves claim that there is *a* problem with the world system and that there is *a* desirable condition which should be aspired to. This can be seen to defeat the whole point of critiquing knowledge claims which are tautological.

There has been criticism of earlier work done by Critical Theorists which emphasised class conflict as the main characteristic of world politics and economics. Realists, for example, see weaknesses in any analysis which fails to acknowledge the contrasts between the same social class in different states. The elite or bourgeoisie is seen by Critical Theorists to be the dominant class in control of state and private sector policy and resources. However, this does not explain why states often go to war with each other, thus pitting bourgeoisie against bourgeoisie and proletariat against proletariat. Of course, the Critical Theory response to this critique is to suggest that the proletariat class is deceived and manipulated into fighting on behalf of *their* state by hegemonic forms of knowledge. Furthermore, conflict can often be profitable and beneficial to the bourgeoisie. Nevertheless, realists would still question why the bourgeoisie would engage in conflict. The two World Wars are used as examples of when conflict between states could not be seen to have benefited the bourgeoisie.

In terms of the methodology of Critical Theory, positivists argue that without following a rigorous and scientific methodology no solid conclusions can be formed from any study. Critical Theory is, therefore, unable to produce convincing conclusions and unable to solidly predict or prescribe in international relations. The rejection of positivist forms of study and the advocacy of more subjective and interpretive methods means that the conclusions that Critical Theory produces are not infallible. This is especially problematic as one of the core aims of this approach is to highlight problems with the global system and call for change in it. Critics simply ask how Critical Theory can highlight problems as true and prescribe courses of action in order to achieve a better world when knowledge and theory are said to be subjective and for someone and some purpose.

Summary

In considering the above alternative approaches they cover a range of concepts and interpretations of IR and IPE. They each emerged as a response to either an existing set of theories or particular issues and events. Constructivism, postmodernism and Critical Theory are all concerned with the presentation and perception of socially constructed phenomena. As such they emphasise the inherently subjective nature of knowledge and so-called truth claims. Feminism is also concerned with socially created institutions and structurally determined relationships. However, feminism has more of a normative dimension in that this approach not only highlights deficiencies and inequalities in existing structures, it also provides an alternative scenario and prescriptions for change. Finally, green thought is perhaps the most varied of the approaches considered here, particularly with regard to the position of individuals. The lighter green environmentalists share the anthropocentric view adopted by the other approaches discussed above. Deep green eco-centric approaches reject subjectivity as they are more concerned with physical/natural processes.

This chapter concludes the section of this book which considers the wide range of theories applied to the study of IR/IPE. We now move on to look at a series of issues that are central to processes of globalisation.

Reflective questions

Constructivism

1   To what extent does constructivism remain engaged in the inter-paradigm debate within IPE?
2   What is the role of subjective perceptions and interpretations on actor behaviour?
3   Is anarchy what states make of it?
4   What are some of the risks associated with considering the subjectivity of individuals in IPE analysis?

Feminism

1   What do feminists claim have been the primary negative characteristics of the relationship between men and women in most societies throughout history?
2   Feminism has become a widely advocated and used approach to study in IPE. In what ways is it a useful approach to understanding international political economy?
3   In a feminist critique what are the major causes of forms of inequality and exploitation in the contemporary world?
4   Is there a problem with focusing on the agency and experiences of individuals at the expense of other types of actors such as the state or MNCs?

Postmodernism

1   What 'agendas' can you identify in relation to various approaches' truth claims?
2   How useful is postmodern thought if it refuses to allow a foundational basis from which to explore ideas and concepts?
3   What types of language might be used to frame an argument in such a way that postmodernist writers would critique such terms?

Green thought

1   To what extent do you agree that non-human species and environmental habitats should be seen wholly in terms of their direct benefit to humans?
2   Does Lovelock's Gaia hypothesis make 'sense' in a world of sovereign states?
3   What do you consider to be the major contemporary environmental concerns and how might they be addressed?
4   What role do states, MNCs and civil society actors play in the environmental issues you have identified?

Critical Theory

1   In what ways is knowledge a social and political phenomenon?
2   What are the Marxist roots of Critical Theory and how have they informed arguments for change in social relations?
3   What structures are inherent in the capitalist world system which seem to perpetuate inequalities between people?
4   What forms of action do Critical Theorists advocate in order to achieve change in the world system?

Suggestions for further reading

Constructivism

Ashley, R.K. (1988) 'Untying the sovereign state: a double reading of the anarchy problematique', *Millennium: Journal of International Studies*, 17(2) (Summer), 243.
Onuf, N. (1997) 'A constructivist manifesto', in Burch, K. and Denemark, R. (eds) *Constituting Political Economy*, New York: Lynne Rienner.
Ruggie, J. (1998) *Constructing the World Polity: Essays on International Institutionalisation (New International Relations)*, London: Routledge.
Wendt, A. (1999) *Social Theory of International Politics*, Cambridge: Cambridge University Press.
Zehfuss, M. (2002) *Constructivism in International Relations: The Politics of Reality*, Cambridge: Cambridge University Press.

Feminism

Azaldua, G. (2010) *The Gloria Anzaldua Reader* (edited by A. Keating), Raleigh, NC: Duke University Press.
Ebadi, S. (2003) *Democracy, Human Rights and Islam in Modern Iran: Psychological, Social and Cultural Perspectives*, Bergen: Fagbokforlaget.
Enloe, C. (1989) *Beaches, Bananas and Bases: Making Feminist Sense of International Politics*, London: Pandora.
Friedan, B. (1982) *The Feminine Mystique*, new edn, London: Penguin Books.
Pettman, J.J. (1996) *Worlding Women: A Feminist International Politics*, London: Routledge.
Staeheli, L., Kofman, E. and Peake, L. (eds) (2004) *Mapping Women, Making Politics: Feminist Perspectives on Political Geography*, London: Routledge.
Wollstonecraft, M. (1996) *A Vindication of the Rights of Women*, new edn, New York: Dover Publishing Inc.
Whitworth, S. (1996) *Feminism in International Relations: Towards a Political Economy of Gender in Interstate and Non-governmental Institutions*, London: Palgrave.
Zalewski, M. (2009) *Feminism and the Transformation of International Relations*, London: Routledge.

Postmodernism

Ashley, R. (1996) 'The achievements of post-structuralism', in Smith, S., Booth, K., and Zalewski, M. (eds) *International Theory: Positivism and Beyond*, Cambridge: Cambridge University Press.
Baudrillard, J. (2004) *The Gulf War Didn't Take Place*, Sydney: Power Institute of Fine Arts.
Herman, E. and Chomsky, N. (1988) *Manufacturing Consent: The Political Economy of the Mass Media*, New York: Pantheon Books.

Der Derian, J. and Shapiro, M. (eds) (1989) *International/Intertextual Relations: Postmodern Readings of World Politics*, Lanham, MD: Lexington Books.

Derrida, J. (1997) *Politics of Friendship* (trans. G. Collins) London & New York: Verso.

Foucault, M. (2002) *Archaeology of Knowledge* (trans. A.M. Sheridan Smith) London: Routledge.

Heidegger, M. (1991) *The Principle of Reason* (trans. R. Lilly), Bloomington: Indiana University Press.

Rosenau, J. (2007) *Distant Proximities: Dynamics Beyond Globalization*, Princeton, NJ: Princeton University Press.

Walker, R. (1993) *Inside Outside: International relations as political theory*, Cambridge: Cambridge University Press.

Green thought

Bookchin, M. (1997) *The Politics of Social Ecology: Libertarian Municipalism*, Montreal: Black Rose Books.

Carson, R. (1962) *Silent Spring*, London: Penguin Books.

Conca, K. and Dabelko, G.D. (1998) *Green Planet Blues: Environmental Politics from Stockholm to Kyoto*, Oxford: Westview.

Dodds, F. and Pippard, T. (2005) *Human Security and Environmental Change: An Agenda for Change*, London: Earthscan.

Durkin, M. (2007) *The Great Global Warming Swindle*, Pinnacle Vision.

Eckersley, R. (1992) *Environmentalism and Political Theory: Towards an Eco-centric Approach*, London: UCL Press.

Guggenheim, D. (2006) *An Inconvenient Truth*, Los Angeles: Paramount Classics and Participant Productions.

Homer-Dixon, T. (1994) 'Environmental scarcities and violent conflict: evidence from cases', *International Security*, 19(1) (Summer), 5–40.

Lovelock, J. (2000) *Gaia: A New Look at Life on Earth*, 3rd edn, Oxford: Oxford University Press.

Paterson, M. (2006) *Consumption and Everyday Life*, London: Routledge.

Vogler, J. and Imber, M.F. (eds) (1996) *The Environment and International Relations*, London: Routledge.

Critical Theory

Adorno, T. and Horkheimer, M. (1997) *Dialectic of Enlightenment*, London: Verso Books.

Cox, R. (1987) *Production, Power and World Order: Forces in the Making of History*, New York: Columbia University Press.

Falk, R. (1995) *On Humane Governance: Toward a New Global Politics*, Cambridge: Polity Press.

Frank, A. (1967) *Capitalism and Underdevelopment in Latin America: Historical Studies of Chile and Brazil*, New York: Monthly Press Review.

Galtung, J. (1984) *There Are Alternatives! Four Roads to Peace and Security*, Nottingham: Spokesman Books.

Gramsci, A. (1998) *Selections from Prison Notebooks*, London: Lawrence & Wishart.

Habermas, J. (1972) *Knowledge and Human Interest*, London: Heinemann.

Horkheimer, M. (1982) *Critical Theory: Selected Essays*, New York: Continuum.

Linklater, A. (1990) *Beyond Realism and Marxism: Critical Theory and International Relations*, London: Macmillan.

4 Globalisation and IPE

Chapter learning outcomes

After reading this chapter students should be able to:

- Engage in the main theoretical debates about the nature of globalisation.
- Understand the concept of globalisation as a set of processes of integration and to understand the debates between hyperglobalists, transformationalists and sceptics as to whether or not globalisation is actually taking place and to what extent.
- Explain the expansion of the European system since the 1500s and how this relates to the emergence of globalisation.
- Understand the roots of the global financial system.
- Comprehend contemporary processes of globalisation in a number of issue areas including: trade and finance, media, environmental challenges, the rise of MNCs and elements of an emerging globalised culture.

Introduction

Globalisation has become one of the key terms in describing and analysing life in the contemporary world. Different authors have focused on different parts of the structures and processes that contribute to global trends and phenomena. There is some disagreement in terms of what should be the primary focus of such studies. Moreover, there remain disputes over the significance and implications of so-called global trends. Hirst *et al.* (2009) question many of the underpinnings of basic assumptions about globalisation. In particular, they have queried the extent to which current trends are essentially 'new'. Rather, they ask whether such trends should be seen as an extension of a nascent global economy with historical roots stretching back several centuries. This chapter will consider the manner in which current aspects of globalisation have developed, and continue to evolve, over time. It will also give you a sense of how the theoretical perspectives, outlined in the first section of this book, have addressed the actions and issues associated with globalisation. As such this chapter is the bridge between the earlier theoretical chapters and the following issue-based chapters.

First of all there remain fundamental disagreements and debates surrounding what it is that constitutes globalisation. Differing schools of thought focus on various aspects of international relations. What is focussed on can clearly colour one's analysis and, therefore, conclusions. This applies to all aspects of IR and IPE. The study of globalisation is no exception. Here we highlight how each of the, broadly defined, three main paradigms of realists and neo-realists, liberal pluralists and structuralists/ Marxists consider globalisation in terms of how it impacts on national interests. We also go on to outline the response from feminism, green theories and postmodernism.

Realism/neo-realism

For realists the basic idea of interdependence between states is contradictory to their core beliefs. States are seen as unitary actors in a zero-sum game scenario of absolute gains and losses. That said, processes of globalisation could be acknowledged within this paradigm in terms of the domination and subordination roles of various states relative to each other. Globalisation might have altered the means by which states attempt to maximise their power. For example, there is generally less emphasis on invasion and occupation by military means. More likely in contemporary relationships, power and influence are increased by way of biased trading relationships and, perhaps, socio-cultural factors. This point on the increased role of the economic sector in promoting state power, or weakness, is more closely associated with the neo-realist variant. The neo-realist approach can be seen as highlighting the economic dimension of globalisation, whereas classical realism continues to adhere to the political dimension.

Liberal pluralism

Liberals, in contrast to realists and neo-realists, do not view the state as the only/predominant unit of analysis. As such this range of views is more in tune with the complex interactions characterised by globalisation. They consider the role of various institutions, IGOs, INGOs and a wealth of civil society groupings. Importantly many liberals highlight the individual as a significant unit of analysis. This is undoubtedly a more complex milieu of actors and processes than the 'simple' state-centric approach. It is important to note that part of this complexity is the dual processes of greater connectedness at some levels (transport, communications and so forth) yet also wildly differing experiences and opportunities at the individual level. Liberal pluralism highlights both political and economic dimensions of globalisation. Political liberalism focuses on issues such as human rights and forms of governance. Economic liberalism is more concerned with economic growth. The 'greater good for the greater number' idea might mean that particular individuals suffer or are marginalised from the benefits of such growth. Currently economic liberalism is at the forefront of the dominant states' 'programme' for the twenty-first century. The political liberalism of the pro-democracy agenda can be seen as part of this programme, but running well behind that of the economic drivers.

Structuralism/Marxism

This range of approaches is concerned with the historical evolution of structures and processes that determine and reinforce patterns of power, domination and resistance. Unlike the above approaches this paradigm is explicit in highlighting levels of exploitation within various structures. Here globalisation is predominantly seen in negative terms, with an emphasis on working conditions and resource depletion. Yet simultaneously this paradigm also acknowledges that aspects of globalisation, such as improved communication networks, actively aid resistance to the negative effects. In terms of distinguishing between the political and the economic, structuralists/Marxists concentrate on the economic sector as the means by which political power is maintained. Importantly this can be seen at both the domestic and international levels. Political power is discussed at distinct levels with, on the one hand, recognition of the ongoing power of governments. On the other hand, political power is often described in terms of individual and collective action for equality of opportunity, with globalisation seen as an inequitable process.

Feminism

As with liberal approaches the emphasis within feminism is based at the level of the individual. It could also be argued that there are connections with structuralism in that many feminist writers high-light the position of women in patriarchal structures and societies. Issues of cultural relativism can also be seen as relevant here. Just as the political and economic spheres can be viewed differently by various approaches, equally cultural issues can be highlighted as significant factors when comparing experiences of globalisation. Also the emancipatory dimension of structuralism is evidenced within feminism. In terms of globalisation feminism is relevant with regard to the concept that 'the personal is political'. Feminism, arguably, goes further than liberal approaches in pointing out the role and re-sponsibility of individuals to recognise their own position in relation to others, and to work towards greater equality and opportunities for all. The UN Conference on Women, held in Beijing in 1995, represented an acknowledgement by the international community that women have particular issues to be addressed. The specialised agency UNIFEM promotes women's health and education issues. Processes of globalisation, such as the general shift towards cash-based economies, have been cri-tiqued as disadvantaging certain groups. Women, in particular, may be seen as disadvantaged if they are employed in a low-earning capacity while also maintaining a relationship that is gender stereo-typed. This could include taking on paid employment while simultaneously also maintaining house-hold and child-rearing responsibilities.

Green theory

Green theories are particularly associated with trans-boundary issues and the need to view the world as a totality rather than artificially fragmented units. There is a huge range of what has been described as 'light' and 'dark' green thought. 'Light' green environmentalists refer to lobbying national govern-ments to reform policies on resource usage and pollution. In contrast, 'dark' green activists call for far more radical measures involving a revolutionary approach to overthrowing capitalism. More extreme elements take exception to the anthropocentric nature of most international relations. They prefer to think in terms of eco-centrism, which does not assume that humans are the centre of the universe. Given that the dominant process of globalisation is the pursuit of a model of development that extols mass consumerism, it is unsurprising the green analysts and activists are concerned about how sustain-able such a model is. Pollution and resource degradation, including loss of biodiversity, are side-effects of globalisation. There are arguments that it doesn't have to be this way and the promotion of issues such as technology transfer from the developed to the less-developed parts of the world are potential responses to these problems. The Earth Summits of 1992 and 2002 are evidence that the international community, at the level of national governments, can come together to discuss environmental issues. Yet, to date, there has been scant progress in reversing the more negative trends associated with processes of globalisation. The 2009 Copenhagen climate change summit largely failed because of the drive for short-term economic growth continues to be the dominant factor in relations between states. The deep green theorists also place emphasis on individuals to reflect upon and amend their patterns of behaviour in response to environmental problems. This can be seen as a further example of the per-sonal being political.

Postmodernism

A central concern of postmodernism is the use of language. With regard to globalisation it should already be apparent that there are numerous definitions and explanations as to what is happening at the global level and what the ramifications might be. As with the above approaches it is important to note what aspects of politics, economics or socio-cultural factors are being considered. For post-modernists the state is but one of many possible foci for understanding the contemporary global political economy. Similarly issues of personal identification can be seen as relevant and powerful forces. The actual processes of globalisation, such as the apparent reduction of time and space in trade and other patterns of interaction, are important. While not discounting the ongoing relevance of the nation state system, postmodernists stress the need to challenge dominant world views, such as state-centrism. Unlike other approaches discussed here they do not offer an alternative vision. On the contrary they suggest that all views are open to question and, controversially, have equal validity. As argued above, individuals have differing experiences of globalisation. Therefore, it is understandable that there will exist myriad interpretations and views on the relative merits and disadvantages of various aspects of globalisation. In this respect postmodernism can be seen as useful in helping to recognise the variety of experiences, although perhaps less useful as a tool for rigorous analysis.

The globalisation debate

The above outlines of differing approaches to interpretations of processes of globalisation is a useful starting point in understanding how globalisation is differently viewed and interpreted. In many ways this is simply an extension of an ongoing inter-paradigm debate. To take this a stage further we will now consider more specific disagreements over the extent to which globalisation is an essentially new phenomenon and how far-reaching the consequences of it might be. In particular this will address the debate over the existence of an emerging global economy and the promotion of human rights.

'Hyperglobalists' are those that believe we are experiencing an era of unprecedented global connectivity and political, economic and social change on a scale never previously experienced. They are made up of a diverse range of analysts who are either positive or negative in their assessments of this scenario. For the positive camp globalisation represents the promotion of neo-liberal economics and democratic forms of governance. This camp would include authors such as Kenichi Ohmae (1999) and Martin Albrow (1996). They can be associated with the so-called 'trickle-down' effect whereby, in the longer-term, all people will benefit from an emphasis on economic growth. They often downplay the role of governments in this process and advocate development via market forces. Negative hyperglobalists, such as Hans-Peter Martin and Harold Schumann (1997), agree that there is unprecedented connectivity, but they highlight the non-sustainable level of resource exploitation and poor working conditions and lack of individual freedoms as economies compete in what these critics see as a 'race to the bottom'.

In contrast to the hyperglobalists there are also a number of globalisation 'sceptics'. These authors, such as Hirst et al. (2009), argue that many of the processes associated with globalisation have a long-standing history. They point to the expansion of the imperial and colonial systems and the way in which resources and labour were exploited across the globe. However, they make a distinction between these international connections and a system that is truly global in terms of coordination and governance. It is also noted that the greatest level of integration and cooperation is at the regional level, and usually in the more developed parts of the world, for example the European Union. In terms of trade and the movement of goods and services, the greater percentage of such trade is found within the EU, rather than between the EU and the rest of the world. Similarly, roughly two-thirds of the international transfer of capital and goods happens between the subsidiaries of MNCs rather than by way of engagement with other companies or states. Also, in opposition to the idea that the world is becoming increasingly uniform due to the spread of dominant ideas and values, the sceptics point to areas of resistance and what Samuel Huntington (2002) has described as a 'clash of civilisations'. Sceptics would argue that despite the rise in rhetoric regarding human rights, the reality is that state power and the demands of market forces continue to have priority over the establishment of a meaningful human rights regime at the global level.

There is also a middle position located between the two outlined above – the transformationalists. They believe that we are in the midst of a period of significant change, experiencing phenomena of a new and unique order. However, they do not take their claims as far as the hyperglobalists. As with the sceptics, the transformationalists do not see these changes as having yet evolved to the point of a global world order. It should be noted that the transformationalists do not suggest any particular form that the process of globalisation is leading towards. Rather, they place their emphasis on the dynamic of change. There clearly are changes taking place in the fields of, for example, information and communication technologies and the types of issues on the international agenda. Transformationalists accept that new relationships and divisions are emerging, both within and between states. This in turn is impacting on the agendas of governments and a range of non-state actors. Manuel Castells' (2009) work on the 'network society' is an example of highlighting these new forms of relationships and the issues that arise from them. Transformationalists tend not to express views as dogmatically as either the hyperglobalists or the sceptics. They adopt more of an observational position, simply stating how institutions and related actors are evolving. For example, with regard to coordinating economic issues, GATT has evolved into the WTO. Similarly, concern about environmental issues has resulted in the Earth Summit process and related conventions. In terms of human rights, transformationalists would note that international human rights campaigning has certainly raised its profile in recent years. Yet at the same time the post-9/11 era can also be viewed as one where individual rights and freedoms have been undermined in the fight against terrorism. In each of these examples change has clearly taken place; what is debatable is whether these changes are positive or negative.

Table 4.1   Conceptualising globalisation: three tendencies

	Hyperglobalists	**Sceptics**	**Transformationalists**
What's New?	A global age	Trading blocs, weaker geogovernance than earlier periods	Historically unprecedented levels of global interconnectedness
Dominant features	Global Capitalism, global governance, global civil society	World less interdependent than in 1890s	'Thick' (intensive and extensive) globalisation
Power of national governments	Declining or eroding	Reinforced or enhanced	Reconstituted, restructured
Driving forces of globalisation	Capitalism and technology	States and markets	Combined forces of modernity
Pattern of stratification	Erosion of old hierarchies	Increased marginalisation of South	New architecture of world order
Dominant motif	McDonalds, Madonna etc.	National interest	Transformation of political community
Conceptualisation of globalisation	As a reordering of the framework of human action	As internationalisation and regionalisation	As the reordering of interregional relations and action at a distance
Historical trajectory	Global civilisation	Regional blocs/clash of civilisations	Indeterminate: global integration and fragmentation
Summary argument	The end of the nation state	Internationalisation depends on state acquiescence and support	Globalisation transforming state power and world politics

Source: Held *et al.* (1999).

Origins of globalisation

Jan Art Scholte states that 'globalisation has no origin' (Scholte, 2005). At best we can pinpoint certain events that herald the start of a significant era. For example, the invention of the printing press, the first manned flight or the first photograph of planet Earth taken from space. In their own ways each of these can be seen as symbolic, even iconic, examples whereby the world is somehow 'transformed' for its inhabitants. Not all of these had immediate widespread impacts. The initial print runs of the Gothenburg press were very limited, not only in terms of the numbers of copies produced but also the distance they could be distributed and the number of people able to read them. Similarly the Wright brothers, at the start of the 1900s, represented the infancy of manned flight. From these early pioneers of this technology there quickly developed an industry that had major implications for warfare, trade and more widespread movement of people and ideas. Finally, and perhaps the most literal example of the concept of globalisation, the images of Earth relayed back from Apollo 9 in 1969 gave many people a sense of substance to trends that had been occurring for centuries. These trends could previously have been thought of as occurring in bilateral or multilateral arrangements or in regional terms. The image of the 'blue planet' suspended in space highlighted that this was a finite area with finite resources. Until space programmes are developed to take us to the next stage of exploration, and possibly off-planet settlement, humans are going to have to interact within certain limitations. Patterns of interaction at individual through to state level are still evolving. Processes of globalisation are increasingly a part of humans', and non-human species', interaction. Before looking more closely at specific examples of such interactions in the fields of communication, trade, environmental issues, culture and military issues, it is useful to briefly review the historical roots of each of these areas. Each of these will then be discussed in more depth in the following chapters.

Expansion of the European system

The development of technological advances in travel, communications, trans-shipment of goods and multi-centred production processes has evolved over several centuries. Non-European civilisations, such as the Chinese, have a history of exploration well beyond their borders, with evidence of Chinese traders venturing as far as Africa by the 1400s. However, it is the experience of European exploration and settlement that can be argued to have had the most profound and longest-lasting impacts. Beginning with the explorations of the Portuguese and Spanish and their appropriation of resources (gold and silver from Latin America) followed by the more reciprocal trading relationships of the Dutch and then the imperial competition among other European powers, notably France and Britain, there evolved a pattern of domination and subordination/resistance between Europe and the rest of the world. This has been characterised by patterns of colonial rule, preferential patterns of trade, social and cultural impacts and the establishment of a global economy that has underlying socio-economic and political structures.

World-system theory (WST), as outlined in Chapter 2, places great emphasis on the historical evolution of relations between imperial powers and their colonies. Crucially this approach highlights the ongoing dynamics of these relations that have their roots in the colonial era. Even when formal independence was achieved, for many states in the 1960s and 1970s, a fundamental determinant of their future development has been the manner in which their economies continue to be linked to their former rulers. Dependency theory also looks at relations between the global North and the global South. It should be noted, though, that 'dependency' can be viewed as a two-way process. By this we mean that although the dominant model of dependency would be one whereby the South would be dependent on the North, for development assistance or other forms of support, equally it can be argued that the North is reliant on both raw materials and markets in the South. As such, a complex pattern of relationships can be seen to be involved within the global economic system of trade and related socio-political and cultural influences. That said, there remain identifiable advantages and disadvantages for the various actors and institutions involved. Again WST is relevant here as these are structural determinants. A notable feature of the processes of globalisation being considered here is that structural features, such as dominance of key political and financial institutions, has led to the embedding of certain powers to the point whereby they dominate the international system. Such a situation has arisen on several occasions over previous centuries as particular powers have gained predominance.

Hegemonic stability theory (HST) is relevant here in terms of explaining the various periods when certain powers, for various reasons, have come to the fore. In relation to European expansion and imperialism it is important to be clear what constitutes a hegemonic power. Although Spain and Portugal were important powers with regard to the amount of wealth they extracted from Latin America and the relative advancement they therefore enjoyed in comparison to other European powers at that time, this is not an example of structural power; it is relational. In contrast the Dutch developed a trading system that involved the acquiescence of trading partners, despite the Dutch gaining relatively more in the course of each transaction. In a sense this might be seen as a quasi-structural relationship. Although their trading partners will have experienced some advantage, it was the Dutch who were the dominant partners controlling shipping routes and, to some extent, market prices. The first truly global hegemonic power did not emerge until the 1700s with the rise of Britain as the predominant naval and trading power. Earlier examples might be cited, such as the Roman or Mongol Empires; however, these were mainly based on continuous territorial expansion of their respective 'known' worlds. Britain went beyond this in that, by control of sea-lanes of trade and communication, they established an extensive network between the major trading ports around the globe. This influence and control was expanded further after the Industrial Revolution with the development of railways into the interiors of various countries. This practical control was reinforced by the active governance of large swathes of territory to the point when, at its height, 'the sun never set on the British Empire'.

After the Second World War there was a significant decline in the power and international influence of the European powers. In some respects this redistribution of power was in line with previous rises and falls of empires. The United States emerged as the dominant power in the post-Second World War era, to some extent balanced by the Soviet Union but having the distinct advantage of sustaining no infrastructural damage on its continental landmass and leading the formulation of the major post-war political and financial institutions. HST is again relevant in explaining the significance of the US role in directing the emerging post-war order. Just as Britain had come to dominate the maritime world, the US not only filled the power vacuum left by Britain's decline, but it also took advantage of emerging trends in global trade and development. These include a greater openness in trading and political relations, as they were no longer as closely tied to former colonial relationships. Some of the newly independent states of the 1960s and 1970s were drawn towards the Soviet-influenced command economic approach with clearly directed government intervention in the market. Many more though were capitalist-driven economies. This was a direction that was actively supported and encouraged by the US. The operations of the leading multinationals of this time, which were predominantly owned and operated by US citizens, reinforced the rise of the US to the position of a global hegemonic state. Simultaneously this was further characterised by developments in the fields of technology, notably the emergence of nuclear weaponry and advances in lines and methods of communications.

The development of nuclear weapons was significant for two main reasons. First, once parity in nuclear capability had been achieved by the Soviet Union, a nuclear stand-off emerged which meant that direct confrontation was largely avoided for fear of escalation to the nuclear level. Yet ideological competition continued between the two superpowers. Part of this competition involved the active promotion by the US of liberal democratic systems of governance, at least in terms of stated political intent. Second, was the promotion of free market economic policies. This approach dominated not only the direction of the US economy but also that of Western Europe and the majority of the newly independent states. Despite actively disavowing territorial gains from its involvement in the Second World War, the US undoubtedly gained from the way in which the post-war world order evolved. The 'empire' of the US is based on much more than territorial expansion. It is characterised more by extending influence in the fields of economics and, increasingly, culture.

The movement of goods and services in increasingly large amounts, at cheaper costs and greater speed, enhanced the position of the leading powers, enabling them to dominate this sector of the emerging global economy. For example, larger cargo ships with the capacity to 'globalise' the production cycle of many goods and the technology to disperse the production process. The emergence of a global economy is most notably characterised by the shift away from local patterns of production to one increasingly reliant on imported goods and services. An extreme example of this would be to consider the spectrum of economic activities ranging from subsistence, drawing solely on local resources, to those that are completely divorced from the local environment and rely on cash income to buy in all goods and commodities, including foodstuffs. Each individual and community is placed somewhere along this spectrum. A key point to note though is that the dominant trend in current economic practices, and even the dominant discourse of what constitutes 'development', appears to be moving towards the cash-based economic model. Later chapters will discuss in more detail the implications of how sustainable such a model of development might be. At this point we wish to focus on the primary architecture and actors that are facilitating and encouraging such a trend. We will also cover additional aspects of globalisation and at the end of each section we will consider how each of these issues is reflected upon by hyperglobalists, sceptics and transformationalists.

Globalisation of trade and finance

Following the end of the Second World War a major conference was held in San Francisco in 1945 to manage the transition from the League of Nations system to that of the United Nations. A key dimension of the emerging order was the role and influence of the main financial systems designed to monitor and control post-war economic developments. This was the first time that multilateral agreements had emerged that took into account the increased connectivity of trading relations on a global scale. Below are brief descriptions of each of the leading financial institutions.

CONCEPT BOX

The International Monetary Fund (IMF)

Headquarters: Washington, United States

Aims: The IMF was established to create a multilateral system of payments between nation states based on fixed exchange rates and the full convertibility from one currency to another in order to maintain currency stability and world trade. All members had to peg their exchange rates to the US dollar or gold while the US pegged the dollar to $35 per ounce of gold. Furthermore, each member would have to pay a subscription charge that would be used to support those states that ran into temporary balance of payments problems. Following the 1971 'floating' of the US dollar and the subsequent collapse of the regime, the IMF was left without its central purpose. It is now one of the main advocates of the 'Washington Consensus', which is a narrow view of the world economic system based on market efficiency and the free flow of capital, goods and services. This is also known as the neo-liberal economic model. IMF assistance to states in crisis is now dependent on reforms aimed at advancing this system.

Website: www.imf.org/

CONCEPT BOX

The World Bank (WB)

Headquarters: Washington, United States

Aims: Following the Second World War the International Bank for Reconstruction and Development (IBRD), now known as the World Bank, was established to revive the war-torn European economies. This mandate was later extended to all developing states. The Bank raises its funds through borrowing from international markets and by dues from member states. The loans made by the Bank to developing states are given at a lower interest rate than commercial banks and are aimed at supporting the construction of infrastructure projects (roads, power plants, hydroelectricity dams and so on). Similar to the IMF, the WB has also been a staunch supporter of the 'Washington Consensus'.

Website: www.worldbank.org/

CONCEPT BOX

The World Trade Organization (WTO)

Headquarters: Geneva, Switzerland

Aims: The WTO replaced the General Agreement on Tariffs and Trade in 1995. GATT was one of the original Bretton Woods initiatives created to establish rules for the governance and liberalisation of international trade. The main goals were to lower tariff and non-tariff barriers (NTBs) to trade that had crippled the global economy prior to the Second World War. Seven rounds of negotiations, often lasting several years, were carried out to reduce tariffs and NTBs, finishing with the Uruguay Round (1986–1994) which resulted in the creation of the WTO. The WTO includes the core agreements of GATT but solidifies them and expands the capabilities for the enforcement of the agreements through trade sanctions and provides greater avenues for future agreements. While GATT focused on trade in goods, the WTO also includes negotiations for the liberalisation of trade in services through the General Agreement on Trade in Services (GATS). GATS covers areas such as telecommunications, banking and transport. There are also agreements that cover trade-related intellectual property rights (TRIPS) and trade-related investment measures (TRIMS).

Website: www.wto.org/

Both the actuality of the process of globalisation of world politics and the study of this process require the occurrence and study of the parallel process of the globalisation of economies. As most scholars in the field of IPE will advocate, politics and economics are inseparable and need to be understood and explained in conjunction with each other. The distribution of power and its application to world affairs (politics) is integral to the distribution, exchange and use of resources (economics) and vice versa. As countless discussions have shown, contemporary international politics have become increasingly global in their nature. At the same time advancements in technology, communications and transport as well as the often sporadic process of industrialisation have resulted in a globalisation of the production process and, by extension, trade. It is now possible to produce a product almost anywhere in the world, using resources originating from anywhere and for sale in any market which at each stage of the process requires trade. The globalisation of trade has largely been a 'natural' phenomenon due to advancements in the human condition dating back to the nineteenth century. However, since the end of the Second World War and increasingly since the 1970s this process has been consciously facilitated by a number of states and international and global institutions, which have as their agenda the globalisation of both trade and finance.

Advocates of globalisation describe contemporary globalisation of trade and finance as a stage in the long-term development of a global society. In this view the globalisation of trade and finance are not merely a more intensified version of the processes of internationalisation and regionalisation but rather the breaking of official (state) controls on the movements of goods, people and services. This 'liberalisation' of the international political economy allows for the replacement of 'international' trade, finance and production with 'global' trade, finance and production. This emergent globalised economy characterised by global trade and financial processes will (as advocates argue) lead to a more prosperous, developed, democratic and peaceful world for all. In this view (often termed neo-liberalism) the occurrence of economic depression, authoritarian regimes and intra- and inter-state conflict in the twentieth century is attributed to the disruption of the process of the globalisation of trade and finance by tightening border controls in the first half of the last century.

During the latter half of the twentieth century trade liberalisation and globalisation increased markedly. Through the General Agreement on Tariffs and Trade (GATT) a number of inter-state accords were reached that led to major reductions in customs duties, quotas and other non-tariff barriers that had previously restricted cross-border trade. In the more prosperous states, for example, the average tariffs on manufactured products fell from over 30 per cent in the 1930s to less than 4 per cent at the turn of the century. This was largely facilitated by GATT. From 1986 to 1994 the Uruguay Round of international trade negotiations were held with the aim of progressively advancing globalisation of trade. The result of these negotiations was the establishment of the World Trade Organisation (WTO) as a replacement for GATT. The WTO was established to be a more homogeneous institution with greater ability to enforce existing agreements and to pursue at greater pace further trade liberalisation.

From the 1950s onwards national borders have also opened considerably to money flows. This was facilitated by the adoption of a 'gold-dollar standard' exchange mechanism that emerged and was enforced by the International Monetary Fund (IMF) in 1959. under this international exchange regime the major currencies such as the United States dollar could circulate the globe freely and be converted into local currencies at an established and fixed exchange rate. Following the unilateral decision by the United States government in 1971, a 'floating' exchange rate regime emerged in 1973 and was formally inaugurated by the IMF in 1976. Furthermore, increasing regional integration throughout the world led to the bilateral and multilateral reductions in the import and export of national currencies. Combined, these developments led to unprecedented levels of foreign exchange which by 2000 had reached over $1 trillion.

Hyperglobalists point to the creation of the above institutions, especially the WTO, as evidence of a concerted attempt to coordinate, integrate and govern global processes at the economic level.

Sceptics acknowledge that there is increased interaction between economies, but deny that this represents an undermining of the basic autonomy of national governments. Some states may indeed be advantaged or disadvantaged under this system. Yet the system itself remains one of individual states interacting, rather than a form of global governance.

Transformationalists focus more on the dynamic of change and the opportunities this creates for some, although others may be actively disadvantaged by such changes.

Corporate globalisation

Globalisation is about more than moving towards a generally common mode of production. The ownership and control of economic activity has increasingly moved away from government control and has also become more centralised in the hands of a relatively small group of parent companies coordinating various multinational corporations. The implications of this are that global trends are becoming ever-more uniform. It is important to note, however, that this does not necessarily lead to uniformity of experience for various individuals and communities around the world. Far from it, as the emphasis on cash-based economies has led to a wide diversity of income generation and amount of disposable income available to individuals. The rise of multinationals is indeed characterised by a spread of branded products, albeit with some regional variations in how they are marketed. Yet this global profile does not mean that all of these products are equally available to all consumers.

Corporate globalisation is the spread of big business across the world. As big business grows, it gets more powerful, often meaning that other actors in the international arena, such as national governments and people, witness varying degrees of loss in sovereignty and autonomy. There are five main identifiable trends in corporate globalisation, each of a controversial nature:

1 The first is that the private market place is becoming dominated by large multinational corporations (MNCs).
2 A second trend is the accumulation of wealth within a small number of economic actors, both public and private.
3 Third, the divide between the rich and poor, which can refer to individuals, states or companies, is growing both within and between states.
4 Fourth, the divisions of labour and multi-centred production are also contributing to growing differences of experiences and opportunities.
5 Finally, the political, social and cultural influences of the corporate sector are increasing in line with their economic influences.

The rise of the MNC is not a recent phenomenon. The spread of imperial rule referred to above coincided with the growth in private investment in international trade. Famous examples of this include the Dutch East India Trading Company and the Hudson Bay Trading Company. The operations of such companies had the dual effect of disrupting existing local economies and reinforcing the emerging dominant position of the 'core' states. MNCs outperform smaller companies and locally owned and operated family businesses. For example, high-street coffee stores around the globe are continually replaced by chainstores such as Starbucks. This is a result of the greater efficiency and profitability of the larger firms. Patterns of wealth accumulation also include takeovers and mergers between MNCs. A result of this has been the ever greater concentration of wealth under the control of a decreasing number of larger and larger firms (see Table 4.2). This accumulation of wealth, and prestige, can also be identified at the level of the state. Neo-realists argue that MNCs can be viewed as 'agents of the state', thereby acting as conduits for enhancing the power bases of MNCs' home states. However, it is important to recognise that, with the exception of arch realists, most analysts acknowledge that the state is not a unitary actor. Therefore, although the overall power and prestige of some states may be enhanced by processes of globalisation, there can also be many divisions emerging both within and between states.

These divisions are significantly driven by the spread of capitalism. Indications of this are clearly evident; of the more than 6 billion people in the world, approximately 2.8 billion live on less than $1.20 a day. Over 60 states had lower per capita income in 2004 than they did in 1990. Furthermore, the 475 richest individuals have a combined wealth that is greater than the poorest half of people in the world. As will be discussed in more depth in subsequent chapters, there are contentious arguments with regard to the ideology of capitalism. Whereas some, such as World Bank economists, consider free market economic policies to be the solution to poverty, others hold diametrically opposed views. For anti-capitalists the problem lies in the lack of accounting of social and environmental costs in 'free' market economics. They point to environmental pollution, non-sustainable resource usage and poor working conditions as evidence that capitalism is fundamentally exploitative and, therefore, flawed. While acknowledging that processes of globalisation, including the spread of free market economics, has created more connectedness between economies and societies, this does not

Table 4.2 Top 25 MNCs by rank based on composite scores for sales, profits, assets and market value

Rank	Company	Country	Industry	Sales ($bn)	Profits ($bn)	Assets ($bn)	Market value ($bn)
1	HSBC Holdings	United Kingdom	Banking	146.50	19.13	2,348.98	180.81
2	General Electric	United States	Conglomerates	172.74	22.21	795.34	330.93
3	Bank of America	United States	Banking	119.19	14.98	1,715.75	176.53
4	JPMorgan Chase	United States	Banking	116.35	15.37	1,562.15	136.88
5	ExxonMobil	United States	Oil & Gas Operations	358.60	40.61	242.08	465.51
6	Royal Dutch Shell	Netherlands	Oil & Gas Operations	355.78	31.33	266.22	221.09
7	BP	United Kingdom	Oil & Gas Operations	281.03	20.60	236.08	204.94
8	Toyota Motor	Japan	Consumer Durables	203.80	13.99	276.38	175.08
9	ING Group	Netherlands	Insurance	197.93	12.65	1,932.15	75.78
10-	Berkshire Hathaway	United States	Diversified Financials	118.25	13.21	273.16	216.65
10-	Royal Bank of Scotland	United Kingdom	Banking	108.45	14.62	3,807.51	76.64
12	AT&T	United States	Telecommunications Services	118.93	11.95	275.64	210.22
13	BNP Paribas	France	Banking	116.16	10.71	2,494.41	81.90
14	Allianz	Germany	Insurance	139.12	10.90	1,547.48	80.30
15	Total	France	Oil & Gas Operations	199.74	19.24	165.75	181.80
16	Wal-Mart Stores	United States	Retailing	378.80	12.73	163.38	198.60
17	Chevron	United States	Oil & Gas Operations	203.97	18.69	148.79	179.97
18	American Intl Group	United States	Insurance	110.06	6.20	1,060.51	118.20
19	Gazprom	Russia	Oil & Gas Operations	81.76	23.30	201.72	306.79
20	AXA Group	France	Insurance	151.70	7.75	1,064.67	70.33
21	Banco Santander	Spain	Banking	72.26	10.02	1,332.72	113.27
22	ConocoPhillips	United States	Oil & Gas Operations	171.50	11.89	177.76	129.15
23	Goldman Sachs Group	United States	Diversified Financials	87.97	11.60	1,119.80	67.16
24	Citigroup	United States	Banking	159.23	3.62	2,187.63	123.44
25	Barclays	United Kingdom	Banking	79.70	8.76	2,432.34	62.43

Source: De Carlo, S. and Zajac, B. (eds) (2008) 'The world's biggest companies: The global 2000', *Forbes*, 2 April 2008.

necessarily mean that all are sharing in a common experience of these processes. Far from it, as processes such as multi-centred production practices are increasingly creating distance between the production and consumption of goods and services. Compare, for example, a locally-orientated subsistence-based economy with that based on the export of manufactured or assembled goods. In a mass consumer society labour costs are driven down by the contracting out of certain aspects of the production process to labour markets with low unit costs. This has a knock-on effect in terms of relative purchasing power. In the field of computers and related technology the consumer is benefiting from both better products and cheaper prices over time. In contrast, the workers producing such goods, although arguably benefiting from the expansion of this sector, are often not in a position to be able to afford the goods they produce.

Hyperglobalists see the operations of MNCs as further proof of the extension of a global economy. Their emphasis is on the global networks that have arisen with multi-centred production processes.

Sceptics recognise the operations of MNCs but view them more in terms of state power and the re-inforcement of a system based on national economies.

Transformationalists focus more on the relationship between MNCs and the state. This can include both the positive aspects of MNCs as agents of a particular state, and also where states (mainly but not exclusively in the developing world) are in an inferior power relationship with the MNCs they interact with.

Global culture?

For the greater part of human history separate cultures have existed in a state of relative isolation from the influence and impact of others, with the exception of intermittent trading. The processes of political, economic and social globalisation have brought cultures into closer contact. Technological and communicative advancements and expanding interaction between cultures have highlighted the problems and possibilities different cultures face with regards to maintaining traditional patterns of culture and social order. Furthermore, cultural interaction and homogenisation no longer requires the direct physical contact of different people. Through channels such as television and the Internet, cultures can interact and blend. As relations between separate cultures have developed further through activities such as trade, migration and even conflict, the level of isolation and individuality of cultures has slowly decreased. In this sense there are relatively few contemporary cultures that are wholly unique. Despite some distinctive features most cultures now share a degree of commonality. By this we mean cultures are open to increasingly common phenomena, such as the free flow of capital and information via the Internet. However, such phenomena may be experienced differently and 'filtered' through local norms and values.

The intense interaction between the different cultures around the globe has not evolved evenly in scope and range of effects. The dominance of what is labelled 'Western' or occasionally simply 'American' culture has been the source of much controversy since the 1970s. The key practices, features and ideologies of Western/American culture can be found in practically all regions of the globe and most if not all cultures. 'Fast-food' chains such as McDonald's and Kentucky Fried Chicken and the related Coca-Cola franchise are good examples of the American and, in general, Western impact on the rest of the world. In addition to influencing dietary habits, and patterns of health, American influences have also been noted in more fundamental aspects of culture. An example would be the promotion of individualism as the focus of a society, where previously the broader community would be the focus. Although this shift to the individual might promote greater equality at the political level it can also promote greater rates of mass consumption and inequality at the economic level.

However, it is questionable whether we can talk of a world of over 6 billion people becoming a monoculture. It is true that the process of globalisation is resulting in increasingly close contact between cultures and rising, albeit asymmetrical, influence of some cultures on others. Nevertheless, as mentioned above, cultures are rarely insulated from outside influence and globalisation does not necessarily result in the loss of traditions and values. New forms of media such as the Internet have in fact proven a powerful means of strengthening the customs, norms and values of traditional culture. For example, many diasporic groups have actively reinforced their sense of cultural heritage by way of developing interactive websites. In the 'liberal' conception of global cultural homogenisation the constant quest of capitalism to produce and sell necessitates a level of multiculturalism. In this way, cultural integration and homogenisation does not necessarily imply the loss of many traditional values, practices and ideas, rather a synthesis of these at one level of culture while preserving others at another level.

Alternative interpretations regarding the impacts of globalisation on culture do exist. As well as the homogenising impacts of globalisation on all cultures also comes the development of reactionary forces. The largely 'Western'-dominated macro-culture that is seen as being spread by the asymmetrical dominance of American and European cultural influence has resulted in large levels of resistance in less-dominant cultures. The West has widely been discredited for its irresponsible individualism, lack of moral responsibility and capitalist ideology that has been perceived as exploitative and unequal as opposed to emancipatory. Harvard Professor Samuel Huntington, in his article and later his book with the same title, *The Clash of Civilizations* (1993), presented a more negative outlook of the results of cultural interaction in the globalising era than the 'liberal' idea. Huntington argues that the interaction at the highest level of culture, that is the civilisation, will determine world affairs in the post-Cold War world. This interaction is likely to be characterised by resistance and confrontation rather than homogenisation and cooperation.

AUTHOR BOX

Samuel P. Huntington

The Clash of Civilizations is Huntington's seminal work on the future prospects for world affairs. In this article that was later developed into a book Huntington offers a new paradigm which focuses on patterns of international conflict and cooperation. He argues that civilisations (the highest point of cultures) will shape these patterns in the decades to come rather than nation states or private actors. Huntington suggests that there are eight identifiable civilisations that will determine world politics. These are Western, Confucian, Japanese, Islamic, Hindu, Slavic-Orthodox, Latin American, and African.

While for Huntington the history of the international system has fundamentally been about the conflict and cooperation between monarchs, nations, states and ideologies within Western civilisation, the end of the Cold War has altered this. In the post-Cold War era non-Western actors are now important 'agents' within the international system. Furthermore, there are four main processes at work in the international system that is facilitating this clash of civilisations. These are: first, the decline of the West in relation to other regions; second, the rise of the Asian economy, with China potentially going to become the greatest power in global affairs; third, the resurgence of Islam due to increasing Muslim populations and the end of imperial domination; fourth, the impact of globalisation on flows of commerce, information and people and subsequent impacts on cultural identity.

The emergence of 'resistance' to global cultural integration or 'dominance' in an ever smaller world plays a major role in ushering in this era of a clash of civilisations.

Regardless of one's position in relation to the clash of civilisations debate it is undeniable that culture is an important factor within all societies. Processes of globalisation can be seen to have aspects of both challenging and, on occasion, reinforcing cultural identity.

Hyperglobalists generally concur with the view that there is an emerging global culture.

Sceptics: Huntington would be firmly in the sceptic camp with his clash of civilisations thesis.

Transformationalists again focus on the dynamic of change. They acknowledge the forces driving a nascent global culture, but also highlight the forces of resistance.

Media

One of the main conduits for both the presentation and, possibly, promotion of globalisation is the wide array of media channels. Marshall McLuhan (2005) famously said that the 'medium is the message'. McLuhan is also credited with coining the phrase 'global village' and his work focused on both how the world appeared to be 'shrinking' and the methods employed that gave this impression. For McLuhan the term media was expansive, including not only print and broadcast journalism, but also wider cultural phenomena such as films and television programmes. The rise to prominence of the Internet takes McLuhan's ideas to another level. Part of the medium of the Internet is whether you are even connected. This has become known as the 'digital divide'. It is not simply what information is being presented but also how it is being received, if at all. We can identify a historical progression of media which can be traced back to significant developments, such as Caxton's printing press from the fifteenth century through radio transmissions, long-distance undersea cabling and on to satellite-based communication. As each type of media has developed, so too have the issues that surround them. Issues of editorial control, accessibility, interpretation, ability to act as a result of information received are all relevant to a discussion of the media. In terms of globalisation, the relationship between the local and the global is becoming more complex. This also applies to the manner in which this relationship is reported.

The numbers of people that can be reached by different forms of media has grown exponentially over time. The early printing presses were not the first examples of the promotion of texts. The library of Alexandria, for example, or the illustrated religious scripts of the early Christian era clearly pre-date the invention of the printing press. But the advent of print technology began the process of moving towards greater circulation of texts. Of course, the level of literacy had also to rise before mass consumption of printed texts could take place. Here there is a link to cultural issues, especially with regard to the expansion of empires. Both the British and the French have placed great emphasis on the promotion of their own languages in their former and current overseas territories. As such there is a clear link between the level of technology being used and the political agenda that underscores its usage. In the context of power relations the example of imperial control and resistance is pertinent here, and relevant to many contemporary situations. The manner in which different types of media are utilised is illustrative of this point. Imperial powers would communicate to their subjects via mainstream media, such as newspapers and later broadcasting. Resistance movements might use similar techniques, but on a smaller and usually more localised scale. By definition, imperial powers had a form of global reach and global interests. In contrast, pro-independence movements have a more localised focus, and more restricted resources to draw upon. A typical example would be the circulation of *The Times* or *Le Monde* compared with pamphlets produced by local political activists. Here it is not so much the numbers of people being reached as much as the content that is being provided.

Increasingly there is a division among various types of media where some might be described as 'corporate' and others as more 'independent'. By corporate we are thinking of businesses such as Fox News and other arms of Rupert Murdoch's media 'empire'. An example of a more independent form of media would be Indymedia (www.indymedia.org) which presents itself as an 'alternative' news source, often highlighting anti-globalisation actions. In terms of relative power the corporate examples have greater access to financial resources, often raised by way of advertising. They are also in a privileged position in terms of access to politicians and the corporate business community. Furthermore, they are seen by many in the mainstream audience to be a trustworthy source of information. In contrast, the smaller more independent providers of 'news' tend to have far more limited financial resources to call upon. Although the growing Internet usage provides Indymedia and similar sites with a potentially vast audience, they have to be proactively accessed by their audience. The same might be said of needing to buy a mainstream newspaper or to tune into a mainstream radio or television broadcast. However, the latter is far more part of the cultural background that surrounds people. Increasingly the mainstream media are extending their reach by means of embracing new technologies; they now exist in print, broadcast and electronic formats. The implications of this are that the underlying political agendas of the corporate media are being promoted, perhaps implicitly rather than explicitly. As with the spread of cultural norms and values cited above, corporate media plays a significant role in delivering such images and views. Simultaneously the spread of independent websites, down to the level of the individual site developer, can be seen to be presenting a wide range of alternative views. Despite such developments there remains a structural bias that favours and reinforces the role of the mainstream providers of news and commentaries.

In addition to the news media it is important to also consider the role and impact of the entertainment industry. As above, there is a sense of division between what can broadly be described as the mainstream corporate industry, especially in relation to the Hollywood studio 'system', and that of more independently minded (and financed) film-makers. In addition to the world of cinema, the same can be said of the music industry with major and independent record labels. Although there will be cultural differences in various parts of the world, it is possible to identify an underlying power dynamic involving a corporate core of mainstream entertainment media and a generally subservient periphery of more marginal independent producers, and consumers. Just as the news media is important in presenting a particular view of the world, albeit challenged by some counter-views, the entertainment industry can have an impact in terms of influencing audience beliefs and attitudes. This is clearly related to issues of culture but focused upon here due to the manner in which these cultural products are presented, distributed and accessed. As with the Indymedia example above, the role of technology in allowing greater accessibility to these products is telling. The phenomenon of file-sharing on the Internet has allowed an ever greater platform for the presentation of such products. This includes raising the profile and accessibility of film-makers and musicians who remain outside their respective corporate mainstream. There is also an issue of the illegal file-sharing of products that bypasses the traditional routes of access, and therefore also bypasses the generation of some of the revenue for the larger players. There is an ongoing debate surrounding the morality and business implications of such practices, inside as well as outside these industries. With regard to globalisation, file-sharing is a truly global phenomenon, it bypasses national and regional distribution agreements. It also changes the previously existing dynamic between the core mainstream of these industries and their peripheral or marginalised components. As such, in line with McLuhan's argument, both the media and the mediums of communication are evolving, and important.

The position and role of various media are closely interrelated to processes of globalisation. This is in terms of both actively promoting aspects of globalisation, highlighting some of the criticisms of these processes, and more generally informing, or perhaps misinforming, debates about globalisation.

Hyperglobalists see forms of media as the conduit for dispersing the norms and values of the dominant powers, thereby continually reinforcing their position of dominance.

Sceptics present a counter-argument whereby the processes of globalisation actually stimulate an oppositional dynamic that can provide a greater sense of local identity.

Transformationalists recognise the role of media sources in presenting images and views of the wider world, but that this is more likely to result in evolving forms of cultural hybridity.

Global environmental degradation

The aim of this section is to highlight the core environmental issues that have emerged and worsened since the 1970s and that are of a 'global' nature (as in affecting multiple states and regions) and the 'global' responses to such issues. The main issues included here are as follows: greenhouse gases due to increased industrialisation and fossil fuel consumption and associated global warming; rising sea levels due to global warming; resource degradation including forests, water and fish-stocks. Fossil fuel consumption is a twin problem with both depletion of stocks and also increased pollution due to their usage.

A key factor regarding environmental issues is that the liberalisation of international trade and investment risks worsening the impacts of human activity on the environment. Critics point to many channels through which globalisation may adversely affect the environment. First, with the increasing levels of, and greater opportunities for, global trade there is the potential for further exploitation and use of oil and other non-renewable resources. The result of these is a rise in levels of land, air and sea pollution, deforestation, soil erosion, floods and other ecological imbalances. Second, more trade often means goods and people travel a longer distance and in greater numbers, resulting in even more consumption of fuel resources and subsequent emissions of pollutant gases. While on the one hand global networks of trade and consumption increase choice in the marketplace, for those that can afford to buy these goods, it also creates a false impression of the true cost of many of these goods. With the exception of the niche market of Fairtrade products, the dynamic of the free market rarely passes on social and environmental costs to the consumer. One of the dominant trends of globalisation continues to be the spread of mass consumerism around the world. Unless this is checked, or technological improvements allow for more environmentally friendly patterns of growth, this is a scenario that is likely to be increasingly divisive and create increased conflict between individuals and states.

Attention towards environmental issues began to emerge in the 1970s and by the turn of the millennium environmental problems had become a focus of international concern. Understanding the causes, impacts and possible responses to global environmental problems has become increasingly urgent. Since the early 1970s an awareness of the number and severity of environmental problems has emerged. Some scientists dispute the more pessimistic predictions for resource depletion. Yet the majority agree that not only is this depletion occurring but also that the more negative impacts on the environment are as a direct result of human activity. As such it should, therefore, be possible for humans to correct their behaviour and activities to improve this situation. The difficulties in achieving this are twofold. First, we continue to operate in an international system driven by individual national governments. Although some progress has been made in terms of binding conventions and treaties, these are currently insufficient to address the serious nature of most of these problems. Second, a lot of environmental problems are a result of lifestyle options and choices at the level of the individual. It is difficult to legislate against such behaviour, especially when the two main strands of the dominant development process are market growth and personal freedoms. For example, indicators for development tend towards levels of economic growth and a population's ability to consume.

Advocates of globalisation highlight other tendencies fostered by the processes of globalisation. They would argue that increased trade liberalisation allows for the spread of more environmentally friendly technologies and practices. Integration with the global economy should lead to increased wealth and industrial development, allowing for the more efficient use of resources and the means to regulate and combat negative impacts on the environment. This position is correct, in theory, but in practice the mass consumer society tends towards greater divisions of wealth, opportunity and environmental conservation (Rostow, 1971). There are some examples of altruistic redistribution of wealth; however, the general tendency is for 'developing' societies to become more focused on self-interested individualism and materialism. This can still include technological advances to enable greater efficiency of use of resources, but these are usually relative savings in the context of a net increase in resource use. For example, fuel efficiency of the internal combustion engine has advanced over time, yet these savings have been more than overtaken by the rapid increase in the number of cars. Therefore, the key determinant here is not so much the level of technology but rather the way in which this is applied. Similarly, awareness of environmental issues needs to be distinguished from practical action to address relevant policies and individual behaviour.

The nature of many approaches looking at environmental issues often describe them in global terms. Concepts such as global warming and the description of certain resources such as forests or oceans as 'global commons' build up a holistic picture of the issues to be addressed. While there is some validity in this perception it is also the case that these issues are generally moderated through the ongoing system of national governments. As such there is a fundamental conflict between short-term national interests and longer-term global interests. This problem is also exacerbated by the previously mentioned drive towards individualism and mass consumerism. Under such circumstances there continues to be a significant divide between the growing awareness of environmental issues and the desire to actively confront these, at both the level of the individual and the state.

Hyperglobalists can envisage environmental issues in both a positive and negative light. Negatively they consider resource degradation on a global scale, highlighting issues such as global warming, climate change, over-fishing and excessive deforestation. More positively they also draw attention to the Earth Summit process and the ability of nation states to come together in a global forum to agree, or at least debate, global environmental concerns. The dominant model of development is relevant here with multi-centred processes of production and manufacture feeding into the ever-expanding spread of mass consumerism.

Sceptics cast doubt on the very existence of some environmental issues, such as global warming. They also doubt the ability of essentially selfish states embracing a global environmental agenda at the expense of their individual national interests. In terms of concerns about mass consumerism the sceptics are less concerned about this as they would allow for the 'technical fix' argument to off-set the worst aspects of resource depletion.

Transformationalists acknowledge that environmental issues are now part of the international diplomatic agenda. However, they see this as only the beginning of a process that has much further to develop before national interests are subsumed by a truly global agenda. Moreover, the transformationalists are less committed to a determined outcome. One outcome could be that societies and economies continue to 'develop' in a non-sustainable manner with resulting resource exhaustion and conflict over dwindling supplies. On the other hand, growing awareness, national legislation and international cooperation could lead to a more sustainable future.

Multi-globalisation

In looking at processes of globalisation it is apparent that there are a variety of approaches and explanations as to the extent and likely consequences of these processes. Moreover, it is possible to discuss globalisation at many different levels, to the point that apparently competing viewpoints are more accurately seen as describing differing phenomena. For example, the above sections have placed emphasis on political, economic, socio-cultural and environmental issues and agendas. Each of these has also been impacted upon by technological developments.

At the political level many national governments are experiencing difficulties in maintaining autonomy, or sovereignty, over their policies. Rather, although they maintain the right to adopt whatever policies they choose to within their own territories, many are increasingly restricted in their policy options due to external factors. Hyperglobalists would point to this as an example of how all states are becoming interconnected. However, as sceptics would point out, this is not the same as saying a truly global community of states is emerging as some states are more profoundly impacted upon by these interconnections than others. Also at the political level is the role and influence of civil society. Just as national government experiences should be differentiated from each other, this is even more the case at the level of the individual. With a global population now in excess of 6 billion there are myriad personal experiences of the processes of globalisation. For the individual the political sphere encompasses issues such as national citizenship. Yet it is also much more. Beyond identifying with a particular state, individuals think of themselves in terms of family affiliations, sexual orientation, ethnicity, religion or simply personal tastes and interests. Processes of globalisation can have a bearing and impact on each of these categories of identification. This then leads to a further complexity in the shaping of individual and collective responses to these processes.

One of the key components of globalisation is the relationship between the political and economic spheres. Even those who are sceptical of the degree of global interconnectedness would accept that this is a key relationship in international relations. Although explicit political agendas can be identified, such as the promotion of human rights, these tend to be subsumed within the dominant ethos of the promotion of economic growth. Furthermore, the drive towards economic growth also has both domestic and international political consequences in terms of the securing and exploitation of resources, some of which may be located in territories under another political jurisdiction. This can lead to either policies of cooperation or of conflict. Again hyperglobalists would highlight the level of symmetry in bringing together economic systems and institutions to facilitate international trade and consumption. A more sceptical view may well acknowledge that such structures are in place, but that they continue to be dominated by certain powerful states and related interest groups. Similarly, some MNCs now have annual turnovers well in excess of the gross domestic product of some national governments. Despite this indisputable fact there remains a debate around the extent to which this represents a true separation of the political and economic spheres. Neo-realists, for example, would dispute the extent to which MNCs are autonomous actors, preferring to describe them as 'agents of the state'. It would be more accurate to view MNCs as being part of a public/private spectrum along which some states and MNCs are in a more privileged position than other states and MNCs. At any given time, each of these international/global actors will be either more or less advantaged or disadvantaged along this spectrum. Put another way, some are closer to the core of the international trading system while others are more peripheral or marginalised from the potential benefits of this system. This analysis can also be applied at the level of the individual. Disparities of opportunities and achievements exist at all levels of community, be it sub-national, national or international/global. Globalisation is, understandably, normally perceived and articulated on a grand scale. However, at both the political and economic levels the opportunities and restrictions of this are experienced at the individual level.

As discussed above, there is a sense that globalisation is leading to a more common political, economic and cultural environment. This view is controversial with active resistance to this process taking place. There is even an argument that it is the very processes of globalisation that are reawakening aspects of cultural identity at a more localised level. This has led to some hybridisation of local cultures and external influences. In part this is a result of the mixing of cultural influences due to the increasing exchange of both goods and services. Processes such as urban drift are also playing a part in the mixing of various influences. The spread of communication technologies and related media sources have also enabled a greater mix of ideas, interests and activities. Therefore, although the concept of cultural imperialism or cultural homogeneity can be challenged, there are identifiable influences that ensure cultures are dynamically evolving. It is, of course, a value judgement to say whether they are developing for better or worse. Even allowing for an element of impartial objectivity there is a strong position to be taken with regard to the equity and sustainability of any given system.

Summary

This chapter has outlined the three main theoretical positions with regard to the existence and extent of processes of globalisation. It has also highlighted the manner in which different theoretical approaches emphasise particular actors and issues, thereby arriving at differing conclusions about the impact of globalisation. Attention was drawn to certain issues that illustrate both the positive and negative aspects of globalisation. These issues will now be explored in further detail in the following chapters of this book. It is recommended that as you read these chapters you consider how the various schools of thought outlined in the first section of this book would interpret and analyse these issue areas.

Reflective questions

1   What arguments are used to support or deny the existence and/or extent of processes of globalisation by hyperglobalists, transformationalists and sceptics?
2   What factors led to the spread of the European/US system and its influence around the world from the 1700s?
3   How are various divisions within the global political economy exemplified in terms of who gets what, when, where and how?
4   Explain the origins and evolution of the contemporary global financial system.
5   What roles do MNCs play in facilitating and promoting processes of globalisation?
6   In what ways are issues of environmental sustainability being addressed at the global level?

Suggestions for further reading

Albrow, M. (1996) *The Global Age: State and Society Beyond Modernity*, Cambridge: Polity Press.
Appadurai, A. (ed) (2005) *Globalization*, London: Duke University Press.
Bhagwati, J. (2004) *In Defence of Globalization*, Oxford: Oxford University Press.
Castells, M. (2009) *Communication Power*, Oxford: Oxford University Press.
De Carlo, S. and Zajac, B. (eds) 'The world's biggest companies: The global 2000', *Forbes*, 2 April 2008.
Held, D., McGrew, A., Goldblatt, D. and Perraton, J. (1999) *Global Transformations: Politics, Economics and Culture*, Cambridge: Polity Press.
Hirst, P., Thompson, G. and Bromley, S. (2009) *Globalization in Question: The international economy and the possibilities of governance*, 3rd edn, Cambridge: Polity.
Huntington, S.P. (1993) 'The Clash of Civilizations', *Foreign Affairs*, 72(3), 22–49.
Huntington, S.P. (2002) *The Clash of Civilizations: And the Remaking of World Order*, Reading: Cox & Wyman.
Martin, H.P. and Schumann, H. (1997) *The Global Trap: Globalization and the Assault on Democracy and Prosperity*, London: Zed Books.
McLuhan, M. (2005) *Understanding Media*, 2nd edn, London: Routledge.
Ohmae, K. (1999) *The Borderless World: Power and Strategy in the Interlinked Economy*, 2nd edn, New York: Harper Paperbacks.
Rostow, W. (1971) *The Stages of Economic Growth: A Non-Communist Manifesto*, 2nd edn, Cambridge: Cambridge University Press.
Scholte, J.A. (2005) *Globalization: A Critical Introduction*, 2nd edn, Basingstoke: Palgrave Macmillan.
Stiglitz, J. (2002) *Globalization and Its Discontents*, London: Penguin Books.

5 National, international, regional and global governance

Chapter learning outcomes

After reading this chapter students should be able to:

- Understand the concept of governance and be able to differentiate it from coordination and management.
- Explain how governance differs/remains consistent at the national, international and global levels.
- Engage with theoretical debates which discuss the nature of globalisation and its impact on international and global governance and how both state and non-state actors are involved.
- Understand and explain how processes of international cooperation have intensified over the past century and how this intensification is leading to forms of governance.
- Understand a range of contemporary issues in international relations and the global political economy which require some form of governance, including: security, health, travel and transportation, trade, communications and finances.

Introduction

This chapter considers how far the governance of processes of globalisation is being managed at a national, international or global level. Hirst and Thompson (1996 – also discussed Chapter 4) contend that despite an increasing number of issues having a global dimension, they continue to be responded to at the governmental level, and by ad hoc collectives of states rather than by an overarching global governing authority. While the popular belief of some conspiracy theorists might be that the UN fulfils the role of a global government, the number of UN resolutions that are ignored or actively broken contradicts this view. Important UN agencies contribute to global governance, but do not 'do' global government. Certain aspects of the work of the UN, notably its specialised agencies, have a very important role. However, this is not a *supranational* organisation. It does not have coercive power. Rather, it is a voluntary collective of states that all retain their sovereign autonomy. It works by consensus (although, as we shall see later in the chapter, consensus can also be powerful). This raises questions about the fundamental definition and workings of international and/or global governance. Is 'governance' simply the coordination of national policies, or does there have to be a greater sense of the rule of law and, crucially, of its enforcement? Does this create a different kind of authority in international relations? Or does it reinforce and develop existing patterns of domination – global hegemony?

The nature of governance

The answer to these important questions might well be 'neither'. Governance is first of all the coordination of national policies. But in order to make this policy coordination work, quite a lot of authority may need to be transferred to a global level. Some aspects of that authority may be changed in the process, some not. This is especially the case where technical decisions require technical knowledge. And other actors, non-state actors, might well have important roles even if the lead role is formally held by states and state-run international bodies. It is also the case that governments very often do much less than appears at first because their actions at national level are shaped by consultation with a range of trade associations, firms, NGOs and advisory bodies which, while they do not carry formal authority, have both knowledge and the capacity to act effectively without which government cannot function. Rather crudely, we might use the word 'government' for those areas of international economic activity where there is a united structure of authority and where decisions have a relatively direct impact on implementation. We might then use the word 'governance' for those kinds of coordinated inter-institutional management of policy where there is no single authoritative body able at the same time to make and to implement policy (see Table 5.1). To think that power and authority in complex international situations is only held by states may often be confusing. Even if states hold the formal role, they are not able to manage the responsibilities that role brings without working with both other states and other actors. This is especially the case in three situations: in markets, in highly technical areas of policy management, and in areas where complex networks have evolved to coordinate policy responses. To repeat, even if (and this is not always the case) states have the formal legal authority, and so retain formal sovereignty, they may well have conceded both authority and effective action to others. Governance is thus about complex multilateral policy management; it is not primarily about law or formal sovereignty, although of course it may have a bearing on both. Confusingly, some commentators and some politicians may use the word interchangeably with 'government'; but it is much more clearly

Table 5.1 Global governance vs global government

Government	Governance
Direct control	Indirect control
Direct authority to act (usually rooted in constitutional arrangements)	Authority achieved through consensus and often risks evaporation at crucial moments
Although some governments may be coalitions, most governments do not require the remaking of the coalition to initiate policy	Rooted in a coalition of different types of actors (which may include governments, private agencies, firms, international organisations, NGOs and regulatory bodies)
Not all governments are centralised – e.g. federal systems – but governments generally have a measure of central control over policy implementation as well as policy making	Decentralised and dependent on cooperation of a range of actors for implementation as well as decision making – and sometimes on different coalitions for implementation and for policy making
Ideally described in a hierarchical structure	Although may have elements of hierarchy – some actors are more senior or powerful than others – the essence of governance is a relatively 'flat' structure of power and authority
Power in this structure rests on constitutional position	Power in governance rests on technical expertise and ability to deliver at least as much on formal position

Note that this table represents both as 'ideal types' for purpose of explanation – there are plenty of variations on the main themes.

understood as distinct from government, and that is generally the way it is used in academic discourse including across the IPE literature.

Governance at the domestic level can be reduced to the fundamentals of law making and enforcement along with domestic and foreign policy making and implementation. In political economy, much of this activity will be some form of regulation. Yet within these fundamentals there can be myriad differing examples between states, especially when one considers the relationship between the individual citizen and the ruling regime. Some regimes are far more authoritarian than others. To transpose this to the global level, such differentiation is, by definition, not possible as we are referring to something which is supposed to be universal in character and action. Therefore, governance at the global level would need to include aspects of law making and enforcement plus policy making and implementation. The 'domestic' level would become redundant, and 'foreign' would presumably refer to any off-planet relations that might occur at some point in the future. That said, there remain difficulties in extrapolating concepts such as citizenship, rights and duties to the global level. These are not universally agreed ideas and practices across various states. As such they will not easily transfer to a system of global governance. This issue is, therefore, perhaps best understood in terms of a range of possibilities with regard to levels of governance, some of which are more straightforward to implement than others. As a tool of analysis and explanation, the framework adopted in Chapter 4 that refers to hyperglobalists, transformationalists and sceptics can also be utilised here. These positions will be considered in relation to political, economic and socio-cultural aspects of governance.

One important debate here is concerned with the extent to which issues in international political economy are actually subject to some form of governance, and whether this governance is international, regional or global in scope. We can identify a great many issues such as trade, conflict, environmental change, democratisation and integration in various forms. Most of the issues which we can identify can also be seen to be managed to some extent at the international level. Around the globe many conferences, for example, take place with state and non-state actors being represented, organisations and regimes are established with a particular agenda and so on. However, it is more difficult to identify when issues are governed at the international level. For example, climate change issues such as rising sea levels and the impacts on coastlines are often addressed by the international community but are these activities about reacting to, managing or governing these issues? Furthermore, who is involved in these processes and who is not? To take another example, global financial governance has failed in the financial crisis of 2007–9; the story of which organisations have been involved and how and why they have failed is an important and complex one which illustrates much of this debate – but it will not be discussed further here since it is discussed at some length in Chapter 7.

Hyperglobalists would argue that the processes driving globalisation are resulting in radical changes in the nature of how issues are dealt with at the international level. There is, in this perception, a change over time in international relations which means that as modernity progresses, the way issues such as trade are dealt with evolves. Initially states would seek bilateral and then multilateral mechanisms to manage and govern the relations between them. But as the complexities of a global system emerge, so too does the need for greater cooperation. The result is a change from bilateral to multilateral to international and then global management. Further integration and cooperation leads to governance at the international or global levels.

The counter-argument, however, is that very little has changed since the end of the Second World War, and that in fact states and non-state actors respond to international issues by managing them at the regional level at most. Advocates of this view claim that any attempts at global management are ultimately unsuccessful. Furthermore, there is little credence given to the concept that international governance takes place.

Yet others argue that not only is management taking place at the international level but a level of governance also takes place between states at the regional level as well. The EU, as mentioned above, is the prime example of this level of governance but not the only one. This camp does not, however, perceive there to be any real measure of governance at the global level.

A separate important theoretical debate is between those who broadly see the growth of global governance as an extension of liberal activism and plural management of the international system and those who see it as the extension of some form of hegemonic or imperial power. This question has dominated much of the discussion of global governance in IPE since the early 1990s. The debate includes, in the first camp, those who are inclined to welcome globalisation but who do not see it as an unqualified benefit (such as Thomas Freidman, 2007, 3rd edition). It also includes liberal theorists who have welcomed the extension of global governance so long as it meets conditions of transparency and accessibility (such as Barnett and Finnemore, 2005). The second critical group of writers includes Gramscian scholars such as Mark Rupert (2000) and James Mittelman (2005) (this question was discussed in more detail earlier in Chapter 3).

How does international governance (regional, global or whatever) arise? One answer would be to look at the theory of the state itself. Over the past 200 years, the modern state has evolved in response to a series of pressures on it for territorial and military security, but also for economic security. In the mid nineteenth century, an increasing number of states started to provide technical education and basic standards of education mainly to respond to economic needs, but also to try to promote social stability in the face of rapid and socially fragmenting growth in the Industrial Revolution. An enlargement of state education was followed by the beginnings of welfare systems such as pensions and basic healthcare. After 1918 this was extended in many countries to housing and to state support for other welfare systems, including state aid for higher education. By the 1950s, most states had extensive welfare agendas, and although the US federal government was only spending around 18 per cent of GNP, most European states and many elsewhere were spending in the region of 40–50 per cent of GNP. Some of this was on defence, but much of it was to meet welfare demands of different kinds, including full employment and high levels of education, training and healthcare. This produced a crisis of the state in the 1970s, a crisis of expectations where governments facing much greater demands than they could match looked for ways to respond. One part of the response was a neo-liberalism which proclaimed the need to reduce the role and power of the state in the economy and in social life. But although this argument produced a great deal of noise and conflict, the percentage of state involvement in GDP hardly fell, and in some cases (notably Mrs Thatcher's Britain) it actually rose. In practice, one key strategy adopted by many states was to internationalise the problems and demands they faced. Developed countries created a series of institutions (such as the G7) or adapted others (such as the European Community) to address complex demands from society and economic actors. It was the state which demanded an expansion of international governance. As Alan Milward (2000) has suggested in the case of the EU, we might even see international organisations as being the saviours of nation state institutions. What Anthony King (1997) called the 'crisis of overload' on the state in the 1970s was managed partly by depressing expectations, and partly by political manoeuvres in domestic politics, but it was also managed by the creation of international institutions which offered governance-based solutions to failures of government. In some cases these organisations actually took on the role of the state more and more, and in some cases they provided smokescreens or scapegoats for the state authorities to pass blame to. It is fair to say that the most important such body, the European Union, has in turn taken all three roles.

International cooperation

One of the earliest examples of international cooperation and a form of governance was the creation of the International Telecommunications Union (ITU) in 1885. In the previous few years European states had been developing their telegraphic capabilities and were entering into numerous bilateral arrangements with neighbouring states. As the telecommunications sector expanded, the number of such agreements was becoming unmanageable and, in a 'form follows function' response, an international body was created to oversee this sector. Twenty European states agreed a framework convention to facilitate and govern the process of trans-border communication. Common rules were agreed to standardise equipment, adopt uniform operating instructions and create international tariffs and accounting rules. This feature of commonality is something that will be returned to in several parts of this chapter. It is important to make a distinction between commonality with regard to overarching principles and processes and the actual 'content' or practices adopted by the actors who are party to such agreements. For example, the ITU would embed its position as a governing body as more states join or more television or radio stations are granted broadcasting licences. However, although this reinforces the role and position of the ITU this does not necessarily lead to greater homogeneity of content. The reverse is more likely as the increased mass of programming creates a growing diversity of broadcasts. Conventional thinking might equate growing coordination with a subsequent reduction in diversity. As referred to in the previous chapter, hyperglobalists equate coordination at the global level with concepts such as cultural imperialism and less heterogeneity. Globalisation sceptics, of course, would highlight ongoing, or even exacerbated, differences.

Similarly at the political level the history of emerging structures of governance has been both incremental and contentious. A certain trajectory can be traced from the creation of the League of Nations (LoN) (1919) to the United Nations (UN) (1945) and to the first truly supranational body, the European Union (EU) (1957: Treaty of Rome). The LoN had a particular historical context being formed in the immediate aftermath of the First World War. Its explicit aim was to foster greater understanding and cooperation between member states as a form of conflict avoidance. It had more of a managerial remit rather than explicit governance of member states. The UN took this approach to another level after the Second World War. This organisation had a much broader membership, which further expanded following the political independence of former colonies. It also expanded its remit, as characterised by its specialised agencies such as the World Health Organisation (WHO), UN Educational, Scientific and Cultural Organisation (UNESCO) and the Bretton Woods institutions. Despite this expanded role and capacity the UN's style is also more managerial rather than governing. In political terms the only international body with a truly governing role and capacity is the EU. All member states of the EU are subject to the rules and regulations that they agree to upon accession to this body. Although this remains a voluntary system a key principle of membership is that the sovereign rule of national governments is superseded by the rule of the *governing* bodies of the EU.

The structure of the EU comprises the European Commission, the Council of the European Union, the European Council, the European Court of Justice, the European Central Bank and the European Parliament. The decision-making process of the EU is a combination of achieving consensus between member states and supranationalism where decisions may be imposed on dissenting members. The latter point is also very significant in relation to the concept of sovereignty. Although membership of the EU is voluntary, no state which has joined has ever left and in fact the EU has continued to expand its membership. As such we can conclude that while occasionally individual states may not always achieve all of their objectives, they do, on balance, gain more from membership than they lose.

The above example of the EU is the exception rather than the rule in terms of international governance. While the UN is widely recognised as the forum for dealing with global issues it remains a collective of individual nation states. State-centric interests, even rivalries, continue to inform the debates and processes of managing global issues. States can be seen as agents of change. In addition, the relative power capabilities of the various member states continue to be of relevance. The ability of states to react to and influence the global agenda differs greatly. Non-state actors in the private and voluntary sectors are increasingly involved and influential in discussions on and actions related to issues arising from processes of globalisation.

Actors

Some approaches to the study of IR and IPE continue to be predominantly state-centric (as discussed in Chapter 2). This section will consider the different power capabilities and roles of individual states before moving on to examine non-state actors.

Power can be based on material resources, military capabilities, financial resources, technology, diplomatic expertise and the historical accumulation of these power-related factors. For example, the expansion of the British Empire was based on and driven by certain technological advantages in the realms of maritime superiority and a leading role in the applications of the Industrial Revolution. Similarly, the United States was able to rise to hegemonic status during the twentieth century via a combination of military might, a favourable economic environment and as a result of the relative decline of European powers. Some other states are in a far less powerful position. This may be because they lack the quantity of material resources, military capabilities, financial wealth and are simply too small to compete at the global level. Other states may have some of the above resources in significant quantities but lack the political control to maximise the benefits of these resources. Former colonies in Africa, for example, may be in this last category, being resource-rich but disadvantaged in the current global economic system. Some connections can be made between the relative poverty and disempowerment of some parts of the world and the relative wealth and empowerment of the dominant powers.

Relative power capabilities are relevant to both bilateral relations and also within the context of intergovernmental organisations. Those states which possess greater power capabilities tend to be in a better position to influence outcomes in terms of reactions to and policies towards issues at the global level. On the other hand, states with limited power capabilities tend not to have a great influence.

In order to most effectively promote individual state interests many states will act in concert with others to achieve shared goals. This has the advantage of pooling resources and creating a larger power base from which to negotiate. The motivations behind such actions can vary. For example, the creation of the EU can be viewed in relation to both the geographic proximity of the member states and also as a reaction to previous conflicts between some of its original members. In contrast, the Alliance of Small Island States (AOSIS) is drawn from several geographic regions but the members, many of which are micro-states, have identified a shared interest in highlighting the problems of, and lobbying for solutions to, issues such as sea levels rising.

Table 5.2   Actors in the global system

Actor type	Total number (2009 approximates)
States	200
MNCs	60000
Single-state NGOs	10000
International NGOs	5800
Intergovernmental organisations	2500+

Sources: Collated from *Forbes*, OECD and UN data.

EXAMPLE BOX

The League of Arab States

Consisting of 22 member states, the League of Arab States (often referred to as the Arab League) offers an example of an intergovernmental organisation whose envisioned purpose is much like that of the European Union. Created in 1945 and headquartered in Cairo, Egypt, the League originally consisted of six member states – the independent Arab states at that time: Egypt, Iraq, Jordan, Lebanon, Saudi Arabia and Syria, with Yemen joining later on in that year to become the seventh member. Following independence and accession negotiations a further fifteen states joined through the 1950s, 60s and 70s (these are: Algeria, Bahrain, Djibouti, Kuwait, Libya, Mauritania, Morocco, Oman, Palestine, Qatar, Somalia, Sudan, Tunisia and the United Arab Emirates; Comoros was the last state to join in 1993).

The League was established in order to coordinate the international relations of its member states in terms of relations between them and relations between the Arab world and the broader international community. Furthermore, following many years of political and economic domination by external powers the Arab world sought to ensure its sovereignty and independence by encouraging greater integration and cooperation between the Arab states. The League was thus also established in order to offer some form of governance over the Arab world while respecting the sovereignty of each member state. There are administrative zones within the League and member states vote on policy, laws and regulations with resolutions often being agreed upon. However, the ability of the League to implement the decisions which are made and enforce the laws and regulations which are agreed upon is in practice limited. For example, in 1997 eighteen of the member states agreed to establish an integrated, single market which would have no barriers to trade such as taxes on exports/imports, tariffs, quotas or non-tariff barriers. This single market is called the Greater Arab Free Trade Area (GAFTA) and came into effect on 1 January 2005. However, while member states agreed to this project, barriers to trade still remain and states such as Egypt have been slow to meet their requirements in terms of fully liberalising their trade system. The department within the League of Arab States which governs economic issues is the Arab Economic Council. This council has little real power in enforcing the agreement when states such as Egypt do not comply with their duties.

In this way, the League can be seen to seek to govern the Arab world but in practice governance is limited and coordination and management are terms which better describe the purpose of the organisation. As noted above, there is also a difference between international and global governance/management. The League of Arab States, while dissimilar to the EU in terms of its capacities (the EU, as discussed above, being much more of a supranational authority), is similar in that it only operates at the international level and not the global level. It only seeks to govern/manage its 23 member states and not a broader global community of states.

A different example of how states promote their interest by working cooperatively is the Organisation of Petroleum Exporting Countries (OPEC) where the member states are geographically dispersed but have a common interest in a primary export commodity.

OPEC

In theory the Organisation of Petroleum Exporting Countries (OPEC) acts as an inter-governmental organisation which governs the oil sector activities of the twelve member states: Algeria, Angola, Ecuador, Iran, Iraq, Kuwait, Libya, Nigeria, Qatar, Saudi Arabia, United Arab Emirates and Venezuela. Here, the member states agree to submit to the governance of OPEC in order to control the levels of oil production, refining and export. The organisation was established in 1961 to regulate the international oil market and control oil prices. In practice, though, the problems of international governance are evident and OPEC does not successfully govern either the activities of its member states very effectively or the global oil market. In the first instance, member states often exceed the production, refining and export quotas they are set by OPEC in a self-interested pursuit of greater export earnings for themselves in the short term. In the latter case, the global oil market is now relatively saturated with suppliers and OPEC only accounts for approximately a third of global production. Its capacity to govern the global oil market is, therefore, heavily restricted as cutbacks in OPEC production and exports can relatively easily be picked up by other exporters. Furthermore, by only having twelve member states OPEC certainly cannot be seen to either govern or even just coordinate state behaviour at the global level. It is, instead, simply an international organisation which attempts to govern one aspect of a small number of states' behaviour.

States also work together to promote their economic objectives. Interestingly, while many states compete economically with each other, there is also a high level of monitoring and coordination in the economic sphere. In the post-Second World War order a central pillar of the UN structure was the Bretton Woods Trio of the International Monetary Fund (IMF), the International Bank for Reconstruction and Development – later renamed the World Bank (WB) – and the General Agreement on Tariffs and Trade – later renamed the World Trade Organisation (WTO). (See the information boxes on these institutions in Chapter 4.) These institutions act as key elements in the global economic system. The IMF is responsible for ensuring relative stability within global financial markets and domestic economies by providing financial resources via loans and grants to national governments. These payments are conditional in terms of expectations that these national economies will be run along prescribed lines. In order to receive support from the IMF national governments have to adopt policies such as encouraging foreign direct investment (FDI), cutting back on domestic expenditures, privatising national companies and opening up markets. In effect these conditions are aimed at homogenising the global economic system by encouraging universal acceptance of free market liberal economic policies.

In addition to the above global institutions a similar ideological model of liberalism can be identified within various regions around the globe. The EU, the North American Free Trade Area (NAFTA), the Association of South East Asian Nations (ASEAN) and the Asia-Pacific Economic Council (APEC) all adhere to this model. On occasion economic and other disputes occur between member states of each of these organisations. Each organisation has a procedural mechanism in place for dispute resolution. So too does the WTO, which is a significant development in governance compared to the GATT system, which did not include such a mechanism.

All of the above examples are intergovernmental organisations. Civil society actors have the opportunity to discuss economic issues with state representatives when they meet as part of the World Economic Forum (WEF). This forum, established in 1971, brings together politicians and civil society lobbyists to debate important global economic issues and their consequences. This is not a formal mechanism of governance in the same manner as intergovernmental organisations like the WTO, but it is an important forum for generating dialogue and policy recommendations. It must be noted that one of the characteristics of globalisation is the increasing role of non-state actors in engaging and influencing state policy decisions.

Socio-cultural issues are relevant in both the domestic and international arenas. Identity formation, partially in response to aspects of globalisation, is now far more complex than a simple reading of national identity. Multiple identities can exist in an individual simultaneously. These can involve elements of race, class, gender, religion and a whole range of issues and situations that individuals can either identify themselves with or be identified by others. Classical realism does not focus at the level of the individual or collective at the sub-state level. With the emergence of a range of global socio-cultural issues that impact on individuals regardless of their state of origin, the personal experience is rarely if ever shared across a nationality. There are a number of organisations at governmental and non-governmental levels which try to address these issues.

UNESCO is a specialised agency within the UN which deals with issues of socio-cultural relevance. It has an explicit global remit, although its work is often mediated through national governments. The primary mission of this organisation is to promote cooperation and collaboration towards shared understanding of concepts of justice, freedom and human rights. This manifests itself predominantly in the fields of education, science and culture. For example, there is a specific 'Education For All' programme which aims to provide basic education for all children and adults by the year 2015. Key stakeholders include national governments, multinational corporations and a range of civil society groups. Public/private projects are increasingly common as national governments and intergovernmental organisations attempt to fund such ambitious endeavours. Similar examples can be found in relation to health.

The World Health Organisation (WHO) is a specialised agency of the UN. As such it is an intergovernmental organisation, but in fulfilling its mission it works closely with a range of non-governmental actors. For example, in addressing issues such as HIV/AIDS, heart disease, diabetes, malaria and a range of potential and actual pandemics various stakeholders coordinate their efforts. The Alliance for Health Policy and Systems Research has more than three hundred partner institutions from around the world. This brings together medical researchers and practitioners with relevant policy-makers and other interested partners. Although having some country-specific projects, this alliance has an explicit global remit. In relation to tackling malaria a holistic approach is adopted, looking at both preventative and curative measures. This involves local environmental conditions which may be a factor in the prevalence and control of malarial vectors. The private sector includes key actors such as pharmaceutical companies. The role of private companies can be controversial as they are primarily driven by the pursuit of profit. As such it may be more profitable for such companies to invest in research to create products like effective slimming medication or hair loss treatments. There is a profitable market for such products in the more developed states. Whereas there are concerns with regard to the growing levels of obesity, diabetes and other lifestyle-related disorders, in terms of rates of mortality greater numbers of people die from malaria. Therefore, it is arguable that the private sector should prioritise its research and development activities towards the types of illness and diseases that are responsible for the highest rates of mortality.

The relationship between various public and private stakeholders is interesting and complex. Government agencies increasingly look to public–private partnerships to achieve their objectives. Private companies are beginning to use phrases such as 'corporate social responsibility' but remain accountable to their shareholders who have a reasonable expectation of a profitable return on their investment. Although sometimes presented as having diverging priorities, governments and MNCs can also be seen as having compatible interests. In the field of healthcare, pharmaceutical companies are understandably driven by the profit motive. In comparison governments are often seen as having an altruistic duty of care responsibility towards their citizens. While this is not a wholly inaccurate view, there is also an argument that governments are equally 'profit-driven,' albeit in a different manner. Citizens are a form of social capital. High rates of illness and mortality are both a drain on national health services, necessarily drawing money away from other potential government expenditure, as well as reducing workforce capacity. Some non-governmental organisations (NGOs) take a much more critical view of the role and impact of the private sector.

One of the leading networks for addressing social/cultural and environmental issues at the non-governmental level is the annual World Social Forum (WSF). Beginning in 2001, this event brings together a wide range of civil society activists who campaign for social and environmental justice. Although explicitly non-governmental in terms of its membership the WSF does receive some funding from national and local governments to support the annual meetings, which take place in different parts of the world (Brazil 2001, 2002, 2003; India, 2004; Brazil, 2005; simultaneously in Mali, Venezuela and Pakistan, 2006; Kenya, 2007; Brazil, 2009). In 2008 the event was not focused on a particular location but related events were held throughout the world with the common theme of the Global Call for Action. WSF is centrally supported by a permanent head office in Brazil and an International Council which consists of representatives of 129 organisations. This council includes six commissions with responsibilities for the areas of methodology, content and themes, expansion, strategies, resources and communication. While not strictly representing governance in the same manner as that of national governments and intergovernmental organisations, this does represent a high level of coordination and consensus building. The issue of communications is particularly relevant as the emergence of the Internet has vastly increased the ability of diverse civil society groups to offer mutual support and coordinate their campaigns.

The impact of media and information technologies is not, of course, simply restricted to civil society. National governments are sometimes described as losing elements of sovereignty and autonomous control as a result of such technologies. For example, rapid communication both within and across borders between citizens, possibly reporting on events such as heavy-handed policing of political demonstrations, is very difficult for national governments to monitor and censor. On the other hand, national governments are also able to utilise such technologies to actively enhance and embed political control. This may be via closed circuit television systems, the monitoring of personal communications and financial transactions. Access to digital information can therefore be seen as a blessing and a curse depending on who is using it and how.

In terms of governance, the power of such technologies has been recognised by states, MNCs and NGOs, leading to the World Summit on the Information Society (WSIS) which was held over two phases, first, in Geneva, Switzerland, in 2003 and, second, in Tunis, Tunisia, in 2005. This was a multi-stakeholder forum which included national governments, MNCs, IGOs, NGOs and specialised agencies. Following the meeting in Tunis participants agreed to create the Internet Governance Forum (IGF). This is an ongoing body which continues to promote the discussion of public policy issues related to the Internet. There is active engagement from the information technology private sector and NGOs concerned with developments in the use and potential misuse of these technologies. One particularly significant aspect of communication technologies is various forms of print, broadcast and digitally available media. These forms of media are major factors, possibly determinants, in the formation of world views.

The reporting of various civil and military conflicts, the representation of minority groups, environmental issues and many other phenomena can actively influence individual and societal opinions and actions/reactions. Controversial issues such as the Palestinian–Israeli conflict, the extent or even existence of global warming, the wearing of the *hijab* and civil partnerships are all issues that can arouse strong and conflicting opinions. Given that most people will not have personal experience of many of these issues, the influence attached to their reportage can be a crucial factor in how they are understood. There has been an evolution and proliferation in the forms of media. For example, a century ago a citizen in London would be heavily, if not solely, reliant on information provided by the *London Times*. Subsequently other print-based media emerged, followed by radio and then television. At each stage the speed and immediacy of reporting was taken to another level. The development of the Internet has taken the field of communication to an unprecedented level. In addition to existing media outlets the Internet has disseminated the ability of very small groups or even individuals to compete in the presentation of 'news'.

Until relatively recently the main institutions of news reporting have been concentrated into a relatively small sector. For example, notable press barons such as Robert Maxwell and Rupert Murdoch have tended to dominate the sector via their ownership of a vast range of publications and broadcasting companies. The Internet has allowed groups such as Indymedia, or the Independent Media Centre (IMC) to present alternative information. IMC describes itself as 'a network of collectively run media outlets for the creation of radical, accurate, and passionate tellings of the truth.' They gather information directly from local activists, rather than relying on the major press release agencies. This may be seen as an attempt to 'democratise' the news. The immediacy and relative lack of control over these news sources have radically transformed the news landscape and how information is presented. Of course, the greater supply of information may actually create greater confusion rather than clarity. It also raises questions about the political control of information.

Indymedia's web servers are based at numerous locations around the world, each one therefore coming under the political jurisdiction of a particular government. There have been several occasions where national governments have attempted to disrupt Indymedia's operations. In 2004 the US government seized the web servers, followed by a similar incident in the UK in 2005. Around twenty Indymedia websites were disrupted during this period. Subsequently equipment was returned and there were no criminal charges as a result of these actions. This suggests that while national governments are unable to legally prevent these sites from operating they can adopt policies of inconvenience and disruption. This disruption represents a form of governance, albeit a rather negative one. National governments sometimes appear to be trying to interfere with 'alternative' news services. Although it would be too much to claim that mainstream media sources are extensions of government they certainly seem able to operate more freely than groups such as Indymedia.

Having considered a range of actors relevant to aspects of governance we now move on to examine a range of issues that have a governance dimension to them.

Issues

In classical realist terms security is thought of as pertaining to the protection of national borders and sovereignty. It does not tend to consider the level of the individual other than as a human resource to promote the interests of the state. Processes of globalisation have challenged this concept of sovereignty and individuals' perceptions of their own security are not necessarily indivisible from that of the nation state. Critical security studies have a much broader definition of both security and insecurity. This applies at the levels of individual governments, IGOs, the business sector and a wide range of NGOs.

At the individual state level the more developed states tend to have a high level of domestic political control. Their main security concerns are economic and the protection of access to foreign resources such as oil. There will be a very different set of national security priorities in states where there is less political stability and governments have much shorter-term goals. Collective security arrangements can be identified in previous centuries. However, these tended to have the dual purpose of protecting from external threats and to increase cooperation within the collective. In contemporary international relations military security still remains a very important issue for national governments.

The advent of nuclear weapons and the (practically universally recognised) risk of mutually assured destruction (MAD) have served to solidify military security and its management as key problems. The vast majority of state actors do not seek nuclear weapons capabilities but a number of states do possess such weapons. Due to the destructive nature of nuclear weapons both states that possess them and those that do not have an interest in coordinating policies at the global level to try to ensure they are not used. The Treaty on the Non-Proliferation of Nuclear Weapons (NPT) is a UN-negotiated treaty which manages the development and use of nuclear technology. Membership in the treaty is voluntary but only a small number of states have not signed it. The NPT acts as a policy guide to when and how national governments may employ nuclear technology for peaceful purposes and offers safeguards on this activity. While the NPT is a good example of how national governments have sought to govern nuclear technology on the global scale it has not been entirely successful. Some states, such as India and Pakistan, have not signed the treaty and have developed nuclear weapons capabilities which are not subject to any form of international governance.

The management of the global Internet captures the complexity and technical difficulty of governance. Although the United States has a great deal of power over the Internet, no one part of the US political economy controls it – different actors worldwide play important roles in its regulation and management, and in its growth and innovation (see Table 5.3).

The security agenda of the twenty-first century is qualitatively different in that threats may not come from another state but from non-state sources ranging from global warming to terrorist groups like Al-Qaeda. State-centric governance is increasingly pursued through cooperative action rather than wholly individual national policy making. The concept of security has therefore evolved to require governments to consider a much broader range of issues, as considered below, as part of their security policy-making process.

The issue of health necessarily has an individual dimension. National health services vary tremendously from welfare states' provisions to no provision at all. The so-called health transition, or the shift from predominantly communicable to non-communicable or lifestyle-related illness, has broad implications. Globally there have been some successes in reducing infant mortality rates but this has been accompanied by longer life expectancies and a growing incidence of ill-health. The prevalence of non-communicable illnesses in modern societies can be explained by processes such as urban shift and the move away from traditional subsistence agriculture. Dietary habits are moving towards more processed foods, which are high in fat, sugar and salt. Modern societies also lend themselves to more sedentary lifestyles with many office-based jobs and transport systems that require the minimum of exercise. The combination of these trends has implications for both personal health and the overall health of broader national societies.

At the global level modern advancements in transport technologies have resulted in the increasing mobility and ease with which individuals can travel around the world. Advancements in air transport have been very important in allowing more people to be able to travel large distances in a relatively short time. The continuous increases in flight services and the relatively cheap cost of flights have also helped to make international travel easier and prevalent. As people travel around the world more the mobility of communicable illnesses, such as flus of various kinds, also increases. The result is that national governments have had to focus on the international and global levels with regards to health issues. In early July 2009, for example, the Tunisian government placed restrictions on Muslim pilgrims travelling to Mecca in Saudi Arabia out of the fear that H1N1 (swine) flu could be transmitted back to Tunisia. Processes of globalisation have thus significantly affected how governments manage some health problems, increasing the need for international coordination.

The advancement in means of transport has become an issue of importance. This is due to the problems associated with organising the mass movements of people and goods across national borders. The private sector has a large role in international transport by offering the goods, services and logistics of transport. Private sector airlines, shipping companies, rail networks and train companies,

Table 5.3 Stakeholders in the governance of the global Internet

Actors/Stakeholders	Process	Power/Capability	Scope
The US government, including military and government regulators	Technical Legal Consultative Participation Still provides the core hardware on which the Net sits	Monitoring Surveillance Innovation Core rules	Very important but not in control
National governments other than the US	Technical Legal Consultative Participation	Variable commitment and capability for censorship	Some significant players – e.g. China – but none in control
Internet Service Providers (ISPs)	Businesses which use innovative systems to manage the Net/web	Have crude power to switch off, but difficult to differentiate between different users	In day-to-day control – but do not own the system or the material that goes on it
Innovating individuals Firms Copyright holders	Technical Consultative Participation Legal – copyright etc.	Copyright protection on political will to prosecute	Primarily dealt with in national jurisdictions
UN bodies (WIPO etc.)	Consultative Participation Some limited technical capability	No independent legislative power, but influential in TRIPs discussions	Low-level monitoring – have sought a greater role without success
World Trade Organization	Important but strictly limited power – not primary regulator	Formal dispute mechanism	So far limited – some actors would like its power increased over Net
Sub-national actors (including regulators, courts and prosecutors)	Regional or local courts have played significant roles in regulation – but often overturned at federal/national level	Limited as they defer to federal/national level	Sub-national
E-commerce actors (e.g. Amazon, Bloomingdales, etc.)	Few formal powers	Limited independent power, but these actors represent the actual phenomena of e-commerce	Have acquired great informal power through commercial and copyright/brand control and through advertising spending
Financial markets – equities and debt	Funding e-commerce and technical innovation	Finance market instability has power to upset or slow innovation and growth	Global with some key regional and national centres
Pornography businesses	Much informal capability – part of e-commerce (see above) but the biggest and most innovative part until recently	Well-funded and embedded in virtually all networked communities	Declining but still important innovators and actors despite their bad reputation
'Netizens' – Net users and lobby groups representing them	Includes Net citizen action groups, illegal downloaders, small innovators, bloggers, etc. – a very large but uncoordinated constituency	Potential to hack into systems for political and non-political reasons	Attempts to democratise the Net/web have largely failed – user groups have some power esp. through 'open source' innovation rather than by direct democracy

automotive companies and fuel suppliers are the main actors. As such, the private sector has to a certain extent been influential in the management of international transport. In the air transport industry, for example, a number of airline companies jointly created the 'Oneworld Alliance' in 1999. Membership in this alliance has since increased rapidly. The aim of this alliance is to standardise specifications for engineering, maintenance and servicing operations within the airline industry in order to facilitate air transport. It is worth noting that member airlines of the Oneworld Alliance seek to manage the global air transport sector in a manner which maximises their profits.

National governments have also engaged in international cooperation in order to manage transport policies. In order to facilitate international transport, national governments have had to coordinate policy decisions as well as actual infrastructure and modes of transport. An example of international coordination in a transport sector is the EU-backed project called The European Rail Traffic Management System (ERTMS). This project aims to achieve a homogeneous railway control and command system which will cover the whole EU. As part of this project there are two key elements: the European Train Control System, which standardises on-board train control, and a single system for mobile communications. This project builds on previous mechanisms for railway management in Europe which include the establishment of a single set of specifications for railway infrastructure.

One of the most visible changes in human relations that have accompanied globalisation has been the rapid expansion of international and global trade. Trade between states, in effect, comprises the majority of *international relations* on a day-to-day basis as individuals as well as public and private corporations exchange goods, services and financial resources over national borders in increasingly large quantities. Advancements in communications, transport and logistics technology have contributed to the ability of economic actors to sell the products, services and capital to others in different states all around the world. At the same time, the socio-economic development of practically all societies to some extent has resulted in increased demand for imports. No state can now supply all its needs domestically. Instead, states must import products, services and even capital to maintain themselves. With the proliferation of trade around the globe since the end of the Second World War has come the need to organise how trade is conducted. The main issues regarding the governance of trade relate to tariff and taxation levels on external trade, protection of intellectual property rights, reciprocity and fairness, and encouraging 'open markets'.

As mentioned above the WTO acts as the main intergovernmental organisation involved in managing international trade. It does this by providing member states with the forum to negotiate bilateral and multilateral agreements and rules which are enforceable as legally binding once approved. An example is the WTO-negotiated agreement on Trade Related Aspects of Intellectual Property Rights (TRIPs). This agreement came into effect in 1994 and stipulates that all member states must respect the intellectual property rights of public and private entities once those rights have been claimed and approved by a member state's government. This prevents infringements such as the illegal production of pharmaceutical goods which have not been approved by the company which originally developed them.

Other examples of effective global governance structures in which state authority, firms, international institutional frameworks and NGOs interact include the management of global telecommunications (Fuchs, 2008). In human rights policies, there is a higher degree of politicisation and a greater degree of conflict, especially over the use of torture in the so-called 'war on terror'. But, even if imperfect, the global regulation of human rights has proved to be of value for people in some countries and some situations, and NGOs such as Amnesty International and Human Rights Watch find it valuable to have the key norms they wish to promote, and which democratic governments generally claim to support, institutionalised in frameworks such as the International Criminal Court (ICC) and the various other UN institutions that deal with human rights. Another example of a systemic framework of global governance is found in international police cooperation through Interpol (see example box below), while global finance, which offers an important body of regulation, norm building and communication of values as well as negotiation on detailed policy management are discussed in Chapter 7.

EXAMPLE BOX

Interpol

The International Criminal Police Organisation, commonly known as Interpol is one of the largest IGOs in the world in terms of membership and operations. First established in 1923 in Austria, Interpol has been headquartered in France since the end of the Second World War. It is the primary agency which coordinates and facilitates international policing operations and at the time of writing has 189 members. As explicitly stated in its constitution, Interpol does not take part in any policing or anti-crime operations that do not cross state borders. Its purpose is exclusively to act as a body which helps national police forces when crimes are transnational or when those perpetrating crimes cross from one state to another.

The need for increased cooperation and coordination between national police forces emerged in the first half of the twentieth century. As processes of globalisation resulted in greater integration between people and increased exchanges such as trade, criminal activities also began to internationalise/globalise. The need for an organisation which would act as a means to combat crime on an international level was clear and in the post-Second World War era has become essential. However, Interpol's activities are limited to a certain extent and its role as an IGO is restricted by its constitution and its budget. The former determines Interpol as a 'coordinating' body rather than a 'governing' body, while its annual budget is only approximately US$60 million – a relatively small amount of money for an organisation with a global remit.

The most striking example of world leaders coming together to address an issue of global governance took place in 1992 with the Rio Earth Summit. Under the auspices of the UN this meeting brought together representatives from 172 nation states, including more than 100 heads of state or heads of government to discuss a perceived crisis of environmental degradation. This was unprecedented in both scale and range of issues under discussion. Civil society was also present but it was noticeable that NGOs had a separate meeting area some miles from the main conference centre. Two major conventions were established, one on climate change and one on biodiversity. Not all states ratified these conventions but their establishment meant that they remained in place beyond the Summit to act as a focal point for ongoing negotiations over environmental issues. Disagreement over the accuracy of the science of climate change has continued and there are complex negotiations regarding the targets to be set for limiting greenhouse gas emissions. That said, the Earth Summit process and work of the Intergovernmental Panel on Climate Change demonstrates a serious attempt to monitor, coordinate and govern a range of issue that impact on all states, communities and individuals.

Summary

This chapter has explored the types of national, international and global governance which take place in the contemporary world. The core debate in IPE which has been engaged with here is whether or not 'governance' actually takes place and at what levels. There are competing schools of thought here ranging from the position that true governance does not actually take place apart from at the national level to the view that governance does take place both within states and between them; a middle-ground approach claims that only 'management' and 'coordination' take place at the international and global levels. Furthermore, governance no longer can be seen as exclusively a function of national governments. Instead, non-state actors from the private sector can also be seen to be involved in management and governance in international relations. In the contemporary world there definitely are issues of a global scope, such as global trade, environmental change and health issues; however, in most cases governance does seem to remain limited to the national or international levels at present.

Reflective questions

1   What is the distinction between coordination, management and governance?
2   Can you identify the differentiating characteristics of governance at the national, international and global levels?
3   The primary function of national governments is to 'govern'; however, can you think of examples of non-state actors engaging in forms of governance also?
4   International cooperation in international relations is not new, but have processes of globalisation intensified the nature of interdependence and thus the need for international or global governance as opposed to just cooperation?

Suggestions for further reading

Barnett, M. and Duvall, R. (eds) (2004) *Power in Global Governance*, Cambridge: Cambridge University Press.

Diehl, P. (2005) *The Politics of Global Governance: International organisation in an interdependent world*, 3rd edn, London: Lynne Rienner Publishers.

Barnett, M. and Finnemore, M. (2005) *Rules for the World: International Organisations in Global Politics*, Cornell: Cornell University Press.

Friedman, T. (2007) *The World Is Flat 3.0: A Brief History of the Twenty-first Century*, New York: Picador.

Fuchs, C. (2008) *Internet and Society: Social Theory in the Internet Age*, London: Routledge.

Hirst, P. and Thompson, G. (2009) *Globalization in Question: The International Economy and the Possibilities of Governance*, 3rd edn, Cambridge: Polity Press.

Hughes, S. and Wilkinson, R. (eds) (2002) *Global Governance: Critical Perspectives*, London: Routledge.

Karns, M. and Mingst, K. (2004) *International Organisations: The Politics and Processes of Global Governance*, London: Lynne Reinner Publishers.

King, A. (1997) *Culture, Globalization and the World-System: Contemporary Conditions for the Representation of Identity*, Minneapolis: University of Minnesota Press.

Mattli, W. and Woods, N. (eds) (2009) *The Politics of Global Regulation*, Princeton NJ: Princeton University Press.

Milward, A. (2000) *The European Rescue of the Nation State*, 2nd edn, London: Routledge.

Mittelman, J. (2005) *Whither Globalization? The Vortex of Knowledge and Ideology*, London: Routledge.

Pease, K. (2009) *International Organisations: Perspectives on Global Governance*, Harlow: Pearson Education.

Rupert, M. (2000) *Ideologies of Globalisation: Contending Visions of the New World Order*, London: Routledge.

Wilkinson, R. (2005) *The Global Governance Reader*, London: Routledge.

6 Trade

Chapter learning outcomes

After reading this chapter students should be able to:

■ Understand and engage with the mainstream theoretical debates regarding trade in IPE.

■ Understand differing interpretations on the importance of trade and its impacts on international relations.

■ Comprehend the characteristics of the contemporary global trade system and its growth in the last few decades.

■ Be able to explain free trade agreements, their proliferation over the last decade or so and to offer conclusions on their significance.

■ Be familiar with the role played by MNCs in trade and to be able to explain patterns of increasing MNC-related trade.

■ Understand contemporary criticisms of the global trade system, free trade agreements and the trade-related activities of MNCs.

■ Relate discussion of trade to theoretical debates discussed earlier in this book.

Introduction

This chapter returns to assess some of the different theoretical views on world trade. Only some approaches that have been outlined in previous chapters will be discussed here depending on their relevance to the contemporary trade structure and contemporary discussions of it. The initial sections of this chapter should thus be read while keeping in mind the discussions of theoretical approaches in Chapters 1, 2 and 3. The development of the global trade system after 1945 is surveyed and particular attention is paid to the multilateral management of this system and its successes and failures, as well as key issues of debate. Pertinent issues in world trade are discussed, including the position of developing countries, the role of MNCs and the 'free trade versus fair trade' debate.

Liberalism

Within IPE liberalism has been said to be more successful as a school of thought than other theoretical approaches (see Chapter 1). This is in part to do with the dominance of trade as an issue of study in IPE and the relationship between liberal economic thought and the development of the global trading system since the end of the Second World War. Liberal economic thought dates back to around the late seventeenth and early eighteenth centuries. Adam Smith (1723–1790) was one of the earliest advocates of notions of free trade which would later be referred to as a single classical liberal approach. Smith's work, including *The Wealth of Nations* (1776), suggested that trade is the predominant form of interaction between people within a state and between states. The exchange of resources, goods, services and even capital from a supplier to a buyer using money as the medium is seen as a natural and peaceful form of international relation. Furthermore, trade between people requires a level of cooperation in order to take place. While liberals share realists' assumptions of anarchy in the international system, they claim that cooperation between people which is centred on trade is possible and desirable.

For liberal economic thought, trade is not a zero-sum game but is in fact a plus-sum game, a form of interaction which actually benefits all who are engaged with it. In this sense the realist/mercantilist assumption that trade benefits one actor at the expense of another is refuted. By exchanging goods and services, for example for money, one state (or market of people) can gain products which it otherwise would not possess or gain products at a lower cost. At the same time, by supplying another state (or market) it is possible to make greater profits than supplying just your own. At the same time as trade being beneficial for purely economic reasons, liberals also claim that trade has other positive effects on international relations. For example, liberals such as Michael Doyle, argue that trade results in greater integration between the trading societies, thus allowing them to become more familiar with each other and strengthen shared interests. The result of this integration is a decrease in the risk of conflict and an increase in cooperation and stability. Early liberal scholars including David Ricardo (1772–1823) developed notions of trade as being a key to economic growth and prosperity. By trading more a state (or market) can further develop economically through developing economies of scale (having large markets to sell many goods and services to), lower costs and increase efficiency (by exploiting comparative advantages in the production of certain goods or services).

As discussed in Chapter 5, there are elements of national governments being involved in the management and governance of global trade through IGOs such as the WTO. However, liberal economic thought calls for the exclusion of national governments from playing a significant role in the economy. Governments, it is claimed, are not capable of organising entire economies efficiently. The free market with its invisible hand of supply and demand is said to be the most effective organiser of economic activity. Liberals say that national borders therefore act as a form of governmental restriction on trade and a restriction on the growth and prosperity it brings. As a result of governmental involvement in the economy, as well as the existence of 'unnatural' borders between markets in the form of state borders, trade is hindered. Thus, liberals suggest a system of limited governmental involvement in trade and the removal of national barriers to trade such as taxes on imports/exports, tariffs and quotas on how much one state may export to another. Many observers, such as David Harvey in his book *Introduction to Neoliberalism* (2005), point to the embedded nature or hegemony of liberalism in the contemporary free market global economy. There is, quite simply, a liberal dominance in the decision-making processes which shape the ways in which trade is facilitated and deregulated to the extent that it often seems there is no other game in town. This discussion is taken further in the section below on the contemporary trade system.

Realism/mercantilism

Realists tend to place less emphasis on economics in general than liberals do. Nevertheless, trade is seen as an area of significance for realists in IPE and mercantilism has a long tradition of thought as well. The key tenets of realist thought on trade are closely linked to its concern with international anarchy, national security and power. In order to maximise one's own national power capabilities with regards to rivals a state must expand its military power base as well as its diplomatic capabilities. Realists argue that in order to do this it is necessary to develop a strong economic base in order to be able to out-compete rivals by purchasing or developing weapons. One way of doing this is to develop an industrialised economy and encourage an affluent domestic society which can provide economies of scale. However, where domestic populations and markets are insufficient to drive economic growth, new markets to sell goods and services in are needed. Therefore, realists suggest that states seek to engage in international trade in order to gain wealth. However, unlike liberals, realists believe that trade is a zero-sum game and that states can gain trade surpluses at the expense of other weaker states (who subsequently have a trade deficit).

Trade for realists is a means to get richer and more powerful in order to strengthen national capabilities and be able to pursue national goals in the international arena. While liberals argue for free trade and the exclusion or limiting of government involvement in the economy, realists argue for the opposite. Free trade in this sense is about competition between economic actors and if a state is weaker or less rich than its trading partners it will be automatically disadvantaged and unable to compete. The result is a trade deficit and the further weakening of the state. The economy or economic actors in a state should thus be supported by the national government if they are to be able to compete with others in the global market. This policy is termed economic nationalism and is put into action through the protection of domestic markets via barriers to imports such as tariffs, taxes and quotas. Direct financial and technological support from national governments to support domestic industries is also used here.

Realists are adamant in their conception of international anarchy and the lack of ability for cooperation between states and peoples under such conditions. While liberals see cooperation and stability stemming from greater levels of trade, realists see no such connection. Trade makes some rich and some poor and is an extension of the competition for power between self-interested states. Cooperation and stability are therefore not directly linked to levels of trade.

Structuralism

Structuralist notions of trade can be complex and positive or negative, seeing trade as a very important aspect of the modern world but one which has many different effects. In some cases structuralists see structures of global trade which very much resemble previous economic structures that existed in the era of European imperialism. Here rich states trade with poorer and less economically developed states in a manner which seems to benefit the former. In terms of exports, the less developed states tend to produce low-value products such as raw materials, low-technology manufactured goods and food. At the same time, more industrialised states tend to export high-value goods and services such as high-technology manufactured goods and financial services. Structuralists, such as Immanuel Wallerstein (1981), see a clear distinction between exports which are worth a lot of money and those which are worth little. The result of trading in this manner is for the advanced economic states to continuously record trade surpluses with their poorer partners. This adds to the *underdevelopment* of the global South and is claimed to be a relationship of exploitation.

Because the global economy is split up into exporters of different types of products, for example with Japan exporting high-technology computing products and Chad exporting cheap clothing, a relationship of dependency has also emerged. Here, Andre Gunder Frank (1978) claims that poorer states need to trade with richer states to get a range of products which they cannot supply themselves with. This causes an endless cycle of trade deficits and economic stagnation, meaning these poorer states can never really compete in global trade for more expensive products. At the same time, some structuralists see the benefits of 'fair trade' as a means to transfer some technology and financial resources to poorer states. However, this is a marginal group.

The contemporary trade system

Of the major theoretical approaches to understanding trade, liberalism has become dominant in international relations. Realist thought on trade had provided most European states with a guide for economic policy during the early modern era. However, by the late eighteenth century and early nineteenth century liberal economic thought had gained in prominence and was influencing policy making in the major European states. The contemporary global economic system is, to a large extent, based upon the dominant themes in liberalism and was consciously formed at the end of the Second World War by the victorious Allied powers. The United States and the United Kingdom led the way in developing institutions which would guide the global economy in the post-war world. The economic structure which was established in the early post-war years largely remains today, with liberalism *embedded* in the global system. So, the cornerstones of international and global trade are the liberal notions of free trade, limited government involvement in economics, global institutions such as the WTO and the primacy of the private sector.

It is extremely important to stress that while the global system of trade is governed in a way which is based upon or informed by liberal economic thought, for many states international trade is not entirely characterised as free and without governmental involvement. However, constant efforts have been made over the last half century to move towards a global system where free trade is universally adhered to. It is in many ways very difficult to organise a set of relations such as trade on a global scale and it takes a great deal of time. Nevertheless, the liberal vision of free global trade is, in some ways, getting closer with the proliferation of free trade agreements and the adoption of liberal economic thought by most governments. That said, many impediments to free trade do exist. While trade in manufactured goods is increasingly becoming liberated and total volumes of traded manufactured goods have risen significantly in the last two decades (largely due to free trade agreements), trade in services, raw materials and agricultural goods remain regulated to a large extent. The result is that trade in these sectors is far from free. Indeed the processes of negotiating the full liberalisation of trade in these areas have proven to be unsurpassable since the mid 1990s and have helped block progress in multilateral negotiations in the WTO.

National governments meet via the WTO in order to negotiate agreements which will result in the creation of further rules and norms governing global trade. These 'rounds' of negotiations last for a number of years each and focus on ways in which to reduce barriers to trade between states. There have been nine rounds of negotiations under both the GATT framework and the WTO. Perhaps the most important aspect of WTO-led trade liberalisation is the principle of most favoured nation (MFN) status. Upon joining the WTO states have to automatically agree to certain norms and rules. Here, the concept of MFN status states that any preferential treatment between two WTO member states in terms of the framework governing trade between them must be given to all other members and reciprocated. So, if Japan and China, for example, agree to bilaterally lower barriers to trade in a given economic sector they are seen as giving each other preferential treatment over other states. This runs counter to the aim of the WTO and the liberal values embedded in the global economic system of facilitating free trade on a global scale. Therefore, if Japan and China reduce barriers to trade between them they must also lower their barriers in the same way with all other WTO member states. In theory this would lead to the level playing field of liberal economic thought and would lead to a global free trade regime. However, in practice often MFN status is not recognised or reciprocated. Indeed, bilateral and regional FTAs actually directly run counter to the MFN principle as they are exclusive to the states party to the agreement. At the same time WTO member states have to treat all companies and economic activity as it would treat its domestic companies. This principle of non-discrimination (by not favouring domestic over international actors) is also often difficult to monitor and enforce. However, there are dispute settlement mechanisms within the WTO system which states can appeal to if they feel that the MFN and/or non-discrimination rules have been broken by another member state.

Joseph Stiglitz and Andrew Charlton: *Fair Trade For All: How trade can promote development*

The dominance of liberal economic thought in contemporary debates and policy with regards to trade (what is called neo-liberalism) is not without its critics. While realists and structuralists present their own critiques of the concept of free trade and the direction in which the contemporary trade system is going, there are those from within the broad umbrella of liberalism who also voice caution. Joseph Stiglitz, a former World Bank head and Nobel Prize winner, and Andrew Charlton raise some concerns about the pursuit of global free trade. At the same time as supporting the claim that trade can lead to greater economic prosperity, international cooperation and stability, Stiglitz and Charlton temper optimism about when this is possible. Here it is argued that free trade among competitive markets and industries will improve productivity and efficiency. However, where underdeveloped markets and industries are concerned, issues of competitiveness and survivability are raised. The lack of ability to actually compete in global markets which have been created through trade liberalisation often leaves poorer states out of the process of trade and therefore the benefits it brings.

In order to fully develop a global economic system which is integrated, characterised by co-operation and peaceful interaction, and is founded on free marketeering Stiglitz and Charlton suggest that *fair trade* should be pursued. This notion is based upon the principle of increasing trade in much the same way as free trade. However, fair trade implies free trade between advanced and competitive states while allowing for varying levels of openness with regards to developing states. Rather than rapidly opening up economies to competition through free trade, the developed world should allow developing states to gain greater access to their markets by reducing barriers to trade. The latter should be allowed to retain some barriers to trade in certain sectors in order to develop domestic industries, allowing for the full liberalising of trade once these industries are competitive enough to engage with the global economy. The core argument of this concept, according to Stiglitz and Charlton, is that the current global economic system, with its pursuit of free trade, only works for half the planet at best. The other half gets left out and is impeded from developing economically.

The latest round of WTO negotiations began in Doha, Qatar, in 2001 but has failed to produce new agreement on the further reduction of barriers to trade. The key sticking points here have been over trade in agricultural products and services. Developing states, led by India, Brazil and Kenya, have pursued liberalisation of trade in agriculture – wanting greater access to the rich markets of the developed states for their agricultural exports. At the same time, the majority of developed states, led by the G7 block, have sought greater access to developing states' services markets for their service exports. However, developed states have so far refused to reduce remaining barriers to agricultural imports or to reduce agricultural subsidies to their domestic industries (the EU has been the most significant actor to refuse this latter point). In return, developing states have refused to lower barriers to services – asking the question of why should they allow developed states' industries access to their services markets (in which developing states' domestic industries are less competitive) while the developed states' agricultural sectors are protected. At the time of writing, there seems to be very little progress in concluding the Doha round.

In part as a response to the lack of progress in multilateral negotiations many states have turned even further to bilateral or smaller-scale multilateral negotiations. The United States, for example, had only three FTAs (with Israel, Canada and Mexico – the latter developing into NAFTA) prior to 2001. By 2009 it had 17 bilateral FTAs in effect and a number of others being negotiated. Regional

FTAs have also begun to proliferate or strengthen. In the Middle East and North Africa, the Greater Arab Free Trade Area (GAFTA) agreement, for example, came into effect in 2005 and steady progress has been made in reducing all barriers to trade in manufactured goods – natural resources, agricultural products and services are somewhat more restricted still. There are fears that the proliferation of bilateral and small multilateral agreements will detract from the WTO-led global efforts to liberalise trade. Here, states may feel that the WTO process is too difficult and slow and will not serve their national interests. Instead bilateral or regional FTAs may be more likely to result in greater success in facilitating trade. If this is the case then barriers to trade will be removed within regional blocks but will remain between different regions, therefore further limiting inter-regional trade. It may also be the case, however, that the proliferation of bilateral and regional FTAs simply will lead to global free trade by a cumulative process of trade liberalisation.

At the same time as institutions are created and engaged with to pursue free trade on a global scale there are many political impediments which restrict this goal. Political impediments continue to exist even when some form of FTA is in effect or when WTO membership is in place. Normalisation of trade relations between Israel and its Arab neighbours that are members of the WTO and which also share FTAs with the United States along with Israel is far from a reality. Even trade between Egypt and Israel is extremely limited, regardless of the facts that they are both WTO members and privy to the MFN rule, as well as having a peace treaty which calls for economic normalisation between them. Furthermore, being close geographically and having economic characteristics which would complement each other it is surprising that Israel and Egypt engage in so little trade with each other. However, when considering the unofficial boycott of Israel by Egyptian businesses and consumers (due to the Israeli occupation of Palestine and the unresolved conflict between Israel and a number of Arab states) the limited levels of trade and lack of free trade between the two is not so surprising.

Rising levels of trade

Globalisation has entailed the expansion of trade to the extent that we can now truly talk of a global trading system (see Table 6.1). International trade has expanded so rapidly and so widely that virtually every market on the planet is linked to many others via the exchange of goods and services. Historically, over the past three centuries international trade was concentrated into two forms. The first was trade between imperial centres and their colonies. The second was between the imperial centres themselves (largely this meant trade between European states). However, the modern global system is characterised

Table 6.1 Trade across regions, 2008, including intra-regional trade (value in US$bn)

The total volume of world trade in 2008 was $15.7tr
The total volume of world GDP in 2008 was $65.4tr

Exports from/to	North America	EU	Africa	CIS	Middle East	Asia
N. America	1014	369	33	16	60	376
EU	475	4695	186	240	188	101
Africa	122	218	53.4	1.5	14	114
CIS	36	406	11	135	25	77
Middle East	117	126	37	7	122	569
Asia	775	127	121	108	196	2181

Source: World Trade Organization (2009) *International Trade Statistics 2009*, Table I.4, p. 9, Geneva: WTO.

by literally all states engaging in some form of trade with others. This assent of trade as a daily interaction between markets and peoples regardless of whether they are from an economically advanced state or not is a relatively new phenomenon. While the global economy has a GDP of approximately US$65 trillion, international trade totalled approximately US$16 trillion in 2008 (World Bank data). As a total amount and as a percentage of global GDP, trade levels have risen very rapidly since the 1950s. It is worth noting that prior to the First World War international trade levels were also very high in terms of a percentage of global GDP. The level of trade dropped significantly in the inter-war period and during the Great Depression but then began to rebound after the Second World War. Many liberal scholars argue that there was a direct causal link between the low levels of international trade after the First World War and the onset of economic crises, global recession, rise of nationalism and ultimately the Second World War. The embedding of liberal economic values in the revision of the global economic system that followed the Second World War was largely based upon these liberal observations. The architects of the post-war system, including economists and scholars such as John Maynard Keynes, argued that in order to ensure that economic recessions, nationalism and conflict did not return an open and integrated economic system was needed. Therefore, the foundations of the contemporary global economic system were developed in a deliberate attempt to facilitate and encourage global trade.

The patterns of trade have also evolved rapidly so that now trade takes place between all areas of the world and in practically all sectors of production. Rising levels of trade have traditionally been seen between the areas of the 'Triad' of North America, Western Europe, and Japan and Australia. These areas constitute the most economically advanced markets in the world where a majority of economic production has taken place in the last half a century. The Triad represents the most prosperous set of markets in the global economy. Trade between Western Europe and North America, for example, has grown rapidly from around US$50 billion a year in the 1950s to over US$528 billion in 2008. This is compared with much lower levels of trade between other markets in the world over the same period of time. While the Triad markets trade quite heavily, sub-Saharan Africa and the Middle East, for example, have seen much more restricted levels of trade. The Middle East has the most limited levels of intra-regional trade in terms of a percentage of regional GDP and sub-Saharan Africa comes a close second. Furthermore, these regions have not had as much success trading with other regions such as Europe or North America as others have. Natural resources such as oil and gas do constitute major exports from the Middle East and North Africa in terms of total value and percentage of GDP. However, if we remove these commodities and only consider non-oil or gas exports, this region does not export very high levels of products to the rest of the world. The same can also be said for other developing regions. Table 6.1 illustrates, among other things, not only the regionalisation of global trade, but also the very powerful differences in levels of engagement in world trade between regions.

At the same time as levels of trade between the less economically developed regions and the more developed ones have been limited since the 1950s, trade between less developed regions has also been quite low. Trade between South Asia and South America, for example, has traditionally been very limited. So, the majority of trade that has taken place between regions since the Second World War has been between more advanced markets. The intensification of processes of globalisation has begun to transform these traditional patterns of trade. Levels of trade have been increasing quite rapidly over the last two decades. Much of this increase in trade has not included the Triad markets but has actually taken place between emerging markets. The emergence of China as a major trading state is the perfect example here. China's levels of trade have increased very rapidly since the 1990s and China now has the world's second largest levels of trade. The development of both low-technology and high-technology manufacturing industries have led to very large increases in Chinese exports of products such as clothes, toys and now even cars. Rising levels of affluence have led to greater purchasing power and subsequently increased imports of consumer products such as high-technology equipment. Industrialisation has also brought a greater need for resources and China is now the second largest importer of oil and gas. But China's trade has not just taken place with the richer markets

Table 6.2   Selected ranking of imports and exports in merchandise trade (value in US$bn)

Rank	State	Exports	Rank	State	Imports
1	Germany	1461	1	US	2169
2	China	1428	2	Germany	1204
3	US	1287	3	China	1133
4	Japan	782	4	Japan	763
5	Netherlands	633	5	France	706
6	France	605	6	UK	632
7	Italy	538	7	Netherlands	573
8	Belgium	476	8	Italy	555
9	Russian Federation	472	9	Belgium	470
10	UK	459	10	R. of Korea	435
11	Canada	456	11	Canada	418
12	R. of Korea	422	12	Spain	401

Source: World Trade Organization (2009) *International Trade Statistics 2009*, Table I.8, p. 12, Geneva: WTO.

in Europe, North America, Japan and Australia. Instead, China is trading at high levels with almost every region. Other developing states have also witnessed similar patterns of economic growth and rising levels of international trade. India and Brazil are cases in point which have managed to develop economically in recent decades and now have many trade links with all regions.

Table 6.2 illustrates world ranking for leading exporters and importers. It demonstrates the growing power of China in world trade, the trade deficits of some countries (the US and UK in particular), as well as some possibly surprising leading players (Belgium and the Netherlands). It does not show the mix of trade (high/low-technology products) and it excludes services and primary products including raw materials.

EXAMPLE BOX

Shifting patterns of trade

Through the course of the seventeenth to the twentieth centuries patterns of trade have tended to follow forms of imperial and colonial expansion. In the twenty-first century, while remnants of such forms can still be identified, new patterns are also emerging. Imperial expansion can be seen as politically driven and centred on territorial expansion. The dominant trade dynamic of today emanates from the private sector. Multinationals are not territorially bound. The free-flow of capital allows their operations to react to the market demands of production and consumption. They are not driven by political allegiance, even though at times political issues will affect MNC behaviour. Instead they are driven by corporate agendas and the pursuit of profit.

For example, India was referred to as 'the jewel in the crown' of the British Empire. The vast majority of its trade flowed towards Britain and other parts of the empire. Today, India has one of the highest levels of trade within an increasingly diverse portfolio of goods and services. Brazil's experience is quite different in terms of colonial inheritance. In part this is because of the very different nature of Brazilian geography and society. Furthermore, Brazil gained independence from Portugal much earlier than India did from Britain. As a result Brazil did not have access to the technologies associated with the Industrial Revolution which formed a significant part of India's economic development.

Figure 6.1 Regional trade flows

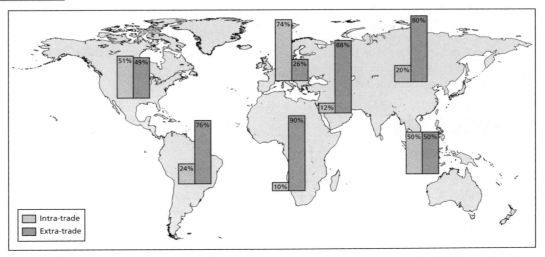

Source: World Trade Organization (2008) *International Trade Statistics 2008,* Geneva: WTO, Chart 1.4, p. 2.

Free trade agreements

One of the key features of the contemporary global economic system is the proliferation of FTAs between states. The primary purpose of an FTA is to facilitate trade across state borders by reducing or removing barriers to trade. This is done by two or more national governments negotiating an agreement as to how they can reduce or remove entirely administrative mechanisms such as tariffs, taxes, quotas and non-tariff barriers on imports and exports. These mechanisms often restrict trade by raising the costs of the products and services that are imported or exported. This is because the companies seeking to sell or buy products and services will always try to maximise their profits. If a national government enforces a tax on a given product that is imported or exported then this cost is transferred to the market and not the company, thus raising the cost to the purchaser and making the product less desirable and restricting market demand.

FTAs are based on classical liberal economic thought. In the works by Adam Smith, for example, trade is described as a natural human interaction but governmental management of international trade is not natural. The benefits of trade are restricted by barriers to trade and so a single free market which is unified by the removal of national barriers to trade should be pursued. The benefits of trade will then allow for the maintenance of a peaceful and stable global system which is prosperous. This position is not without its criticism, however, as many scholars, NGOs and civil society groups often highlight. This is discussed in more detail below. The dominant actors which have established and shaped the institutions of the modern economic system have advocated FTAs as a primary mechanism. The WTO is in itself largely a forum for states to meet in bilateral or multilateral settings to negotiate FTAs. The WTO also acts as a forum to ensure that FTAs (once agreed) are respected as international law and are abided by.

There have been two main forms of FTAs in the last few decades. The first type is bilateral FTAs which are negotiated between two national governments. These agreements can cover trade in all goods and services which are exchanged between the states or only some economic sectors. They also cover trade only between the two parties, although provisions for trade with other states are also accounted for. In the case of the latter point, FTAs have provisions that ensure that a third state does not simply export products to one of the FTA signatories and then re-export them to the other signatory, thus in effect gaining free access to this state without actually reciprocating such access. FTAs are often seen as very desirable for states which are seeking to maximise exports. Gaining free access to a large market such as the United States offers the opportunity for greater exports and greater economic growth. However, reciprocal free access to your own market also raises competition for domestic companies and can therefore be seen as undesirable.

EXAMPLE BOX

The Jordan–United States FTA

In many ways this FTA was a first in terms of US foreign trade policy and how FTAs are constructed. The agreement was the first between the United States and an Arab state and only the fourth FTA the United States had signed at the time. It also included provisions for labour rights and environmental protection. Subsequently the United States signed a large number of FTAs and several of these have been with states in the Middle East. The agreement requires the removal of all tariffs, quotas and taxes on all forms of bilateral trade in goods and services. Some observers claimed that this agreement was a reward given to the Jordanian government for its support of US policies in the Middle East. This observation was based on the belief that gaining free access to the US market would result in greater Jordanian exports and economic growth. The United States, on the other hand, was not seen as gaining much from the greater access to the Jordanian market as it is small in size. As such, the agreement was seen as a political one rather than an entirely economic endeavour. Nevertheless, others claimed that the FTA was designed as a purely economic project aimed at increasing trade.

The result of the agreement has been quite profound and since 2001 when the agreement came into effect bilateral trade between Jordan and the United States has increased from US$390.2 million in 2000 to US$2.1 billion in 2008. This fivefold increase in trade in just eight years is quite a dramatic rise and is clearly attributed to the FTA. Importantly the increase in trade value was mostly because of a rapid expansion of Jordanian exports to the United States. Jordanian exports rose from US$73.3 million in 2000 to just under US$1.5 billion.

The second form of FTA has been regional multilateral agreements such as the North American Free Trade Area (NAFTA) agreement. Here, the United States and Canada negotiated an agreement with Mexico in 1994 which added free trade between the three states to the bilateral FTA already in existence between the United States and Canada. This multilateral agreement created a single market with free trade in goods and services (but not labour). The EU, in effect, has a multilateral FTA also and states wishing to join the union have to accept this agreement. Because of this FTA the EU represents a single economic market with liberalised movement of goods, services and people across state borders.

Many states now use FTAs as major foreign and economic policy tools. The United States has pursued bilateral FTAs at an increasing rate since 2000 as a means of meeting its political as well as economic objectives. Up until 2001 the United States only had FTAs with Israel, Canada and Mexico. Following an FTA with Jordan which came into effect in 2001 the United States has signed a further fourteen and at the time of writing is negotiating a number of others. The United States has largely focused on signing bilateral FTAs with South American, Middle Eastern and North African states. With regards to the latter two, FTAs form a key element in broader US foreign policy aimed at engaging more with the region.

There are many criticisms of FTAs by individuals and groups that do not share the liberal assumptions about their benefits. Many people see FTAs as damaging to economic development of poorer states. It is argued that by reducing barriers to imports domestic industries, which are often in their infancy or are relatively uncompetitive internationally, will not be able to survive. The increased competition from external actors, which are often more efficient and competitive, will out-compete domestic rivals and thus reduce economic growth in the poorer states. In this argument, barriers to trade are there to protect domestic industries and economic growth and not to impede trade. Some states such as North Korea follow some policies which encourage barriers to imports in order to strengthen or protect domestic industries.

Other criticisms of FTAs are that they encourage the deregulation and removal of governance of the economic sector. Here, MNCs can pursue their activities without the hindrance of national governments regulating their behaviour. In some states, such as the United Kingdom, governmental laws stipulate things like minimum wages, the right of association in unions and working conditions. However, in many developing states such regulations are not in existence and national governments are unwilling to discourage MNCs from operating in their countries. In effect, the modern liberal economic system necessarily entails a race to the bottom as governments seek to offer the most profitable terms for MNCs and foreign capital to invest in their economies. Critics of FTAs claim that these agreements only encourage this process. Exploitation of labour and the environment is seen as a negative result of FTAs. Regardless of whether FTAs are seen as economically and morally desirable or not ultimately has little impact. FTAs have proliferated rapidly and the liberalisation of global trade has resulted in greatly expanding levels of this type of exchange.

One of the most important contemporary debates with regards to global trade is the importance of regional FTAs and their impact on the WTO-driven pursuit of global free trade. Since the 1980s there has been an emergence of regional trading blocs such as NAFTA, Mercosur (a South American regional trade agreement aimed at creating a fully integrated single market in Latin America) and the EU. These regional trade agreements create preferential treatment for the member states at the expense of states not included. As discussed above, there are concerns that the development of regional trade agreements and the regional blocs they create will actually hinder global trade. This is in direct contradiction of the liberal economic thought that has inspired the contemporary global economic system which seeks free trade on a global level. It may be the case, however, that regional trade agreements and trade blocs are actually steps on the way to a fully integrated and free trading global system. The EU, for example, negotiates FTAs with other states or groups of states as a single actor. This helps to streamline the process, as is evidenced by the Barcelona Process of integration between the EU and the Middle East and North Africa. States on the southern Mediterranean such as Tunisia only have to negotiate one agreement instead of twenty seven, making the process of integration more efficient.

MNCs and trade

Much of the global trade that takes place today is carried out by and on behalf of MNCs. Private sector MNCs account for over US$5 trillion in trade, which is equivalent to nearly 50 per cent of all international trade that takes place; trade within individual companies but across international boundaries – intra-firm international trade – accounts for an estimated 23 per cent of total world trade (all figures from WTO 2009 *Yearbook*; authors' estimates). It is often said that MNCs are the engines that drive global trade. In the liberal point of view, therefore, MNCs are the engines which drive global economic growth via trade. Realists would also argue that MNCs are very important in encouraging international trade and so they are important to the economic development of their 'home' state.

Structuralists, on the other hand, acknowledge the link between MNCs and trade and suggest that this relationship is extremely intense. Ultimately, though, they see MNCs as having an exploitative and damaging role on people and the environment via international trade. Almost all the international trade that MNCs are engaged with is actually inter-firm trade or intra-firm trade. This means that they trade largely with other MNCs or with different branches of their own corporation which are situated in different states. In the case of the latter it is very interesting to note that while goods or services may be transferred from one branch of a single corporation to another, if these branches operate in different states this transfer counts as international trade. Intra-firm trade actually constitutes a large percentage of trade involving MNCs. It has also become much more prevalent as the operations of MNCs have become increasingly geographically dispersed.

MNC-related trade is driven by global divisions of labour which allow for the combination of material, labour, infrastructure, technology and financial resources from around the world to be pooled together in one economic endeavour. The utilisation of different markets for different parts of a manufacturing process, for example, helps MNCs to maximise profits. This is done by locating the cheapest labour, resources and infrastructure which are appropriate and employing them in the manufacturing of goods. Of course, divisions of labour which are global in scale are only possible due to advanced and cheap technologies in communications and transport. The nature of the global economy with these divisions of labour mean that MNCs pursuing more profits will move their operations around the world, possibly quite rapidly. This means that states can attract investment from MNCs as they move the operations into new markets. For developing states this is a key source of income and economic activity. Because many states around the world are so keen to attract MNCs to their markets, they are often in competition with each other, putting MNCs in a preferable position where they get to choose where and when to invest. The result can be seen as a 'race to the bottom' where developing states (and in some cases developed states also) will offer incentives to MNCs such as tax breaks, low labour wages and so on. Combined, these processes allow MNCs to be extremely flexible with where they operate and the terms under which they move their activity to other states. Because of this position MNCs are often criticised for evading normal forms of governance – they quite simply can be above the law in many states or move on if national governments cause them trouble.

EXAMPLE BOX

Rolls-Royce

One of the world's most famous MNCs is the Rolls-Royce Group. It has total assets of US$22.5 billion, annual profits of US$1.2 billion and operates in over twenty-five different states. Its products and services include aircraft engines and automotive vehicles. It operates in highly competitive high-technology manufacturing industries. In order to remain competitive and maximise profits Rolls-Royce has developed a complex division of labour in the research, development, manufacturing and distribution of its products to a global market. This division means that various operations are conducted in different states and resources and labour are sourced from around the world. By having operations in these different states Rolls-Royce has to transport material from one branch to another, which often are in different states. This transfer constitutes international trade. At the same time, the goods that Rolls-Royce produces are purchased in many states and are traded from one market to another.

An example of how Rolls-Royce's chain of production and transport works is as follows. One of the company's main products are engines for commercial aircraft. The engines are manufactured at the company's facilities in Derby, UK, but much of the materials and parts which go into the engines are sourced from other branches and from other corporations from around the world. The fuel piping, for example, is purchased from a number of corporations based in Texas, USA.

For structuralist as well as liberal interpretations, global trade is driven to a large extent by the activity of MNCs. As mentioned above, MNCs do account for a large share of global levels of trade. However, the role of MNCs in enhancing trade is not straightforward. In many ways MNCs act as the channels or conduits between markets, facilitating the movement of goods, people, capital and services in myriad ways. The ability of MNCs to exploit markets for resources, labour, production and sale around the world is quite extraordinary and with modern forms of communication and technology trade is greatly enhanced by the pursuit of maximising profits. Put in other words, MNCs require trade in order to be profitable and to grow.

Criticisms of trade

There are a wide range of criticisms of trade and its impacts on the world. These can be categorised into three broad camps or schools. One camp is very much against international trade, claiming that the impacts on the human and natural worlds that come from trade are very damaging. A second camp argues that international trade is structured in a manner which is unfair to many of the world's poorer and less economically developed people. This argument is based on the perception of the global economic system as being based on open competition between economies. In this system those economies which are more advanced and industrialised automatically are in a more advantaged position to compete. The third key school of criticism is made up of those who see international trade as encouraging conflict between states by leading to imbalances in power capabilities as well as relationships of dependency.

For those who see international trade as very damaging there are two key elements of concern. It is argued that international trade and the deregulation of the global economy weakens labour rights and leads to exploitation of workers. Here, the actions of MNCs and how they treat employees is of great concern. Low wages, poor working conditions, long hours, no holiday or illness allowance and even in many cases modern forms of slavery are cited as some of the problems which international trade brings. Furthermore, the movement of goods and people which international trade entails is seen to be adding to environmental problems. As larger amounts of fuels are consumed in order to transport goods and people from one market to another greater levels of pollution are witnessed. Of importance here, again, are the operations of MNCs. As mentioned above, MNCs often transfer material and people from one branch to another as part of global divisions of labour. By manufacturing products in different states and transporting the different components in the production chain MNCs add to pollution. Some would argue that international trade does in fact add to economic growth. This may be good in terms of raising incomes and national GDP levels. However, this also means that greater levels of consumption and pollution will follow.

We might add that there should be real doubt about whether many governments actually support free trade. Even those which use the rhetoric of free and open trade most effectively jealously guard particular industrial sectors and particular firms. The United States, European Union and Japan each have very elaborate systems of trade control. As powerful agricultural exporters (such as Australia and Argentina) have pointed out, this applies especially to food products. But protection against low-cost products from newly industrialised countries is rife; using health and safety regulation, regulations on common standards, and many other forms of non-tariff barriers is widespread. This is partly because trade protection is so fiercely lodged in domestic politics. But many countries, including those in east Asia which grew rapidly in the 1960s and 1970s under state management (Taiwan, the Republic of Korea and Malaysia among them) and those in continental Europe, the Middle East and Latin America which have a long state tradition of government management of economic activity (France, Italy, Argentina and Egypt among them) have not created a political culture in which ideas of free trade stand unchallenged. The ideas of state protection as a basis for growth enshrined in the writings of Friedrich List, the nineteenth-century father of neo-mercantilism, may be disreputable to most economists, but they are still important in political and media views of the economy, especially in response to crises.

One major concern for many in the contemporary global economic system is the problem of fair competition. Advocates of free trade claim that open markets and the removal of barriers to trade will create a 'level playing field' where economic actors all have the same opportunities. Critics would agree that by adopting liberal economic policies of free trade and open markets economic competition is actually encouraged. While liberals see competition as leading to greater efficiency, lower costs and increases in economic activity, others, such as structuralists, see competition as relatively undesirable. They point to the fact that the more advanced economic states achieved their high levels of advancement not through free trade and open markets but by economic nationalism, conquest and the protection of domestic industries. At the same time, critics ask how less advanced economies can expect to successfully compete with the more advanced ones. In this view, therefore, the global economic system of free trade is simply not fair. This position is often referred to as the 'free trade versus fair trade' debate. Advocates of this position suggest that barriers to trade should remain in place for less developed states so that infant industries can be nurtured and economic development can take place. We could say that this second camp of trade critics is actually pro-trade, but refuses to support 'free trade' in its current form.

EXAMPLE BOX

The Fairtrade Foundation

Following are excerpts from the Fairtrade Foundation's website (www.fairtrade.org.uk):

> The FAIRTRADE Foundation is the independent non-profit organisation that licenses use of the FAIRTRADE Mark on products in the UK in accordance with internationally agreed fair trade standards. The Foundation was established in 1992 by CAFOD, Christian Aid, Oxfam, Traidcraft and the World Development Movement, later joined by the National Federation of Women's Institutes. Member organisations now also include Banana Link, Methodist Relief and Development Fund, Nicaragua Solidarity Campaign, People & Planet, SCIAF, Shared Interest Foundation, Soroptimist International, Tearfund and the United Reformed Church.
>
> Our vision is of a world in which justice and sustainable development are at the heart of trade structures and practices so that everyone, through their work, can maintain a decent and dignified livelihood and develop their full potential.
>
> To achieve this vision, fair trade seeks to transform trading structures and practices in favour of the poor and disadvantaged. By facilitating trading partnerships based on equity and transparency, fair trade contributes to sustainable development for marginalised producers, workers and their communities. Through demonstration of alternatives to conventional trade and other forms of advocacy, the fair trade movement empowers citizens to campaign for an international trade system based on justice and fairness.
>
> The Foundation's mission is to work with businesses, community groups and individuals to improve the trading position of producer organisations in the South and to deliver sustainable livelihoods for farmers, workers and their communities by:
>
> 1 being a passionate and ambitious development organisation committed to tackling poverty and injustice through trade.
> 2 using certification and product labelling, through the FAIRTRADE Mark, as a tool for our development goals.

3 bringing together producers and consumers in a citizens' movement for change.
4 being recognised as the UK's leading authority on fair trade.

Our key areas of activity are:

1 Providing an independent certification of the trade chain, licensing use of the FAIRTRADE Mark as a consumer guarantee on products.
2 Facilitating the market to grow demand for fair trade and enable producers to sell to traders and retailers.
3 Working with our partners to support producer organisations and their networks.
4 Raising awareness of the need for fair trade and the importance of the FAIR-TRADE Mark.

Source: Fairtrade Foundation, Mission Statement (www.fairtrade.org.uk).

A more radical perception of the impacts of international trade is one based on realist assumptions. The belief that trade leads to relative increases and decreases in economic wealth and therefore power capabilities is utilised here. This view suggests that national governments do follow policies of economic nationalism despite the claims to be trading freely and openly. Trade is thus seen as a form of competition between states in itself. Furthermore, rising levels of trade are leading to the transfer of resources, wealth and power from some states to others. For example, economically advanced states tend to have trade surpluses in their trade with less-developed states, resulting in an overall transfer of wealth to the more developed world. This is, in short, a continuation of former imperial economic relationships. The effect can be to further tip the balance of power capabilities in favour of the wealthier states.

Summary

Building on the previous chapters on theory, globalisation and governance this chapter has introduced trade as one of the most important contemporary forms of international relations. The ideological foundations of the structure of global trade have been considered. Here, classical liberal economic thought has been very influential in the establishment of the post-Second World War global economy and the role international trade plays in it. Over the past half a century or so international trade has expanded very rapidly and now we can refer to global trade. At the same time, while international trade traditionally was dominated by the Triad of North America, Western Europe, and Japan and Australia, international trade is now prevalent in all regions. The more economically advanced states still tend to dominate in trade relationships with less-developed states but trade between less-developed states is increasingly important. Also, less-developed states such as China are becoming very large traders.

The proliferation of bilateral and multilateral FTAs since the 1990s has helped to reduce and remove barriers to trade. The facilitation of trade has helped to drive greater levels of international trade. Through these agreements and the global trading regime dominated by the WTO, trade is likely to continue to increase rapidly. At the same time, MNCs play a very important role, accounting for a large part of global trade. Much of this trade is between firms or even between different branches of the same MNC. The expansion of global trade has served to highlight very different opinions on its impact. Liberals claim that trade is good for economic development and international stability and should be promoted. The structure of the global trading system is based on these ideas. The realist position is one of economic nationalism and mercantilism which suggests that trade is good for building power capabilities but only if a state has a trade surplus. Finally, more critical observers, such as structuralists, argue that the manner in which global trade is carried out is damaging to both people and the environment.

Reflective questions

1   What is the significance of international/global trade on international stability and economic growth according to liberals, realists and structuralists?
2   How significantly have levels of international/global trade increased since the end of the Second World War?
3   If FTAs seek to encourage trade by reducing or removing barriers to trade, does the proliferation of such agreements necessarily mean that trade will continue to increase? And to what extent?
4   How far can we say that international/global trade is driven by MNCs?
5   Are there negative impacts of international/global trade?

Suggestions for further reading

Baghwati, J. (2003) *Free Trade Today*, Princeton: Princeton University Press.

Bernstein, W. (2009) *A Splendid Exchange: How trade shaped the world*, London: Atlantic Books.

Dunkley, G. (2000) *The Free Trade Adventure: The WTO, the Uruguay Round and Globalism – a critique*, London: Zed Books Ltd.

Gunder, F.A. (1979) *Dependent Accumulation and Underdevelopment*, London: Macmillan Press.

Harvey, D. (2005) *Introduction to Neoliberalism*, Oxford: Oxford University Press.

Madeley, J. (2000) *Hungry For Trade: How the poor pay for free trade*, London: Zed Books Ltd.

Marrewijik, C. van (2002) *International Trade and the Global Economy*, Oxford: Oxford University Press.

Narlikar, A. (2003) *International Trade and Developing Countries: Bargaining Coalitions in the GATT and WTO*, London: Routledge.

Sampson, G. (ed.) (2008) *The WTO and Global Governance: Future Directions*, New York: United Nations University.

Stiglitz, J. and Charlton, A. (2007) *Fair Trade For All: How trade can promote development*, Oxford: Oxford University Press.

World Trade Organization (2008) *International Trade Statistics 2008*, Geneva: WTO.

World Trade Organization (2009) *International Trade Statistics 2009*, Geneva: WTO.

7 Global finance

Chapter learning outcomes

After reading this chapter students should be able to:

- Offer a description of how a global financial system has emerged.
- Understand the core ingredients of global finance and the process of state/market interaction.
- Explain the international debt crisis, its origins and contemporary impacts on global financial relations and development.
- Comprehend the processes which led to financial crises and explain the 2007–2009 global financial crisis and subsequent recession.
- Be familiar with the leading global financial institutions, how they operate and how they try to (de)regulate the global financial system.
- Relate discussion of global finance to theoretical debates discussed earlier in this book.

Introduction

In this chapter, we will look at the core elements of the world financial system, how it works, how the different markets for money and finance interact, and what institutions there are which manage the system. At a fundamental level, the system is regulated to an extent – it consists largely of market forces, but the markets are often not 'free markets' except in a relative sense. The regulators include national actors (especially in the more powerful states), banks and inter-banking institutions, international bodies such as the IMF, and a number of key agents which are entirely private (in the sense that they are not at all under state control), including major accounting firms, businesses which insure financial transactions, and credit rating agencies. The chapter also tries to explain why the world went into financial crisis in 2007 and what might be needed to get it out of crisis without creating the causes of further problems (if that is possible). This also provides a case study of some important aspects of globalisation processes in IPE which relates to other chapters and other discussions in this volume.

The global financial system is at once (i) a market in which money itself and financial products, representing credit, debt and risk, are bought and sold, (ii) a structure of exchange, which accountants would call a pattern of flows of funds, in which first Britain, then the United States, then Japan and, most recently, China has acted as the dominant provider of funds for the major debtor nations and firms, and (iii) a set of institutional arrangements, including regulators and rules and institutional procedures, most obviously exemplified in recent years by the continuing rise of the G20 bloc of leading developed and developing nations along with global institutions and key market actors which, it could be said, both largely caused the 2007–2009 crisis and enjoyed success (so far) in resolving it.

Two stories of financial globalisation

The financial crisis which began in 2007 demonstrated the vital importance of global finance (Cable, 2009). It also demonstrated that the financial system that emerged from the 1980s was a good deal less stable than many had imagined when it was leading world economic growth in the early 2000s. Sixty years ago, the total volume of financial transactions in the international system were determined largely by the volume of trade and foreign direct investment (FDI), together with an element for the repayment of debts. But the proportion of international financial transactions grew throughout this time. In the dollar and oil crises of the early 1970s, it already made sense to say that the world economy was dominated by financial structures and processes. It had become a finance-driven global economy. Globalisation did not start then; but it did continue to accelerate. In the 1980s, led by the US, German and British governments, formal state regulation of financial markets was significantly reduced, markets grew very rapidly, and new kinds of banking were created. World finance became what the distinguished financial specialist Susan Strange called a 'global casino' (Strange, 1997), driven by high risk-taking for high rewards, and stoked by the circulation of huge amounts of what she called 'mad money' (Strange, 1998). Many of these funds circulated very quickly around the world system in ways that governments found hard to grasp, never mind control. In this stage of the globalisation of financial activity, financial transactions became significantly but not totally disconnected from the 'real economy' of trade in goods and services, tourism, and international investment and job creation. Rapid flows of 'hot money' – money borrowed for very short terms for speculative investment – came to dominate the financial system, where bankers dealt in risky investments but also provided the finance which fuelled mergers and acquisitions and corporate growth. The globalisation of finance is a relatively recent transformation, perhaps partly a flight from common sense. We are where we are today because of globalisation, and most of the globalisation of financial services has happened since the 1980s.

That at least is one story. It is the story that, according to many newspapers and blogs, explains the origins of the 2007–2009 crisis. It contains *important elements* of truth; but it is actually *far from being the truth*. Finance has *always* been international, and the roots of modern capitalism, which lie in the creation of modern banking in the fourteenth and fifteenth centuries, were international from the start. Globalisation is not new, and global finance has been at the heart of most economic activity, including the growth of the modern state, since then. There are important new elements in the post-1980s financial system, of course, but they need to be much more carefully examined than the general story of the previous paragraph. The story of the origins of banking are important here. Rich merchants in wool and metals found themselves with spare money in one place (where they sold their goods) and a need to pay debts (for the wool or spices or precious metals they had bought) or save for future investment in another place far away. This was at a time when much of Europe was in continuous warfare, where mercenary armies dominated much of the Continent, and where moving money around in the form of gold and silver was especially risky. The solution was the letter of credit rather than moving cash itself. The letter of credit was guaranteed by the signature on it and by the reputation of the banking house that issued it. But at the same time, governments cast jealous eyes on the money that these merchants were gathering. As a banker, you might have two choices. Some monarchs simply took your money on some pretext or other, some of which involved taking your life at the same time. Or you could give cash to the state to fund its wars and bureaucracy in exchange for the same kinds of letters of credit, hoping they would be worth something later on, that the state would redeem them and pay back the loan they represented. You took big risks: when, in order to pay for a great war with France in 1346, English King Edward III reneged on all his debts (what we would call bonds) to Italian banks, having already looted everything he could to pay for his war with France from English Jewish merchants, in a stroke he destroyed all the newly emerging Italian banks he had borrowed from. It took thirty years, and the aftermath of the impact of the Black Death

(1348–1351), to recover. This gave the opportunity for a second generation of newer banks, including most famously the Medici in Florence, to emerge later in the century (Parks, 2006).

Early merchant capitalism was intrinsically linked to early banking, trade and the beginnings of government finance through the creation of a market for letters of credit from merchants and governments. Today letters of credit are still used in international trade. But much of the debt in the international system takes the form of bonds. Bonds are simply corporate or state debt which can be bought and sold. This market financed the activities of trade and state power. They were sold on, giving the buyers freedom to turn their paper back into liquid cash, and redeemed – given back to the issuer in exchange for cash – when their time period ran out. The creation of the letters of credit and what becomes the bond market is the first piece in the jigsaw of capitalism, not a relatively recent invention, although of course there have been many changes since the mid fourteenth century. Governments can benefit from this: it hugely increases the amount they can spend. So long as they are able to continue to pay the interest on debts, they can continue to borrow. They do not have to pay back the principal they borrowed. The growth of 'big government' in the sixteenth century depended on it. The growth of even bigger government in the nineteenth and twentieth century followed the same pattern. Small powers that were good at managing debt – for example Holland – flourished at the expense of larger but incompetent rivals. Failure to effectively manage their debt reduced the greatest European Empire of the early seventeenth century, Spain, to ruin. They were replaced as system leader first by Holland, then for a longer term by France. The link between governments and merchant capitalism is fundamental to the whole economic system. All governments (including most which proclaim themselves anti-capitalist) have depended on their ability to raise money on international markets to fund wars and increased public spending. But it is not only governments that depend on bankers. The growth in trade and big government in the nineteenth century produced a further evolution in the state, and the growth of industrial capitalism into the twentieth century produced further refinements. But the model was in significant ways the same as before. And the banking system has also always depended on the state and its regulation, its judicial powers, and its capacity to enforce contracts and establish international agreements. The relationship also works in reverse. When the global banking system collapsed in 2007–2008, only state action could protect the system. This action was taken by central banks such as the US Federal Reserve and the European Central Bank, and committed huge reserves to finance and also to insure the system. A few individual banks and bond dealers were allowed to go bust. But the state had an overwhelming interest in protecting the system, even at the cost of several trillion dollars of extra public spending. This financial system took three hundred years to establish. But what is characteristic about the modern state and the modern financial system is that they are not merely 'interdependent'; they are symbiotic – they have evolved together and each could not exist without the other.

In 1907, 1929, 1987, 1997 and 2000/2001 there were significant shocks in the global financial system. The recent 2007–2009 crisis is therefore part of a pattern. A sudden and apparently unpredictable crisis is not new. The biggest and most violent of these was undoubtedly the crisis of 1929. While economic historians debate in detail whether the financial crisis caused the economic depression of the 1930s, or whether it was preceded by the start of the depression, the two together forming a perfect storm of crises. The impact of 1929 was very important not just for its tragic consequences in the 1930s, but also for the future of economic diplomacy. International institution building at the end of the Second World War and in the subsequent crises of the 1950s and 1970s was directed primarily to ensuring that the experience of 1929–32 would not be repeated. Central banks and governments cooperated with the market to achieve this. In the Asian financial crisis of 1997, some banks went bust, mainly in Japan and South East Asia, and there was a knock-on effect on Western financial markets. But the main gainers in the crisis were the US, which reasserted its power over what had seemed to be rising Japanese and Asian institutions, and China, which mostly stood apart from the bad loans which had helped to cause the crisis. In the 2000/2001 crisis (the dotcom collapse), financial markets were not undermined by a powerful shift in investor confidence, partly because of effective government-led responses to stabilise global finance. It looked as if financial crises – famously described over and over by politicians and commentators as 'boom and bust' – were a thing of the past.

A word on 'stability': the international financial system is not stable, and nor is the international economy. This is, to put it at its crudest, because global capitalism is not stable, and does not seek stability. Global capitalism is dynamic, and only functions effectively if there is instability. Political commentators of all parties invariably say that they want 'stable growth' (does anyone want stable recession?). But stable growth is a contradiction in terms. What they probably mean is that they want manageable or sustainable growth rather than periods of explosively rapid growth followed by dramatic recessionary collapses. But stability has been a feature of international financial markets only if they are measured on a particular timescale. Day-to-day, they are dynamic, and that dynamism enables markets to trade, and traders to make money out of the changing margins they find. Over longer time periods, financial markets are also unstable, reflecting not just a 'business cycle' of trade and exchange, but also a cycle of the creation and destruction of credit and asset value in markets for financial products. The task of regulation is not to eliminate instability (which would kill the market) but to control its extremes and their consequences. This has never proved easy to do.

The core ingredients of global finance

Global finance involves the buying and selling of particular assets – money, credit and debt, and financial instruments linked to them. Some of this business is investment – money committed for projects which, in the longer or shorter term, are directed to produce profits. Some is the repayment of earlier debts. It also includes deals between governments and government-backed institutions such as the International Monetary Fund (IMF) and Bank for International Settlements (BIS). But most of this activity is done in the market by banks, firms and insurance companies with money to invest. These markets are regulated where they operate in particular national jurisdictions by a mixture of private and government bodies. But international markets have become increasingly complex, and at the same time have evolved less certain forms of regulation, to which we will return shortly. International trade is still a very significant factor in the demand for money in the world system. But, as already noted, it has for quite a long time not been the determinant of demand for finance. If you buy a foreign car, a Japanese brand electronic item, which was probably made in South East Asia, American software, Indian financial services, Scottish life insurance, or when you book your holiday abroad, you are creating a demand for currency. This is so because people, including workers, suppliers and shareholders, in the country your product or service comes from want to be paid in the currency they use, not in the currency you use. Trade creates a pattern of cash and currency movement which mirrors the movement of the goods and services themselves. Trade in insurance, including insurance for trade, adds to this pattern. But these 'real economy' flows are only a relatively small proportion of global financial flows, not more than 10 per cent, and arguably now as little as 5 per cent, depending on how the measure is done.

The global financial system is thus not a single market. It consists of a set of separate but interconnected markets. There is, first, a market for money, and part of that is demand and supply for money borrowed at very short notice (called in the London market 'at call'), and capable of moving very quickly around the global market ('hot money'). There is a separate market for capital. And there are markets for debt and debt-based financial instruments. There are also markets for foreign exchange. Finally there are markets for commodities, which may substitute for money, most obviously gold, but also for anything in which investors might have confidence, from oil in transit (in other words, oil actually in a tanker at sea may change hands many times before it arrives at a destination port if investors are drawn to short-term investment in the commodity), to land, and to Chicago pork bellies (an investment vehicle invented at a time when the Chicago commodities exchange was right next to the meat market, and less surprising to Chicagoans than to most other people).

All these markets are not just ways of getting access to funds or ways of investing. They are without exception also channels for speculation. And they are ways of quantifying risks – putting a price on the risk of holding *or not holding* a particular asset over a given longer or shorter time period – in ways that allow those risks to be passed on or hedged in a market. All financial markets have this role, which we could describe as an insurance function – they enable dealers to insure against possible changes in price or availability in the future. So financial markets manage several different kinds of risk at the same time. First of all these include the risk of price movements in a given commodity. But they also include the risk of holding a given commodity or bond or debt as against the risk of not holding them, and as against the risks involved in holding any other alternative. Since any risk can be measured (at least in theory), complex mathematical models can measure the trade-off between different kinds of risk; this is the difference between *risk* and *uncertainty* in the jargon of the market. Risks may be greater or smaller, but can in principle be measured; uncertainty is insecurity of a kind which can be imagined, but not reliably measured. In general, financial markets like risk; this is because they can speculate in it. Furthermore, they hate uncertainty; this is because it creates loss of confidence. On a large scale this can also undermine confidence in the markets themselves, not just in individual items the markets sell. 'Derivatives' are financial products whose value is derived from that of other products or processes. Using some version or other of mathematical models for calculating the price or expected change in price of a package of investment products, derivatives are established. These emerged in the 1990s as important investment vehicles. By the 2000s, they had taken so many varied forms that it had become impossible to define very accurately what a derivative is or was. Those selling derivatives had to understand both the mathematics and the markets they were dealing with if they were to succeed without simply engaging in a dressed-up gamble. As Susan Strange pointed out in the later edition of her compelling critique of these markets, *Casino Capitalism* (1997), most people involved either did not understand the maths or did not understand the markets. In the reports into the financial crisis after 2007, it became clear that quite a lot of market players did not really understand either.

INFORMATION BOX

Global finance: basic facts

The total volume of world GDP is approximately US$65 trillion.

The total volume of world money supply including credit and debt, credit card debt, government debt, short-term lending and derivatives, excluding 'hot money', is approximately US$600 trillion. The world financial system is thus much larger than the world volume of trade in goods and services, and much larger than the world volume of production and exchange.

Bonds are debt which is tradable (they often used to be called 'commercial paper'). All debt carries risks. The risk together with the lifespan of the bond defines its value at any one time – since the risk changes over time, the value also changes. Buying debt, including bonds and derivatives based on debt (such as mortgage-based collateralised debt obligations or CDOs), is also often called 'buying and selling risk'.

Global derivatives trading was worth approximately US$1.6 trillion in 2006. It was predicted to rise to US$2 trillion in 2008, but due to the financial crisis collapsed to US$0.6 trillion in 2007.

Total US debt held abroad is approximately US$3 trillion of which 25 per cent is held in China, most of that by the National Bank of China.

The main international reserve currencies are the US dollar, the yen, the euro and the Swiss franc, but the renminbi is also starting to assume a reserve role.

The total volume of world foreign direct investment (FDI) in 2007 was approximately US$16 trillion.

The total volume of debt of the world's developing countries (G77) is approximately US$2 trillion. The total volume of the debt of the world's richest countries (OECD group) is approximately US$11 trillion.

The International Monetary Fund (IMF) acts as a kind of 'lender of last resort' for governments but it is not, strictly speaking, technically an LLR, and it does not have the role of other international credit creators – banks and funds.

All national economies aim to regulate the national creation of credit, and generally aim to do so under strict rules. There is, however, no comparable regulation for the international creation of credit where it does not fall clearly under national jurisdiction. This lack of credit creation regulation was widely (but not universally) thought to be a virtue – until August 2007.

The growth of a global financial system: a little more history

The global financial system evolved fairly rapidly throughout the nineteenth century for four main reasons. First, there was a continuing growth of industrial capitalism which created a growth in trade in industrial goods, and the equally important increases in exchanges of raw materials and foodstuffs to pay for those products, creating a growing demand for money and investment. Second, there was rapid growth in financial speculation, especially in government, railway and banking bond issues, particularly in the last thirty years of the nineteenth century. Third, as the 'modern state' emerged, with its greater role in the economy and in social affairs (education, pensions, social provision, local government), as well as the greater cost of advanced-technology military equipment, this led to a transformation of the larger states' economies, with a steadily increasing reliance on finance based on the sale of short- and long-term debt. Fourth, imperial competition was an important driver in the growth of global financial interests, and investment patterns (German money in Turkey and the Balkans, France in North Africa, Britain in South America) followed political as well as commercial interests. At the start of the twentieth century, these formed a relatively balanced system under the broad hegemony of British-run institutions. Those institutions included the pound sterling, the Bank of England and London money markets. Investment channelled from London funded the growth of the American and Russian rail systems and the beginnings of global oil markets in the 1880s. Rules set largely by British institutions, with some consultation with others, especially French and American banks and investment houses, dominated the global economy. But there was virtually no formal regulation of any international activity other than trade by international intergovernmental institutions. There was little perception that formal regulation could be necessary. This was partly because the system seemed to work, despite the instability of growth and recession over the business cycle. It was also because there was a theory which appeared to explain effectively why the global financial system worked and why it would go on working – free trade liberalism. Free trade liberalism was never universally accepted, and most politicians and businesspeople in Germany, France and Russia had grave doubts about it. But at the core of the system, including in the main British institutions, the theory was largely accepted by those who managed the 'rules of the game'.

The First World War changed all that. The relative stability of the global system was wrecked from the onset of war. Britain had been the world's leading exporter of capital throughout the nineteenth century, even if German, French and American capital exports started to challenge the British leadership from about 1870 onwards. Quite suddenly, in the spring of 1916, Britain became a net importer of capital for the first time since at least the mid seventeenth century, as it sold off foreign assets as well as vast quantities of bonds in order to pay for the war. It was the US which replaced Britain as the world's main lender. Nationalist-minded political and business leaders in the US may have felt that the switch was only right, but the US was ill-prepared to take on the role of global hegemonic state which was implicit in this fundamental underlying shift in the structure of global capitalism, and it was not until 1944 that the US assumed a role of effective system manager. The US role in the 1920s was important, especially when US loans underwrote the partial recovery of the global economy and paid for much of the costs of German currency stabilisation after their crisis in 1922–23. The crash of 1929 and the incompetent management by all governments of its economic aftermath produced a wave of economic nationalism which helped to bring about the Second World War. The instability of the years 1914–1949 was of a different kind to any that had gone before, at least since 1650. The stabilisation of global finance, which included the stabilisation of exchange rates, the creation of a new institutional framework, the greater regulation of government and corporate borrowing by credit rating agencies and banks, and the introduction of more transparent rules for bond markets all helped to create growth. International trade and international finance were together the moving forces of global economic growth and global economic integration in the period from 1949 to 1970. This produced very important benefits. But it is also important to say that it produced an important skew in the distribution of the benefits. The wealthier countries – the OECD group – got much more out of this growth than many developing countries, although it is also true that a small group of developing countries, mostly in East Asia, benefited greatly too (Stubbs and Underhill, 2005).

In the 1950s and 1960s, the global financial system was also anxious to maintain stable exchange rates. The Bretton Woods System tried to guarantee 'fixed but flexible' exchange rates by linking the value of all major currencies to that of the dollar. The IMF acted to support governments when they could not keep rates fixed. The US Treasury also in effect acted as an important international player. This was seen as desirable because it provided predictability for investors and stability to boost trade. It worked well for twenty years, but was dependent on the stability of the dollar. In the later 1960s, the dollar lost value due to domestic inflation and the costs of the US international role. The US government lost its willingness to support stable exchange rates if it would cause deflation and unemployment at home. In 1970–71, the Nixon Administration abandoned the system, a unilateral move which caused enormous disruption for a short time. The phenomenon of rising deposits of dollars in banks outside the United States, known as Eurodollars, encouraged this decision. But the rise of other currencies and economies was bringing the dollar's dominance to an end, and the new system of flexible exchange rates proved more workable than had been thought. Some countries developed currency collaboration, including several different structures in the European Union before the decision to develop a common currency, the euro, at the end of the 1990s. But the system of flexible exchange rates, which still exists, has proved durable. One main effect has been that, on the whole, exchange rate policy has become depoliticised, and attention has focussed on other financial problems. But exchange rate instability remains a potential problem, evidenced today by concerns about the continuing relative rise in China's currency and the relative decline in the value of the dollar long term. We cannot rule out a future major currency crisis, marking shifts in global financial power between major players as in the past, but flexibility has tended to create markets where adjustment happens more gradually rather than in sudden shocks (Sinclair and Thomas, 2001).

EXAMPLE BOX

Credit creation

In most national economic systems, it is lawful only for banks or the government to create credit. Other financial institutions – funds of different kinds, insurance companies, investment houses' hedge funds and so on – can trade in money and credit and financial instruments which represent them, but cannot *create* money or credit. Governments have the power of credit creation as the issuers of legal money – they can decide how much to issue at any time in order to balance the need to grow the economy and control inflation. But when government-backed currency collapses other forms of money may be introduced – ranging from the currencies of other countries (often dollars, as in Zimbabwe in the late 2000s, and much of Central Asia after the collapse of the USSR in the 1990s) to cigarettes and silk stockings (in Germany in the mid 1920s and again in 1945–49), to almost anything else where people trusted its value more than that of formal money. In desperate food crises, food too, including international aid supplies, have acted as currency. This is obviously harmful since it encourages the hoarding rather than the distribution of the food.

Credit is most often created when a bank lends out more than it has taken in deposits. This is normal banking behaviour, because bankers know that at any one time their customers will only require back a proportion of the money they have put in the bank. If this 'normal' behaviour changes, because customers lose confidence in the bank or the currency, it causes a 'run on the bank', where customers demand all their deposits back at once. Governments normally in effect insure the banks against this by acting as 'lender of last resort', being willing to cover a run on the bank, but at interest rates high enough to discourage the banks from abusing their right to create credit. In both British and American law (and in other legal systems too), banks' rights to create credit are very specifically defined, with some banks having greater independence than others, and, as noted above, non-bank financial institutions having no right to create credit. On international markets, however, they may be able to find ways of getting round that restriction. This weakness of regulation was a factor – although not the principal cause – of the 2007–2009 crisis.

Capital ratios are created when governments impose limits on how much money banks can create by requiring them to keep liquid assets (things that they can use in a crisis to pay demands for money – cash, short-term debt, gold) in accounts in the national bank, and by requiring them to hold a percentage of the credit they issue as liquid assets themselves. This ties up bank resources so that they are restricted in the credit they can issue. Normally, careful banks would want to do this anyway. But careless or dishonest banking can threaten the banking system and the whole economy.

Measuring the amount of credit and money in an economy is a difficult and controversial art. Measuring the total amount in the world system is even more difficult. The solution has been not to arrive at a 'true' verdict', but to set accounting standards so that equivalent and comparable measures are generally used. Figures from some states, and some banks, are highly unreliable because those standards are not universally maintained.

What is the 'international debt crisis' and where did it come from?

One aspect of global finance which has been of continuing difficulty is global debt, usually meaning 'third world debt'. This emerged as a problem at the end of the 1970s (Herman, et al., 2010). At various points since Mexico defaulted on huge debts in the early 1980s, a number of countries have created enormous piles of debt which they have then either defaulted on or threatened to default on if the banks did not radically change the terms and conditions of their loans. Sometimes, as with Argentina's repeated difficulty, the main cause has been persistent government incompetence. But there are usually more complex causes, and the structure of global finance and the working of global markets have been the principal causes of much of the debt crisis.

The origins of the global debt crisis lie in the willingness of investors, some might say investors with more money than sense, to put money into bad business around the world. It is not that simple, but that is a valid starting point. At various points in the history of international finance, good money has gone down a great many bad drains. In the 1840s and 1850s, waves of investment poured into railway companies. Most of the original rail businesses went bankrupt because they were badly run or over-ambitious (or both) and some were merely scams to attract investment and steal it. The railway boom only came to fruition when much more carefully run second-generation companies came to expand the market after the initial boom and bust. This pattern was so closely repeated in the biotechnology boom of the 1980s and the 'dotcom' boom in Internet business in 1997–2000 that one can only wonder at the ignorance of those who supervised it (banks will pay for most senior executives to do an MBA, but few fund programmes in economic history). In the 1920s, money flowed even faster into the US stock market, whether from large investors, foreign banks or much smaller businesses, only to disappear in the 1929 Crash. In contrast in the 2000s, people with money to invest committed it to mortgage-backed securities in the belief that somehow their risk would disappear in clever mathematics. In the same way, investors put money into the developing world, especially money gathered from oil producers who grew rich in the early 1970s after the price rise of 1973. Much of this money was invested in high-return high-risk investments not in the poorest countries but in those developing countries with some natural resources or oil or strong agriculture to exploit. At the end of the 1970s, material, energy and agricultural prices collapsed. The prospects of these investments showing a return from cocoa, coffee, oil, copper or iron disappeared. Developing countries became saddled not just with large debts, but with growing interest payments they could not make. By the end of the 1980s, and ever since, many countries have faced debt repayments much greater than the total value of foreign aid and investment they received. Several attempts have been made to eliminate this debt. Some countries have found it easier to default, but the costs are great. Some countries are in effect in default, including some large ones, but it is quietly not recognised. The June 2005 Gleneagles Summit of the G8 attempted to resolve this, partly in the aftermath of huge public campaigning to reduce debt for the 2000 Millennium Development Goals, and partly because developed countries recognised that it was in their own long-term interests to have healthy growing markets in Africa and Asia. The Summit reached some important agreements, only part of which have been implemented so far. Developing-country debt remains an ongoing problem, but one positive side-effect of the recent global crisis might be that lenders might become more careful about lending too much to countries that cannot afford it.

The financial crisis of the 2000s

Suppose you are a relatively ordinary student with not much money. You borrow money from the bank or student loan authority to finance your lifestyle, run a credit card or two which maybe your parents have guaranteed and so on. If you owe, say, £6,000 (or $6,000) and the bank for whatever reason suddenly asks for its money back, you have a problem, and possibly a big problem. But suppose you manage to borrow £60 billion (don't think too much about what you might spend it on). At that point, the bank has a problem much more than you do. To lose this amount of money would not simply be a poor image on a balance sheet. It could well threaten the bank's survival, and in turn it might also threaten a national banking system. This is a part of what happened between August 2007 and August 2008 in the Western banking system, when banks found themselves with huge piles of debt, including bonds they had bought at high prices in boom years that had become worthless. The American banking system in particular nearly collapsed because of debts backed by mortgages on houses and land. The British banking system was also threatened, but less so because there was relatively less bad debt, but there was enough to cause a serious crisis. The globalised creation of credit rested on trust in the system as a whole and in its fragmented regulators, including central banks, credit rating agencies, underwriters, banking associations and other market managers. This trust proved to be mistaken. The incentives to drive ahead in creating new financial instruments, including the infamous mortgage-backed securities (and CDOs), outweighed the caution bankers might have felt in dealing with risk in new and very complex ways. Banks had become used to building deals on the back of heavy borrowing from other banks, highly leveraged deals. When, suddenly in August 2008 banks ceased to trust this inter-bank market and stopped lending in it, they equally found it impossible to borrow from it. They could not refinance existing deals, never mind create new ones. For a period of time, much conventional banking activity stopped, until government intervention gradually refuelled the system.

It is often said that the crisis began suddenly and unpredictably with problems in the housing and mortgage sector which were evident in August 2007. But some US and British finance businesses reported warnings about the level of risk they had on their books in January and February 2007. Few people took these as warnings of a systemic problem at the time, but it is clear with hindsight that there was a systemic problem across the structure of world debt markets, and a number of commentators had pointed this out well before August 2007. After then, it was probably too late. By August 2008, banks almost completely stopped lending to each other – the inter-bank lending market collapsed and inter-bank lending rates, when it was possible to get a loan at all, soared through the ceiling. The origins of the crisis have been found in (i) bankers' greed and the bonus system, (ii) excessive debt in both governments and societies, (iii) the globalisation of capitalism and the growth of a global system of credit creation which regulators cannot control in principle, (iv) a failure of central banks to do their core job of managing the banking sector because they trusted the banks to behave, or because they shared the same values as the bankers, (v) a failure of credit rating agencies to issue effective revaluation of debts as it became clear that some of them were toxic and many of them much riskier than their face-value rating suggested, (vi) a failure to implement effectively a set of rules which would work pretty effectively if made to work properly, and (vii) capital markets experience cyclical collapse – there was nothing much new in the crisis except that the exact date when it happened was not predictable (Cooper, 2008).

It was indeed government intervention that saved the banking system. Governments in the United States, UK, the Eurozone and Asia pumped huge amounts of funding in the form of newly created credit into the global system. If they had not done so the entire fabric of Western banking and finance would quite probably have collapsed. But doing so runs the risk of leaving an inheritance of high debts into the future. The calculation was always that present stability was necessary despite future risks, which could be managed in due course. Some banks were allowed to collapse, including the long-established Lehman Brothers in the US. Others were in effect nationalised. This was not wholly strange in countries with a tradition of nationalisation, including Britain and Germany, but in the US it was a radical step which provoked great political opposition. However, with the hindsight of a further year, it is clear that this action was helpful and saved the core elements of the financial system from meltdown. There are future risks, but a short-term catastrophe was avoided – fairly narrowly.

```
EXAMPLE BOX
```

Three countries in the 2007–2009 crisis

Iceland

Icelandic banks had initiated a strategy of borrowing large sums to finance investment and activity around the world over the previous twenty years. This was a strategy of highly leveraged growth – largely dependent on borrowing to finance the deals. This also encouraged other Icelandic firms in retail, marketing and services to do the same. At the onset of the crisis in 2007, it was not clear to bank managers that the world of easily available cheap credit was coming to an end, and they failed to act to cut back on the borrowing – it may already have been too late anyway. When the full force of the crisis hit in 2008, the banks went bust and the government was unable to protect them. It was too small and too indebted itself to act as effective lender of last resort. The banks had borrowed too much, and so had the Reykjavik government. Much of Iceland's economy effectively became owned by foreign banks and governments, mainly in the European Union, which helped it keep afloat. The Icelandic economy suffered a severe shock with high unemployment as well as a loss of prestige forcing the country to give up on its much-prized position outside the EU. In its new dependent relationship it makes much more sense to join the EU. This is seen as necessary, but is hardly popular.

Turkey

Turkey was also highly dependent on global finance in 2007. The financial shock and the collapse of demand for world trade in 2008 were severely felt. Turkey experienced a much higher unemployment rate and GDP fall than EU member states. Banks which were generally highly internationalised survived, but in a slimmed down form. The government introduced tighter structured capital ratio requirements to protect the system. Turkey did nothing especially wrong – certainly nothing different from many others – before or in the crisis, but has paid a high price for doing what many others did.

Lebanon

The Lebanese central bank had introduced a high capital ratio (30 per cent) long before 2007 because the political instability of the country, further threatened after the Israeli invasion in 2006, undermined the banking system. Although it was not intentional, Lebanese banks were in a very strong position to weather the storm of 2007–2009. Their relative stability brought in a sudden flow of further funds looking for a safe haven in a storm. This helped the prestige of the country and affirmed that of its banking system. It also pushed currency values up, which in theory would weaken Lebanese exports because it pushes up their prices. But so much of Lebanese economic activity internally and externally is done in other currencies that it had limited real impact. The Lebanese have, relatively speaking, done better out of the 2007–2009 crisis than any other economy except perhaps China.

Global financial institutions

The global financial system is characterised by some important institutions. Some are very well known; some are powerful but hardly discussed in the media and little known. Some are private, some public, and some in effect cut across the public/private distinction.

The International Monetary Fund: originally created to manage international exchange rate stability in the post-1944 Bretton Woods System. The IMF has become a major actor both in coordinating aspects of financial policy and in acting as lender of last resort to governments, a role it was originally not intended to have. Power in the IMF depends on the money states put in – the more they contribute, the more weighting their votes have. As the mix of leading contributors has changed, the balance of power has changed, but the US (the leading contributor and thus the state which has the most voting power/influence with an almost 17 percent voting quota) and EU (made up of other leading contributors) continue to dominate the IMF despite the rise of China and Saudi Arabia as contributors, at least so long as they agree together.

The World Bank: the World Bank was originally called the International Bank for Reconstruction and Development. That title is a better representation of its main roles, which provide funding for development and guidelines and studies on what makes for effective development. The World Bank was powerfully shaped by the so-called 'Washington Consensus' in the 1980s and 1990s, cooperating with the IMF and US Treasury in imposing a neo-liberal agenda on the organisation. But by the late 1990s, in response to continuing crises in the developing world as well as changes in the Clinton administration in the US, the WB moved somewhat apart from the IMF and the nature of the Washington Consensus shifted and became less dictatorially neo-liberal. The WB's anti-poverty programmes have become a distinctive instrument of funding for development.

Perhaps confusingly, we should note that, in most respects, the World Bank acts as a fund, and the IMF acts as a bank. The IMF does not have the independent credit creation powers of most banks – it depends on the direct authorisation of participating governments, and is not a credit creation agency in the way that governments and international banks are; but with the specific authorisation of governments it can create credit through its loans, and it has done so in the recent past.

The Bank for International Settlements: one of the least known and least understood of global financial institutions. Important not least because central bankers meet more regularly than anywhere else through the BIS. It therefore acts as an effective coordinator even when it is not trying to act as an enforcement body. Its primary function is to act as a clearing house for international payments between governments and central banks – hence its title. But it has become a main tool of international economic cooperation on finance, and has developed a series of tools on capital ratios (the Basle 2 Agreements) which may bring greater stability to international banking if and when they are fully implemented.

The Organisation for Economic Cooperation and Development: the OECD has no executive role over global finance but is an important source of cooperation and policy coordination. It has also been a source of proposals for the management of global trade in services, which would include banking, finance and insurance, and which, if ever implemented, would bring much greater liberalisation to global markets. These proposals are, however, frozen, widely opposed by developing countries.

The G7/G8: founded in 1974 on a French initiative, the G7 was established as a coordinating body to deal with global financial and economic crises after the 1970 dollar and 1973–4 oil crises. Its members are the US, Japan, Canada, France, Italy, the UK and Germany. Russia was later added as the eighth member. The G7 has been widely criticised, and it has sometimes tried to do much more than proved possible in managing financial issues such as responses to the decline in value of the dollar in the 1980s. It has also vastly broadened its agenda to include security, environment, development and so on. This is mainly because the institution has a semi-permanent and very efficient secretariat which has been able to institutionalise the process of agenda setting and issue negotiation.

The G20: the G20 is a much more recent body. As of September 2009, after the Pittsburgh Summit, it has in effect replaced the G7. This gives it a more effective secretariat, wide agenda-setting powers and some executive authority. It includes the leading developing countries, Brazil, China, Indonesia, India and Saudi Arabia, as well as all the G8 members. Africa is seriously unrepresented in the G20, as are other smaller states and non-state movements. But it has the ability to represent core world financial actors. It is too early to evaluate whether the G20 will succeed in the missions it set itself at Pittsburgh, but no other body has the authority or power to do what it is attempting.

Governments and government-led bodies jointly manage the global financial system through agencies such as the IMF, the G20 and BIS. The United Nations as an institution has no overall role, but the IMF and World Bank are UN specialised agencies, although almost entirely independent of the main UN structures. Private actors also play key roles in regulation of global finance.

Leading accountancy firms: accounting firms not only report on the financial health of all businesses, including finance houses and banks; they also set the standards for reporting. In general these standards are adopted by national regulators. Increasingly, the four major worldwide accounting firms and their subsidiaries form a powerful oligopoly which dominates the setting of financial standards. They are, with 2008 turnover in brackets, PriceWaterhouse Coopers (PwC) ($28bn), KPMG ($27bn), Deloitte Touche Tomatsu ($27bn), and Ernst and Young ($24bn). They also do a great deal of consulting and management work which goes well beyond a basic accounting function, and allegedly sometimes clashes with their interests as auditors. They are a relatively hidden power in the global financial system – there is much less IPE research on their role than, for example, on that of the CRAs (see below). They are of roughly similar size – necessary to compete with each other effectively. But their size, and prestige and regulatory role effectively shuts out others – their combined turnover ($106bn) is considerably greater than that of the next 30 leading world accounting firms. It is their role as standard setters which is authoritative, as well as their role in transmitting management cultures and styles. They are key agents of globalisation in the 180 countries in which (separately) they have subsidiaries.

Underwriters: underwriters are institutions which perform the specialist role of backing share and debt (bond) issues. This means they help to value the asset, promote it, and give it the backing of their prestige. When the asset is sold, they have agreed to buy up any unsold stock or debt. If the sale is successful, their commitment is not called on. If the asset fails in the market, they are left with a pile of commercial paper which is going to be hard to sell. In effect, therefore, they act as insurers of new financial products. Mostly, underwriters are banks that have a specialist underwriting division alongside the other business they do. Thus banks in, say, New York or Frankfurt may be acting as insurers of each other's debt sales. Whether this is harmful or not depends on the quality of regulation. Underwriting emerged as a practice in the London markets in the nineteenth century, but is now a worldwide practice, and an important element in the working of financial markets.

Academic standard setters: global finance has its own qualifications, some more widely recognised than others. Mostly, people working in global finance have – or acquire – qualifications in law or accountancy or both. Many have MBAs. But the MBA may be worth quite different things in different countries. The CFA (Chartered Financial Analyst) qualification has become a standardised measure of academic ability in world finance, and it is pretty much impossible to get a job in a number of markets – notably Singapore – without one. The more the system has globalised the more globally recognised qualifications have become a passport to work and a measure of quality. Neither the MBA nor the CFA are innocent technical qualifications. They incorporate an element of ethics, and act as a means of communicating shared standards and practices – it is an acculturation as much as a technical award.

Credit rating agencies: Tim Sinclair and Kimberley Corwin (2008), among others, have, through research over nearly twenty years, shown how important the credit rating agencies have become in the global financial system, at least up to 2008. Credit rating agencies are independent companies which make judgements about firms and governments by rating their debt. In other words, they make a judgement about the riskiness of the bonds they issue – are they a good risk or not? If they are a very good risk, they carry a 'triple A' rating. This means they have a high status, but also that they will pay less to borrow money. If a firm or bank loses its rating, for example downgraded from 'triple A' to 'double A', there are several consequences, including a loss of prestige and almost certainly serious damage to the share price, but also an increase in the costs of borrowing money into the future. Exactly the same happens with countries – government debt, 'sovereign debt', is rated by the agencies, and if they are able to maintain a high rating, the rates they pay to borrow money are lower and their status as trustworthy is reinforced. All this is done by three businesses which are independent of any regulation other than normal company law. They are based in New York and in London, but together act as a global regulator of great importance. Sinclair has argued that they are the only effective regulatory force in the global creation of credit which has been so important in the last twenty years. They rate bonds and debt instruments – specific financial products – rather than the firm or government as a whole, but inevitably their power is seen as a power to award ratings like stars to leading pupils or films in the popular and media mind.

The credit rating agencies are, however, commercial businesses. They act for the firms and governments which they rate. They charge a fee. If a bank launches a new bond, it invites a rating agency to classify it, and if it doesn't like the outcome, at least in theory, it might ask another for a different judgement (although mostly the four agencies follow each other closely). The credit rating agencies thus appear to have a conflict of interest – do they serve the interests of the rated bond-issuing firm, the market or customers of the bonds rated? The conflict of interest is, however, illusory. Rating agencies did not choose the role of global regulator which they have evolved, and their first duty is to their shareholders, and their secondary duty is to their customers.

Summary

Let's draw together the key elements of the discussion so far:

1. International economic activity creates a demand for money – finance for trade, aid, investment, payment of debts, goods, services, holidays.
2. Some currencies are seen as more reliable than others, and trade tends to take place valued in those currencies.
3. All money has two functions: it acts as a store of value and as a medium of exchange. These two roles are not always compatible, for many reasons, but most simply because as a medium of exchange its value will change depending on the demand and supply for money, whereas those who use it as a store of value want it to hold the same value over time and will turn to other forms of value storing, such as buying land or gold, if they cannot be confident it will at least hold its value.
4. Capital is not merely 'money'; it is money invested for a particular purpose, bearing particular kinds of risks and carrying a particular reward – profit (which accountants often call return on investment, or ROI).

5   In the contemporary economy, money takes many different forms, not just cash in your pocket. These include credit card borrowing and other loans. It also includes credit created by both banks and governments. Measuring the total amount of money in an economy is quite a contentious business, and economists do not agree on how to do it; but they do have different measures for different purposes. Measuring the total amount of assets (money + equipment + land + other resources) held by a firm is a matter of accounting conventions as well as of simply adding up. Measuring the amount of money in the world economy is even more difficult since a lot of credit creation occurs across borders, and the conventions globally are not so clear cut. At different times and in different places, 'money' has included gold bars, human beings (slaves), conch shells, cocaine and cigarettes. Now most money in the world system is paper money, which has no intrinsic value (no value in itself or of itself) other than the confidence which markets put in the institutions and governments which issue it.

6   Credit is value created by issuing promises to pay later. All credit is in some way linked to debt. So markets for credit are also markets for debt – most often in the form of government and corporate bonds which are bought and sold on specialist markets. The value of credit depends on the confidence markets have in the capacity and willingness of governments to redeem their promises later. Sovereign debt is debt owed by governments, which can default on their promises to pay much more easily (but not without a considerable cost) than individuals or firms.

7   Complex markets are regulated by a complex system of governance in which no one major agency has control. This system of governance necessarily involves a range of stakeholders. Although sovereign governments have strong powers in this area, they cannot act unless they both agree among themselves and carry the support of markets and leading market actors. The 2007–2009 crisis has called this system of governance into question, and it is in need of revision. But that revision is more likely to be a set of developments and refinements than a major transformatory reform.

This chapter has explored the nature of the global financial system as a group of interrelated markets for money, financial products, debt and insurance. It has stressed the complex nature of governance of the system – regulation is dominated by some major actors, but not all of them are states. International institutions such as the IMF and BIS are important, and the G20 is clearly of growing significance. The largest firms and banks not only play roles in the market as buyers and sellers; they also support each other's dealing, buy shares in each other and act as underwriters for major deals. In some cases, they play crucial roles as regulators – they define the rules and standards for the system as a whole. The interplay of public (state) and private regulation has become an important theme across IPE theory as well as in empirical studies in the last decade or more. It is nowhere more important than in finance.

Reflective questions

1   To what extent is the contemporary financial system rooted in developments stretching back to the fourteenth and fifteenth centuries?

2   What was the impact of the Allied victory in the Second World War on establishing the structure of the globalised financial system?

3   Was the financial crisis of 2007–2009 unique or are there historical examples of similar financial crises? If so, can we say that these types of crisis are built into the modern world of finance?

4   Do international and global institutions manage the financial system or do we live in a liberalised economic environment where financial management is not possible?

Suggestions for further reading

Cable, V. (2009) *The Storm: The World Economic Crisis and What It Means*, London: Atlantic Books.

Cooper, G. (2008) *The Origin of Financial Crises: Central Banks, Credit Bubbles and the Efficient Market Fallacy*, Petersfield: Harriman House Publishing.

Herman, B., Ocampo, J.A. and Spiegel, S. (eds) (2010) *Overcoming Developing Country Debt Crises*, Oxford: Oxford University Press.

International Monetary Fund, *World Economic Outlook – Crisis and Recovery*, April 2009, Washington: IMF.

Parks, T. (2006) *Medici Money: Banking, Metaphysics and Art in Fifteenth Century Florence*, London: Profile Business.

Sinclair, T. and Corwin, K. (2008) *The New Masters of Capital: American Bond Rating Agencies and the Politics of Creditworthiness*, Ithaca: Cornell University Press.

Sinclair, T. and Thomas, K. (eds) (2001) *Structure and Agency in International Capital Mobility*, Basingstoke: Palgrave Macmillan.

Strange, S. (1997) *Casino Capitalism*, Manchester: Manchester University Press.

Strange, S. (1998) *Mad Money*, Manchester: Manchester University Press.

Stubbs, R. and Underhill, G. (eds) (2005) *Political Economy and the Changing Global Order*, 3rd edn, Canada: OUP.

8 Development

Chapter learning outcomes

After reading this chapter students should be able to:

- Comprehend contemporary definitions of the concept of development.
- Explain what liberal modernisation is and how it is seen by many as the key to achieving development.
- Understand and be able to analyse the 'development problem'.
- Understand the UN Millennium Development Goals, how they are being pursued and how progress towards achieving them is going.
- Analyse the agency of the major state and non-state actors involved in pursuing development internationally/globally.
- Discuss examples of major development projects found around the world.
- Relate discussion of development to theoretical debates discussed earlier in this book.

Introduction

This chapter considers the position of development in the world economy. The contested nature of the term is highlighted and the historical understandings are outlined in the first section. The shift towards a neo-liberal orthodoxy in development is discussed and the impact of salient issues such as sustainability, foreign aid and the debt crisis are highlighted.

Mainstream economists predominantly think of development in terms of overall GDP and rates of GDP per capita. A more holistic view of development, however, can be found in the UN's Human Development Index which expands the criteria for the definition of development to include the distribution of wealth throughout societies. Health indicators, such as rates of infant mortality, life expectancy and rates of death, are also considered. Similarly, social indicators, including literacy rates, gender equality and access to secondary and higher education, are seen as key features of development. The development discourse operates at many levels featuring many actors with various, sometimes competing, agendas. These can be broadly summarised as those which favour a 'top-down', economic growth-driven version of development and those more interested in establishing a firm foundation of environmental and social sustainability upon which economic growth can prosper.

Within development discourse there are numerous ideological approaches which encompass views on the political, economic, socio-cultural and environmental dimensions of development. The latter half of the twentieth century was dominated by the confrontation between the United States and the USSR and their respective allies. This can broadly be represented as the division between the capitalist and communist political economic approaches. The early 1970s saw a growing awareness of environmental issues which fed into the debate on what truly constituted 'development'. In the post-Cold War era there has been growing awareness and discussion of world views that are not wholly driven by economic growth as an end in itself. Such views can have an explicitly religious or spiritual dimension, seeing development as the attainment of spiritual purity. In addition to differing conceptions of development there are also differing methodologies and prescriptions as to how to achieve such development.

Fukuyama's *End of History* thesis (referred to previously) explains the end of the Cold War as well as the triumph of liberalism. While having some convincing elements to his argument, it fails to address social and environmental development issues. Below, we first discuss the dominant model of neo-liberal development theories, followed by critiques of this approach.

Liberal modernisation

Central to the liberal perspective is an attempt to theorise and explain issues of economic disparity between states. The end of the Cold War witnessed the formulation of a new geographical political map as many states broke away from the USSR and gained independent status. Many scholars turned their attention away from 'high politics' and began to theorise about economic development. The North/South divide is a geographical term which distinguishes the rich developed North from the poor underdeveloped South. This line of division is not, however, straightforward; splitting the world into two hemispheres is too simplistic. Australia and New Zealand are situated in the southern hemisphere but are essentially rich developed countries. On the other hand, the supposedly rich North includes relatively poor countries such as Turkey and Albania. Despite these inconsistencies the term North/South divide has become an understandable shorthand. It is widely used to explain the distribution of wealth, poverty and decision-making capacities of states in the international arena. It is worth recognising here that there are commonalities in these regional groupings, for example states located in the North have all gone through the process of industrialisation whereas states in the South have all experienced political and economic domination, many acting as colonies to the North. Liberal modernisation is a perspective which seeks to account for the slow economic progress of 'Third World countries'.

CONCEPT BOX

Development terminologies in IPE

The term Third World stems from Cold War terminology and the idea that there were two mutually hostile power blocs and a third which did not align to either superpower; hence, 'three worlds' were depicted. The First World referred to the capitalist market economy states, such as in Western Europe, North America and Australia and Japan. The Second World to the communist/socialist centrally directed economies of Eastern Europe, China, North Korea and Cuba. The 'Third World' was then a residual term which referred to the poorest regions of the world such as parts of Africa and Asia and Latin America. Some have pointed to the possibility of a 'Fourth World'. This includes indigenous populations of the world. Many contemporary writers have pointed to the inadequacies of this 'three world' model, arguing that there exists one world. By using this term it implies that these countries are not a part of the global economic system. What to call poor states is much contested and some prefer 'developing countries' or 'least/lesser developed countries' (LDCs). Some dislike the term developing as it implies that liberal economic development (industrialisation) is the only way forward. Also, the term 'majority world' has been applied in some academic perspectives. What terminology to employ often stems from personal or political preference; however, arguing over terminology does not alter the fact that the gulf between rich and poor continues to grow.

Walt W. Rostow was a leading academic and American policy adviser, who formulated a controversial thesis on development. His book *The Stages of Economic Growth: A Non-Communist Manifesto* (1960) was in stark contrast to Marxist-inspired approaches. Rostow was explicit in his rejection of state interventionist command economy ideas. He outlined how and advocated that in order for lesser developed regions to progress they should industrialise and develop their economies along the same lines as Western liberal economies.

The stages of development theory gained momentum in post-Second World War economics as many formerly colonised states began to gain their independence. This theory was primarily concerned with developing these newly independent nations and development was based on the Western model that industrialisation and market-driven economies are key to a flourishing and successful national economy. As suggested by the title, the theory of stages of growth was an alternative to Marx's theory of social evolution. Rostow argued that underdeveloped economies should follow the path of the industrialised states; in short, they should industrialise. Rostow argued that all the industrialised states had followed the same path and witnessed the same historical stages of development; underdeveloped states were just at an earlier stage on this developmental path. This developmental path is linear and progressive and once states had reached a certain point in this linear path, economies would just 'take off'. An example of how 'take off' can be achieved is given in Rostow's explanation of the different stages of development.

The stages of development fit into five distinct categories. The first of these stages is traditional societies; these are subsistence economies. An example of a subsistence economy would be an agricultural one in which economic product is consumed by producers or bartered rather than sold in a cash-based economy. In agricultural economies labour is intensive, jobs are carried out by hand or animal as opposed to mechanised forms of production. This meant that a ceiling existed on the level of attainable output (tradable produce) per head. Traditional economies could not reach the levels of tradable produce to participate in emerging global markets, thus having limited quantities of capital and not achieving industrialisation.

The second stage of Rostow's developmental model is labelled the 'pre-conditions for take off'. In this stage traditional societies need to create a surplus for trading and this is achieved by industrialising old methods of working, for example technology and machinery is incorporated into agriculture. The infrastructure of the society needs to be built up to support the new industrialised industries, for example roads need to be built in order to secure the easy movement of goods and services. Also, healthcare and schooling sectors need to be built and developed to serve the new workforce. Another important part of this stage is the emergence of entrepreneurs, banks and other institutions which mobilise capital. This stage of development is also referred to as the transitional stage. Rostow argued that traditional societies coexisted with the pre-conditional societies and no time frame was given as to when societies would reach the third stage, which is 'take off'.

In this third stage industrialisation massively increases, with workers switching from land to manufacturing industries, and economic growth is regionalised into a few regions of the country. Cities are established and new political institutions and social institutions evolve to support the industrial economies. 'Take off' is fully achieved when old traditional societies and ways of doing things have been eradicated and modern society becomes the norm. During 'take off' new industries expand, rapid profits are gained, trade relationships are established, and social and political structures are transformed in such a way that steady growth can be maintained.

The fourth stage in this linear process is called the drive to maturity; this means that technological innovation continues to flourish. The entrepreneur class continues to grow, capital is accumulated and 'take off' is sustained with continual steady growth. The last stage is high mass consumption societies; this is where emphasis is on consumption and industry is centred on the consumer society. America and Western Europe have achieved this fifth stage of development, where branded clothes and innovative technology such as the Ipod and wireless Internet access have become the 'must haves'. Industry is always driving towards creating new ideas which the consumer will desire.

However, Rostow's view is based on observations and interpretations of previous economic developments. It does not necessarily follow that future developments would evolve in the same context or follow the same patterns. This approach is seen as deterministic and overly rigid in its predictive nature. It must also be acknowledged that states have not been able to follow Rostow's path to development. His theory presupposes that states operate in the international arena as isolated units; for him there are no systemic forces that prevent or hinder the development process. This view does not take into account structural obstacles to development such as the hierarchical nature of the international arena. Also, Rostow's argument is too simplistic in his assumption that all industrialised economies followed the same path. Rostow could be accused of Western-centrism as he devised the five stages of growth based on observations of the West, and from his title (a 'non-communist manifesto') it is clear that his study is an ideologically motivated blow, struck at the height of the Cold War. If we analysed the most high-performing countries in GDP per head terms since his work was published, which are the East Asia Tiger economies, including South Korea, Taiwan, Malaysia and more recently China, we would find that none were open liberal market economies which combined free markets with open democratic institutions: all of them have been powerfully centralised states with managed industrial growth and very distinctive patterns of human capital by comparison with other developing countries. Their attachment to managed trade and state control of labour markets is hardly a liberal model, but it is perfectly true that they have passed in quick time through the stages of growth. This does not mean that modernising development cannot work; but it is very hard to find contemporary examples which actually fit the narrative Rostow offers.

Nonetheless, Rostow's model can be seen as an orthodox approach to liberal development and still, with adaptation, forms the basis of much liberal development thought. Later development theorists have been critical of Rostow's work, seeing it as too deterministic. The failure of Rostow's model led liberal modernists to re-evaluate their position on processes of modernisation. However, the underlying principles of liberal development and the need for lesser developed states to modernise their economies is still adhered to and modernisation theorists have developed a more refined set of economic principles which are known as the 'Washington Consensus'. This Consensus was a list of economic policy reforms which, it was thought, Latin American states should adopt in order to develop. The principles were later applied to Eastern European countries and also to African and South Asian states.

CONCEPT BOX

The Washington Consensus

John Williamson is credited with coining the phrase Washington Consensus. Below are the ten policy reforms he identified as representing the preferred policy options promoted by the Washington-based financial institutions of the World Bank and the International Monetary Fund.

- Fiscal discipline.
- A redirection of public expenditure priorities towards fields offering both high economic returns and the potential to improve income distribution, such as primary healthcare, primary education, and infrastructure.
- Tax reform (to lower marginal rates and broaden the tax base).
- Interest rate liberalisation.
- A competitive exchange rate.
- Trade liberalisation.
- Liberalisation of inflows of foreign direct investment.
- Privatisation.
- Deregulation (to abolish barriers to entry and exit).
- Secure property rights for key political groups.

Source: Williamson (1990).

The Washington Consensus was an attempt to move away from a tradition of development loans and a move towards linking loans to specific conditions set by the financial institutions of the developed world. The implementation of the Washington Consensus is most clearly illustrated in the promotion of so-called Structural Adjustment Programmes (SAPs).

Neo-liberal ideas point to the positive nature and aspects of such a system; for example, states and non-state actors and individuals share a common interest and aspire to the same liberal economic goals. This idea has been conceptualised and developed due to the advent of communications technology which has enabled greater connectivity between individuals and societies. Also, the movement and flow of consumer goods and the spread of ideas, including mass consumerism, have begun to breakdown cultural divisions and draw the world into what Marshal McLuhan called the 'global village'. However, this conception has been criticised by both realist and Marxist-inspired theories as not all states and individuals share a common goal; for example, Islamic states and individuals, North Korea and to some extent China do not share 'Western' liberal 'common values'. This idea of the international society has also been criticised due to the fact that only rich industrialised states have access to advanced technologies. This has led Anthony Giddens to reinterpret McLuhan's global village into what he describes as 'global pillage' (for a fuller discussion of these ideas, see Chapter 4).

Neo-liberal agendas are also concerned with the diverse processes that characterise the emerging global economy. These include: flows and patterns of trade and resource use; movement of goods and services; technology transfer; technological 'leap-frogging' and knowledge diffusion; the evolution and implementation of international property rights, patenting laws and bio-piracy. Moreover, the formation and management of international regimes and processes of conflict and cooperation are included.

The value of foreign aid as a tool for development has been widely debated. Liberals have tended to promote aid as a useful means of achieving development goals, at least if targeted and managed well. Neo-liberals and structuralists have both criticised aid, the former because they claim it distorts the working of markets and the latter because they see aid as a form of hegemonic domination or, more succinctly, 'aid as imperialism' (Hayter, 1971). Foreign aid is distinct from aid for emergency relief (which most people agree has great value). There is plenty of evidence that foreign aid cannot be the main cause of growth, and its advocates today would argue that it is an adjunct to effective domestic capital formation and the creation of a skills or knowledge base (through education and training). Aid contributes to growth, they would suggest, rather than being its primary cause. Over the last twenty years, aid programmes have been restructured to meet those objectives by Japan, the European Union, the US and major international institutions. But this has not removed the criticisms of those who retain their fundamental objections to aid. One powerfully argued version of this is the debate between two recently published and widely discussed alternative accounts of development. Moyo (2009) advocates a version of the established Washington Consensus in her rejection of most foreign development aid practice, holding firmly to the view that aid distorts markets and undermines domestic capital formation even if it is not encumbered by corruption. Joseph and Gillies (2008) defend the argument that, if given with focus, attention to the context, attention to human development needs and care to avoid corruption, development aid can be 'smart' and effective. This is an argument which has circulated for at least forty years, but which is worth careful attention. What we might also note is the extent to which development issues have vanished from political agendas – in the 2010 British General Election, all the main parties were committed to protect foreign aid and development spending even if other financial cuts were necessary, while in other countries debates about the value of development assistance in whatever form have also been muted in the 2000s.

The development problem

Despite the lessening of political attention, the 'development problem' in IPE is a complex and heavily debated issue. Within liberal economic thought, development is equated with poverty reduction by way of economic growth. However, where growth has occurred it has rarely been accompanied by the so-called 'trickle-down' effect whereby the benefits of such growth reach all sectors of society. A more likely scenario is the accumulation of wealth among the elite and upper middle classes. Structuralists point to this in terms of clear class-based divisions of wealth, where wealthy and relatively Europeanised elites have the ability to reproduce their social and economic power over or against poorer and often indigenous communities. In addition to this division of wealth, there is a further criticism that can be made of mainstream development approaches. The accumulation of capital can be argued to be based on a false premise. This refers to the lack of acknowledgement of the hidden, or overlooked, social and environmental costs that occur in the pursuit of economic growth. Poor working conditions, environmental pollution and non-sustainable resource use are not generally taken into account when assessing indicators of development. The evolution of multi-centred points of production and consumption also add to the difficulty of monitoring and taking into account such costs. On the contrary, the dominant model of development is to rely on market forces free from political oversight and legislation. Without social and environmental costs being factored into the market value of particular goods and services, the imagined benefits of economic growth are liable to contain more negative aspects. Structuralists tend towards a more encompassing view than many other approaches to the study of IPE. The degree to which relevant factors are acknowledged in determining indicators of development goes to the heart of the development problem.

EXAMPLE BOX

The 'development' of Nauru

Nauru is a small island state in the South Pacific. For many years its economy has been based on the mining and export of phosphate (used in the production of fertilisers). Originally this operation was controlled by Britain and then Australia. Nauru achieved political independence in 1968. Successive Nauruan governments have continued to rely upon this export income, despite the known environmental costs the mining was inflicting on the island. At the height of phosphate export Nauruans had one of the world's highest rates of GDP per capita. However, this situation could not be sustained and as the phosphate deposits have been mined out the Nauruan economy has faced a sharp decline. The majority of the land area has been stripped of its surface soil and the rocky outcrops that remain are unsuitable for crop production, even for basic subsistence. Nauruans are now heavily dependent on importing foodstuffs and other goods, while simultaneously having decreased purchasing power for such imports. 'Development' in economic terms has come at the cost of the local environment and also social costs as many Nauruans are now leaving the island to seek employment and improved lifestyles in other countries.

The above example demonstrates two significant aspects of the development problem. First, it shows how economic growth in itself is only one aspect of development. Second, the Nauruan economy post-independence was tied into a form of production and export-led growth that made it very difficult for the newly 'independent' government to diversify its economy and move away from colonial era reliance on the export of a single commodity, albeit one of a limited and finite nature (IBP USA, 2009). Nauru's experience may be seen as an extreme case but it is illustrative of how this small island state is tied into a wider global economy. The historical evolution of the Nauruan economy has clearly had a lasting impact on the options and choices made by subsequent Nauruan governments.

The above section has outlined the predominant (economics-based) development model and the problems that can arise from this. The following section looks at a response to this at the level of the UN.

Millennium Development Goals

The latter part of the twentieth century saw a proliferation of international meetings and summits focusing on poverty alleviation and other development goals. The UN took the lead in organising conferences on themes including Children (New York, US, 1990); Environment and Development (Rio de Janeiro, Brazil, 1992); Human Rights (Vienna, Austria 1993); Population and Development (Cairo, Egypt, 1994); Social Development (Copenhagen, Denmark, 1995); Women (Beijing, China, 1995); Human Settlements (Istanbul, Turkey, 1996); Food (Rome, Italy, 1996). Several of these meetings established standing bodies to institutionalise ongoing negotiations to tackle the issues that were raised.

The momentum of this succession of conferences led to a meeting held at UN Headquarters in September 2000 at which the General Assembly adopted the UN Millennium Declaration. This comprised eight Millennium Development Goals (MDGs) with a timetable set out to achieve each of them by the year 2015. This represents the most ambitious development agenda ever undertaken and on an unprecedented scale. The eight goals are: (1) End Poverty and Hunger; (2) Universal Education; (3) Gender Equality; (4) Child Health; (5) Maternal Health; (6) Combat HIV/AIDS; (7) Environmental Sustainability and (8) Global Partnership. Perhaps unsurprisingly, when the midpoint of this period was passed in 2008, despite some notable progress having been made in some fields, none of the MDG agenda were being fulfilled at a rate that suggested the goals would be met in time. In part, this can be explained by a lack of commitment by the major powers to keep to their promises on overseas aid packages for the poorest nations. There were also unexpected downturns in the global economy and crises in relation to food and energy supplies. While some might argue that the MDGs were always unrealistic in their targets and timescale, it should also be recognised that conditions for development were far from ideal. The MDGs are also significant in their process: they represent a globally arrived at consensus to which pretty much all states, many NGOs and most relevant international organisations have given active consent. From a liberal point of view, this is an important step in norm building and institutionalisation, in practical action for development. From a critical theory point of view it is an important step in the consolidation of a global hegemony which, although apparently beneficial to development, embodies conceptions of development and practices of aid, trade and surveillance which box the poorest peoples and communities into acquiescing in their own domination, in liberal hegemony.

MDG 1 links two of the perennial objectives of development policies. In many ways these two areas may be seen as indivisible. It is hard to imagine one existing without the other. As outlined elsewhere in this text, there is no simple strategy for reducing poverty. Some approaches that focus on wealth creation may be effective for some sectors of society, but actively impoverish other members. For example, the push towards increased privatisation of services may offer business opportunities, but also push some of these services beyond the financial reach of some of the poorer members of a community. Equally, the increased privatisation of water or other infrastructure needs may help boost needed investment while putting the price out of reach of many of the poorest in society.

The complex relationship between poverty and hunger was graphically highlighted in the mid 1980s during the famine crisis in Ethiopia. Despite food aid being shipped to the country it was discovered that there were actually grain stores within the country that could have been drawn on but there were economic reasons why this food was not being distributed. Food aid also risks disrupting national markets with an unintended negative impact on local producers, as it had in 1984/85 in Ethiopia. In other cases a country with serious food shortages may be prioritising non-food cash crops such as tobacco, cotton or flowers in order to earn export revenue. Again, this highlights how there are complex economic factors at play at both the domestic and international levels when attempting to meet essential nutrition requirements.

In spring 2010, when clouds of volcanic ash from Iceland cut all flights around Europe for more than a week, flights of vegetables, salad crops and flowers from Kenya to Europe's supermarkets were disrupted. It was announced that this affected up to 12 per cent of jobs in Kenya, around 11 per cent of Kenyan GDP, and around 30 per cent of export earnings (BBC News, 16 April 2010). This trade is no more than ten years old, having evolved largely through the global activities of European supermarket supply chain managers. It contributes to local economic growth and makes a real difference to employment and skills. But it also impoverishes neighbouring non-exporting farms, uses much more than a fair share of available water, and has a grim carbon footprint. The majority of the profits it generates go to Western supermarkets rather than local farmers; the farmers do benefit substantially too, but given the pattern of post-colonial land ownership in Kenya, that too raises problems about who is really benefiting.

MDG 2 focuses on the provision of universal education. There are stark divides in terms of how life chances are increased, or not, depending on access to education. Even basic literacy and numeracy skills remain beyond the reach of many children and adult learners. Some advances have been made in countries such as Burundi, Ghana, Kenya, Tanzania and Uganda where the governments have abolished fees for schools in the public sector. This has led to a significant uptake in education opportunities, but with a resulting pressure on these governments to now provide sufficient teachers and school buildings of an adequate standard. Inequalities remain with a lower uptake in rural areas and a marked gender divide with girls being more likely to drop out from education. Governments are faced with the dilemma of investing in future generations while at the same time meeting the demands of current budgetary needs in other sectors of the economy. Education may well be recognised as a priority for longer-term development goals, but may be seriously restricted due to the practicalities of budgetary constraints and shorter-term priorities.

MDG 3 deals with the issue of promoting gender equality. As the UN Development Programme has repeatedly noted, roughly 70 per cent of the actual work done in developing countries is the product of female workers, although because quite a lot of that work is 'domestic' it may not be counted in GDP statistics. Women not only make the greater contribution to past growth; they also, according to the UNDP, have the greatest potential to contribute to future growth – if you seek future growth, educate and empower women. As noted above, educational opportunities are a key factor in providing for gender equality. Since the launch of the MDGs there has been a marked increase in female school enrolments. That said, there remain marked difficulties in retaining these pupils. In rural areas where water is in short supply it tends to be women and girls who can spend large parts of their day walking to fetch water for the household. Lack of water also impacts on levels of sanitation and female pupils may be reluctant to attend schools with no private toilet facilities. Cultural issues such as this extend well beyond primary school years. Many societies have hugely differing norms and expectations running along gendered lines. Even if a girl is able to access primary education, this is no guarantee that she will be able to progress to secondary or higher education, regardless of intellectual ability. Male students have greater employment opportunities and even when females are able to enter the labour market it is far more likely that this will be in low-paid jobs. One indicator of gender equality is the proportion of women holding parliamentary seats in a national government. There are only twenty countries where women hold more than 30 per cent of parliamentary seats. This gender disparity in direct involvement in political decision making is even more marked in the senior ranks of government, with even the most developed states still showing a male bias at ministerial level.

MDG 4 seeks to reduce child mortality. In reviewing this goal there are noticeable regional variations. Some parts of the world have made progress in this field but sub-Saharan Africa stands out as a problem area with very little progress having been made since 2000. Malnutrition is deemed to be the underlying cause of death for many children under five. Poor access to potable water is another major factor, which has also been linked to the need to promote breastfeeding rather than rely on powdered milk preparations. More than one-third of child deaths occur before the infants reach one month of age. This indicates that early intervention is crucial in order to increase survival rates. With targeted food and medical aid, this figure can be brought down substantially, but getting it down and keeping it down has proved a problem in areas affected by civil conflict or widespread corruption such as West Africa. Beyond this age, immunisation programmes are also important and this is a priority area for national healthcare teams. The likelihood of a child surviving is clearly influenced by the environment into which they are born. Poor sanitation, poor diet, limited water supply and the availability of healthcare support systems all play a part in determining rates of survival. This is a good example of how an integrated approach to development is required to tackle the various MDGs cited here. Although each represent distinct areas of concern it is difficult to have a discrete policy initiative to tackle them in isolation from other considerations, in both the policy domain and other aspects of governance.

The connection between MDGs is perhaps most clearly demonstrated in the relationship between MDGs 4 and 5. MDG 5 relates to maternal health. Very often mothers are at risk during the latter stages of pregnancy, during delivery and in the immediate post-delivery period. One of the most shocking examples of the divergence of healthcare provision between the developed and developing world can be found in statistical data relating to health risks during pregnancy. The risk of a woman in Sweden dying from causes that are pregnancy-related is 1 in 17,400. In Niger this figure is 1 in 7. Again there can be numerous factors that lead to this enormous disparity in life chances. These can relate to the overall health of the individuals concerned and their resilience to deal with the physical stress of pregnancy and childbirth. As with rates of infant mortality, a major factor is the level of healthcare and nursing support available during labour and shortly thereafter. Although high-technology healthcare can sometimes be helpful, very often what women actually need in crises at childbirth is simple and reliable care from a qualified midwife within quick reach. Once again the development infrastructure needs to be in place to tackle this particular MDG. The enabling of this has to be set into the context of national governments, and aid agencies, making hard budgetary decisions on the basis of limited funding.

MDG 6 is an interesting case as it deals with the fight against HIV/AIDS. As such it is something that can be seen as a global issue, although as with some of the above examples there can be extreme variations in incidence between regions. This MDG also refers to tackling the spread of malaria and other diseases. The HIV/AIDS issue is one that has been experienced very differently in various parts of the world. Rates of prevalence are diverse, as is the availability of treatment and even popular beliefs about the causes and consequences of infection and cultural attitudes towards sufferers. Sub-Saharan Africa is, again, one of the most vulnerable regions to infectious diseases. The numbers of people in this region living with HIV/AIDS continues to rise, although antiretroviral drugs are making some progress in treatment. A priority area for the use of these drugs is to prevent mother-to-child transmission. Again this demonstrates the overlap between MDGs as this is clearly an area of work that relates to both child and maternal health. With respect to other diseases, malaria is notable as it appeared to be in decline but has more recently re-emerged as a significant health threat in particular regions, once again Sub-Saharan Africa being a case in point. Malaria has been cited as a disease that should perhaps be given a greater priority in terms of research and development among international pharmaceutical companies that have been accused of focusing their efforts more on products aimed at the developed world. For example, slimming pills may be seen as more profitable products than those to treat malaria and other diseases associated with the poorer parts of the world. In contrast, there have been some examples of pharmaceutical companies working with governments and aid agencies to develop coordinated strategies to tackle particular diseases. The Global Polio Eradication Initiative is a good example of this.

MDG 7 is perhaps the most far-reaching as it seeks to ensure environmental sustainability. This clearly ties in with other UN-led initiatives such as the Earth Summit process. Despite this, it is also one of the more vague of the goals in terms of targets. It is broken down into four subsections. The first refers to reversing the loss of environmental resources, but fails to be explicit about what these are and how to reverse such losses. The second calls for a 'significant reduction' in loss of biodiversity, but neither sets targets or proposes a plan of action for this goal. The third calls for improved access to sanitation and potable water. The final sub-goal calls for a 'significant improvement' in the lives of 100 million slum-dwellers. To some extent this is the MDG that reads like more of a 'wish list' than something where a coherent strategy is being promoted via inter-state or multi-stakeholder cooperation.

The final MDG 8 deals with the concept of a global partnership for development. Although the UN is, by definition, state-centric it also promotes cooperative action with a range of stakeholders from civil society and the private sector. In terms of North/South cooperation there has been a long-standing target of 0.7 per cent of developed states' gross national income (GNI) being set aside for overseas development assistance to the less-developed states. This has only been achieved by a small number of Scandinavian countries, with the vast majority of developed states falling well short of this target. The international conferences referred to above routinely include pledges of additional financial packages to aid development projects, but these are often unfulfilled. More recently governments appear to be placing greater emphasis on public/private partnerships whereby MNCs are encouraged to invest in development projects. In part this can be seen in the context of the broader project of neoliberalism and greater emphasis on the private sector driving all aspects of society. Civil society groups are also engaged with in relation to identifying development needs and facilitating the delivery of aid. This can lead to some eclectic alliances of stakeholders and tensions can occur with MNCs being essentially profit motivated, NGOs tending towards the more altruistic and governments seeking to balance pledges of aid with myriad other budgetary pressures.

Table 8.1 charts the progress of each of the eight Millennium Development Goals.

Major groups

The multi-stakeholder concept has its origins in the UN Commission on Sustainable Development's Agenda 21 and the designation of 'major groups' with identifiable interests and roles in the promotion of sustainable development: (i) business and industry, (ii) children and youth, (iii) farmers, (iv) indigenous people, (v) local authorities, (vi) NGOs, (vii) scientific and technological community, (viii) women, and (ix) workers and trade unions. Each of these groups represents a particular constituency of actors and agendas. The following section looks at each of these groups in turn and locates them within the broader development process.

Business and industry has been seen in both a negative light as one of the main reasons for environmental degradation, and more positively as a source of potential solutions. Either way this is a sector that clearly plays a key role in the development debate. The text of the Agenda 21 document calls on businesses to look towards more efficient forms of production, to minimise pollutant discharges and to recycle and reuse component parts of the manufacturing cycle as much as possible. For its part, the private sector has responded in a rather ad hoc manner with some businesses engaging much more fully with this process than others. Some of the larger MNCs have formed the World Business Council for Sustainable Development (WBCSD). Some of this group's members are drawn from the oil, gas and mining industries. These are precisely the companies that environmental groups have targeted their

Table 8.1 Millennium Development Goals progress chart 2009

Goals and Targets	Africa		Asia				Oceania	Latin America & Caribbean	Commonwealth of Independent States	
	Northern	Sub-Saharan	Eastern	South-Eastern	Southern	Western			Europe	Asia
**GOAL 1	Eradicate extreme poverty and hunger**										
Reduce extreme poverty by half	low poverty	very high poverty	high poverty	high poverty	very high poverty	low poverty	—	moderate poverty	low poverty	high poverty
Productive and decent employment	very large deficit in decent work	very large deficit in decent work	large deficit in decent work	very large deficit in decent work	very large deficit in decent work	very large deficit in decent work	very large deficit in decent work	moderate deficit in decent work	small deficit in decent work	moderate deficit in decent work
Reduce hunger by half	low hunger	very high hunger	moderate hunger	high hunger	high hunger	moderate hunger	moderate hunger	moderate hunger	low hunger	moderate hunger
**GOAL 2	Achieve universal primary education**										
Universal primary schooling	high enrolment	low enrolment	high enrolment	high enrolment	moderate enrolment	moderate enrolment	—	high enrolment	high enrolment	high enrolment
**GOAL 3	Promote gender equality and empower women**										
Equal girls' enrolment in primary school	close to parity	close to parity	parity	parity	parity	close to parity	almost close to parity	parity	parity	parity
Women's share of paid employment	low share	low share	high share	medium share	low share	low share	medium share	high share	high share	high share
Women's equal representation in national parliaments	very low representation	low representation	moderate representation	low representation	low representation	very low representation	very low representation	moderate representation	low representation	low representation
**GOAL 4	Reduce child mortality**										
Reduce mortality of under-five-year-olds by two-thirds	low mortality	very high mortality	low mortality	low mortality	high mortality	low mortality	moderate mortality	low mortality	low mortality	moderate mortality
Measles immunisation	high coverage	moderate coverage	high coverage	moderate coverage	moderate coverage	moderate coverage	low coverage	high coverage	high coverage	high coverage

Table 8.1 *(Continued)*

Goals and Targets	Africa		Asia					Latin America & Caribbean	Commonwealth of Independent States	
	Northern	Sub-Saharan	Eastern	South-Eastern	Southern	Western	Oceania		Europe	Asia
GOAL 5 | Improve maternal health										
Reduce maternal mortality by three-quarters*	moderate mortality	very high mortality	low mortality	high mortality	high mortality	moderate mortality	high mortality	moderate mortality	low mortality	low mortality
Access to reproductive health	moderate access	low access	high access	moderate access	moderate access	moderate access	low access	high access	high access	moderate access
GOAL 6 | Combat HIV/AIDS, malaria and other diseases										
Halt and reverse spread of HIV/AIDS	low prevalence	high prevalence	low prevalence	low prevalence	low prevalence	low prevalence	moderate prevalence	moderate prevalence	moderate prevalence	low prevalence
Halt and reverse spread of tuberculosis	low mortality	high mortality	moderate mortality	high mortality	moderate mortality	low mortality	high mortality	low mortality	moderate mortality	moderate mortality
GOAL 7 | Ensure environmental sustainability										
Reverse loss of forests	low forest cover	medium forest cover	medium forest cover	high forest cover	medium forest cover	low forest cover	high forest cover	high forest cover	high forest cover	low forest cover
Halve proportion without improved drinking water	high coverage	low coverage	moderate coverage	moderate coverage	moderate coverage	high coverage	low coverage	high coverage	high coverage	moderate coverage
Halve proportion without sanitation	moderate coverage	very low coverage	low coverage	low coverage	very low coverage	moderate coverage	low coverage	moderate coverage	moderate coverage	high coverage
Improve the lives of slum-dwellers	moderate proportion of slum-dwellers	very high proportion of slum-dwellers	high proportion of slum-dwellers	high proportion of slum-dwellers	high proportion of slum-dwellers	moderate proportion of slum-dwellers	moderate proportion of slum-dwellers	moderate proportion of slum-dwellers	—	—
GOAL 8 | Develop a global partnership for development										
Internet users	moderate usage	very low usage	high usage	moderate usage	low usage	moderate usage	low usage	high usage	high usage	low usage

The progress chart operates on two levels. The words in each box indicate the present degree of compliance with the target. The colours show progress towards the target according to the legend below:

■ Already met the target or very close to meeting the target.   ■ No progress or deterioration.
■ Progress sufficient to reach the target if prevailing trends persist.   ▨ Missing or insufficient data.
■ Progress insufficient to reach the target if prevailing trends persist.

*The available data for maternal mortality do not allow a trend analysis. Progress in the chart has been assessed by the responsible agencies on the basis of proxy indicators.

Source: United Nations Department of Economic and Social Affairs, Statistics Division (2010) Millennium Development Goal Progress Chart 2009.

campaigns towards, citing them as being some of the worst polluters and responsible for environmental degradation on a massive scale. The more cynical or, at least, sceptical in the environmental movement are suspicious of the WBCSD and the whole concept of 'corporate social responsibility' (CSR). It is difficult to judge the extent to which corporations are truly trying to make their operations more environmentally benign, or if this is simply a public relations exercise to counter the campaigners' arguments – and to attract the 'green pound' of environmentally-conscious consumers.

Children and youth are the group that are arguably the most relevant to sustainability, given they are likely to be inheriting either the ongoing problems or the more positive solutions of the current environmental crisis. The UN has a long-standing commitment to the promotion of children's rights via agencies such as UNICEF, the above MDG on child healthcare, special reports on child soldiers, access to primary schooling and so on. Many of the UN's publications are aimed at a younger audience, highlighting the organisation's peace and development work and the need for intercultural understanding and cooperation. This attitude is also mirrored in many local and national governments' documentation that is distributed via school networks. Similarly, many NGO groups have a youth membership category with their campaigning messages pitched at younger age groups. Children and youth comprise roughly one-third of the world's population. In many parts of the developing world there remain relatively high birth rates, which means that in these states the younger age group is beginning to outnumber the older population. Demographic patterns vary between states but there is a growing correlation between the areas where environmental vulnerability is at its most extreme and a high level of children and youth as a proportion of the population. In that regard, getting the message of sustainability across to the younger age groups is even more important.

Farmers are highlighted as a significant group in the context of sustainable development. This makes sense given the relationship between the agricultural sector and the natural world. The use of pesticides and the evolution of genetically-modified crops may be cited as examples of some farmers moving away from a reliance on the 'natural' balance of eco-systems. That said, this only applies to certain sectors of the farming community and the underlying principle for the vast majority of farmers is that one needs to care for the land if they want to have successful crops year on year. About one-third of the world's land surface is given over to agricultural production and this is the foundation of most rural communities. As such it is crucial to sustain this sector. This is doubly important when one considers that it is this production that also sustains urban dwellers. A distinction needs to be made between the small-scale subsistence farmer who may produce little more than what is required to feed an extended family, and the huge conglomerates that represent farming on a massive industrialised scale. This is not to say that small-scale farming never includes harmful, non-sustainable practices. However, it is farming at the industrialised level where most criticisms of environmentally-damaging methods can be cited. For example, extensive use of chemical fertilisers and pesticides can create toxic run-off which pollutes local water supplies. High levels of nitrogen in water has been noted as having damaging impacts on numerous fish and amphibian species. Such pollution can also be harmful once it enters the food chain, up to the human level.

Indigenous peoples are cited as a major group for several reasons. They are recognised as having a special connection to their lands. This point can be contentious in some areas where land ownership is seriously contested and also where indigenous peoples are no longer the majority group in their home state. The latter point can raise questions of identity and the perceived legitimacy of the national government. Although all states can lay claim to having some element of an indigenous population this is more easily identifiable in some parts of the world than others. For example, in areas where there was expansion of European influence and colonisation the indigenous population is more easily identifiable, such as in Australia or New Zealand. The same applies in the US where, although no longer formally part of a European-led imperial strategy, the post-independence US drove westwards into the territories of many indigenous tribes. Over the years mixed-race relations have blurred the indigenous/non-indigenous divide. That said, there remains a strong sense of indigenousness in many parts of the world and traditional concepts of stewardship of the land, as opposed to over-exploitation of resources, is being turned to as a more sensible and sustainable model. There are also powerful models of development which draw on indigenous knowledge and indigenous practice in agriculture, aquaculture and medicine. It is clearly a mistake to see a dramatic opposition between the demands of indigenous peoples and the prospects of development when the know-how which specific groups in Amazonia, the Pacific Islands or elsewhere can offer provides a basis for bottom-up patterns of sustainable growth, as organisations such as Survival International have been arguing for some time.

Local authorities have been at the forefront of promoting the Agenda 21 message. Local Agenda 21 projects have been particularly successful in the UK and other parts of Europe, notably Germany. One of the mantras of the environmental movement is to 'think globally – act locally'. Local authorities, such as city and district councils, are particularly well-placed to communicate 'green' initiatives and policies to local communities. They are also often significant employers in terms of both numbers of staff employed and also the environmental impact the provision of their services can have. To some extent they represent the interface between national governments and citizens. They can act as promoters of recycling in relation to waste management schemes, they are providers of public transport systems to reduce car pollutants, and they can support environmental education initiatives in schools and colleges. Many local authorities in the developed world are involved in twinning projects with counterparts in the developing world, thereby fostering education opportunities and potential exchange visits. Such projects can be somewhat unbalanced as one partner will tend to have considerably greater access to resources than the other. However, recognising this is part of the education process.

Having NGOs as a major group is appropriate, even necessary, but this represents one of the most diverse of the groups. The breadth of this group covers representatives from several of the other groups such as farmers, women and, of course, women farmers. The groups are not mutually exclusive and the diversity of the NGOs represented here illustrates the tremendous range of interest groups related to the field of development. Some issue areas are covered by several different NGOs. If one were to take tropical deforestation as an example, then there are interest groups in both the NGO sector and within the other major groups. Survival International has campaigns that deal with protection of tribal peoples threatened by logging operations (see: www.survivalinternational.org). Similarly, the Rainforest Alliance is attempting to protect rainforests, but may have a greater emphasis on the overall eco-system rather than the more anthropocentric approach of Survival. The Worldwide Fund for Nature may focus efforts on the protection of a particular endangered species living in a rainforest habitat. The interests and agendas of these groups lead them towards cooperative actions, although priorities and action plans may sometimes differ. Through the mechanisms of the Cotonou Convention (2000), the European Union has adopted a programme of active involvement of civil society groups in development programmes, which is also an important source for the legitimisation of specific programmes and for genuine involvement of local communities (see: ec.europa.eu/development/geographical/cotonouintro_en.cfm). This is, however, not always welcome to national governments which quite often – but not always – try to control or undermine civil society NGOs, which they see as a source of opposition, and the African, Caribbean and Pacific (ACP) governments in the Convention have a veto over EU development programmes. In giving formal recognition, some power, and sometimes not a little authority to NGOs through the Cotonou programme and through Echo (its emergency relief organisation), the EU is following behind what is widely seen as the 'good practice' of other regional and UN-led institutional frameworks.

The scientific and technological community plays a very important role in development policy making. If one looks at the debate on climate change there have been serious disagreements on the causes, rapidity and consequences of changes in climatic conditions. Without a firm basis for predictions on what will happen in the future it is difficult to plan accordingly. While strongly reliant on scientific input, the climate change debate has become heavily politicised. Various interest groups have lobbied to present scientific findings as either over-dramatising the likely impact of climate change, or even disputing the methodology and interpretations of these conclusions. The Global

Climate Coalition (GCC) was formed in 1989 with an apparent remit to counter the claims being made by scientific advisers to the IPCC. For the better part of a decade it included prominent members from the oil, gas and automobile manufacturing industries. These were the sectors deemed most responsible for producing high levels of greenhouse gas emissions and most at risk from tighter regulation of harmful emissions. As the science of climate change became better understood and more difficult to dispute, many of these members left the GCC and began to investigate how to reduce their carbon footprints. The nature of scientific inquiry is such that it is virtually impossible to achieve 100 per cent certainty on outcomes and scientists prefer to present findings in terms of probability percentages. That said, there is now a widespread acceptance that not only is climate change occurring, it is also significantly impacted upon by human activity. Therefore, human activity needs to be modified in order to reduce the more extreme negative impacts of climate change. This has a direct bearing on development policy in that the transfer of knowledge and skills in renewable energy and low-carbon technologies is an important goal of development policy actors including the EU and Japan. It also provides an area of development action which offers commercial advantages to the stakeholders, which are able to research, develop and promote green technologies more efficiently: economic development is not invariably an obstacle to environmental improvement – or vice versa.

Technology is therefore double-edged and, depending on its application, may lead to greater environmental degradation or greater protection. It plays a key role in the promotion of development goals. Science and technology are fundamental elements in meeting the majority of the UN's MDGs, be it in healthcare, agricultural production or sustainable energy supplies. Technical fixes are sometimes cited as the solution for many development problems. There is an argument to be made here, and *some* technologies may have a demonstrable development and environment benefit; but it does risk avoiding the underlying issue of what is creating a problem in the first place. For example, there is a very lively debate on what types of energy supply should be utilised from a range of fossil fuels, renewable sources or the nuclear option. There is less discussion on reducing energy consumption and, perhaps, even slowing economic growth. There is also a risk of assuming that technology will continue to advance and we will find future answers to problems that we are currently aware of. For example, in the 1950s it was suggested that nuclear power would be 'too cheap to meter' and that there would shortly be a solution found to the problem of the safe storage or disposal of harmful radioactive waste. Nuclear waste remains a problematic issue and the cost of nuclear power generation, when waste disposal and decommissioning costs are factored in, is actually far more expensive than originally predicted.

Women are undeniably a major group and play a very important role in the context of the MDGs. This is partly because they are often at the centre of many of the development issues to be addressed. This is especially the case in rural communities where it is women who are often at the forefront of providing food and water for households. They are both the bearers of and main care providers for children. The UN has recognised the importance of promoting gender equality and highlighting the role women play in development issues, especially since the 1995 UN Women's Conference in Beijing (which was actually the fourth UN Women's Conference). Embedded within the UN framework are bodies such as the Division for the Advancement of Women, the Development Fund for Women (UNIFEM) and the International Research and Training Institute for the Advancement of Women (INSTRAW). There are also a great many NGOs that focus on the issue of women's rights or development issues where women are the central focus.

The final major group involves workers and trade unions. Again this is a very large sector to cover and it includes a broad range of workers drawn from all aspects of rural and urban economies. While there may be less formal employment in rural areas there are often mining or agricultural workers, some of whom may be unionised but many who are not. Workers' cooperatives are increasingly seen as a way in which land use can be retained in the control of local communities. This is not to say that MNCs do not continue to engage in interaction with such groups; but they may play more of an intermediary role by sourcing their supplies from cooperative farms and then selling these on to the international market.

This has the advantage of allowing the cooperatives to have access to markets they might not otherwise have, but also maintains a greater sense of stewardship for the land than might otherwise be felt by MNCs with no personal connection to the land. Involving workers and trade unions in a more engaged manner also provides some sense of shared planning and 'buy in' to development planning. The whole thrust of the major groups initiative is to recognise that there are shared interests and to try to avoid some potential tensions and conflicts, such as between workers and employers.

Having considered how development has been defined, explored potential problems with this, and reviewed the main development goals and the major development actors, it is useful now to look at some specific examples of development projects to assess how they are implemented and how successful, or not, they have been.

Development projects

In the 1960s and 1970s, there was a wave of decolonisation, with many states achieving political independence from their former colonial rulers. It is important to note here, however, that political independence as represented by a head of state, government officials, national flag and national anthem does not necessarily equate to full economic independence. Many of these states were, and to some extent remain, tied into neo-colonial patterns of dependence. They often sought development aid in the early years of independence with a view to increasing their infrastructure capacity and investing in major schemes such as large hydroelectric power generation schemes. The large dam schemes, such as the Aswan High Dam in Egypt, are classic examples of such large-scale investment projects. While they have undoubted benefits in terms of both power generation and flood control, there are also some serious negative consequences of such projects. The initial building of such dams almost always involves the forced relocation of communities. The silt that would normally flow with the river that has been dammed is held back in the reservoir that has been created by the dam. This has two significant impacts. First it prevents the nutrients in the silt enriching the land downstream, with a result that farmers there are then forced to use artificial fertilisers which may have a harmful environmental effect. Second, the amount of silt is often underestimated and as it builds up it shortens the projected productive lifespan of the project. More recently the World Bank has recognised that the negative impacts of such major dam projects outweigh the benefits. The World Commission on Dams has led a review of such projects and they now have considerably less support with international funding reduced or withdrawn altogether from several projects. India's Namada, Turkey's Ilisu and, perhaps most controversially of all given the scale of the project, China's Three Gorges Dam have all faced significant international criticism.

At the opposite end of the development planning scale there are also examples of much smaller-scale projects. Many development consultants and campaigners prefer the grassroots or community-based approach. A UK-based development NGO called Practical Action highlights the role of intermediate technologies to provide low-cost community projects such as the digging of wells and other irrigation projects and micro power generation (see: www.practicalaction.org.uk/home-uk). Solar cookers and wind-up radios are also examples of very small-scale initiatives that don't grab the headlines in the same way that the major projects do, but have a far-reaching impact in terms of the lives improved by these small initiatives. This reflects two very different approaches to development. As highlighted elsewhere in the chapter, it is possible to take either a top-down or a bottom-up approach to development. The MDGs and the major groups discussed above can be seen to combine elements of both approaches. Almost by definition something emanating from the UN may be be seen as top-down as it attempts to coordinate action on a global scale. That said, when one looks at the majority of practical plans within the majority of the MDGs they tend to be focused at the individual and local community levels. Some of the major groups are more community-focused than others. Yet even with some of the more economic-growth-first-and-then-'trickle-down'-later members, such as the main MNCs, there appears to be a growing awareness that development has to be inclusive and is not something that can be simply directed from above. Development is a combination of global processes and local impacts, and responses.

Critical frameworks for rethinking development

A variety of studies offer more critical ways of looking at development issues, drawing on the kind of literature we have already discussed in Chapter 4 above. These include more radical approaches, sometimes looking at resistance to globalisation and its development dimensions from a neo-Gramscian perspective (e.g. O'Brien et al., 2000) or a feminist approach (e.g. Peterson, 2009; Parpart and Marchand, 1995). Much of this critical work begins by questioning the very conception of development, going back to the arguments rehearsed earlier in this chapter and asking how we can better understand what development actually means, how specific discourses and social practices associated with development have been produced, and how their meaning is controlled. Probably the most influential work in this field is Escobar's *Encountering Development* (1995 – although there are several competitors for this title). Escobar invites us to question the project of development as envisaged in both the liberal/radical and neo-liberal/neo-realist camps, drawing particularly on Foucault's work on understanding the construction of discourse and the forms of power it involves. This also turns attention in development studies to the varieties of forms of power which are involved within the academic discipline of development studies itself, as Pieterse (2000) shows. The extensive literature on development theory and sustainability and the varieties of liberal arguments about development can also be explored through a reading of his account.

Critical theory and postmodern theory raise at least one question in application to development, which is at the same time an ethical and a policy concern. This body of broadly critical analysis of development processes has great value in formulating sharp questions and suggesting research strategies to find answers to them. But at the same time, their approach is one of critique which, as Robert Cox argued (see discussion in Chapter 4), make a sharp division between practical knowledge and critical thought. But development, although it might justify a critical approach, surely also justifies a practical approach, one which engages with practical realities and needs which people face every day – surely it cannot afford the luxury of merely thinking critically without some form of effective response. But while this raises some important theoretical questions, the shorter answer to the dilemma is that it is a false distinction, and that most development debate is at once critical (from whatever standpoint, including that of Gramscians and postmodern Foucauldians and neo-liberal writers such as Moyo (2009)) and practical, at least in its aspirations. The more important question may be to ask, who controls development processes, in whose interests, and with what assumptions?

Summary

This chapter has aimed to introduce a range of ideas and arguments about development. These touch on questions of political economy, of course, but they also confront political economy with questions of justice and ethics, with questions of how political economy itself studies its subject, or, less abstractly, it challenges the choices we each make when we choose to study aspects of it. And it raises questions about the wide range of groups and organisations which have become increasingly involved in the 'delivery' of development policies.

Reflective questions

1   Why is the concept of 'development' considered to be problematic?
2   Who are the key actors in the development process? And what role do they play?
3   What factors are impeding progress towards the MDGs?
4   Is there simply a technical fix for development problems, or are there more deep-rooted problems which need to be addressed?
5   What is the core discourse of development? How far does it pit liberal and neo-liberal ideas in opposition to each other and how far does it absorb them into a single structure of ideas and social practices?

Suggestions for further reading

Adams, W.M. (2008) *Green Development: Environment and Sustainability in a Developing World*, London: Routledge.

BBC News (2010) 'Kenya flower industry hit by flight cancellations', *BBC News Online,* 16 April 2010.

Brinkerhoff, J.M. (2002) *Partnerships for International Development: Rhetoric or Results?* London: Lynne Reinner.

Chari, S. and Corbridge, S. (eds) (2007) *The Development Reader,* London: Routledge.

Escobar, A. (1995) *Encountering Development: The Making and Unmaking of the Third World*, Princeton, NJ: Princeton University Press.

Hayter, T. (1971) *Aid as Imperialism*, London: Penguin Books.

Hopkins, M. (2008) *Corporate Social Responsibility and International Development: Is Business the Solution?* London: Earthscan Ltd.

IBP USA (2009) *Nauru Recent Economic and Political Developments Yearbook*, Washington: International Business Publications.

Joseph, R. and Gillies, A. (2008) *Smart Aid for African Development*, Boulder, CO: Lynne Rienner.

Moyo, D. (2009) *Dead Aid: Why Aid Is Not Working and How There Is a Better Way for Africa*, London: Allen Lane.

O'Brien, R., Goetz, A-M., Scholte, J-A. and Williams, M. (2000) *Contesting Global Governance: Multilateral Global Institutions and Global Social Movements*, Cambridge: Cambridge University Press.

Parpart, M. and Marchand, J. (1995) *Feminism/Postmodernism/Development*, London: Routledge.

Peterson, V.S. (2009) *Global Gender Issues in the New Millennium*, 3rd edn, Boulder, CO: Westview Press.

Pieterse, J.N. (2000) *Development Theory: Deconstructions/Reconstructions*, London: Sage.

Roberts, J. Timmons and Hite, A.B. (eds) (2006) *The Globalisation and Development Reader: Perspectives on Development and Global Change*, Oxford: Wiley Blackwell.

Rostow, W. (1960) *The Stages of Economic Growth: A Non-Communist Manifesto*, Cambridge: Cambridge University Press.

United Nations (2010) *Human Development Report 2010*, New York: UN.

Williamson, J. (1990) 'What Washington means by policy reform', in *Latin American Adjustment: How Much Has Happened?*, chapter 2. Washington, DC: Peterson Institute for International Economics.

9 Environment

Chapter learning outcomes

After reading this chapter students should be able to:

- Describe how environmental issues have emerged as an important element of the international political agenda.
- Explain the role of a range of actors in creating/responding to environmental issues, including governments, MNCs and international non-governmental organisations.
- Understand and explain a range of contemporary environmental issues, including resource depletion, deforestation, biodiversity, reef systems, fisheries and energy security.
- Analyse global processes of dialogue and cooperation which focus on responding to, or resolving environmental issues.
- Discuss how the role of the media is creating awareness of environmental issues.
- Discuss the role of individual lifestyles in causing global environmental issues.
- Relate discussion of environmental issues to the theoretical debates discussed earlier in this book.

Introduction

Environmental issues have always been a part of human interaction from the earliest hunter-gatherer groups through to the settlement and cultivation of territories, and subsequent competition for land and associated resources. That said, it is only relatively recently that environmental issues have come to the fore as a significant part of the political agendas of states and an increasing number of non-state actors. As outlined in Chapter 3, numerous factors contributed to the growth in environmental awareness in both the public and private arenas. The late 1960s and early 1970s was a time when environmental consciousness was raised and the environment became a strongly politicised issue. This chapter will look at the actors, issues and processes relevant to the political economy of the environment.

The interaction between actors, issues and processes can be viewed in a variety of ways. None of these categories are homogeneous. There are enormous differences between the material situations of various states in terms of their physical resources and the impact that environmental change can have as a result of exploiting these resources. Similarly, MNCs and NGOs are also broad categories that mask a variety of agendas and capabilities. The issues that will be referred to below have varying degrees of impact and importance to the diverse range of actors under consideration here. It therefore follows that the processes involved in the interaction between this complex array of actors and issues will also be variable. While there is a case to be argued that there may be a single 'process' of global environmental degradation taking place over time, it is important to highlight that this process will be experienced, understood and acted upon differently by different actors depending on their individual interests and level of agency.

Figure 9.1   Survey of attitudes towards environmental protection in the EU

Question: How important is protecting the environment to you personally?

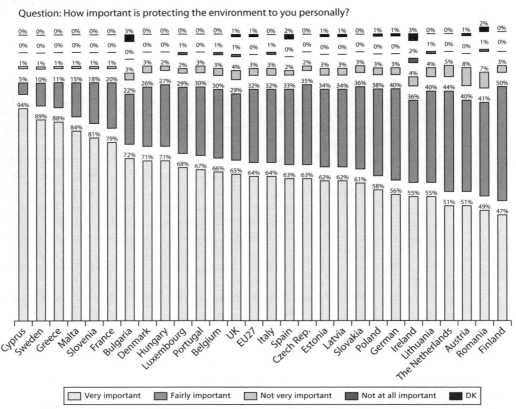

Source: European Commission (2008) 'Attitudes of European citizens towards the environment', *Special Eurobarometer*, 295, p. 11. Copyright © European Union, 2008. Reproduced with permission.

The huge variation in interests and agendas of the various actors concerned with environmental change means that it will always be problematic attempting to reach a consensus on what action needs to be taken, if any. The December 2009 Climate Change Conference held in Copenhagen dramatically illustrated the difficulties in reaching agreement between nearly two hundred states. This event was also subject to intense lobbying from both MNCs and other civil society NGOs.

Figure 9.1 illustrates public perceptions and attitudes towards environmental protection within EU member states. There are clearly variations across this region, as there will be in other regions of the world. In part this reflects the manner in which environmental issues are ranked relative to other social concerns. How these concerns are formed and addressed will be determined by a range of actors and issues, as outlined in the following pages.

Actors: governments

Although national governments have not always acknowledged the importance of the global natural environment within which they operate, they have played a large part in the development of processes that have led to the current pressures on this environment. Governments are not a homogeneous group and some have more impact on the environment than others. Looking at how the global economy has developed over the last few centuries it is reasonable to argue that the economic growth that has driven the accumulation of power among the core states has largely not taken environmental degradation into account. Far from it, as natural resources have been plundered in many parts of the world in order to fuel this growth. Even when colonial rule has been supplanted by political independence for former colonies the underlying economic dynamism has tended to rely on the extraction of primary products to generate export income. Multinational corporations, thereby highlighting the combination of actors that feed into environmental politics, facilitate much of this. In addition, numerous civil society groups, such as Friends of the Earth and Greenpeace International, have been extremely active in highlighting environmental problems and lobbying both governments and MNCs to move towards more sustainable economic development practices. This initial section will consider how governments, MNCs and civil society actors have responded to the emerging environmental agenda from the early 1970s onwards.

The UN Conference on Environment and Development, held in Stockholm in 1972, marked a significant breakthrough in international diplomacy whereby the major powers acknowledged that there was a clear connection between economic development and environmental conservation. It was recognised that it was not possible to continue to emphasise economic growth without an understanding of associated environmental costs that accompany this growth. The Brundtland Commission's report 'North/South: a programme for survival' highlighted the vested interests that the governments of the global North had in avoiding the social disruption that would be caused by excessive environmental degradation taking place in the developing world. This was in terms of ensuring access to a steady supply of primary resources, and also to secure markets for their manufactured goods. There was also a desire to maintain stability in the developing world to avoid pressure to intervene, by military or other means, should political control in the global South break down to the point that Northern strategic interests were threatened. However, despite a growing awareness of the interconnections at a global level the majority of international relations have continued to be based on relatively short-term national interests.

All governments face difficult choices when trying to address environmental issues. The more developed ones have more diverse economies and the capital to provide for some environmental conservation, both domestically and as part of their overseas aid programmes. Even these, though, have been criticised by environmental groups for failing to restrict pollution, managing vulnerable species and habitats appropriately and generally continuing to prioritise economic growth over sustainability. The less developed states are often at the forefront of major environmental crises in the forms of spreading desertification, deforestation and loss of biodiversity. These are also the governments that tend to have fewer budgetary resources to draw on for conservation projects. Their position in the global economy is such that they draw heavily on their natural resources for government revenue. This may be in the form of mining operations, which often have severe polluting characteristics, or the clear felling of swathes of tropical rainforest. The latter raises some export income but the environmental consequences can be far-reaching. These include loss of habitat, reduced biodiversity, increased soil erosion and even damage to mangrove and reef systems as a result of higher levels of silt in river systems. Governments may be fully aware of the environmental consequences of some of their policies but feel unable to take more direct conservation measures due to the short-term economic costs involved.

The latter part of the twentieth century saw some headway being made with national governments at least opening discussions on how to address perceived environmental problems. Initially this was focussed on the fear that fossil fuels were being depleted at such a rate there would be significant energy shortages and potential conflicts over access to dwindling fuel supplies. Some of the more extreme 'doomsday' predictions of the early 1970s suggested that coal, oil and gas supplies would be close to exhaustion by the turn of the century. This has clearly not come to pass but it should be acknowledged that this is largely because of the willingness of consumers to pay significantly more for these fuels. Because of this, reserves that had not previously been considered economically viable to exploit were added to the overall reserves available. Although these secondary fuel supplies continue to be depleted far in excess of the natural processes that would replace them there is now less concern regarding the amount of fossil fuels available for use. Rather, the concern has shifted to the pollution associated with such usage, not exclusively but predominantly in relation to greenhouse gas emissions. This issue has formed the basis of the main international negotiations at the governmental level, as illustrated by the Earth Summit process and the formation of the Intergovernmental Panel on Climate Change (IPCC).

The Rio Earth Summit of 1992 will be looked at in more detail below but it is worth noting here the significance of this event. This Summit meeting built on the environmental platform established in Stockholm in 1972, but took this debate to a more profound level. This was in terms of both the number of governments that were represented at Rio and also the fact that this included a great many heads of state and heads of government, including those from the most powerful developed nations. There were also legally binding agreements presented for ratification in the form of Conventions on both climate change and biodiversity. Not all of the states present were wholly enthusiastic in ratifying these agreements. George Bush, the US president at the time, had appeared reluctant to even attend the meeting and in a speech shortly before his arrival he had stated that he would not sign any agreement that would cost US jobs. His agenda was still focused very much at the level of national interest and not acknowledging that global environmental concerns necessarily included the national interests of all states. This attitude goes to the heart of the dilemma of dealing with global issues at the national level. Pursuit of national interests has been a central part of international relations since the creation of the Westphalian nation state system. Although this socially constructed political system simply overlies the reality of the natural world and environmental processes it has gained a predominant role in how humans interact with this wider environment. There may be a mismatch between what is actually happening and how we deal with it but national governments retain a key role in how these events are mediated and dealt with, or not in many cases.

Although the above point highlights the ongoing significance of national governments it is worth reiterating that some are in more powerful positions than others to deal with environmental crises. For example, the low-lying island states of the Pacific region contribute virtually nothing in terms of greenhouse gas emissions, yet this issue is a threat to their very survival with some of these islands already being inundated as a result of sea-level rise. Adapting to a rising sea level via building coastal defences is not a viable option for most of these states. Mass migration is also problematic both in terms of where to relocate to and issues of identity. Ideally the problem should be dealt with at its source, which are the emissions generated by the industrialised states. The only way these small island states can influence this scenario is by arguing their case at international forums such as the IPCC. This reinforces the state-centric nature of international relations, but also highlights the power politics dimension of this whereby the interests of a few thousand Pacific islanders is unlikely to alter the course of the major powers of the United States, China, Russia and other significant greenhouse gas emitters. Although the major powers are discussing reductions in such emissions they are generally rather modest targets in comparison to what would be required to halt, or even significantly slowdown, the encroachment of the ocean being experienced in low-lying regions of the world. One of the problems with the 'front lines' of environmental crises is they happen in particular places and unless this is within the boundaries of a major power they are unlikely to be acted upon in a significant manner. Despite the recognition that problems such as sea-level rise or tropical deforestation have global consequences they largely continue to be seen as something to be managed at the national level.

While national governments are geographically fixed in terms of their sovereign territory the same cannot be said for their interests. The above example graphically demonstrates the Pacific islands' interests being intertwined with events taking place well beyond their political boundaries. Similarly, the

Table 9.1 Regional distribution of protected areas

WCPA region	No. of sites	Total protected area (km^2)	% of land area protected
Antarctic	126	70,294	0.0%
Australia/New Zealand	8,724	1,194,800	9.6%
Brazil	1,277	1,575,986	18.3%
Caribbean	952	69,468	11.7%
Central America	762	145,322	24.8%
East Asia	2,118	1,031,813	8.5%
Eastern and Southern Africa	4,418	1,682,989	14.6%
Europe	43,019	750,225	13.3%
North Africa and Middle East	1,133	1,272,840	9.7%
North America	13,280	4,204,468	16.8%
North Eurasia	17,724	1,816,735	7.2%
Pacific	410	368,926	2.1%
Hispanic South America	1,472	2,387,218	24.9%
South Asia	1,477	308,826	6.8%
South East Asia	2,656	759,788	14.8%
Western and Central Africa	2,575	1,125,261	8.7%
Grand Total	**102,123**	**18,764,958**	**11.6%**

Source: Chape *et al.* (2003).

most developed states have overseas interests in terms of access to resources and markets. When looking at the emerging environmental agenda from an international political economy perspective it is difficult to maintain a wholly state-centric view as so many relevant issues cross national boundaries. The growth of transnational and interdependent relationships is a key feature of processes of globalisation. Within that context it is important to look at the role that MNCs play with regard to environmental issues.

Actors: multinational corporations

Chapter 4 outlined the significance of MNCs as major international actors. Regardless of seeing them as wholly independent actors or as 'agents of the state', their impact is undeniable. Many of the environmental crises currently taking place around the world are a direct result of MNC activities. Resource depletion and resultant pollution from all manner of manufacturing processes are overwhelmingly conducted with MNC involvement. With the minor but worthy exception of the very small percentage of international trade that can accurately be described as 'fair trade', the vast majority of international trade does not factor in environmental, or social, costs when fixing the price of tradable goods. This is not to say that no MNCs have any sense of environmental awareness or the need to promote sustainability. Some of them do have long-term strategies and recognise that in order to protect their business interests this requires at least some degree of environmental sensitivity. But these tend to be the exceptions to the rule and the latter part of the twentieth century saw the emergence of the phrase the 'race to the bottom' as both governments and MNCs tried to pursue economic growth by any means necessary. The consequences of this have slowly emerged with a growing recognition that such practices are short-sighted and need to be fundamentally reassessed. That said, just as national governments are a wildly varying collective, so to are MNCs with some much further advanced in their environmental awareness and strategies than others.

The World Business Council for Sustainable Development (WBCSD) is a coalition of some of the world's largest MNCs. These include major fossil fuel companies and representatives of the mining, shipping, airline and automobile industries. As such it features many of the companies responsible for the most dramatic environmental issues on the planet. In recent years the phrase 'corporate social responsibility' (CSR) has been coined to acknowledge the central role that MNCs play in impacting on the environment. As with many such phrases it is open to a wide range of meanings and interpretations. The companies themselves, understandably, say this highlights their environmental and social concerns. Others, notably some of the civil society environmental campaign groups, have criticised this approach as 'greenwash' and a shameless public relations exercise to both divert attention from ongoing environmental damage caused by these companies, and also to attract the 'green pound' of environmentally aware and concerned consumers. Short of an admission of guilt from the MNCs this is a debate that cannot be satisfactorily resolved one way or the other. No doubt there are some who work in the private sector that do have sentiments that extend beyond the basic profit motive. The Body Shop and Ben and Jerry's are both examples of MNCs that have gone out of their way to source, manufacture and promote their respective products in a sustainable manner. They do also highlight this in their advertising but this does not diminish the value of these practices.

Energy companies are at the forefront of the climate change debate. They are also among the most high profile when it comes to flagging up their CSR credentials. British Petroleum is a good example of this with a redesigned logo that resembles a green flower and a marketing slogan that reads 'Beyond Petroleum'. This is a reference to their research and development work on renewable energy sources and products. This certainly exists but it represents a very small proportion of the company's overall business, which remains firmly based on highly polluting and non-sustainable use of fossil fuels. The major automobile manufacturers are also developing hybrid products that highlight fuel efficiency and reduced carbon emissions. Again, this is to be welcomed but the underlying problems of resource depletion and pollution associated with an emphasis on multiple car households as opposed to investment in public transport infrastructure remains in place. In the broader context of development policies based on consumerism MNCs are the principle actors in facilitating this. Governments can play a role in terms of taxation and other forms of market intervention, such as health and safety legislation. Individual consumers are also clearly crucial as the 'end users' of manufactured products. Yet it is MNCs that provide the drive and momentum for this by way of both producing products and actively promoting them, often creating a market that would otherwise not exist. Markets can also be artificially created by built-in obsolescence. Added to this the constant redesigning of products to create a sense of them coming in and going out of fashion demonstrates this is a system that is built on ever-expanding levels of consumerism, and related environmental degradation. Very few markets are ever truly saturated and with many millions of new consumers entering these markets in India and China alone this is a process that has potentially very serious environmental consequences.

Governments and MNCs have both been the target of a broad range of environmental lobbying groups covering an equally diverse array of campaign issues. The early 1970s were again a significant period for this group of actors as it saw the formation of some of the leading organisations, such as Friends of the Earth and Greenpeace International. Their agendas and methods have evolved over time but they remain fundamentally concerned with environmental conservation and sustainability. Initial campaigns were based on the detrimental impacts of human activity on the environment. The Greenpeace organisation was born out of protests against US nuclear testing in the north Pacific. Success in this campaign led to protests against the French nuclear testing programme and the remit of the organisation quickly evolved to cover many other campaigns. Notable among these was their opposition, along with other conservation groups, to the annual seal cull conducted in Canada and Newfoundland. Both the cull and the protests remain ongoing. Greenpeace was one of the first campaign groups to highlight both the role of direct action and the importance of recording and publicising these actions. MNCs are not alone in their public relations exercises. The protest groups operate at various levels. They highlight the environmental damage caused as a result of MNC activities. They attempt to influence governments to adopt more environmentally aware and responsive policies and legislation. They also encourage members of the public to join their organisations and to lobby both MNCs and governments on their behalf. Advances in telecommunication technologies have radically enhanced the latter point.

Actors: non-governmental organisations

NGOs previously relied on writing to newspapers or conducting high-profile actions that would ensure their arguments would receive press coverage. As these actions became more commonplace their newsworthiness subsequently declined. However, the Internet has provided a valuable platform for highlighting issues via these organisations' own websites and it is also becoming a conduit for the practical coordination of campaigns and related actions. This also enables connections to be made highlighting how the consumption of products, for example in the UK, may have far-reaching consequences for people, other species and habitats far across the globe. The organisation of consumer boycotts, or at least raising awareness of more sustainable-sourced alternatives, has played a significant part in these groups' actions. The role of the individual has become increasingly important as patterns of consumption have evolved to such a degree that lifestyle options and choices have impacts well beyond a person's immediate locality. NGOs have capitalised on this by highlighting these connections and illustrating the level of empowerment this bestows upon individuals. It is no longer the case that citizens are restricted to exercising a level of political power once every few years by casting a vote in an election, assuming they have the right to vote. Now many people are making actively 'political' choices in relation to thinking about the implications of their consumption of all types of goods and services. This can be in relation to where they take their holidays, how they travel, whether they are using energy-saving light bulbs or avoiding leaving electrical items on stand-by. These are day-to-day activities that are increasingly recognised as having environmental consequences.

EXAMPLE BOX

Stakeholder Forum for a Sustainable Future

This section has looked at how different types of actors interact in the pursuit of their various interests in relation to environmental issues. At times national governments may be the key players. Often the economic interests and processes the MNCs represent can be crucial determinants. The role of NGOs and civil society more generally is another important factor. The relationship between these differing actors can cover the full spectrum from conflict to cooperation. There are few arenas where a dialogue between all three sectors can be successfully facilitated. One of these though is the Stakeholder Forum. This was initially created in 1987 as the National Committee for the UN's Environment Programme in the UK. It then became an international multi-stakeholder organisation called Stakeholder Forum for our Common Future, hosted by the UN Association of the UK from 1993 to 2004. It is now a fully independent NGO which facilitates close links and dialogue between representatives of national governments, intergovernmental agencies, the private sector and a broad range of civil society actors. It has a particular focus on the international negotiations organised by the UN's Commission of Sustainable Development. This example is illustrative of the recognition that environmental issues cannot be adequately addressed within a single sector but must recognise the need for dialogue and cooperation right across the range of actors and interests relevant to these issues.

Having looked at the range of actors that are influential on and impacted by environmental change we now turn to look at specific issues and how each of these actors relate to them. None of the following are completely 'stand alone' as, in line with Lovelock's Gaia theory, they are each interconnected as part of a global eco-system. Some have very locally specific dimensions, but all are best understood in terms of their place in relation to broader environmental impacts.

Issues: resource depletion

Resource depletion has been a concern since the earliest days of the environmental movement. As mentioned above, there have been varying predictions and disagreements over the rate at which supplies are becoming exhausted. However, there is virtually unanimous agreement that the vast majority of resources are being consumed in excess of natural replenishment. Fossil fuels appear to have a degree of market elasticity, which means that supplies can 'expand' in relation to their market value. The same cannot be said for other resources such as forests or fish stocks. Both of these have been excessively exploited, to the point of systemic collapse in some areas. These are interesting examples in terms of issues of ownership and sovereignty. Forests are obviously located within a specific sovereign territory, yet they have also been described as the 'lungs of the world' and should therefore be seen as a form of global commons. This is obviously a contentious point with states that wish to exploit their forest resources arguing that they have political autonomy and every right to use these resources in any way they see fit. A fair point in the current nation state system, but one that is at odds with the more holistic perspective that recognises the importance of these forest areas as carbon sinks which play a crucial role in the global climate system. Some developing states, notably Malaysia, have been very forthright in condemning the more developed states for what they see as the denial of development and the opportunity for these states to better themselves. The UN has devised a set of 'Forest Principles' that attempt to monitor, if not police, the use of forest resources in a sustainable manner. This is directed towards governments but has implications for the MNCs involved in the timber industry and also NGOs such as the Rainforest Alliance, which promotes forest conservation.

Issues: deforestation

The debate surrounding forest resource use and conservation is highly politicised with potential disagreement over land use at the domestic and intergovernmental levels. Added to this is the economic dimension with big business involvement, plus numerous NGOs that campaign for forest conservation. The latter include those that may be campaigning for the protection of a particular species, such as the orang-utan. They argue that the best way to protect a species is to protect its natural habitats, in this case tropical rainforest. There are other groups that campaign on behalf of indigenous peoples, for example the Yanomani in Amazonia, who are threatened by loggers and mining prospectors. Tropical rainforest is home to the most concentrated and diverse range of biodiversity on the planet and this also raises its profile as both a resource, notably for medicinal plants, and as an eco-system to be valued in its own right beyond the market value of any extractable timber. The political economy of tropical rainforest is as complex as the flora and fauna that inhabit this

Table 9.2 Forest area and area change

Region	Extent of forest, 2005			Annual change rate			
	Forest area (1,000 ha)	% of land area (%)	Area per 1000 people (ha)	1990–2000		2000–2005	
				(1,000 ha)	(%)	(1,000 ha)	(%)
Central Africa	236070	44.6	2020	−910	−0.37	−673	−0.28
East Africa	77109	18.9	346	−801	−94	−771	−0.97
Northern Africa	76805	8.2	392	−526	−0.64	−544	−0.69
Southern Africa	171116	29	1303	−1152	−0.63	−1554	−0.66
West Africa	74312	14.9	269	−985	−1.17	−899	−1.17
Total Africa	**635412**	**21.4**	**673**	**−4375**	**−0.64**	**−4040**	**−0.62**
East Asia	244862	21.3	160	1751	0.81	3840	1.65
South East Asia	203887	46.8	361	−2790	−1.2	−2763	−1.3
South Asia	79239	19.2	52	213	0.27	−88	−0.11
Oceania	206254	24.3	6096	−448	−0.21	−356	−0.17
Total East Asia and Pacific	**734243**	**25.8**	**201**	**−1275**	**−0.17**	**633**	**0.09**
CIS	826588	46.7	4065	103	0.01	−73	−0.01
Eastern Europe	43042	32.8	341	71	0.17	150	0.35
Western Europe	131763	36.8	328	703	0.56	583	0.45
Total Europe	**1001394**	**44.3**	**1369**	**877**	**0.09**	**661**	**0.07**
Caribbean	5974	26.1	146	36	0.65	54	0.92
Central America	22411	43.9	557	−380	−1.47	−285	−1.23
South America	831540	47.7	2197	−3802	−0.44	−4251	−0.5
Total Latin America and Caribbean	**589925**	**47.3**	**1870**	**−4147**	**−0.46**	**−4483**	**−0.51**
North America	677464	32.7	1537	17	0	−101	−0.01
Central Asia	16017	3.9	214	9	0.06	9	0.06
Western Asia	27571	4	93	25	0.09	5	0.02
Total Central and West Asia	**43588**	**4**	**117**	**34**	**0.08**	**14**	**0.03**

Source: Data derived from Food and Agriculture Organization of the United Nations (2009) *State of the World's Forests 2009.* Reproduced with permission.

eco-system. There are a wide range of actors with competing interests and agendas involved over the fate of this habitat.

Issues: biodiversity

One aspect of protecting biodiversity is to reduce the number of extinctions of species that occur. The International Union for Conservation of Nature (IUCN) produces a 'red list of threatened species'. This currently lists over sixteen thousand species at various levels of risk up to highly endangered. As the natural world has evolved, unless you are of a creationist persuasion, many distinct species have emerged and subsequently disappeared. This raises some interesting points on the 'value' of species. Does it matter that we no longer share the planet with the dodo? The answer to this question is likely to revolve around the extent to which species and habitats are perceived as having inherent value, or if this only occurs in terms of a 'use' value for humans. This is an illustration of the distinction to be made between those who separate out humans from our natural environment and the deeper green approach which sees humans as simply another species, albeit one with a disproportionate ability to impact on all other species. Here we are touching on the realms of moral philosophy but the answer to the above question is of great significance to some of today's most pressing environmental debates. To return to the rainforest example, protecting biodiversity can be on the grounds that it is the most remarkable, even beautiful for some observers, environment on the planet. Equally from a human use perspective the plants of the rainforest have provided the basis for many medicinal drugs and it is quite possible that further medicines could yet be discovered that would provide cures for some of the most widespread and lethal illnesses. Whichever position is taken, the rainforests represent one of the front lines of environmental destruction and conservation debates.

Issues: reef systems

The world's reef systems have been described as the 'rainforests of the oceans'. This is a reference to their comparable levels of biodiversity, and also the fact that they are similarly under threat. The big difference of course is that the reefs are underwater and often subject to the old adage 'out of sight, out of mind'. Awareness of the importance of reef systems, and mangrove to a lesser extent, has grown in recent years but remains largely restricted to marine scientists, divers and those who rely directly on reefs for fishing resources. Reef systems are under pressure due to a number of factors. Unsustainable fishing methods, such as the use of explosives to stun fish, can damage reef systems but the greatest threat comes from pollution of coastal waters and the bleaching of coral due to fluctuations in water temperature. In another example of how environmental issues are connected, the end result of damage to reef can be traced back to issues as apparently unconnected as deforestation many miles from the sea or the use of nitrogen-rich fertilisers in agricultural production. Both of these processes have impacts on river systems that then drain into the sea carrying either silt that suffocates the reef, which is a living organism, or the nitrates from fertilisers that can over-stimulate marine growth, creating algae blooms that also damage the reef. Climate change and the warming of the oceans have also been cited as one of the main reasons why coral reefs lose their natural colourfulness and die. The implications of the loss of this habitat can also be far-reaching. Reef systems act as a nursery for many species of fish. If the reef dies and no longer offers this form of protection then a whole generation of fish species can be impacted upon. Fish stocks are under threat from more advanced fish-finding technologies and the use of drift nets and other methods that are non-selective in the fish that are caught. Again this can have a major impact on fish stocks if immature fish are caught before they have had chance to spawn a following generation of fish.

Issues: fisheries

There have been several cases of previously well-stocked fisheries being exploited to the point of collapse. One of the most infamous is the case of the northern Atlantic cod stock, which experienced a devastating collapse in the early 1990s. The Canadian government had been warned that it needed to reduce quotas for catches but refused to act to the level required because of the political consequences of the number of job losses that would result from such drastic measures. There was a further factor of long-distance trawlers operating outside Canada's twelve-mile nautical jurisdiction, which also contributed to over-fishing in this region. Again we can see both domestic and international politics in action over this issue. Short-term policies were adopted when longer-term vision and strategies were required. A similar situation has occurred with regard to European Union fishing quotas and trying to balance the needs of local economies based on fishing and related industries and the sustainability of these stock for the longer-term. The EU example has the added complication of a supranational body ruling on an issue that is highly emotive within certain regions of its member states. For example, the northeast and southwest of the UK both have long histories of fishing industries and the local economies there have struggled to adapt to the decline in these industries. Again what makes good environmental sense with regard to conserving stocks may be for the longer-term benefit of this industry, but in the shorter-term some difficult and unpopular policies may have to be introduced.

Issues: energy security

Gaining popular support for environmentally-friendly policies is always going to be a challenge for governments. This is mainly as they are going to be expensive, either in terms of direct taxation to raise funds for eco-projects, or in the costs of goods if a 'polluter pays' principle is adopted. As already indicated, most aspects of modern life have environmental costs associated with them, even if they are not always immediately apparent. Although the majority of people are likely to endorse conservation measures in principle this position could be severely tested if the true cost of goods and services were to be calculated in terms of environmental impacts. For example, energy security has come to dominate many aspects of domestic and international politics. There is a huge range of potential energy sources from fossil fuels to nuclear power to many variations of renewable energy. The political economy of energy production has numerous environmental aspects. Fossil fuels pollute and access to supply is not always guaranteed. Nuclear power has the advantage of not producing greenhouse gas emissions, but there remains no fully acceptable solution as to what to do with the radioactive waste that is produced during this process. There are also massive costs involved in safely decommissioning nuclear power stations at the end of their productive lifespan. Renewable energy sources, by definition, would appear to be an obvious solution to our energy needs, but even these are subject to political issues with regard to initial investment and where they should or should not be sited, and they also face active resistance from those with interests in maintaining the status quo in energy markets.

EXAMPLE BOX

Energy production

The production of energy can be seen to be one of the most basic of concerns in the contemporary world. Food security is obviously a major issue but many aspects of food production are reliant on secure and sustainable energy supplies. Energy security operates at all local levels but also informs the geo-strategic thinking and policies of the world's major powers. This is particularly the case in ensuring supplies of oil and gas. Arguably many of the military conflicts involving the major powers in recent years have, at least to some extent, been informed by energy supply considerations. By now it should be apparent that when looking at environmental issues it is extremely difficult to separate out the natural science of environmental degradation or conservation from the whole range of economic and political factors that inform domestic and international relations. A nomadic tribe on the edge of the Saharan desert may gather firewood for heating and cooking in what appears to be an act of local subsistence. It is, but it also feeds into a much bigger picture of advancing desertification, which in turn has climatic effects and can be related to major environmental negotiations and agreements such as the Kyoto Protocol or the UN Convention to Combat Desertification.

The key to understanding the impact of all of the environmental issues considered here is to recognise that none of them happen in isolation from each other. They are all interconnected, even though some of these connections may not be clear even to those most closely associated with each localised event. The following section looks at the political, economic and socio-cultural processes that relate to environmental issues.

Processes

Fundamentally environmental conservation or degradation is a natural, physical process. Even before the emergence of Homo sapiens the natural world experienced significant changes in the natural environment, including waves of extinctions. Earth's eco-systems are dynamic and constantly changing, both within relatively discrete micro-habitats and in the interaction between these and the overall system. Humans are not the only species to disrupt the lives and habitats of other species, but we have 'advanced' to a stage where, unlike any other species, our combined actions are having impacts at the global level. Climate change scientists continue to debate their predictions on how such change will impact on the planet, and at what rate. However, there is now near universal agreement that climate change is happening, it is largely due to human activity and the consequences of changing climatic patterns are becoming increasingly severe.

The natural environment has its own dynamism but this can be modified by human actions in the political, economic and socio-cultural fields. Most IPE approaches highlight the interconnections between the realms of politics and economics. This position is not being challenged here but for the purposes of this analysis this section will begin by looking at the political processes relevant to environmental issues. These operate at national and international levels with some aspects of sub-national politics to be considered, and also a number of standing intergovernmental agencies such as the IPCC, UN Environment Programme and UN Development Programme.

Figure 9.2 illustrates climate change over time using two different models, one derived from natural processes and the other taking into account human impact. Although there are variations between regions, each area under consideration demonstrates a marked increase in both greenhouse gas emissions and related rises in temperature.

| **Figure 9.2** | Human-induced climate change by region |

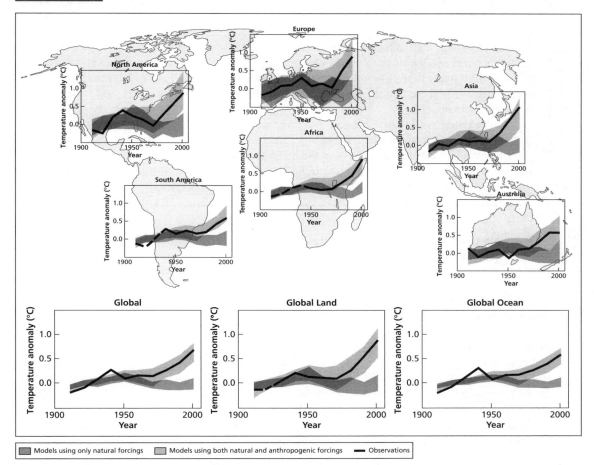

Source: Intergovernmental Panel on Climate Change (2008) *Climate Change 2007: Synthesis Report*, Geneva: IPCC, Figure 2.5, p. 40.

EXAMPLE BOX

Earth Summit process

The UN Conference on Environment and Development took place in Rio de Janeiro, Brazil, from 3 to 14 June 1992: 172 states attended with 108 of these represented at the head of government or head of state level. This was an unprecedented gathering of political leaders drawn together to discuss environmental issues. There was also a parallel NGO forum with representatives from 2,400 civil society groups. MNCs attended, but in a lobbying of governments capacity rather than a discrete conference mode. Resulting documentation included the Rio Declaration on Environment and Development, the Statement of Forest Principles, the United Nations Framework Convention on Climate Change and the United Nations Convention on Biological Diversity. Follow-up mechanisms were the Commission on Sustainable Development; Inter-agency Committee on Sustainable Development and the High-level Advisory

Board on Sustainable Development. This was an important process as it established standing bodies and a rolling agenda to maintain discussion and policy-making forums to address international environmental issues. Several follow-up meetings have taken place with regard to the conference of the parties of the above convention plus five- and ten-year review conferences of the Earth Summit, held in New York and Johannesburg respectively. The 2002 ten-year review conference was notable because the developing states complained that the developed states had failed to fulfil many of the commitments they had pledged to at the Rio conference. It also occurred post-9/11. The era of the 'war against terror' has seen many states shift their focus away from environmental issues.

The Copenhagen Climate Change Conference of December 2009 was widely regarded as a failure as it did not produce a legally binding agreement to reduce greenhouse gas emissions. A partial agreement was reached between the major powers with a marked shift in the dynamic within the developing world as China, India and Brazil distanced themselves from the positions adopted by the smaller and more vulnerable states, such as Tuvalu.

The main political unit remains the national government. With over two hundred such bodies in the international system there is an understandable variance in how environmental issues are approached. Most of the more developed states have advanced governmental bureaucracies that include ministers with specific responsibilities for environmental issues. Their departments may be subdivided to sections dealing with specialised policies on energy, agriculture, transport, wildlife conservation and other aspects of the environment. Importantly, some of these posts will be 'mirrored' by government officials working in other sections of the administration. For example, an official in the department of transport would have a portfolio that related to those in the departments of both energy and environment. In some respects this should accommodate some coherent 'joined-up' policy prescriptions. While this may sometimes be the case it is also a recipe for conflicting bureaucratic politics to take place, especially if each department is competing for a slice of their government's overall budget. In addition to potential conflict over policy priorities within an administration, environmental issues have become something of a party political football with opposition parties routinely disagreeing with the standing government's policies in this area. In some respects this is no more than an extension on normal party politics within the regimes that allow for this. That said, it is noticeable that environmental issues have moved from being relatively marginalised in most parliamentary debates to becoming one of the central issues of political and popular debate.

The above point on departmental budgets immediately connects the political realm with the economic. Many government officials may have the best will in the world to adopt environmentally sustainable policies but do not have access to the material resources to do so. Very often, especially in the developing world but also in the most developed states, it is the drive for economic growth that is the root cause of the environmental problems that need to be addressed. The process of economic growth continues to hold a central position among most governments, and the majority of economic consultants and advisers. This is not to say that it is not possible to have economic growth without environmental degradation, but the dominant model of development currently reflects this trade-off between growth and sustainability. This is illustrative of the long-standing approach to development that argues for a top-down or 'trickle-down' approach where the political priority has to be growth first, then environmental conservation and, possibly, social justice. This approach has long been supported by MNCs, which obviously have a vested interest in promoting economic activity as a priority, and criticised by NGOs, which tend to favour more bottom-up, grassroots approaches.

The economic processes involved in environmental issues have two distinct aspects. One can be seen in terms of the degradation that is caused by undervaluing the environment in market calculations of the worth of a particular good or service. In contrast, the value of the environment is becoming increasingly realised in some quarters, including some MNCs. The process by which the environment is calculated into the private sector can take many forms. As noted above, it can be referred to as part of an MNC's publicity campaign in an attempt to bolster its CSR credibility, which may or may not be wholly genuine. Other examples can be where the natural environment itself becomes a commodity. This would concern nature reserves operated as profit-making businesses and a range of activities that would come under the broad heading of eco-tourism. An example of the latter is the relatively recent addition of Japan as a whale-watching destination. Japan continues to be one of the few nations in the world to undertake whaling, allegedly for scientific purposes although at least some of the meat is subsequently sold in commercial markets. There has been an awareness gained that you can only kill and sell a whale once, but you can profit repeatedly by selling whale-watching trips. Hence there is a financial incentive to conserve rather than deplete the whale population. Similar financial incentives can be found in other sectors. Deforestation was referred to above as a serious environmental issue; it is, but this is not to say that forest resources cannot be harvested in a sustainable manner. Clear felling often results in a one-off payment to local landowners and resulting environmental damage caused not only by the heavy machinery required to fell and transport the logs but also the loss of other forest resources accessed by local people, especially if they retain a subsistence lifestyle of hunting and gathering from the forest. A more appropriate method would be selective logging, which utilises timber resources but also maintains the surrounding eco-system. This may be a slower process and income would be generated over a longer period, but a similar amount of income could be generated without the negative impacts that are almost always associated with industrial-scale logging practices.

The above examples demonstrate that the process of making a profit does not necessarily have to result in significant environmental degradation. MNCs, by their basic characteristic of economies of scale, do tend towards the larger and therefore more damaging practices. Moreover, as they rarely have a particular association to a piece of land, other than as a source of wealth creation, they are less likely to see 'value' in the land other than how profitable it can remain. Once its profitability has been maximised the MNC is free to move on to exploit new territories. On the other hand, local inhabitants are far more likely to have social, cultural and even spiritual connections to their natural environment. This is something that is difficult, if not impossible, to calculate in terms of a financial worth. There are examples of indigenous peoples accepting relocation packages from governments and MNCs in order for their traditional lands to be mined or flooded for a hydroelectric power scheme or some other sort of resource usage. There are, of course, many other examples where locals have been forcibly evicted and even killed to remove them from particular sites. Arguably in the former case there is, perhaps, a case to be made for a market price having been found to replace the feeling of identity associated with a particular piece of land. Yet this seems to be conflating two quite different world views of 'value' in the realms of the financial and the spiritual.

Considering socio-cultural aspects of the environment might appear out of place in a section looking at the processes that surround these issues. Yet in all of the above, whether it is with regard to governments, MNCs, NGOs or individuals, the common thread on the emergence of the environment as an agenda item is a process of consciousness and the raising of environmental awareness. NGOs explicitly aim to do this with the majority of their campaigns, which rely on mobilising popular support. MNCs do this, to some degree, in relation to their CSR campaigns. Governments also attempt to justify their policies, particularly those that are dependent on being re-elected. In each case awareness of environmental issues is a crucial factor. Added to this is the politicisation of these issues, as mentioned at the start of this chapter. Awareness suggests there is a single reality about the nature of environmental issues and how they might best be addressed. In outlining the range of actors, interests and agendas referred to above it is apparent that this is far from the case.

Summary

This chapter has considered the wide variety of actors, issues and processes relevant to environmental issues. Each sector is complex in its own right so this is necessarily intensified as they interact. Neither governments, MNCs nor NGOs are homogeneous groups and each sector includes tremendous variances. Even if one were to adopt a very state-centric view towards environmental issues you could not look at the issues and agendas of the US and a small island state and say you were comparing like with like, although they may share some common interests. Similarly, some MNCs may be taking CSR very seriously, while others continue to be entirely profit-driven. NGOs are a wildly diverse sector in terms of the issue areas they campaign on and their size and capabilities.

The issues referred to above have only scratched the surface of what might be considered relevant to the environment. By definition everything is, so it has not been possible in the space allowed here to do more than highlight some of the key issues in the contemporary environmental agenda. The way in which environmental issues are reported in the media is clearly important in informing popular debate surrounding these issues. In this respect the media itself, especially when seen as an MNC, becomes an important actor in relation to these issues. How government policies, MNC activities and NGO campaigns are reported are important as part of the process of informing and shaping the environmental agenda.

Finally, the processes of environmental change can be seen as operating at two distinct levels. First, there is the 'real world' physical process of environmental change, which can either be towards degradation or sustainability. Second, consider the political processes that impact on these physical changes. These involve the myriad actors referred to in this chapter. Both sets of processes are constantly being played out and interrelating with each other.

Reflective questions

1   What factors led to environmental issues coming on to the political agenda in the early 1970s?
2   What interests can you identify in relation to the various actors involved in the debates surrounding environmental issues?
3   What incentives and impediments are there with regard to addressing various environmental issues?
4   How has the Earth Summit process evolved since the Rio conference of 1992?
5   What role does the media play in highlighting environmental concerns?
6   How might individual lifestyle choices have an impact on global environmental issues?

Suggestions for further reading

Berkhout, F., Leach, M. and Scoones, I. (2003) *Negotiating Environmental Change: New Perspectives from Social Science*, London: Edward Elgar.

Carter, N. (2007) *The Politics of the Environment: Ideas, Activism, Policy*, 2nd edn, Cambridge: CUP.

Chape, S., Blyth, S., Fish, L., Fox, P. and Spalding, M. (compilers) (2003) *2003 United Nations List of Protected Areas*. UNEP-WCMC and WCPA. IUCN: Gland, Switzerland, and Cambridge, UK.

Clapp, J. (2005) *Paths to a Green World: The Political Economy of the Global Environment*, MIT Press.

Connelly, J. and Smith, G. (2002) *Politics and the Environment: From Theory to Practice*, London: Routledge.

Dodds, F., Higham, A. and Sherman, R. (2009) *Climate and Energy Insecurity*, London: Earthscan.

Dodds, F., Howell, M., Onestini, M. and Strauss, M. (2007) *Negotiating and Implementing Multilateral Environmental Agreements*, New York: UNEP.

European Commission (2008) 'Attitudes of European citizens towards the environment', *Special Eurobarometer*, 295, p. 11.

Food and Agriculture Organization of the United Nations (2009) *State of the World's Forests 2009*.

Intergovernmental Panel on Climate Change (2008) *Climate Change 2007: Synthesis Report*, Geneva: IPCC, Figure 2.5, p. 40.

Middleton, N. and O'Keefe, P. (2003) *Rio Plus Ten: Politics, Poverty and the Environment*, London: Pluto.

10 Technology

Chapter learning outcomes

After reading this chapter students should be able to:

■ Engage in debate about the nature of technology and in particular the ways in which technology can be seen as both process of thought and product.

■ Understand and be able to explain how technologies act as a major tool in economic competition and how new inventions drive competition forward.

■ Comprehend the use of technologies by MNCs in economic competition.

■ Explain the global division of labour and the influence of technology in determining this division.

■ Understand the ways in which the role of technology is limited in international relations.

■ Be familiar with the concept of intellectual property rights and their role in economic activity.

■ Offer interpretations on the nature of the individual and the influence of technological developments on the person as subject.

■ Relate discussion of technology to the theoretical debates discussed earlier in this book.

Introduction

International political economy involves technology a great deal, and in many ways. Discussions of the relative power of leading multinational companies often hinge on their ability to use technologies to compete; discussions of the dangers of their activities often hinge on the threats their products and practices present. Technology also provides a vital resource for governments, but a focus on state-to-state relations is likely to simplify and underestimate the importance of technology as a factor in international relations. Much debate on environmental policy, and nearly all discussion of energy security, engages with questions of the merits (and problems) of present and future technologies. The same is true of food security and information security. Production technologies, communication technologies, technologies of surveillance and the self, technologies which can destroy the planet and those that can save humankind: the list of potential issues is very long. It touches on nearly every aspect of IPE, including 'classic' questions about states and markets and inequality, and emerging questions about the changing world order and the growing power of new actors – firms, networks and social movements – in world politics. But IPE, although it discusses all of this, does not always theorise these issues very well. It does not always have a very clear idea of how to conceptualise technology or technological change. And it fails quite often to think critically about them.

So in approaching this chapter there is a great deal to discuss, but the intellectual resources to look critically at technology have to be found and clarified. Despite the importance of all the issues in the previous paragraph, most IPE texts do not even have a chapter on technology. However, there are also writers in IPE who explore questions of innovation, technique, technological competition, techno-structure and the philosophy of technology. Very often, they draw on business studies or cultural studies. Together, they provide good starting points. And there is a rich literature in political economy which scholars in IPE have learned to draw on (perhaps rather late) that provides a vital resource for understanding.

Five questions get us into detailed discussion of the main issues here. They form the main structure of the chapter:

- What is technology here/what do we mean by 'technology'?
- How does it shape the ways firms behave and compete?
- How does technological change affect global conflict in IPE?
- How does technology shape *individuals* and *groups of people* as *agents* in world economy, and how does it create capacities for the *state* as an *agent*?
- How can we best locate technology within theories of IPE so as to take account of it as seriously as we should (which of course implies a debate about how seriously we should take it)?

Here, we will try to answer the problem of conceptualising technology in the first section. The problem about theory arises in all sections but especially the last. The issues about thinking critically will also arise in each section in turn.

What is technology?

At first, our idea of technology might seem simple. We are surrounded by technology – mobile phones, the web, downloading software, the systems that provide electricity, water and sewage management that we take for granted until they break down, logistical systems that fill supermarket shelves and the technologies of military power from the suicide bomber's belt to the advanced cruise missile. Isn't technology just the stuff we use? Are we (humankind, not just one culture or another) not 'man the tool maker'? But these things, this 'kit' comes from somewhere. We learned to use it. Everything in this list requires infrastructure. Most of the things we use would not be manufactured at all if the cost of individual items reflected the cost of research and development directly. They can only be produced efficiently if, like mobile phones, they are produced in large numbers for a global market. How did that global market come about? Some technologies triumph over others – not all good ideas work commercially, and some technologies work so well, or are marketed so well, that others struggle to get noticed. The obvious example is the success of Microsoft's operating system MS-DOS, but there are innumerable others.

One example of a set of common assumptions about technology occurs right at the start of Stanley Kubrick's film *2001: A Space Odyssey* (1968), in which a group of hominid apes seem to discover a technology – the use of basic tools, bones, as weapons to kill. Kubrick directly links these technologies to the advanced computer technologies which the film cuts to over the credits, which are part of a space mission, and where the computer eventually takes over from human operators and kills them, apparently to defend the mission it was programmed for. The film reflects a set of deeply embedded ideas not just about the threats of technologies, but also about the fact (alleged fact) that technologies are 'taking over', and that technologies have determined the fate of humankind in very strong ways throughout our history. Kubrick's view in the film is influenced by a then-prevailing set of attitudes about technological determinism that we find in work that welcomes the power of technology, in communications and media technologies, in life sciences, in ideas of what drives economic progress and in images of everyday life, such as the dominance of the car and the capacity of ever-improving domestic tools to bring an end to housework, and perhaps the end of all work. These attitudes were quite widespread in the 1960s, although they were never un-challenged, and have become less popular today. They are reflected in different ways in another very influential film, the satirical masterpiece *Dr. Strangelove* (1964), which is also shaped by technolog-ical determinism, but where the technologies of nuclear war drive decision-makers who rapidly lose all control of the conflict they start. In both movies, technology is clearly very powerful, but it is also embedded in social institutions. Technology is as much a reflection of a set of values and social practices as it is a toolkit or body of practical knowledge.

So it is possible to say that a 'technology' is a thing or an artefact, but also that it is a *created thing in a social and economic context*. Technology is as much about organisation, management and competition as it is about producing things. And technology generally consists of a set of things em-bedded in cultures and values rather than a single object, however significant some individual ob-jects may be. When we ask what managers do, what 'entrepreneurship is', it certainly cannot be reduced to questions of technology, but it involves technology – how work is organised, how busi-nesses exploit technical advantages they have, logistics and information technologies, as well as productive systems. The complexity of managing these variables is a key part of the challenge of modern management. If you doubt this, look up online the biography of leading entrepreneurs such as Steve Jobs (Apple Computers), Marjorie Scardino (Pearson Group), Anne Mulcahy (Xerox) or Paul Ottelini (Intel).

Furthermore, technologies have and create meanings which are often critical building blocks of a culture. The invention of the automobile involved basic underlying technologies (metatechnologies) – the invention of the internal combustion engine, the electrical systems for instrumentation, the rub-ber processes to make tyres. It created a metal box where people, often on their own, travelled in long convoys on freeways in total separation from each other, in a kind of idolised individualism. Or at least until they had an accident, at which point individuals and social groups collided, something observed (in very different ways) in two films both called *Crash* (1996 and 2006). The culture of the car mapped a great deal of the world of the 1950s and 1960s – the Beach Boys sang about how 'she'll have fun, fun, fun, till her daddy takes the T-bird away'. The Ford Thunderbird may have been *the* car North American males wanted to be seen in, but the song went round the world and quite a lot of people who heard and danced to it must have had no idea at all what the girlfriend's father had done – one artefact, but many meanings in different cultures. The systems of meaning that surround all of our technologies, including the military ones and the production systems hidden within factories, are at least as complex, and change as rapidly as the systems that produce them and keep them working.

Technology is, then, what? A thing, an artefact (a thing made by human ingenuity), a social sys-tem, a thing embedded in a particular organisation, a set of cultural meanings, or a global structure of power capable of creating inequalities, winners and losers? It is not one of these rather than the others. It is *all* of the above. At the same time, although it may appear that technology so underpins everything in social and economic life that it is everything, this is not a very useful idea expressed in this way. If we say that technology affects nearly everything in our experience of the world, that implies we can at least separate technology (cause) from 'nearly everything' (effect). But if tech-nology and the world it changes are wholly embedded in each other, we need another strategy to make sense of it. Technology is, one can propose, all of the above, but it is important for the sake of clarity that we state which we mean at any one time. In saying this, we are admitting that tech-nology cuts across the traditional boundaries of academic disciplines, that it touches on much more than traditional IR or IPE.

CONCEPT BOX

Summary: What is Technology?

Technology is stuff – machinery, equipment, kit. It is, at least to a minimum effect, made by people – artefacts used for a purpose, as an extension of human capabilities (but often these days an unimaginable development of human skills).

But technology is also a social system – it is used by groups of people or societies, and it has come to define the nature of those societies. Prehistoric societies are often defined by the tools or technologies they used, but so too are modern societies.

Technologies involve innovation – in new *products* and in new *processes*. Process innovation is a vital element of industrial research even though it may seem less glamorous than the creation of new products. Process innovations often facilitate the design and creation of new products. They also help firms to get costs down and to gain the potential learning effects of production.

Innovation systems vary from one country to another, so some countries (notably Sweden and Finland) have highly effective innovation systems which sustain very active international companies (ABB, Nokia) even though they are relatively small countries. 'National innovation system' models are widely used to explain different patterns of innovation. But companies are mostly international, and have their own distinctive research cultures (e.g. 'the HP way' in Hewlett Packard) which cuts across national boundaries. Often, the study of individual sectors and individual companies will throw more light on the behaviour of KBIs than focus on state- or country-based analysis.

Metatechnologies or 'base technologies' are technologies which form the basis of a whole economic system. Examples include the development of arms-making and cotton-spinning machinery (both sectors used automated pattern-based machines) at the start of the Industrial Revolution, the internal combustion engine – the car engine, also of course used for aircraft – in the first half of the twentieth century, and the microchip. On each of these technologies, other industries and technologies were based, and they formed the basis for widespread growth and new forms of employment and skills.

Technologies as a principal tool of global economic competition

Obviously, technologies change. The process of technological change – innovation – may involve either product innovation, the development of new products, or process innovation, the development of new techniques or new ways of making things. The more spectacular side of technical innovation which gets on the top of news stories generally involves new products – new drugs to treat a danger-ous disease, new technologies to save energy, new weapons systems, new capabilities on your mo-bile phone and so on. But process innovations are at least as important in business. They may take place step-by-step, so there is no obvious breakthrough moment. But they help firms to reduce costs, to become more efficient, to become more competitive. Some of the most important innova-tions in the automobile industry, for example, were those process improvements made by Japanese engineers which enabled them to produce cars with much more reliable engines and transmis-sions, with longer lasting systems which demanded less service time, and which enabled them to out-compete European and American firms in the 1970s and 1980s by simply producing cars that were more reliable and cheaper to run as well as cheaper to buy. In doing this, they were copying what Japanese firms had already achieved in textile machinery, machine tools and electronics. It was process engineering innovation which made possible much of Japan's global economic power in the 1980s and onwards.

Large firms in specialist areas such as pharmaceuticals, computing software and aerospace use technological innovation to compete in a wide variety of ways. Innovation is so important in some of these sectors that firms will spend huge amounts of money investing in research and development. Inevitably, some of this investment will produce no returns at all, but other investments may well produce not only large increases in income, but also major gains in market share and the ability to dominate competitors and markets. For example, the major pharmaceutical companies, with a turnover in the several hundred billions of dollars a year, spend 12 to 15 per cent of turnover on research and development. Major electronics firms typically spend 5 to 10 per cent of income on research. Oil, gas and energy firms also spend around 5 per cent on research and development, a figure which excludes investment in exploration for new sources of supply, and which includes money spent on energy retrieval techniques and downstream technologies (in other words, investment in oil and gas processing or refining as well as pipeline technologies). Excepting relatively small firms, which may specialise entirely in particular aspects of research and spend most of their income on research activities, it is possible to analyse global competition in terms of the levels of spending on research and development (R&D). As this paragraph suggests, what emerges from such an analysis is a pattern where major firms in any individual sector commit roughly comparable amounts to research: if we study individual sectors, we find that they have common patterns in the way research impacts on business strategy and in the characteristics of major players as sources of knowledge as a factor in competitive behaviour.

It is also possible to compare innovation systems as a way of analysing patterns in the advanced technology industries. This kind of analysis originated in the 1980s in the analysis of national innovation systems. Some economies were observed to have advantages over others which were not merely questions of size and economies of scale, including the successful innovating economies of Sweden and Finland, the dynamic economies of some of the (then) newly industrialising world, and some regions within countries which had the capacity to help to lead the economy out of recession in the 1980s through technological strength (Silicon Valley in California, the 'M4 corridor' and 'Silicon Glen' in the UK, the second in Scotland, Catalonia in Spain, and the Rhone-Alpes region of south-eastern France. While to some extent the first two of these regional examples were strongly oriented towards defence investment, which gave a relatively easy explanation, the attention of researchers focused on why some national economies seemed to outperform others.

This national innovation systems literature has pointed towards two criticisms which are both important in understanding international high-technology activity. For in a globalised world, technical innovation is often not nationally based, and technological capabilities, although they are unevenly spread across the world system, are not easily confined by national boundaries. Cross-border regional innovation systems may be important (most obviously between France, Switzerland and Germany, but there are plenty of other examples). International intra-firm innovation is also important. Large firms concentrate research capability in some countries rather than others for a mixture of reasons (which include tax advantages, access to university expertise, access to a pool of highly skilled labour, and access to suppliers). But many firms, including most of the largest, have research centres in different countries. These may be set up to compete with each other, on price or intellectual property ownership of their successful research, or they may cooperate in networks. Either way, trade within a single major company across international boundaries in intellectual property and components accounts for a significant proportion of all international trade, at least 12 per cent (estimates vary quite widely).

Kondratieff cycles and major innovations

There is an important argument about the nature of technology and its role in economic development which originates in the work of a Russian economist, Kondratieff, in the 1920s, which was refined by Schumpeter in the 1940s, and which was developed by a range of scholars in the 1970s and 1980s (notably Christopher Freeman).

The scholars argue that technology change forms a series of waves – sometimes innovation is more rapid, sometimes there is a period of consolidation. Innovation is not a smooth, steady evolutionary pattern. It is a dynamic and sometimes strongly disruptive force. In order for new technologies and ideas – new intellectual capital – to develop, old technologies and old ideas have to be scrapped. The abandoning of intellectual capital is often difficult for people and social groups (such as a workforce) to bear – they have to give up on old assumptions and practices in order to adopt new ones.

Apart from a relatively short cycle of growth followed by recession – the business cycle, typically of five to seven years – which both liberal and Marxist economists had discussed throughout the nineteenth century, Kondratieff suggested that there was a longer term and more fundamental cycle of roughly 25–30 years. Each wave – each Kondratieff cycle – is associated with a new technology which forms the basis of the new economy. It shapes the social and cultural changes of the day as well as the patterns of trade and production. It may also have an influence on the rise and fall of dominant powers, a view which Schumpeter held quite strongly, although more recent writers have tended to say only that changes in technology cycles are one factor among many in shaping patterns of world hegemony. Each Kondratieff cycle has been associated with a deep recession – much more powerful and much more painful than those associated with a shorter trade cycle. These slumps have also had important political and cultural effects.

The first Kondratieff defines early industrial capitalism, and is associated with iron, factory production of cotton and wool products and of firearms, and the adoption of steam and water power in new and more efficient forms. Its emblems are often said to be the cotton gin (in the US), the mass production of firearms with interchangeable parts (in the US and Britain, but also elsewhere) and the iron bridge over the gorge at Ironbridge in Shropshire, UK (late eighteenth century into the 1820s).

The second Kondratieff is associated with early chemical engineering, large volume steel production, more sophisticated textile and machine tools production, and a much greater concentration of capital in the hands of large firms, many of which are either operating internationally or form parts of emerging international cartels – deals which firms use to undermine competition. The great railway boom starts in the first Kondratieff, but pretty much all of the companies in every country which start making railways in the 1830s is bust by the 1840s. It is the second Kondratieff which sees rail and steam shipping, as well as the early electric telegraph, really take off as economic powerhouses.

The third Kondratieff (1890s to 1930s) follows a slump in the 1890s which is not as serious as that in the 1840s, except in world agriculture, but which is profoundly important in promoting greater industrial development, further increases in firm sizes, and a shift of population from the land to industrialised cities. Associated with the development of new forms of power – electricity, oil and gas – and with the development of the internal combustion engine, as well as more advanced communication technologies (radio) and mass consumptions (cinema, early vacuum cleaners and other domestic goods), it produces mass car production ('Fordism') and a capacity to produce standardised arms in enormous quantity, especially in the First World War. It takes mechanical engineering and machine tools to a very high level, but is dependent on the organisation of the labour force in a hierarchy with a great emphasis on the role of the semi-skilled worker who assembles or builds products through a repetitive set of processes which are highly controlled – the control of the labour process is the most important key to making money in this Fordist, production-line-based form of economic system.

The fourth Kondratieff (late 1930s to 1970s) is generally associated with more advanced electronics, the jet engine and space technologies, plastics, agricultural chemicals such as DDT and fertiliser production, penicillin and aspirin (and more advanced pharmaceuticals more generally), more sophisticated production techniques in many industries, and a widening of education and skills across a larger workforce (including many women workers and managers). It is more research and development intensive. It produces the first computer (for decoding purposes during the Second World War), the first microprocessor (in California in the late 1940s), the further extension of much that is associated with K3 (mass consumption spreads from the US to Europe in the 1950s and 1960s), and the development of advanced factory production. The rate of technology change increases, and so does the wider public awareness of some of the (good and risky) implications of technology change.

Oligopoly competition in high-tech sectors: how multinational firms use technology to compete

Most high-tech ('knowledge-intensive' or 'knowledge-based industry' – KBI) sectors are dominated by a small number of producers which operate globally and compete intensively both for customers and for the attention of governments and international regulators. This is known as oligopoly competition – classic oligopolies or monopoly theory predicts that where only a few firms act in a market, they will collude in reducing competition, but contemporary theory and case studies suggest something different happens.

Why oligopolies at all? Five reasons: knowledge is key in advanced technology: (i) patents and intellectual property rules create barriers for new firms to enter, keeping new players out; (ii) research and development is expensive – only large, relatively established firms can afford to do it; (iii) existing large firms will take over successful rising star firms to exploit their knowledge, skills and strength, deny them to others and so reduce competition; (iv) successful large firms are able to build big stocks of cash and the support of large shareholders, enabling them to use M&As aggressively to grow still larger, making them more immune to competition and creating important national champions which governments may often protect from the 'normal' rules of anti-trust and competition policy – what economists call 'rent-seeking behaviour'; (v) as the largest players address each other in competition, they naturally push each other to grow and succeed, but at the same time grow apart from 'the rest' – smaller firms in the sector.

The tendency to oligopoly is always increased when the major customers of producers are also large firms – where there is oligopsony as well as oligopoly, because the customers have established links with suppliers, and because there is a high degree of specialised knowledge on both sides of the market. Power systems, robotics and aircraft engine manufacture are good examples (see below). As a result, KBIs tend to be characterised by a distinctive structure: a very small number of powerful lead actors, few or no convincing middle-sized competitors rising to challenge them, and a very large number of small firms which provide services and specialist roles, including aspects of activity outsourced from the big firms and high-risk marginal research which the larger firms are reluctant to try until they see it works. The small firms often act as subcontractors for the majors, and may sometimes have been set up by teams of former staff at a major who have gone independent. If they succeed, the large firm will buy them back up, creating enormous instant wealth for the entrepreneurs who set them up – but inevitably most fail.

EXAMPLE BOX

Examples of oligopolies

Civil aviation: two major world players, Airbus and Boeing. Former third player McDonnell Douglas lost out to the other two and was bought by Boeing in 1997. Russian production has made no impact on world trade since 1990, and China has been hoping to develop a competitor business but shows no sign as yet of breaking into world markets. Military aerospace has quite a distinctive different structure dictated by government involvement in the sector in the various countries heavily involved in production.

Pharmaceuticals: many active players, but only a small number are large enough to afford to research across most of the field. Most firms are specialist researchers. Top two firms in 2008 were US firms (Pfizer and Johnson & Johnson), but this is a sector with strong European presence: the next biggest are Bayer (Germany), Hoffman LaRoche and Novartis (both Swiss), GlaxoSmithKline (UK) and Sanofi (France). The largest firms are investing most in cash terms, but some are much more research intensive while others rely more on producing standard or more mature products. The most research active larger firms spend 15 per cent of turnover on R&D, more than any other sector (in small specialist firms the figure is much higher but does not tell you much).

Robotics: world market is dominated by a group of Japanese firms which have been developed out of automotive, computing and automation businesses. Some are independent and some subsidiaries of larger groups such as Kawasaki Heavy Industry. Similar patterns in the weaker European and US sectors. This structure means that robotics is not so dominated by a handful of huge players – this is a function of the business history as well as knowledge ownership. But there is still a tendency towards oligopoly – large firms include FANUC, Nachi, Toshiba Machine and Intelligent Actuator (IAI), all in Japan, KUKA in Germany, ABB (Swiss/Swedish), and Intelitek and ST Robotics (both US based). But the largest players include firms whose main business is something else – Toshiba (computing), Renault Automation (part of the automobile group) and General Electric (defence, power systems, advanced engineering).

Industrial gases: Linde Group (includes the former British and Commonwealth market leader BOC, which it bought in 2006) (Germany): 21 per cent market share; Air Liquide (France): 19 per cent also a major player worldwide, especially dominant in the EU and francophone world; Praxair (US and the Americas): 13 per cent; Air Products and Chemicals (US): 10 per cent; Nippon Sanso (Japan): 4 per cent; Airgas: 3 per cent but specialises in medical gas applications.

Technology, work and patterns of global labour

Technology shapes patterns of work. It affects what people actually do at work day to day. The shift from home working in cottage industries to large factories in the nineteenth century is one example. The growth of more flexible working systems in the 1980s and since is another. Thus, the use of robotics and computer control, as well as computer design, has reshaped manufacturing. People and automated systems work in teams to participate in a division of labour that has been repeatedly re-engineered, as we know from the language used to describe it: 'teamworking in a culture of continuous change', 'working together in a perpetual quest for quality' and so on. This kind of self-promotion by giant multinationals is not mere nonsense – it reflects an ideology of how competition works. Writers such as Mark Rupert have pointed to the direct connections between the culture of work, the culture of training, and the globalisation of the ways in which not just managements but also whole workforces think. Firms such as McDonald's and Pizza Hut are so influential across the global system because they train staff in service industries to adapt to very specific patterns of work linked to very specific technologies designed to deliver those services more effectively. Critics would say the language used by multinationals to sell themselves and at the same time train their workforces is a dangerous nonsense, but it is also a very powerful production of social relations. Continuous adjustments to the mix of what people, machines, software and control systems do have become the essence of technology in business. They also affect a range of other activities – how healthcare systems and universities work, for example.

This is clearly the case in manufacturing, and one can see it if on a visit to a manufacturing plant. It is equally clear in service industries, although it may be harder to see the nature in a shipping or insurance office. And it is true too of what happens at the top of a business. All boards of companies (especially all boards of holding companies) manage the sources of capital. The functions of senior managers and boards of directors have changed in so far as much more rapid information is available, and decisions need to be taken more rapidly, because of the information technology available to them providing that information. This also means that boards can often cut out layers of management which were previously created to organise information flows to the board which IT now manages. This enables a wider variety of corporate structures than in the 1970s. It also helps smaller companies which are able to use the technology more effectively than large competitors to survive by being quick and aggressive in their markets. Using technology in comparable ways, we could point to similar examples in the development of complex global supply chains (networks that provide components or maintenance services or other expertise) or the global trade in skills (especially in buying in key managers or researchers and their knowledge), again often on a global level. Logistics management, the management of the supply chain as efficiently as possible in shipping and truck services, saves on the costs of transport and of holding stocks, and helps to drive competition. It is, of course, entirely dependent on sophisticated uses of information technology.

Limitations on the role of technology

At the same time, there are important factors which limit the spread of innovations and which may reduce the rate of technological change and limit its social effects. These include the availability of finance for investment and the degree to which managers and other financial decision-makers are risk averse. Investment in riskier technologies is likely to be less in a recession, or in the period coming out of a recession, than in a boom, when investors are generally much more open to new ideas. Individuals, firms and social systems have different capacities to absorb technological innovations. India, with a surplus of graduates, and very different levels of education in different regions, found it had a relative advantage in developing an IT industry in and around Bangalore which has become world class even while much of the rest of the country has remained relatively disadvantaged in new technology. China, with a strongly centralised direction of education policy, has succeeded in developing a comparable leadership in creative media industries in the Shanghai region, but this has not necessarily helped other regions of the country's economic development as much as central government expected. The factors at work here are as much cultural as economic, although they also reflect institutional capacities. It is when we look at different patterns of technological change and their real results in economic and social change that we discover how much innovation patterns are *not* merely a result of market forces.

To take another example, in 1958, Ghana and Malaysia both gained independence from the UK. At that time, they had comparable literacy rates, similar population numbers, and similar levels of GDP and of engagement in the world economy. Fifty years later, Ghana has achieved some respectable levels of growth by comparison with other countries in Africa, has a highly developed civil society and a democratic state (despite quite long periods of military rule in the past), and a great deal more political stability than some other west African countries. But it has developed at a far slower rate than Malaysia, which now enjoys a GDP approximately ten times that of Ghana ($386 billion as against $34.4 billion). There are many explanations for this, some of which are complex and some of which make sense at a regional rather than a purely national level. But technical innovation and education in technology are two of the most important. Malaysia made a series of decisions (very much state focused rather than market focused) to develop large oligopoly firms designed to compete within its region with South Korea, Taiwan and Hong Kong, to develop higher education, to develop technical education at all levels, and to attract capital in advanced technology industries. The aim was to build a domestic technical capability through spin-offs from multinational firms and to build human capital across Malaysian society. Part of this was a political deal – ruling political elites offered goodies in the form of rapid and sustained economic development in exchange for little opposition and little questioning of how they did business. But at an economic and social level it worked, and at the same time most Malaysian commentators would say this has preserved social stability in a country which experienced a serious civil conflict before the British withdrew. High technology education and the skills which went with it have helped to make Malaysia a successful, if not a very open, society. But none of this would have happened if the state – what has been called the 'competition state' – had not played a leading role in managing the transition.

The previous discussions also suggest that 'technology' does *not have a fixed meaning*. It means one thing in firms, usually the definition just used. It means another to the individual. The person who gets up, switches on her TV, runs a bath with clean water, takes her iPod to the gym before boarding the train to work is very conscious of the systems she uses in some respects, and has a range of very sophisticated skills. But she is almost certainly not very aware of the systems that underpin what she does each day, and it is probably true that all of us have a 'horizon' of awareness of technologies beyond which quite a lot of important things happen or where systems operate which we have little understanding.

To check this, imagine you go to Baghdad as it is today. The city works, after a fashion, surprisingly well. Individuals, families and larger communities have adapted to the conditions which people in the advanced economies would think were unbearable. There is little electricity, no reliably clean water, and dreadful failures of the sewage system make the Euphrates River dangerous and obnoxious. The land-based telephone system, never very good, has largely been abandoned. Instead, people use their own electricity generators, systems they can maintain themselves, which use diesel or petrol, at huge environmental cost. The relatively wealthy drink bottled water; the poor get ill with water-borne disease. The mobile phone system works relatively well, and has been the fastest growing business in a damaged economy. Years after the 2003 invasion, the electricity, water and sewage systems fail the people and the invaders alike. Humans can, and of course do, live in all kinds of conditions that people today would find appalling. The situation in Baghdad, which reminds one of how much we all depend on basic technology systems we can often take for granted, is a result of a technological and political choice. In the Second World War, US army and navy combat engineers were legendary for their efficiency and their ferocity under fire. Two brigades of combat engineers (one for electrical engineers, one for water and sewage) could have restored the key systems in Baghdad and then improved them. They would have worked under fire if necessary, and they would have won the proverbial 'hearts and minds' battle. Instead, a careful decision was made to give contracts for this work to private companies which treated the contracts as a giant milking machine. In turn, when they said they had to be paid but could not work because of security concerns, they were then protected by 'security' companies that provided bodyguards and convoys and communication systems. Although this has, by 2009, delivered a little bit of restoration of electricity services, on the whole it can only be evaluated by use of language which would have an academic text barred for obscenity. The decision to privatise to large multinational firms all those key functions was a reflection of a particular neo-liberal ideology. It was not in principle a poor decision, providing the contracts had been regulated, had severe penalty clauses, and had been effectively policed. As much as $6 billion has disappeared in these contracts, which the US government refused to police, to protect the private firms which enjoyed their benefits.

LITERATURE BOX

Frankenstein's legacy

Mary Shelley's novel is one of the most sophisticated tools for starting to think about the relationship between science, scientists, technology and society you can find. It does not try to tell us that all science is wrong, and it does not say that scientists should be ignored in favour of some naïve kind of romanticism. It does suggest that science without ethics is dangerous and that scientists – such as Dr Frankenstein himself – are most dangerous when they become powerful and arrogant.

Put into contemporary terms, this is not an argument against science but an argument for having strong ethical restraints on scientists. If we want to understand the impact of technology on IPE, we need to remember that – as elsewhere in this book – 'IPE' itself has an enlarged and critical definition. It is not just about firms and markets or regulation and states. Cultures of technology impact on political behaviour, but also constitute political behaviours. Asking questions about Frankenstein leads us to ask questions about the interaction of cultures and globalisation and business. It also leads us to ask about the value of Shelley's many successors in film and literature who explore questions of ethics, the culture of difference, the importance of valuing knowledge and using it wisely, in writing about science and technology in society. See, for example, the very varied works of Arthur C. Clarke, William Gibson, Donna Haraway, Philip K. Dick and J.G. Ballard (and many others).

Intellectual property and technology

Intellectual property is knowledge which can be bought and sold. It includes patents, copyrights and designs. The purpose of intellectual property rules is not to keep ideas and techniques secret, but to enable them to be traded in an orderly way. There is a balance of interests here – it is in the general public interest that firms should innovate, and that those innovations should be diffused around the economy as quickly as practically possible. This requires that individual inventors and firms which specialise in innovation should do research, develop new products and processes, test them for safety and efficiency and market them. It also needs firms to encourage others to buy their innovations and adopt them, since this produces greater competition and brings the price of the innovation down more quickly. But of course none of this is necessarily in the inventor or innovating firms' interest. Benjamin Franklin is said to have encouraged innovation as one of the main qualities of the new republic of the US: 'Make a better mousetrap and the world will make a path to your door!' But if you make a better mousetrap and do not have legal protection, the world may well leave your door alone and merely reverse engineer your product to copy it. Individual firms will only innovate if they know that they are going to be able to secure a good level of returns on their investment.

Advanced technology sectors are dominated by concerns about how intellectual property rules work. Software is covered by copyright rather than patents, this changes the way the rules work, meaning that software producers get added protection for much longer. This provides an incentive to put computer power into the market in the form of software rather than embedded in hardware, a point which has shaped the development of the personal computer market. Pharmaceutical companies take longer than others to bring new products to market because of the extensive safety and testing requirements of new drugs. This justifies drug patents having a much longer life – so the companies can recover their investment in research and testing – than, say, engineering products. Research in industry is structured around the intellectual property rules that apply, and the legal and political control of intellectual property rights (IPRs) is of growing importance.

This is also reflected in international trade negotiations. Firms anxious to use their strengths in IPRs to compete in the marketplace push governments and international trade organisations and industry associations to adopt principles which support their own position and weaken those of rivals. As a result, negotiations such as those in the WTO Doha Round, which are formally conducted by governments, are always surrounded by major firms and their representatives, pressing negotiators to move in particular ways. Most WTO trade disputes, again formally brought by governments, have trade associations on both sides pushing the case of individual firms. This can be seen as somehow illegitimate rent-seeking activity, but it is also a natural corollary of the nature of the negotiating process. The problem is that some actors, notably developing countries, are weakened in this kind of situation unless they are able to organise in similar ways to the well-resourced industry associations of developed countries. This they have started to do, and countries such as India and Brazil have similar patterns of organisation, and make similar use of specialist consultants, to the most effective developed negotiators.

Firms also engage in mergers and acquisitions (M&As) for a range of reasons, often primarily concerned with financial economies of scale. But they may also seek to buy up a rival in order to get access to its intellectual property or its research potential. More crudely, firms may buy up another not because they want its assets so much as to deny them to a leading competitor. Technology is a major resource, including the knowledge and know-how of a workforce, and counts as a significant asset on the balance sheet of any company engaged in the global knowledge economy. But valuing 'know-how' is formidably difficult, and if the know-how a company owns is its principle asset, this makes for difficulties (especially in recession) in valuing not just companies but whole sectors of the economy.

Technology and the individual person as subject

Traditional studies in international relations tend to neglect individuals, except individual leaders or decision-makers. IPE has often followed an IR agenda, and so individual people and groups of individuals have found little role in the subject because of its fundamental agenda. This fundamental agenda is the ontology of the approach (its 'theory of what exists'). As soon as this is acknowledged, the door is open to ontological critique: why do some actors seem to count for a great deal and other people or institutions do not count, and do not count as 'actors'?

There are a number of leverage points for this critical argument. One, advocated in particular by Craig Murphy and Roger Tooze (1996), starts with a phenomenon which, they argue, IPE neglects and should not: poverty. If we ask operators why radical inequalities occur in global politics, there might be several answers. But if we are to investigate poverty, as they suggest, we need also to ask about the experiences of the poor. How do those people experience, define and understand the world? If we ask that question, we cannot ask it only of 'the poor' for very long. These are, after all, individual people, with a diverse set of responses to their situation. And poverty may not in any case be experienced as *the same* in different cultures and contexts, although no doubt there are many similarities. Individuals use the available technologies, make choices and overcome difficulties or negotiate strategies to survive. People here are 'victims' of poverty, but that is not all they are or what they are essentially: they are also agents, initiators, survivors, witnesses and negotiators. They are both victims and perpetrators of the violence of poverty, as some works such as the two great Brazilian films *City of God* (2002) and *Central Station* (1998) explore. Of course states, large and small, regional power systems and social and economic structures all shape the realities of poverty. But we cannot validly discuss its place in international political economy without also exploring and giving a central place to those individuals and groups who experience it.

Feminist political economists make similar kinds of arguments. They look to the experience of women in development, in people smuggling, in sweatshops, in migratory labour, in house and field work – and in all of this, think they may also look at women in large groups (for example the class of working women). They also often look at the micro-political economy of the chosen topic, which leads directly to individual women as agents, negotiators, witnesses, victims, decision-makers, mothers, entrepreneurs and no doubt more. At the same time, feminist writing goes beyond offering a distinctive agenda of study of a destructive ontology, a theory of what counts and what *ought* to count in the theory of IPE. Feminist scholars have also explored questions of how knowledge is constructed within IPE, and how that knowledge might be critiqued and developed. The epistemological critique opens the possibility of different forms of knowledge in the field, while questioning the privileging of *some* forms of knowledge over others. The newly established forms of knowledge include the work of those scholars who are investigating these questions which other more traditional or orthodox IPE generally neglects. But this heterodox IPE also looks at the knowledge these women identify as previously excluded. This might use some kind of grounded theory or critical discourse analysis approach to explore the meanings people in particular institutions give to their lives, how *they* conceptualise and construct the world, how they use special language and distinctive social practises to do so and how they find *agency* in these experiences. One particular issue here is of women's indigenous knowledge. Women in particular communities hold special knowledge, which may be medical (e.g. knowledge of healing plants) or agricultural (knowledge of particular techniques that suit their own soil or seed or water supply), important when women do most of the teaching, all the midwifery and a disproportionate amount of the agricultural labour in many societies. This special knowledge has a recognised status within some societies, for example in Amazonia, in India and among Arctic peoples. But it is significant also where it may not be recognised. And in the Caribbean and Africa, as in developed societies, women often take roles as heads of families and as key organisers of small businesses as well as their more 'traditional' work.

If one then asks if the discussion had not got a long way from technology, the answer is that both the analysis of the impacts, experiences and meanings of poverty and the role of women in development, business and families involves the day-to-day use of technologies of labour and production as well as indigenous knowledge which in itself is a form of technology. So far in this section we have tended to assert the ability of individuals to take control of their lives, in some part at least, and to negotiate or struggle for themselves using available technologies and ideas and collective as well as individual action. Structural world-system theory, like neo-realism, focuses on the main global structures of power (defining 'structure' in quite different ways). Both tend to agree that dominant structures create and continuously reproduce social systems in which individuals have little effective power to change their lives. This is not to say that they do not try. But for at least some world-system theorists (unlike, for example, liberal or Gramscian theory) the struggles of people to resist, to change the global structures, to achieve either 'agency' or an effective renegotiation of their position, are bound to fail except in the relatively long run when, along with underlying changes in the key structures of power, some more radical transformation can come about. 'Technologies' may well be relevant in these struggles, but they do not in themselves change the main pattern of social and economic relations. Technologies are more evident as part of the tools of domination of the hegemonic power that constitute the driving actors in the world system (again, both world-system theory and neo-realism use concepts of global hegemony but mean different things by them). One can reply that, in giving the account very briefly summarised here, both schools are also giving an inadequate account of the capabilities and meanings and subversive potentialities of different technologies.

Who has technology leadership?

Governments have worried about the loss of something they often call technological leadership. This has been a key element of debates about the decline of US hegemony or its rise to 'unipolarity' both in the US and elsewhere. But countries don't have technical leadership; firms do. The argument matters in IR theoretically as well as in policy terms, as part of a set of claims either that the US holds global hegemony (whether that is seen as very much a good thing or not) or that it has lost or is losing it. Of course, firms with strong records of patenting may appear to have technical leadership – but the majority of world patents are registered in the United States for legal reasons, to get protection of the US courts, whether or not the research on which they are based was done in the US. Nonetheless, US science and technology does have obvious and very broad-based strengths. Other countries with strong positions in technology markets and innovation include the obvious large states, but also some smaller but intellectually well-endowed actors such as Malaysia, Sweden, Switzerland and Canada.

But this is not the way in which global firms work. The main MNCs are global operators. They may be based legally in one country or another, but they operate in many. Where they are based is primarily a question of taxation and regulation. But firms which are 'based' in, say, California or Delaware in the US may have their research division based in Germany and a range of research labs in a dozen other countries. Defining state leadership in many technological fields is thus very hard, although in defence it is usually easier to assess. US firms such as Boeing and General Electric are primarily based in the US and produce their knowledge there – but they are exceptions rather than the rule. And important research operations, including much 'hard' physics and heavy engineering, are so expensive that they are routinely done by multinational consortia of laboratories and countries, and not just in any single state. This is true of non-military space research today, and of fundamental physics and astrophysics. But it is also the case in automotive engineering, advanced robotics and high-voltage power systems, where many large and smaller firms are members of consortia which collaborate both on R&D and on getting new designs to market as quickly as they can.

Having said that, it is clear that in some areas EU firms have a distinctly strong position, including bioengineering, pharmaceuticals and food processing. Japanese firms have particular strengths in biotechnology applications (especially marine biotechnology), anything connected with domestic electronics, and production systems (for example automation and robotics). US firms have strength across a wide range of fields but not in all. The USA's particular strengths lie in defence-related research, because of the long-term impact of very high state funding, but also in software engineering and applications and in business systems. There are quite a number of fields where there is no clear leader, including advanced power systems and renewable energy resources other than wind power (where Denmark is a world leader). Other fields where there is no obvious leadership include chip manufacture, where the US, Japan and China all have strengths, advanced materials, where there are a range of countries with diverse strengths, and nuclear power, where France is the leading exporter, but where Sweden, Canada and the US all have technical strengths. China has an acknowledged strength in a range of existing technologies, but is also emerging as a world leader in electronic technologies (lithium batteries), media technologies and some software applications.

Summary

It has been widely recognised that both 'orthodox' IR theory and more conventional accounts of global political economy tend to underestimate the significance of technology and innovation. This can be verified by looking in most IPE textbooks. However, these are exceptions: the dated but still valuable text by Skolnikoff, *The Elusive Transformation* (1993); and the discussions of the knowledge structure, in which she includes technology issues, in Susan Strange's *States and Markets* (1994). Several journals offer valuable articles, most regularly *Research Policy*, but also the *Review of International Political Economy* and *New Political Economy*, and some of the main business studies journals.

However, looking across the discussion in this chapter, it is possible to conclude that technology makes an enormously significant impact on international political economy. It shapes corporate strategies and patterns of trade and exchange. It creates a world of intellectual property which offers both opportunities and threats to key players. It shapes the distribution of power between states not just because it affects defence capabilities but also because it underpins many of the sources of economic and financial power. It shapes conflicts, but also provides frameworks within which a great deal of co-operation takes place.

Reflective questions

1   Does the term 'technology' refer simply to material things which humans create or does it also refer to processes of thought and manufacturing?
2   How do technological capabilities influence the economic competitiveness of national economies and in particular MNCs?
3   In what ways do varying technologies shape the global division of labour?
4   Is technological advancement the answer to human development? Do intellectual property rights advance or restrict this?
5   When studying international political economy and international relations what benefit do we get from looking at issues of technology?

Suggestions for further reading

De La Mothe, J.R. (2001) *Science, Technology and Global Governance*, London: Routledge.
Dunning, J. and Lundan, S. (2008) *Multinational Enterprises and the Global Economy*, 2nd edn, London: Edward Elgar.
Harris, P.G. (2009) *Climate Change and Foreign Policy*, London: Routledge.
Kofman, E. and Youngs, G. (eds) (2008) *Globalization: Theory and Practice*, 3rd edn, London: Continuum International Publishing Group Ltd.
Skolnikoff, E.B. (1993) *The Elusive Transformation: Science, Technology and the Evolution of International Politics*, Princeton: Princeton University Press.
Stoneman, P. (1988) *The Economic Analysis of Technology Policy*, Oxford: Oxford University Press.
Strange, S. (1994) *States and Markets*, 2nd edn, London: Pinter.
Talalay, M., Farrands, C. and Tooze, R. (eds) (1997) *Technology Culture and Competitiveness in the Global Political Economy*, London: Routledge.
The Economist (especially its excellent quarterly reviews of technology issues).

Company annual reports provide valuable resources for researching key technology businesses.

11 Culture

Chapter learning outcomes

After reading this chapter students should be able to:

- Engage in theoretical debates about the nature of culture, the impact that globalisation has on culture and how cultures can be in conflict.
- Explore the emergence of aspects of global culture.
- Understand and explain resistance to cultural globalisation and in particular the hegemony of Western culture.
- Understand and explain how social institutions shape cultures in a non-coercive manner.
- Recognise various aspects of the political economies of cultures and how they are impacted upon and evolve as a result of processes of globalisation.
- Relate discussion of culture to the theoretical debates discussed earlier in this book.

Introduction

A significant factor in relation to globalisation is its impact on various cultures around the world. It has been suggested that the seeds of a global monoculture have already been sown. This chapter will consider this proposition in light of the issue areas discussed above and related theoretical debates. The potential impact of the spread of a dominant system of production, and the possibility that a common set of intrinsic values necessarily follows, will be critically presented. The emphasis here will be on the promotion of certain types of 'knowledge', values, norms and 'rights'. Huntington's 'clash of civilisations' thesis has attracted renewed attention with regard to competing value systems. The ongoing debate surrounding cultural relativism and/or universality will be reviewed.

The concept of 'cultural imperialism' suggests a monolithic expansion and dominance of a single form of political, economic and socio-cultural order. However, the process of globalisation is more diverse and complex than the imposition of colonial rule. One reason why the Roman Empire was able to expand so dramatically was the manner in which the invading forces adapted and absorbed elements of local cultures. Although this was supported by the military might of the legionnaires it was a more efficient and successful strategy to not wholly alienate and repress the colonised culture. While the dominant control was centralised and directed from Rome there was also a relatively tolerant attitude taken towards the local norms and practices that were not seen as being in direct opposition to Roman rule. In the contemporary global political economy it is worthwhile to consider what aspects of cultural diversity may be viewed as being challenged, and possibly repressed, by processes of globalisation. Is there a sense in which some aspects of globalisation, notably the dominance of neo-liberal economics, are promoted and protected against alternative economic systems? Can multiculturalism be seen as a challenge to the current economic world order, or are economics and socio-cultural issues two distinct and separable areas of the processes of globalisation?

Many authors looking at the spread of neo-liberal economic policies seem to conflate this with the increasing 'reach' and influence of Western media. This may be in the form of music, television and radio programmes and the very active promotion of the teaching of English as a foreign language. The US Peace Corps volunteers of the 1960s onwards where instructed to not only teach English but also to be ambassadors for the American way of life. The fact that the English language was being increasingly taught to non-English speakers was the foundation for these new English speakers to be able to access and, probably, be influenced by wider cultural norms and values of the broadly defined 'English-speaking world'. More recently the shift in the balance of various languages has altered. The demographics of the US means that there is a relative decrease in English-only speaking Americans with a corresponding rise in those whose first language is Spanish. Similarly, an increasing number of non-Chinese are now studying Mandarin as China emerges as an increasingly important international power. Such issues should be borne in mind when considering alleged cultural dominance and expansion. There are examples of 'traditional' cultures being significantly challenged, to the point of extinction in the case of some indigenous languages. Important as this is for the preservation of cultural diversity there are relatively few examples of this in recent times with the more common pattern being the expansion of language skills and cultural awareness, rather than the wholesale erosion and replacement of one cultural form with another. The following section looks at the so-called 'triumph' of neo-liberalism as the dominant economic form in the contemporary world order, but also asks whether this dominance extends to the realm of cultural norms and values.

Liberal triumphalism

There are a range of theoretical positions on the importance of culture in international relations, and the cultural impacts of globalisation. One of the most prominent in academic circles since the end of the Cold War in 1989 has been liberal triumphalism. This school of thought was founded very much on the work of Francis Fukuyama (see Chapter 2) and has remained quite popular even in the post-9/11 era. The main assumptions are that human history has been a constant process of movement from one human condition to another in the search for the most effective systems of political, economic and social governance. Fukuyama claimed that capitalism and Western-styled liberal democracy constitute one such form of human governance. Rival systems of organisation and governance have included fascism, radical nationalism and communism. All of these rivals have been defeated by liberalism over the past century and thus the liberal democratic and capitalist system has triumphed. Liberal triumphalists claim that the human pursuit of development and progress has resulted in this type of system or condition and that it is in fact the pinnacle of human civilisation. No other ideological form of organisation or governance can compete with it and as such all people now desire (or soon will) to adopt capitalism and Western-styled democracy. Liberalism has, in short, triumphed.

The implications of these assumptions for international relations are that processes of globalisation are encouraging the adoption of liberalism around the world. This, in effect, is creating a more homogeneous and cohesive human world in which peoples from different states are increasingly similar in their culture. This is termed cultural homogenisation. While there have always been cultural exchanges of some sort throughout human history these exchanges have tended to be limited in scope and have been relatively mutual. However, in the contemporary world, the combination of the triumph of liberalism with globalisation has meant that cultural exchanges are occurring at extremely rapid rates and at very deep levels. Also, these exchanges are not as mutual as in the past and seem to be dominated more by the export of Western, liberal culture to the rest of the world.

Liberal triumphalism points to examples such as the 'victory' of the West in the Cold War and the perceived defeat of communism as a rival ideology, to prove its thesis. There are, however, many critics of this theoretical approach. These criticisms can be divided into two broad approaches. One approach claims that liberalism has not triumphed and many different ideological and cultural approaches to organising human society still exist. The existence of communism as the national ideology of some states such as China and Cuba is said to undermine the claim that capitalism and Western democracy 'defeated communism' in the Cold War. Furthermore, the existence of Islamic-based ideologies and the prevalence of Islam in the socio-cultural, political and economic characteristics of many states is also used to discredit liberal triumphalism. The second critique of Fukuyama's thesis is based upon the perception of negative results of cultural homogenisation and the triumph of liberalism. This criticism does not refute that liberalism has triumphed and is leading to a homogeneous world culture. Rather, advocates of this critique agree that these processes are taking place but they argue that the cultural dominance of Western, liberal societies is not desirable. Radical groups such as Al-Qaeda are advocates of this second critique.

Clash of civilisations

At the opposite end of the spectrum is the clash of civilisations thesis. This approach can be seen as the polar opposite of liberal triumphalism. Its main advocate was Samuel Huntington (see Chapter 2) who argued that international relations consisted of conflict between different and opposing cultural or civilisation groups. He claimed that globalisation was not leading to the homogenisation of cultures around the world. While it is true that some features of cultures, such as food, clothing and music, are being shared this does not constitute homogenisation. Instead, the sharing of cultural characteristics is something which has always taken place and does not necessarily represent the coming together of cultures to form one. Rather, it is argued that there are large groups of people who, broadly speaking, share the same culture. These groups are civilisations and Huntington argues that there are perhaps eight such groups in the world (see discussion in Chapter 2). Furthermore, these civilisations are inherently opposed to each other in many ways and retain their cultural distinctions through resistance to and conflict with others. There is no constant process of progress from one condition to another as is argued by liberal triumphalism and there will not be an emergence of a single global culture.

This position has also been criticised, not least of all by liberal triumphalists. Again we can identify two broad camps of critics here. The first claims that processes of globalisation have in fact led to greater cultural exchanges and the sharing of cultural characteristics now takes place at deep-rooted levels. In a sense the structure of cultures changes as the adoption of cultural practices, values, norms and so on takes place. In this sense there are no insulated civilisation groups; instead there are multiple linkages between cultures which are increasingly changing societies. At the same time, this critique suggests that even where cultures remain relatively static there is no reason to believe that different cultures are in fact opposed to each other. They simply have different characteristics. The second main critique of the clash of civilisations approach to understanding culture in international relations is subjective and normative. Critics here argue that by defining societies as inherently different from each other and claiming that they are in conflict with each other can only lead to more radical interpretations of international relations. Indeed, people such as Osama Bin Laden would most likely agree with Huntington and advocate the same kind of perception of international relations.

Binary opposition

Binary opposition is a term developed and used by critical theorists, usually structuralists, to analyse how humans construct meanings and definitions. It is claimed here that we define people, objects, processes and issues only by identifying opposites. In this sense people, for example, are defined as one thing because they are not another. Thus, an adherent of Islam is identified as a Muslim because he/she is not a Hindu and so on. Cultures are also defined in opposition to each other. 'Civilised' is found opposed by 'barbaric', 'developed' is opposed by 'undeveloped' and 'enlightened' opposes 'backwards'.

In this sense, seeing cultures as binary opposites can be useful in identifying ways in which social barriers are constructed between people of different backgrounds. By constructing meanings through comparison, perceived differences between cultures are essentially maintained. This view contradicts the notion present in liberal triumphalism that people and cultures can and will all share many similarities and will not be 'opposed' to each other. Furthermore, perceiving cultures as opposite to each other can lead to confrontational attitudes or stereotypes which would encourage a clash of civilisations. At the same time, the definition of binary opposites in a given context can also be seen to be culturally relative. Postmodernists could argue that there are no tautological claims and therefore there can be no binary opposite to such claims.

Anti-globalisation/structuralist and green thought

A third main approach to understanding culture in contemporary international relations and in international political economy can be seen to be, on the whole, critical. This approach suggests that as the world integrates further as a result of globalisation and as people interact more with each other, cultures are changing. These cultural changes take place very rapidly and are quite overarching. This in itself is not seen as a negative development in human history and can be seen to have positive affects. These include the reduction of international conflict and greater cooperation. However, there is much concern about the type of cultural change that takes place and which culture is becoming dominant. This approach shares some of the assumptions present in liberal triumphalism which relate to the unequal exchanges between cultures. Generally it is observed that Western, capitalistic culture is spreading around the world to much greater effect than other cultures. Western music, clothing styles, language (English is sometimes referred to as 'globalish' as a representation of its global usage), ideologies and institutions are more dominant around the world than any other. Figure 11.1 is representative of a particular critique of the spread of global brands and associated lifestyles.

The Marxian critique is that capitalistic culture is based on the concepts of competition and accumulation. The result of these conceptual foundations is the division of wealth, justice and opportunity between people. For example, some people in capitalistic societies will become wealthy and powerful but only at the expense of others who become poorer, weaker and have fewer opportunities for a good quality of life. Capitalistic cultures are, therefore, unequal and unfair. If this is the type of culture which is becoming dominant in the world then there is a risk that increasingly societies will become eschewed in this way. Surely, it is argued, this cannot be desirable.

Environmentalist critiques share this Marxian assumption that Western capitalist culture is dominating others on a global scale. The primary concern of this theoretical approach is not so much to do with the levels of exploitation and inequality between people as much as it is with the human impact on the environment. It is argued that capitalistic cultures express two key characteristics which relate to the environment. The first is the prevalence of consumerism. This means that people express a conceptual

Figure 11.1 Cultural hegemony

Source: Andy Singer/The Funny Times (www.funnytimes.com).

assumption that quality of life is based upon how much you consume in terms of resources, food, manufactured products, entertainment and so on. The desire to consume without inhibitions means that the planet's resources are increasingly used, leading to environmental degradation and pollution. It is important to note that the planet's resources are finite and, as such, consumption of resources is unequal between people. Some will consume more at the expense of others. The second key characteristic of capitalistic societies of relevance here is the dominant perception that the environment is there to be utilised to meet human demands. This is directly linked to consumerism and results in negative impacts on the environment. The dominance of capitalistic cultures is, therefore, seen to be a negative thing by environmentalists as it entails the encouragement of environmentally damaging practices.

Global culture

In international relations new dynamics and processes which relate to culture are becoming increasingly important. With regards to more common issues of concern in IPE, such as trade, finance, globalisation and security concerns, culture issues are now seen to be important. This is in terms of the impact of cultural issues in determining the behaviour of state and non-state actors as well as how culture affects other issues such as environmental degradation. As cultural influences have increasingly spread, the interaction of cultures, as opposed to simply the interaction of individuals or groups of people, has become an important determinant of actor behaviour. As noted above, there are many indicators that certain cultures are becoming more dominant than others and the exchange of cultural features is becoming more uni-directional. Western culture can be seen to be imported by non-Western societies at the expense of existing cultures. This is usually termed 'cultural hegemony'.

The spread of cultural influences has been a combination of 'push and pull' factors. The push factors come from historical experience of imperial expansion and the imposition of institutional structures that require certain language skills and other cultural attributes and sensibilities. In order to progress in relation to a dominant, albeit imposed culture, the colonised population need to assimilate and modify their behaviour to achieve success. To maintain control, imperial powers would often draw from local populations to fill administrative posts, albeit only up to a certain level of authority. It is worth noting that many of the leaders of former colonies had experience of the colonial power's education system, including periods of study at leading European private schools and universities. This facilitated a certain level of indoctrination into the norms and values of elite society of the imperial powers. That said, some of these leaders subsequently adopted harsh authoritarian models of governance. Furthermore, the export of cultures to other societies can be linked to processes of political and economic dominance. For example, English is a widely spoken second language in many parts of the Middle East and French is widely spoken as a second language in many parts of North Africa. The primary language of both of these regions is Arabic. British and French imperialism in the Middle East and North Africa respectively during the 1800s and early 1900s have encouraged the use of these foreign languages.

In terms of pull factors, the processes that lead to cultural hegemony can be related to domestic processes of modernisation and the wilful import of elements of other cultures. The popularity of the late Michael Jackson in many places such as South America and South East Asia is an example of this type of cultural import. Similarly, the growing global audience for football is altering patterns of entertainment consumption in various parts of the world, to the point that Japan and South Korea co-hosted the football World Cup Finals in 2002. American Football also has an increasingly global audience with the annual Super Bowl match receiving the second highest television audience for any sporting event after the football World Cup Final. As an example of a global brand name Manchester United is now recognised in most countries of the world. This is due to the availability of broadcasts, such as those via Sky Sports and also the proliferation of Manchester United merchandise, notably apparel such as T-shirts.

The expansion of the Internet has provided the platform for the spread of ideas and has fuelled the aspiration towards particular cultural forms. This extends well beyond the world of entertainment to the spread of individualism and calls for democratisation. Western democracies have long called for political reforms within more authoritarian regimes. However, the concept of sovereignty and non-intervention remains sacrosanct and the position taken tends to be that popular movements at the local level should drive democratic reform. The Internet has served the dual function of providing a window on to the outside world, showing how civil society engages with the political process in liberal democratic systems. It has also facilitated the organisation of pro-democracy movements within non-democratic states. The spread of democracy has become synonymous with other processes of globalisation. Governments in China and Burma, for example, remain firmly non-democratic. Both of these governments heavily filter and censor Internet communications in an effort to maintain their sovereign control.

Resistance to cultural hegemony

At the same time as there are numerous processes that have led to the emergence of a global culture, there are also differing responses to it. Broadly speaking there tends to be acceptance of or resistance to the exchange of cultures. In the first case, cultural exchanges are seen as positive developments and the emergence of a dominant culture is not necessarily a bad thing. Having similar cultural characteristics can help to develop greater communication, understanding and cooperation between cultures. In the second case, the increasing rates of cultural exchange and the emergence of a dominant culture are seen as undesirable developments. Here, the disruption of existing cultural practices and norms is viewed as damaging to the well-being of the society. Furthermore, there is quite simply a level of resistance to the dominance of other cultures because they are foreign.

Resistance to cultural hegemony is not exclusive to any one culture or society. Instead individuals or groups of individuals in any society may resist forms of cultural exchange or hegemony. Other individuals or groups of people within the same society will, at the same time, welcome cultural exchange. Those who do resist cultural hegemony often express this resistance in non-violent ways. Grassroots movements aimed at raising awareness, supporting existing cultural practices and norms, and 'educating' people on the negative impacts of cultural hegemony are commonplace. Other non-violent practices including the boycott of goods and services that are believed to be too culturally invasive are also evident. For example, the boycott of 'Barbie' dolls in many Islamic societies has come about because of the Western clothing and fashion styles that the dolls come with. These clothes are believed to be too immodest and encourage the import of Western clothing styles to these societies.

Language is often cited as the key indicator of a vibrant and distinct culture. The imposition of non-native languages has already been noted as a central characteristic of embedding colonial power. Many indigenous civil society groups are actively campaigning to reinforce and disseminate traditional cultural skills. For example, Native Languages of America is an NGO which is dedicated to the survival of native American languages. Its website holds a database of material relating to more than 800 such languages. In addition to language skills there are also attempts to preserve and pass on traditional methods of hunting, cooking and craftwork to future generations. Some of these may seem at odds with processes of modernisation and there is often a tension between modern and traditional practices. However, the value of traditional skills can be seen in terms of self-sufficiency and maintaining a distinct cultural identity. For all the benefits of modernisation, many indigenous populations have experienced negative impacts as a result of interaction with the outside world. Difficulties in moving from the traditional to the modern have resulted in social, economic and environmental disruption. Some individuals have assimilated more easily than others. Many indigenous communities have above average incidences of drug and alcohol abuse and high suicide rates among young adults. 'Traditional versus modern' does not have to be an either/or choice. The key issue appears to be one of personal identity and a sense of belonging to a particular community.

Processes of globalisation can be characterised by all manner of impacts on personal interactions. This can be via enhanced transport and communication systems through to the way in which world views have expanded as individuals have a greater sense of their place in the world. Sense of place and belonging to a particular piece of territory is an ancient concept harking back to the earliest forms of human civilisation. Even hunter-gatherer societies and nomadic peoples maintained a sense of territory and how far the range of their territories extended. Identity politics has become one of the central features of the study of international relations in recent years. There has been a long-standing focus on what constitutes national identity in relation to the post-Westphalian nation state system. It is now recognised that this is only one aspect of what can be multiple identities that exist simultaneously as part of each individual. Race, class and gender are the traditional aspects that sociologists have highlighted when looking at social structures. These aspects can be added to in terms of many other dimensions, ranging from political or religious beliefs to the neo-tribalism of modern societies that can extend to identifying oneself with a particular musical genre, such as those represented by punks or goths. The latter example may appear somewhat trivial but, for the individuals concerned, this can form an important aspect of self-identification.

As national governments are confronted with processes that appear to be lessening the level of control they command over certain aspects of their affairs, individuals are looking beyond the level of the nation state in terms of cultural identity. National pride can still be evoked at times of war or major international sporting events but beyond that national identity is now simply one of many, rather than the determining factor in forming and maintaining cultural identity. One interesting phenomenon in this regard is the development of the concept of global citizenship. This is a departure from the traditional understanding of citizenship which would be associated with belonging to a particular national group. As world views have broadened there has been a resulting awareness that it is insufficient, even actively dangerous, to assume that the world consists of discrete political units with no conception of broader processes, such as global warming.

The cultural dimensions of global citizenship are extraordinarily complex. On the one hand they involve a recognition that humanity lives on a shared, finite planet and that cooperation is required to meet the common interest of environmental sustainability. Yet in addition to this awareness there is also a recognition that the world is divided by competing world views that, in some cases, appear wholly incompatible. This is one of the greatest challenges for conflict resolution. Disputes over territory can be mediated to some extent and political jurisdictions can generally be agreed upon, although some parts of the world do have long-term disputes of this nature. Cultural differences are more difficult to resolve unless one takes the position of cultural relativity and a fair degree of tolerance of counter-views. This generally works between governments where the concept of sovereignty still holds significant meaning and, although some practices may be criticised, there is unlikely to be intervention in the domestic affairs of another state, apart from rare and extreme examples such as the prevention of genocide. With growing multiculturalism within domestic jurisdictions it is in this arena that cultural issues are coming to the fore and presenting some potentially problematic issues.

Tolerance of minority belief systems and behaviours is a growing concern for many societies and their governments. The French government has taken a very direct approach to this issue with the suppression of certain religious and cultural symbolism. This can extend to forms of dress, notably for Muslim women. Ironically this is within a society that maintains a political right to free speech which allows a platform for extreme right-wing groups to present their views, which are often abhorrent to other sectors of French society. The ability to present controversial views is an aspect of the Western system of political freedoms that characterises political liberalism. Such a system can allow the election to the European Parliament of candidates that hold extreme nationalist views and are avowedly anti-EU. This illustrates the level of tolerance that such a system embodies, but it also highlights that tensions remain with some various world views existing, often with cultural differences at the heart of these disagreements.

There are several other examples where cultural differences can be highlighted with reference to domestic legislation. Dignitas is a Swiss-based organisation which promotes the assistance of suicide for terminally ill patients. This would not be allowed within any of its European neighbours. The issue of abortion is highly charged with emotion and illustrates a rare example of diversity within EU law, for example. Different EU member states have varying laws with regards to this issue, such as the criteria by which an abortion may be legally undertaken and how far into pregnancy this procedure can be conducted. In the United States there is also variance between state legislations. Although not part of the due legal process, it is worth noting that in extreme cases people convicted of murdering doctors who have carried out abortion procedures have claimed a defence of 'justifiable homicide'. There is a marked inconsistency in the logic of a right-to-life campaigner taking a life. However, they would argue a utilitarian position of promoting the greater good by preventing what they would term as feticide. This position is often associated with deeply held religious beliefs.

Resistance to cultural hegemony can also take violent forms. Around the world the targeting and vandalising of symbols of Western culture, such as McDonald's fast food restaurants and Starbuck's cafes, as well as Western banks and shops, occurs during demonstrations or protests. The concept of counter-culture is usually associated with the protest actions of the 1960s: notably the student demonstrations in France, and elsewhere in Europe, and the alternative lifestyle developments of the west coast of the United States around this time. The so-called 'hippy culture' saw the rejection of establishment material consumerism. The stereotype image of this time is one of the promotion of peace and love. That said, this was also the time of more radical confrontational groups such as the Black Panthers and Nation of Islam. Counter-culture in contemporary times maintains some of the anti-establishment ethos but is now taking different forms of protest against different targets. In the 1960s the key targets were national governments and the assumption that 'success' was measured by one's socio-economic position in society. While some of these concerns still remain the protesters at G8 and G20 meetings are now more likely to be highlighting the broader negative consequences of the neo-liberal project. Government policies are still targeted but these are mainly in relation to the extent to which they promote neo-liberal economic policies.

There are also a range of non-state actors which are organised to resist cultural hegemony specifically through violent and armed means. Al-Qaeda is an example of a group which some would argue falls into this category as much of its founding ideology expresses a keen interest in resisting Western cultural dominance of Islamic societies, which some have termed cultural imperialism.

EXAMPLE BOX

Al-Qaeda and cultural hegemony

Al-Qaeda is a loosely structured network of individuals and groups of people around the world, but mostly located in Africa and Asia. It is a non-state actor in international relations and possesses its own ideological belief system which in a sense acts as a constitution or declaration of principles and purpose. Al-Qaeda has been involved in a large number of terrorist attacks ranging from the 11 September 2001 attacks on the United States to car bombings in Afghanistan, Iraq and elsewhere. Founded during the 1979–1989 Soviet invasion and occupation of Afghanistan to fight the Red Army, Al-Qaeda was largely funded, trained and supplied by an anti-communist alliance consisting of the United States, Britain, Saudi Arabia, Egypt and Pakistan.

The Soviet war in Afghanistan represented a Cold War proxy war for the liberal and capitalist West to confront communism, much the same as the Vietnam War had represented a chance for the communist East to confront the West. However, for Al-Qaeda the war was more about resistance to non-Muslim aggression and dominance of Islamic societies. Following the withdrawal of the Soviet forces from Afghanistan, Al-Qaeda began to focus increasingly on armed resistance to cultural penetration of the Muslim world by the West. Thus, in Afghanistan, for example, the Taliban and Al-Qaeda united to enforce strict laws prohibiting certain music, TV, media, dress and literature (largely to counter the dominance of Western culture in these forms).

Al-Qaeda's ultimate goals are the exclusion of all features of Western culture from Muslim lands and societies and the pre-eminence of Islamic culture. Al-Qaeda's support tends to come from disadvantaged segments of Islamic societies that are unhappy with Western foreign policies (such as the perceived support of the Israeli occupation of Palestine). While supporters and members of Al-Qaeda may have legitimate reasons to be unhappy with Western foreign polices, the actual motivation of Al-Qaeda's existence is found in its objection to perceived Western cultural hegemony.

Non-coercive globalisation

The above examples have tended towards oppositional and potentially violent and confrontational dynamics of cultural expansion and resistance. The following examples highlight non-violent but no-less effective means of cultural dominance. These are often implicit rather than explicit forms of persuasion and control. In part they are evidenced in the dominant social norms and values of mainstream culture. Furthermore, these can be represented via various national and international institutions. Mainstream media is also significant in promoting particular cultural values.

Edward Said, drawing on the earlier work of Antonio Gramsci, highlights the significance of social institutions such as education, literature, art and media. Many education departments attempt to impose a national curriculum in schools which reflects a particular viewpoint, especially in relation to national historical narratives. The Textbook Authorisation and Research Council of the Japanese Ministry of Education has faced criticism, particularly from China and Korea, with regards to history textbooks used in Japanese schools which provide a sanitised version of Japan's role and actions during the Second World War. The teaching of one's history is a crucial dimension in identity formation and attitudes towards others. History lessons are important for both what they highlight, and also what they omit. Several countries promote an annual Black History Month to emphasise the particular experiences of the black population. This is important both for the self-awareness and empowerment of black communities as well as inter-race relations more generally. The African American academic Dr John Henrik Clarke (1993) said:

> History is a clock people use to tell their historical culture and political time of the day. It's a compass that people use to find themselves on the map of human geography. The history tells them where they have been, where they are and what they are. But most importantly history tells a people where they still must go and what they still must be.

This quote applies to all peoples and their cultures. History is seen as a dynamic and unfolding narrative and experience. It is not just about the past but also the present and the future. This is important in the context of processes of globalisation, widespread migration and moves towards multiculturalism. Identity politics is a significant factor in community cohesion and/or conflict.

Both fictional and non-fictional literatures play a role in shaping cultural norms and values. Even novels can play a part in challenging and embedding cultural stereotypes and prejudices. Personal histories such as Maya Angelou's *I Know Why the Caged Bird Sings* or Edward Said's *Out of Place* use the format of autobiography to highlight and critique broader socio-economic and political events they have experienced. Many of these encompass the period of decolonisation and resulting changes in circumstances. Although these are the stories of individuals they tell a broader narrative of their times. These forms of literature represent the 'alternative' voices. They stand out precisely because they are new, critical and often dissenting narratives. They are the exceptions that prove the rule. Mainstream literature, by definition, continues to reinforce the majority view. In the fields of international relations and international political economy the majority of the world's university libraries continue to be stocked with texts written by European and American authors. Even in the field of development studies, authors such as the Egyptian economist Samir Amin are exceptional in representing an authoritative academic voice from the global South. The field of international economics continues to be dominated by traditional neo-liberal thinking and policy prescription.

The field of visual arts has been used for political purposes for centuries. Renaissance figures such as Michelangelo were commissioned by Popes to create works of art. The motivation for such commissions may have been justified in terms of illustrating the 'glory of God'. However, there was also an underlying aspect of self-promotion and legitimisation of the political position enjoyed by the Papacy. Similarly, numerous royal families have commissioned flattering portraits of themselves and their children in addition to grand architectural designs of castles and landscaped gardens which also symbolise and reinforce their political position. Other examples include the explicit political art of former Soviet Russia and communist China as well as the wartime propaganda of both the Nazi government in Germany and the Allies during the Second World War. Anti-war art can also be cited with examples such as Picasso's *Guernica*. In the private sector nationalist symbolism has been used to promote particular products. A classic example of this is the frequent use of the Stars and Stripes and the American Bald Eagle in the advertising of Harley Davidson motorcycles. This is a form of subliminal advertising linking a product with aspects of patriotism. One of the company's advertising slogans is 'Free to Ride'. This can be read as symbolising the political freedoms enjoyed in the United States.

The role of the media is arguably the most influential factor in promoting aspects of cultural expansion in an implicit rather than actively explicit manner. Here the media is referred to in its broadest form including print, broadcast and Internet-based news services. In addition, music, film and television are all important conduits by which audiences receive various messages that either challenge or, more commonly, reinforce cultural stereotypes and resulting attitudes. The very act of news reporting, and the role of the editor, is crucial in determining what issues constitute 'news' and also the way in which stories are presented with emphasis placed on certain features which can slant a story in a particular way. News stories are often geared towards perceived audiences, usually along national lines. Editorial adages include 'sex sells' and 'if it bleeds, it leads'. This reflects either an accurate assessment of readers and viewers' interests and tastes, or an active manipulation of this audience. If it is the latter then one might wonder what the motivation for this might be. Conspiracy theorists, and various neo-Marxists, would consider this as an example of a sinister plot to distract citizens from more pertinent stories about power structures and how they are maintained. For example, political demonstrations are often only covered if violence breaks out. Even then the angle taken on the story is one of disruption to law and order rather than whatever the protest was about.

Michael Moore's film *Bowling for Columbine* includes an insightful analysis of the role of the media from US rock singer Marilyn Manson:

> . . . that's not the way the media wants to take it and spin it, and turn it into fear, because then you're watching television, you're watching the news, you're being pumped full of fear. There's floods, there's AIDS, there's murder, cut to commercial, buy the Acura, buy the Colgate, if you have bad breath they're not going to talk to you, if you have pimples, the girl's not going to fuck you, and it's just this campaign of fear, and consumption, and that's what I think it's all based on, the whole idea of 'keep everyone afraid, and they'll consume'.

Fear and consumption is certainly something that can be identified in the dominant culture of the recent past. The Western alliance has had a fear of the spread of communism followed by a perceived clash of civilisations and the so-called 'war on terror'. In each case the response has been to highlight consumerism as either an escape from this fear or as an example of the rightness of the 'Western way'. There are strong vested interests to promote this negative climate. In 1961 US President Dwight D. Eisenhower warned of what he described as the military-industrial complex. This referred to the self-serving agendas of both the armed services and the private sector. The media also plays a significant role in both reinforcing fears by emphasising bad news, and also providing a platform for the advertising industry. The entertainment industry plays a role in the evolution of popular culture, although there is an ongoing debate surrounding the extent to which behaviours may, or may not, be influenced by the consumption of images and text. This is particularly pertinent to the issue of violence in society. The 'flower power' era of the late 1960s referred to above was relatively short-lived and films, television and popular songs have generally gravitated towards the representation, possibly even promotion, of a more individualised and competitive culture and society.

When trends in globalisation are referred to they are usually couched in terms of the spread of mass consumerism. More specifically patterns of consumption are geared towards the personal acquisition of goods. Furthermore, these goods are really one-off lifetime purchases. Many manufacturers adopt an approach of built-in obsolescence whereby goods are deliberately designed to have a relatively short period of productive use. The incentive, of course, is that when the product breaks or simply wears out the consumer will need to make another purchase to replace it. In addition there is also the issue of what is considered fashionable at any given time, with perfectly functional items being discarded if they are no longer in vogue. Advertising campaigns can play a major role in shaping consumer choices but this does not mean that there will necessarily be a drive to persuade people to all buy the same products. Far from it, as diversifying markets, and even producing competition between consumers who may favour differing brand names for similar products, actually expands markets still further. The 'culture' of mass consumption does not necessarily mean that there are shared norms, values or preferred tastes. Great cultural diversity can exist within what might be termed the 'mega-culture' of neo-liberalism. The key elements of the arguments surrounding 'cultural imperialism' are more to do with lifestyle aspirations than political or religious ideologies or traditional cultural norms and values.

The so-called triumph of liberalism is normally referred to in terms of the rights of individuals to vote in a form of democracy and the apparent success of free-marketeering over interventionist command economies. The latter point is open to greater dispute following the overextension of credit facilities and the resulting downturn in the majority of the world's economies. Despite this caveat, the emphasis in both the political and economic fields is at the level of the individual rather than the wider community, and both are also more associated with short-term rather than longer-term perceptions. In the political case one is asked to vote for a politician for a relatively short term of office, perhaps four to five years. The assumption is that if one is not content with that person's performance they can be quickly replaced. There is also a temporal dimension to the economic sphere. Capitalism as a philosophy of economic accumulation can be seen to have longer-term goals, as in maintaining and ideally increasing the amount of available capital. Of course this is simply based on the artificial value given to particular currencies and commodities. The 'true' costs of goods, as in the social and environmental capital costs, are rarely calculated. This is one of the great concerns for many critics, especially green theorists, of the spread of mass consumerism and a culture of individual-based consumerist desires which do not take wider community and environmental costs into account and are, therefore, fundamentally non-sustainable.

Summary

Post-Cold War, the so-called 'triumph' of liberalism has led to the spread of Western culture to virtually all parts of the world. This is not to say that it has been wholly embraced everywhere. As noted above, it is also resisted, in some cases violently. The Westminster model of democracy has been described as an inappropriate colonial imposition at odds with traditional decision-making processes, for example in Fiji where this argument was used as a partial justification for the overthrow of a democratically elected government in 1987. Western styles of dress and behaviour are considered immodest and actively offensive in many cultures, although trends continue to be towards growing Westernisation. The issue of culture has come to the fore in both the study and practice of international political economy. Traditional security concerns remain firmly on the international agenda, but security issues are increasingly being linked to factors that are cultural in origin.

This chapter has highlighted a broad range of cultural issues and the manner in which they influence the evolution of both domestic and international relations. The issue of multiculturalism, by its very existence, questions the extent to which there is some sort of monolithic, hegemonic global culture emerging. However, it is possible to identify some key attitudes and trends which can be said to represent aspects of Western culture which are, at least, having impacts on other cultures around the world. Neo-liberalism has spread around the world, but with varying degrees of acceptance. China is the classic example of a state experiencing the impact of processes of globalisation, but attempting to manage this as far as possible on its own terms. It has largely accepted neo-liberal economic policies while maintaining a strong central political authority. It also retains a very keen sense of its own cultural heritage, as do many societies. Traditional cultural values can be very resilient. Some have even experienced a level of resurgence in the face of challenges from alternative norms and values.

The argument surrounding the possibility of a global monoculture tends to miss two crucial points. First is the strength and resilience of non-Western cultures to maintain a clear sense of their own cultural identity. Second is the fact that it is not that dominant cultural norms and values are being disseminated to other cultures that is the primary issue. Rather it is that the Western culture of individualism and mass consumerism is having an impact on the rest of the world due to depletion of resources, polluting impacts on a global scale and military actions to ensure access to overseas resources.

Reflective questions

1 What role do cultural factors play in ongoing processes of globalisation?
2 Outline what you understand by the term 'cultural imperialism'?
3 What forms of resistance to cultural hegemony can you identify?
4 Can you identify examples of global brands? And what culture do they represent, if any?
5 How important are social institutions in shaping cultural values and norms?

Suggestions for further reading

Ali, T. (2002) *The Clash of Fundamentalisms: Crusades, jihads and modernity*, London: Verso.

Clarke, J.H. (1993) *African People in World History*, Baltimore: Black Classic Press.

Chabal, P. and Daloz, J.P. (2006) *Culture Troubles: Politics and the Interpretation of Meaning*, London: C. Hurst & Co.

Mikula, M. (2008) *Key Concepts in Cultural Studies*, New York: Palgrave.

Moore, M. (2003) *Bowling for Columbine*, London: Momentum Pictures.

Reeves, J. (2004) *Culture and International Relations: Narratives, Natives and Tourists*, London: Routledge.

Said, E. (2003) *Orientalism*, London: Penguin Books Ltd.

Said, E. (1994) *Culture and Imperialism*, London: Vintage.

Tomlinson, J. (2001) *Cultural Imperialism*, London: Continuum International Publishing Group.

Zank, W. (ed.) (2009) *Clash of Cooperation of Civilisations: Overlapping Integration and Identities,* Farnham: Ashgate.

12 Security

Chapter learning outcomes

After reading this chapter students should be able to:

- Understand changes in security studies from a narrow agenda focused on inter-state war to a much broader range of issues.
- Understand and be able to explain the emergence of 'new' security issues in international relations and IPE in the latter half of the twentieth century including the emergence of nuclear weapons, environmental change and related issues, identity politics and the rising power of MNCs.
- Comprehend contemporary processes of change linked to globalisation which is leading to the emergence of more security issues including water, energy and food security, migration and demographic change, capital movements and financial crises, the revolution in military affairs and international terrorism.
- Explain how security issues are no longer simply state- and military-centric.
- Relate discussion of security to the theoretical debates discussed earlier in this book.

Introduction

This chapter is designed to relate to the previous chapters in the context of a dynamic, contentious and evolving set of security agendas. Whereas many IR textbooks will focus on state- and military-centric security, the distinctive nature of IPE approaches, as opposed to IR, tend to adopt a broader interpretation and analysis of security issues. This is the approach taken here. The discussion in this chapter demonstrates the evolution of the study of security issues from traditional analyses to much broader ones which consider both state and non-state actors as having security interests, and which take account of a range of issues. During the latter half of the twentieth century processes of globalisation, technological and industrial development, environmental change and demographic growth, among others, led to the emergence of critical security studies. This field of study has been characterised by a shift away from the dominance of the billiard-ball model of international relations. This model, as was discussed in Chapter 1, sees states as the only important unit of analysis in IR/IPE and power and military security as their primary concern. Furthermore, this model of understanding and explaining assumes that states are unitary and rational egoistic actors, meaning that, in effect, everything that goes on inside the state (the agency of individuals, MNCs, NGOs and so on) is irrelevant to security studies.

A different model to understanding security has come to dominate this area of IPE. This model has developed as a result of the emergence of critical security studies (Booth, K., 2004) and can be seen to offer a drastically different approach to the billiard-ball model. While the state is still seen as a primary actor in international political economy and international relations, other actors are acknowledged. This is done in two ways: first, by acknowledging that non-state actors do have significant degrees of agency and, therefore, can impact upon security issues (whether these be traditional military security issues or others). Second, it is acknowledged that non-state actors themselves have legitimate security concerns and thus deserve attention. At the same time as critical security studies sees a plurality of actors as constituting a main element in security studies, the range of issues which are considered is much larger than the limited set of issues in traditional security studies. In short, what actually constitutes 'security' and what threats to this security there are has drastically changed. Critical security studies does not only see military security as being important. Instead, security has come to denote a vast range of issues which still includes military security but also a range of other issues. The emergence of revised forms of security studies has been caused by developments in both the academic fields of IR and later IPE, as well as events and processes that have unfolded in the real world.

This chapter outlines some of these developments and explores some of the most important security issues in terms of international political economy. The following section thus explores processes following the Second World War and how they created 'new' security challenges for state and non-state actors. The second section deals with key issues in the contemporary era and how they relate to some of the topics discussed in earlier chapters. This is followed by a concluding section which summarises the main points.

The development of 'new' security issues

The nuclear era

Towards the end of the Second World War the United States was able to develop and use nuclear technology in the form of atomic bombs. The scale of the destruction that these weapons brought has few equivalents in human history. The fire bombing of Dresden during the Second World War is a comparable event. However, the ability to destroy entire cities with a single bomb changed the nature of warfare and the meaning of military security. One of the most significant ways in which nuclear weapons changed military security relates to the range of actors involved in any military security dynamic (Hough, P., 2007). As other states developed nuclear weapons and the technology itself advanced and more powerful weapons were created, military security for the vast majority of states throughout the world was altered. The context of the Cold War meant that there was a bipolar world system and the threat of conflict between the two poles and their allies could be felt practically everywhere. This was combined with the destructive power and damaging effects of nuclear weapons (which through the 1960s and 1970s were proliferating) to mean that military security interdependence on a global scale developed. The notion of mutually assured destruction (MAD) existed not just for the nuclear-armed belligerents of any conflict, but also for many states that may be impacted also. In Europe, for example, Germany, France and the UK would most likely have been the first states to have been hit with nuclear weapons in the event of a break-out of nuclear war between the United States and the USSR. Security studies had to evolve to take account of the changing intensity of military security and the rising levels of interdependence this created.

Since the late 1990s the issue of nuclear weapons proliferation has been at the forefront of much international relations (Buzan, B., Ware, A. and Hoffmann-Martinot, V., 2007). The UN Security Council, for example, has focused on this issue as one of the key threats to global instability. The 1998 detonation of a nuclear warhead as part of a test by India and the subsequent Pakistani detonation announced the arrival of the two South Asian rivals as nuclear-weapons-capable states (both tests were conducted underground). While nuclear weapons proliferation has been managed and controlled in most regions of the world, North Korea has been able to develop a nuclear weapons programme and has manufactured up to a dozen nuclear bombs. North Korea's capability was demonstrated in late 2006 with the successful underground detonation of a nuclear weapon. Iran's nuclear programme has been the focus of much scrutiny, with the International Atomic Energy Agency reporting that the programme appears to be for civilian use but also that some research and development into a weapons programme was taking place up until the early 2000s. There is much suspicion and mistrust between the international community and Iran over whether or not the latter is secretly pursuing nuclear weapons. Iran in turn seems to be demonstrating signs of greater insecurity as the West, led by the United States and Israel, put more pressure on the Iranian government to stop some of its nuclear activity. Whether or not some states are pursuing nuclear weapons programmes or will do so in the future, the security challenge of nuclear proliferation remains a key issue on the global security agenda.

International cooperation and coordination is evident, however, in seeking to manage existing nuclear weapons stockpiles and the ability of non-nuclear states to develop nuclear weapons (see Table 12.1). On 8 April 2010 US President Barak Obama and Russian President Dmitry Medvedev signed a new Strategic Arms Reduction Treaty (START) in Prague, Czech Republic. The treaty replaces the previous START II agreement which expired at the end of 2009 and facilitates the reduction of both states' current nuclear weapons by one-third from approximately 2600 for Russia and 2126 for the United States to around 1550 for both. The treaty also requires both states to reduce by one-third the long-range delivery systems (missiles) for nuclear weapons, allows for a vigorous inspection structure and mechanisms for further coordination in non-proliferation activities. The reductions in weapons will take up to seven years to implement and the treaty should be viewed as part of a broader process of reducing nuclear weapons stockpiles globally and preventing the development of nuclear weapon technology in other states. Just four days after the new START was signed, President Obama hosted a two-day summit on nuclear security in Washington in which 47 states were represented. The gathering was by far the most comprehensive international meeting on nuclear security held to date and was focused on the dual issues of reducing nuclear weapons and non-proliferation.

At the same time as nuclear technology was being used for the creation of weapons, this technology was being harnessed for energy production in many states. Use of nuclear technology to produce energy can be very cheap and efficient, making it desirable for national governments and private energy sectors. However, it also produces nuclear waste from spent radioactive fuel as well as polluted water and other material. Nuclear waste is highly radioactive and contaminated and it can take hundreds of thousands of years for the radiation to be reduced to safe levels. Nuclear energy is generally quite safe as long as nuclear material, energy plants and so on are monitored and maintained constantly. However, nuclear energy production can lead to radiation leaks and environmental damage, which

Table 12.1 Nuclear weapons stockpiles by 2009

Country	Strategic	Non-strategic	Total operational	Total inventory
Russia	2,600	2,050	4,650	**12,000**
United States	2,126	500	2,626	**5,113**
France	300	unknown	~300	**300**
China	180	unknown	~180	**240**
UK	160	unknown	<160	**160**
Israel	80 est.	unknown	unknown	**80 est.**
Pakistan	70-90	unknown	unknown	**70-90**
India	60-80	unknown	unknown	**60-80**
North Korea	<10	unknown	unknown	**<10**
TOTALS	**5,600**	**2,550**	**7,900**	**23,300**

Source: Anon. (2009) *World Nuclear Weapons Stockpile Report*, Ploughshares Fund.

are harmful to humans. These facts have caused much concern for human and environmental security. In essence, the threat of nuclear contamination can often be just as significant to individuals and groups of people as, say, the threat of war.

Global environmental agenda

As is discussed in Chapter 9, the environment has become a key area of consideration in IPE. In particular, environmental change and the impacts this has on the human condition have, for many scholars, become central to the study of international relations and international political economy. The environment emerged as an issue in the era after the Second World War as a result of two processes. The first was an intellectual and anthropocentric development. During the 1950s and 1960s intellectual debates in IR were still centred on military security, power and state relations. However, small spaces had begun to open up for debate on other issues relevant to the human world. The environment was one of the topics which benefited from this development. The second process was environmental. Two centuries of industrialisation in Europe and North America, as well as elsewhere, had begun to take its toll on the environment and impacts of human activity were beginning to be noticed. At the same time, demographic growth and urban sprawl meant that people around the world were being affected by the environment in different ways. Regardless, it was not until the 1970s that intellectual attention was really given to environmental issues. Many changes in the environment were being witnessed and recorded including deforestation, climate change, pollution and droughts, to mention just a few.

Studies conducted and conferences held (see Chapter 9) began to highlight that the planet's environment and resources were finite, that humans rely quite precariously on these and that the environment was changing significantly. For many, these realisations began to underpin other security issues such as military security and war. People and governments since the 1970s have had to consider environmental threats to their security and well-being. Climate change, for example, is taking place and has resulted in changes to the human condition for many. Perhaps one of the best examples is that of small island states in the Pacific Ocean which have seen sea levels rise to the extent that their lands are being swallowed by the ocean. Security from invasion by another state is not a central concern when your very land is disappearing beneath the waves. IPE is essentially a discipline which is driven by intellectual debates and real world issues. Environmental change has become a major issue in the 'real world' and so has shaped intellectual debates. This has also contributed to the development of critical security studies and the shift away from state- and military-centric security studies.

Identity politics

As is discussed in Chapter 4, the modern world has seen the intensification of processes of integration in the political, economic, security, environmental and socio-cultural realms. These processes combined are termed globalisation and have increased in pace quite significantly since the end of the Second World War. Perhaps an area which has begun to receive most attention since the end of the Cold War is integration in the socio-cultural sphere. Here, there are a number of processes taking place which are resulting in greater interaction, integration and conflict between different socio-cultural groups. In the first instance, the proliferation of forms of mass media and the domination of these mediums by Western, largely American, products is leading to what can be seen as cultural homogenisation. Western clothing, music, movies, sports and other forms of social expression can be found in practically every society and are fast becoming more poplar than other cultures' counterparts. Second, the mass movement of people around the world in the form of temporary travel (for example, for business trips or

holidays) as well as more permanent forms of migration are resulting in increased interaction between socio-cultural groups. The effects of these processes are sometimes to increase understanding,
familiarity and diversity in societies, thus altering communal identities. On the other hand, cultural
imports and migration can lead to friction between communities.

Advancements in technology for travel and communication as well as increases in availability of
mass media since the 1970s have been coupled with increasing economic and political integration.
The human world has, as a result, changed quite dramatically. Societies around the world are becoming eclectic and diverse, and now share common features with others. The impact on European societies, for example, has been quite dramatic as Europeans themselves have integrated with each other
extensively and as immigration from Africa and Asia has rapidly increased. Questions of national and
regional identity now feature very high on political agendas in European governments and in central
EU institutions. Meanwhile, some communities have resisted (sometimes violently) Western cultural
influences. Afghanistan under the Taliban during the 1990s and early 2000s would be a case in point
here. Questions of Afghani or Islamic identity being eroded are often cited as key elements in the Taliban's ideology and as significant considerations in the motivations of groups such as Al-Qaeda. In
much the same way as the emergence of nuclear technology and the occurrence of environmental
change, issues of identity politics have had a direct impact on security studies, altering perceptions of
what constitutes security, what threats there are to it and for which actors.

The rise of MNCs

Multinational corporations have existed and operated in the global economy for quite some time.
However, only in the last few decades have MNCs been major players in international political economy (Ohmae, K., 1999). The number of MNCs has increased extremely rapidly since the 1950s and
the scale of their operations has also increased. MNCs operate in virtually every economic sector in
the global economy and account for a very large percentage of global trade (some studies conclude
that more than half of world trade is carried out by MNCs). Furthermore, many MNCs have become
so large and prosperous that they have larger annual GDP turnovers than most states. Somewhere in
the region of half of the largest economies in the world are actually MNCs, not states. The meteoric
rise of the MNC in the last half century or so has affected many aspects of the global economy and of
international relations. For example, MNCs are key components in the health of the global economy
and are largely responsible for the maintenance of economic growth. Because many MNCs have
become so large and important actors in their own right, intellectual debates have, since the 1970s,
viewed MNCs as actors in their own right. More traditional approaches (especially realism) still view
MNCs as merely elements of states. In either perception, MNCs are studied as important features of
the modern world.

Yet MNCs are not only seen as economic actors engaged in business activities. They are also seen
through the prism of security studies. In the first instance, the security of MNCs is increasingly considered in critical security studies – usually in terms of the economic well-being of companies and
financial stability, but also in more traditional, physical security terms. Second, the influence MNCs
have on other forms of security has become increasingly important. MNCs, for example, manufacture weapons and supply national militaries with services. This directly influences national military
security. In other cases, MNCs actually engage in warfare themselves, either on behalf of states or in
more controversial scenarios on behalf of themselves of other non-state actors. In terms of economic
security, MNCs (whether seen in state-centric or pluralist ways) are important to other actors. National
economies rely heavily on MNCs for investment, employment, economic activity, goods and services.
The security of national economies, therefore, is directly related to MNCs. Governments are often
willing to offer financial aid to MNCs which are struggling in order to safeguard the health of the

wider economy. MNCs also directly impact environmental security as well, in both positive and negative ways. Pollution and environmental degradation are often caused by large MNCs and so they can be seen to have a major impact on environmental security. Through the development of cleaner technologies or problem–solving technologies, MNCs can also be seen to be remedying environmental problems and so providing environmental security. Critical security studies has been deeply influenced by debates on MNCs and the actual agency of such entities in international political economy.

Emerging issues

Water, energy and food security

Over the past century the global human population has seen very rapid growth, from approximately 1.6 billion in 1900 to over 6.5 billion in 2009. The rapid expansion in population has placed increasing pressures on energy and food requirements (Homer-Dixon, T., 2001). The dual processes of urbanisation and industrialisation, which have been seen most dramatically in Europe, North America and South East Asia but which have also taken place to some extent in virtually all states, have also led to greater need for both energy and food. Furthermore, advancements in healthcare and medicine now mean that most societies around the world have longer life expectancies than they did at the start of the twentieth century. Combined, rapid demographic growth, industrialisation, urbanisation and longer life expectancies have meant that demand for energy and food has often exceeded supply in some areas. On a global scale, there is no overall shortage of either energy or food; however, the political economy of both of these sectors has led to chronic shortages as a result of unequal distribution of resources.

During the 1970s the two oil shocks of 1973–74 and 1979–80 resulted in fuel shortages in much of North America and Western Europe, as well as elsewhere. The 1973–74 period was the first time in the modern era that the industrialised world's overall demand for fuel was not met by available supplies. This was followed by fuel shortages in less-developed states also. In the early 2000s fossil fuel production in the form of oil, gas and coal has steadily increased as new sources have been discovered and developed and as facilities have been upgraded. For example, oil production totalled roughly 45 million barrels per day in the 1960s and 1970s whereas current production totals around 80 million barrels per day. Similar increases in the production of gas and coal have also been seen. Thus, supply of fossil fuels has increased quite significantly since the 1970s. However, demand for energy has soared at an even faster rate. The rise of South East Asian economies, rapid and expansive industrialisation in China and India and economic development in South America, the Middle East and Africa have led to increases in demand for energy. As demand increases, so does competition for the limited amount of energy resources available.

One result has been increases in the international price of oil, gas and coal. A second result has been greater energy insecurity and the creation of national policies to combat this. Many states are now seeking to invest in new sources of energy such as large-scale oil and gas exploration in the Caspian Sea region, the Arctic and the Gulf of Mexico. Other policies aimed at energy security include the development of new technologies and renewable energy sources. Increasingly, states are developing wind power farms, solar power fields and hydroelectricity infrastructure in order to meet energy shortfalls. European Union states, for example, have begun to really harness wind power. Spain and Germany now each generate somewhere in the region of 5000 MW of wind power annually, which represents approximately 12 and 8 per cent of total electricity supply respectively. The EU as a whole now gets around 4 per cent of its energy needs from wind power and a recent report suggests

Europe's wind power potential could fuel the Union several times over. Meanwhile, states in the oil- and gas-rich Middle East are expanding solar power capabilities. Even Saudi Arabia, which possesses the world's largest reserves of crude oil, is beginning to consider expanding its solar power infrastructure. Importantly, Saudi Arabia, along with other Arabian Peninsula states, receives as much solar energy in a single year as all the energy value of all the known reserves of oil, gas and coal in the world – harnessing this energy would provide much energy security for many states. Nuclear energy is also being developed as an alternative or in addition to fossil fuels.

During 2007–2008 world food prices rapidly increased, causing a global food crisis which negatively hit both developed and developing states alike. There were a number of causes of the price increases including rises in oil prices, multiple severe droughts around the world, increased demand due to demographic growth and expanding dietary demands due to increased wealth (Garrison, N. et al., 2009). Whatever the causes of the crisis, its impact was to highlight issues of food security for most societies. Unrest and instability spread throughout many states as people protested against high food prices and limited food stocks. However, there was little national governments could do in the short term. Policies have been created and implemented to secure food supplies by some more prosperous states. Rich states are buying millions of acres of arable land in poorer states, mostly in Africa, central Asia and Eastern Europe, and using the produce exclusively for their own domestic consumption. This has led to fears that as some states secure land in others to ensure their own food security, the food security of the states in which the land and rights to the produce are bought will be hurt. This is especially the case with regards to African states, which already have difficulty in feeding their own populations but which need the economic investment.

EXAMPLE BOX

The GCC and international farm purchases

The Gulf Cooperation Council (GCC) states (Bahrain, Kuwait, Oman, Qatar, Saudi Arabia and the United Arab Emirates (UAE)) have witnessed growing food insecurity. Due to the lack of water and arable land these states have to purchase the vast majority of their food supplies from abroad. The food price crisis of 2007–2008 resulted in huge increases in the GCC's food bill, which topped $20 billion in 2008. In response, these states have purchased agricultural land and food production rights around the world. The UAE, for example, has invested heavily in Sudan, and Saudi Arabia has invested in Ethiopia. Future investments are sought in the Philippines, Madagascar and Kazakhstan to name a few.

These purchases have raised concerns in the food producing states that domestic food supplies will be reduced and concerns in the GCC states that their food security is reliant on the security of farms thousands of miles away. However, in the majority of cases, as has happened in Sudan, the GCC investment is to bring online new arable land and not to simply purchase the rights to existing farms.

Access to fresh water has also become a major global security issue (see Figure 12.1). Fresh water sources are decreasing overall because of a number of factors. Pollution of river and lake systems, growing demand from larger populations and industrialisation, and climate change have led to major water shortages. In many states access to fresh water has never been guaranteed for the entire population due to a lack of infrastructure and limited supplies. In others, fresh water supplies are often disrupted and are not reliable. Yet even in states which have traditionally had plenty of fresh water due to climatic conditions, shortages in recent years have been witnessed. Thomas Homer-Dixon suggests that conflict over fresh water shortages will be the primary cause of international conflict in the

Figure 12.1	Total actual renewable water resources per inhabitant (m³/year)

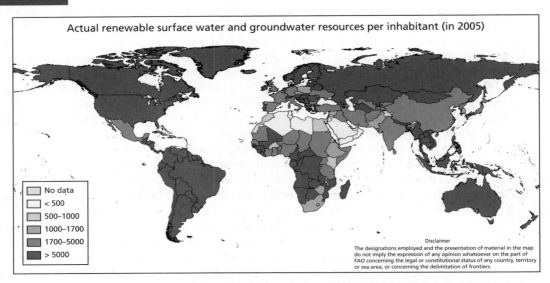

Source: Food and Agriculture Organization of the United Nations (2008) Aquastat Global Map: Total actual renewable water resources per inhabitant (http://www.fao.org/nr/water/aquastat/globalmaps/index.stm). Reproduced with permission.

twenty-first century. Indeed, conflicts over water sources have already been seen in arid regions across Africa and Asia. The issue of fresh water rights in the West Bank and Jordan Valley have complicated the Palestinian-Israeli conflict and contributed to the failure to achieve a lasting peace there.

It is certainly the case that energy and food security have become national and global issues of great importance. The threat to the security of states and peoples of not having enough energy and/or food have increased significantly in recent decades and policy making has reflected this. It also seems that in many circumstances energy and food insecurity is a zero-sum game where one state's security comes at the expense of another in the competition for limited energy and food resources.

Migration

In the modern world the migration of people from one state to another and from one region to another has taken place at increasingly high rates (Castle, S., 2008). The international movement of people in the early twenty-first century far surpasses previous trends. Demographic growth has meant that populations have become so large that people often have had to migrate to another part of the planet in order to secure resources for survival. This also happened on a large scale during the eighteenth and nineteenth centuries when European expansion and colonialism relieved some of the population pressures on resources in Europe. A more contemporary example can be found in Sudan where nomadic and settled communities in the western province of Darfur have come into conflict over territory as their populations grow.

At the same time as demographic pressures are causing more migration, advancements in transport technology have encouraged and facilitated the mass movement of people. The development and proliferation of air travel has drastically reduced travelling times and costs around the world. It is now possible to travel via airplane to the other side of the planet in a little over a day and at relatively cheap prices. Several decades ago long-distance international travel was mostly limited to sea transports and to the segments of society that could afford quite high costs. This helped limit the movement of people around the planet. However, air transport allows people to move quite quickly and cheaply, meaning that travel is open to broader sections of society and not just the elite. At the same time, developments in rail and vehicular transport have provided the means for people to travel internationally. In the case of the former, the creation of large international rail networks has facilitated migration. Furthermore, new technologies such as the magnetic levitation rail allows for trains to travel at relatively fast speeds of up to 550 km per hour and with the potential to travel at faster speeds than commercial aircraft. With regards to vehicular transport, the proliferation of car ownership in most societies has increased mobility.

The technological developments which have allowed for greater movement of people have been utilised for both temporary and more permanent migration (see Table 12.2). People from different states and societies increasingly travel abroad on short business or holiday trips. This form of migration can be very profitable for many tourism markets and is largely encouraged. However, tensions between societies do arise as a result of this form of migration. Very few states now have entirely homogeneous populations and most populations possess minorities which have formed out of immigration. Hispanic immigration into the United States, for example, since the Second World War has resulted in a significant part of the US population (around 15 per cent).

While many of us will likely agree that diversity and cosmopolitanism in our societies has many positive benefits, there are many who would highlight the problems that can arise from rapid migration. For many societies cultural homogeneity is key to communal identity. The Taliban-led government in Afghanistan during the 1990s, for example, formulated a set of laws which prohibited the use of television sets, radios and published media. The purpose of these laws was to limit the influence of Western and other non-Islamic/Afghani cultures on Afghan society. Likewise, the immigration of people that were not Muslims into Afghanistan was discouraged and limited. Even in states which are seen to be culturally diverse and accepting there can be many tensions between citizens and immigrants. Racially motivated crimes are of concern in the UK and other EU states.

Another impact of contemporary processes and patterns of migration is related to illegal activities. Policing and regulation of societies and law enforcement are often complicated and made more difficult by the mobility of individuals. Managing the movement of criminals, contraband and so on has become a major challenge for national governments and international institutions. A crime may be committed in one state and the perpetrators travel to another quite easily. Illegal activities of all kinds, but especially the movement of contraband such as drugs, weaponry and stolen property, are no longer restricted by time and space to small areas. Poppy seeds used to produce opium can be grown in the mountains of Afghanistan, transported through Iran and on to Europe, North America and elsewhere at low cost and in short periods of time. Stopping these operations is very difficult. A major concern of the United States is preventing 'terrorists' from entering the country with weaponry and carrying out attacks.

Financial crises and capital movements

A salient feature of the modern global economic system is the liberalised and dynamic movement of capital from one market to another and from one investment to another. Capital (as in money supplies) has become truly global and no longer restricted to single markets. A capital investor based in one state may wish to invest the capital in practically any market in the world and for almost any endeavour. Most national governments, international institutions and even private sector actors do not now possess the ability to control capital entirely and in many circumstances they have no control at all. The owners of capital, of course, do possess such abilities. As the capitalist global economy intensifies and becomes even more embedded and as trade in goods and services continues to be further liberalised, capital becomes even more mobile. Many observers see the free movement of capital from one market to another as a very positive and healthy characteristic of the global economy. After all,

Table 12.2 International migrants and refugees

Region	International migrant stock					Refugees	Net migration		Remittances	
	Total (000)	% of total population	% female migrants	Average annual rate of change (%)	Net migration among the foreign-born (000)	Total (000)	Average annual net migration (000)	Average annual net migration rate (per 1,000 population)	Total (US$m)	% of total GDP
	2010	2010	2010	2005–2010	2005–2010	End-2008	2005–2010	2005–2010	2007	2007
World	213,944	3.1	49.0	1.8	24,359.8	15,150.4	—	—	380,050	0.7
More developed regions	127,711	10.3	51.5	1.7	14,715.3	2,081.0	2,700.5	2.2	134,457	0.4
Less developed regions	86,232	1.5	45.3	2.0	9,644.5	13,069.4	−2,700.5	−0.5	245,593	1.9
Least developed countries	11,531	1.3	47.4	1.1	1,089.9	1,880.8	−314.6	−0.4	17,334	5.4
Sub-Saharan Africa	18,007	2.1	47.2	1.7	2,245.2	2,133.4	−360.5	−0.4	18,615	2.5
Africa	19,263	1.9	46.8	1.7	2,326.8	2,332.9	−532.0	−0.5	36,853	3.1
Asia	61,324	1.5	44.6	2.1	6,768.6	10,378.2	−1,075.7	−0.3	145,200	1.1
Europe	69,819	9.5	52.3	1.6	8,097.5	1,602.2	1,340.6	1.8	125,429	0.7
Latin America and the Caribbean	7,480	1.3	50.1	1.7	769.1	350.3	−1,049.1	−1.8	63,435	1.8
Northern America	50,042	14.2	50.1	1.9	5,760.4	453.2	1,219.9	3.6	2,972	0.0
Oceania	6,015	16.8	51.2	1.7	637.3	33.6	96.4	2.8	6,161	0.6

Source: UN Department of Economic and Social Affairs: Population Division (2009) *International Migration 2009.*

classical liberal economic thinking (which in many ways forms the basis of the structure of the global economy) claims that the purpose of capital is to generate profits, and even more capital. In order to maximise profits, capital will seek the most efficient and productive use for it, therefore rewarding sound economic endeavours and generating greater economic growth and prosperity. By removing governmental controls on where and when capital can be invested or removed, capital is allowed to be as useful and profitable as it can be.

There are also those observers who do not advocate classical liberal economic theory and who see the liberalisation of capital movement as a very negative and damaging aspect of the global economic system. In this view, if capital is allowed to be invested for any economic purpose (as long as it is legal) and in any market, this can lead to economic growth. However, capital investment may also harm the local community and environment, for example in the creation of factories and polluting industry. At the same time, if capital can just as easily be removed as it is invested then this detracts from economic security in the market in which it is invested. Furthermore, this freedom of movement allows capital to, in a sense, instigate a 'race to the bottom' as markets compete with each other for the capital investment. Markets will make themselves seem as desirable and profitable as possible to the owners of capital in order to out-bid their competitors. Providing capital investors with tax breaks, exemption from labour and environmental protection laws, and other forms of preferential treatment in order to attract it can lead to damaging effects for the people and environment. Even once the capital investment is secured, the threat of the capital moving to another market at any time is constant.

One of the clearest examples of such fears being realised is the Asian financial crisis of 1997–1998. On 2 July 1997 Thailand's baht began to rapidly devalue. The Thai currency suffered an almost 20 per cent devaluation over a two-month period after Thailand started to suffer from large speculative attacks and the bankruptcy of its largest finance company, Finance One. The first devaluation of the Thai baht was soon followed by devaluations of the Indonesian rupiah, the Philippine peso, the Malaysian ringgit and, to a lesser extent, the Singaporean dollar. By early November 1997 Hong Kong's stock market had collapsed, suffering a 40 per cent loss in October of that year. These financial and asset price crises set the stage for a second round of large currency depreciations. This time, not only the currencies of Thailand, Malaysia, Indonesia, the Philippines and Singapore were affected, but those of South Korea and Taiwan also suffered. The result of this crisis was massive negative growth in overall GDPs. Indonesia was worst hit as its economy shrank by approximately 80 per cent during the crisis, while the other states hit by the crisis saw their economies shrink by around 30 to 40 per cent.

In essence, the crisis was caused by fears of lower profits and economic recession in the newly developing states of South East Asia. The owners of capital feared that their investments in these states would not return suitable profits or would even lose money and so capital began to move out of these economies very rapidly (capital flight). As there were limited governmental controls on the movement of capital there was nothing anyone could do to stop the exodus. In short, fears of economic crisis became a self-fulfilling prophecy as the initial withdrawals of capital led other capital investors to fear the worst and withdrew their capital. The free movement of capital had helped these economies grow very rapidly since the 1970s as it flowed into their economies unhindered. But it just as easily flowed out unhindered. This has become a common fear of many governments and people around the world. Capital has become so privileged and controls on capital movement largely removed that states and markets now have to contend with each other and hope that capital comes in and stays in their economies. The threat of capital flight is ever-present and so capital mobility has become a key security issue in the twenty-first century.

At the same time as capital flight has become a major issue in contemporary international political economy, so too have financial crises caused by capital *immobility*. The global financial crisis that began in August 2007 with the sub-prime mortgage crisis in the US market has become the greatest economic crisis since the Great Depression of 1929 (Bellamy-Foster, J. and Magdoff, F., 2009). Practically every state has been hit with recession and the failure of private sector actors. Banks as well as other major economic entities have closed down very rapidly and in large numbers as they have gone bankrupt. Countless projects have been cancelled or put on hold around the world as funding has dried up. The crisis has demonstrated the incredibly high level of interdependence in the global economy and the lack of security against capital forces and trends shared by most states. The crisis has been caused by the slowing down of capital flows around the global economy as capital owners shy away from investing in markets and lending to each other. In effect capital is not moving around the world in large enough quantities and at a fast enough pace to satisfy all demands. Recession and decreased economic activity has followed and will only be replaced with economic growth and dynamic activity once capital begins to move faster again. Again, there are only so many means states and non-state actors have at their disposal to combat problems of capital movement. As has clearly been demonstrated by the economic collapse of Iceland (previously thought to be one of the most stable and healthy economies in the world), security threats are no longer simply about military action.

The revolution in military affairs

There are many phenomena which have shaped contemporary critical security studies and altered the security agenda in IPE. There has undoubtedly been a shift away from considering security as only pertaining to states as actors and military issues. Yet we cannot ignore military security or state security interests if we are going to consider security in IPE. Indeed, developments in the military sphere compel us to consider military security as being perhaps more important than ever before. As discussed above, the advent of nuclear weapons and the systems used to deliver them helped to reshape military affairs in the twentieth century and continue to do so today. At the same time, the nature of military interdependence was highlighted due to the possibility of large-scale destruction. In addition to nuclear weapons, new military technologies have emerged which have transformed the nature of modern warfare. These technologies have made war far more destructive, far more costly in financial terms and more efficient. Modern military technologies are sometimes said to be less costly in terms of civilian casualties as they are more 'accurate'. However, in reality military-industry complexes around the world continue to find more ways of killing and destroying – accuracy is often not sufficient or a matter of consideration.

The revolution in military affairs (RMA) that has taken place since the 1980s has altered the effects time and space have on military warfare. As a result military security has truly become a globalised issue (Benbow, T., 2004). Previously, states had to consider their immediate surroundings when assessing their military security. Stability and the lack of military threat from one's neighbours or near-abroad used to be sufficient to ensure one's own security. In the contemporary world, states must consider military threats from states much further away. The United States now has to think about states as far away as North Korea and even Iran when it considers the military security of not only overseas assets but the actual mainland US as well (in the same manner, practically every other state in the world must consider the United States' military capabilities in their security assessments). The development of intercontinental ballistic missiles (ICBMs), long-range stealth aircraft, fully automated machines and weapons of mass destruction (WMDs) all mean that the military reach of many states now exceeds their near-abroad.

This reorientation of how space impacts warfare also means that some states can engage in conflict from a long distance away while others do not possess the same projection capabilities. For example, unmanned US Air Force and Navy drones are increasingly being used in Afghanistan and Pakistan (even though the use of them in the airspace of the latter is a highly contentious issue) to combat the

Taliban. These drones are able to act as intelligence-gathering spy planes as well as platforms to launch highly destructive missiles. While these drones are launched from bases in the region and not very far from the theatre of operations, they are often 'piloted' by personnel back in the United States using satellite links. Others are programmed and, in effect, pilot themselves. Developments of unmanned drones and other technologies which allow one party to fight battles from far away are encouraging next-generation arms races. The ability of one state to posses these types of capabilities adds to its security yet detracts from the security of others and often renders existing military capabilities obsolete – even defensive ones. The twenty-first century may see many next-generation arms races and the realignment of security concerns.

EXAMPLE BOX

Invisible military forces(?)

By 2008 scientists at the University of California at Berkley in the United States had managed to engineer material which bends visible light around objects. The project is funded by the US military and the material has obvious military applications. By using molecular engineering, the Berkley scientists have been able to create material which has electromagnetic properties. These properties absorb electromagnetic radiation in the form of visible light and direct it around the material. The result is, in effect, the ability to cloak an object in the material and bend light around it. The observer looking at the object would actually see the reflection of light from behind the object, therefore making the object invisible to the naked eye.

The 'invisibility' material could be used to coat military equipment such as tanks, aircraft, ships and other weaponry which would make them appear invisible to the enemy. Coupled with existing 'stealth' technology, which makes objects invisible to radar and other detection methods (but not to direct visual observation), this new technology could mean that future battlefields house entirely invisible and undetectable forces. Suits for combat soldiers may also use the light-bending material to render soldiers invisible on the battlefield. Fears have been raised that this technology has already been used by military forces on individual soldiers in intelligence-gathering operations. However, the US military and the scientists at Berkeley claim that the technology is not that advanced yet and large quantities of the new material cannot be manufactured at this stage.

Clearly the development and application of 'invisibility' technology by military forces (and exclusively the US military at this point) would severely reduce the deterrent capabilities of other states. This would reduce their military security and so could cause further arms races.

The militarisation of space also has become an area to note. Space remains largely demilitarised but the use of satellites for military purposes and plans to develop military material for use in space may change this. Satellites orbiting the planet have long been employed by militaries for gathering information, communication and coordination. Current-generation missile technology uses satellite systems for guidance and targeting. Newer technologies include such things as anti-satellite missiles and space-based missile launch systems. The latter could be developed as part of an international missile defence system planned by the United States and some of its allies. One of the elements of this system would be missile-launching platforms orbiting the planet. Again, these developments would significantly alter existing notions of security and make the current military capabilities of most states entirely obsolete, thus leading these states to rearm themselves with more advanced technologies.

One of the more recent developments in modern warfare has been termed cyber warfare. As use of modern technologies linked to the Internet by governments and non-state actors increases, a new sphere for conflict has arisen. In most states, and especially in the most developed states in Europe, North America and South East Asia, the Internet and related technologies are used very widely. Governments, for example, now utilise the Internet for most of their functions. Military forces also widely use the Internet in some form or another (usually involving complex cyber security systems). Since the late 1990s developments in methods of conflict either using the Internet or targeting online capabilities have been seen. Cyber attacks on government and business targets which use the Internet can severely disrupt communications and standard operations. The advent of cyber attacks has created another form of security issue for both state and non-state actors. This has added to the reinterpretation of security as a concept in the contemporary world system.

An example of this form of security threat can be found in the experiences of the United States. In 1999 the email systems of several US government departments were overwhelmed by a massive surge in incoming spam-like emails which caused the systems to crash. The backlog of incoming illegitimate emails delayed and crowded out legitimate incoming emails and hindered outgoing messages. The disruption to communications and the functioning of various agencies was unprecedented and lasted several days. While never proven or admitted, the events of 1999 have been seen by some as a cyber attack on the United States originating from China. It is suggested that this (supposed) attack was in retaliation for the May 1999 bombing of the Chinese embassy in Belgrade, Serbia, by NATO forces during the Kosovo War.

International terrorism

Acts of terrorism are not something which are particularly new to international relations (no matter how one defines such an act or, indeed, what a 'terrorist' is). But the events in New York, Maryland and Pennsylvania on 11 September 2001 ushered in a new era of international relations characterised by the heightened importance of international terrorism (Halliday, F., 2001). The terrorist attacks on the United States in 2001 were largely unpredicted, at least with regard to the scope that they took place, even though intelligence services had predicted that an attack on the United States mainland was possible/was being attempted. The response of the United States and many parts of the international community to these attacks was to engage (perhaps it is more appropriate to say 're-engage') with an effort to combat terrorist networks (and terrorism itself as a concept) around the world. The initial phase of this 'war on terrorism' was the 2001 invasion of Afghanistan to remove the Taliban from government there and to defeat Al-Qaeda and apprehend its members deemed guilty of orchestrating the 2001 attacks. This phase remains incomplete as the Taliban are at the current time resurgent in Afghanistan and to an extent in Pakistan, and Al-Qaeda remains operational. Other elements of this war on terrorism have included changes in the roles and limitations of state institutions domestically (such as the suspension of some freedoms of speech, association and judicial processes) as well as greater freedom of action at the international level for some states and less for others.

A number of states around the world have utilised the war on terrorism as a pretext for pursuing domestic and foreign policy interests. In the mid 2000s Russia stepped up its campaigns against Chechen and other separatists in the Caucus while Israel reoccupied parts of the West Bank which had been handed over to the Palestinian Authority as part of the peace process there as well as invading Lebanon to stop attacks by Hezbollah, a group considered by many to be a terrorist organisation. Many authoritarian governments (such as Syria, Egypt, China and Uzbekistan) tightened their grips on power under the pretext of combating terrorists within their borders. Even in Western Europe and the United States civil freedoms have been reduced to some extent, as under the US Patriot Act. Meanwhile, terrorist organisations, and other organisations classed by some as terrorist, have been increasingly active. Many terrorist activities are targeted at the domestic level but there has been a significant increase in the scope of these types of activity and many acts of terrorism are now international in nature. As an introductory explanation, terrorist activities include acts of violence such as bombings (delivered using technology such as cars and telecommunication equipment; and people, as in suicide bombings), assassinations, sabotage and kidnappings, as well as the logistical, training and financing operations which support violent acts.

One of the key problems in international relations with regards to terrorism is the analysis of what causes people to engage in terrorism, how we define what is classed as a terrorist act and therefore who is a terrorist, and the impact of the war on terrorism on these things. In many cases the motivations of terrorists are clear and can be easily understood as relating to poverty, lack of political and economic opportunity, responses to policies and actions taken by some states which negatively impact on others and so on. In other cases, though, terrorism is motivated by criminal activity and is intertwined with broader processes of crime. It can be argued that international cooperation in law enforcement can be effective in combating terrorist groups. There has been a vast increase in the level of international cooperation in this field. At the same time, however, analysis suggests that, often, actions taken as part of the war on terrorism simply cause more terrorism. The US-led invasion and occupation of Iraq since 2003, for example, was founded upon a number of foreign policy goals which included combating terrorism. The conflict ultimately acted as a boon for terrorist organisations as well as legitimate resistance movements, both of which experienced rapid rises in numbers of recruits. As Iraq descended into less stability and order, terrorist groups such as Al-Qaeda were able not only to be based and operate in Iraq, but also to carry out attacks internationally. Until the root-causes of the poverty and disillusionment which encourage people to turn to 'terrorism' are studied and addressed, the threat of international terrorism and the war against it will continue.

Summary

The nature of security studies is such that as processes in the 'real world' take place and international relations change over time, the field of study also changes. This chapter has discussed some of the key developments which have led to a more comprehensive and critical approach to studying security issues. The emergence of nuclear weapons, environmental issues, identity politics and non-state actors (most notably the MNC) following the Second World War helped to transform how we define security, whose security we should consider and what security challenges are faced in the modern world. Critical security studies entails the consideration of state and non-state actors as well as individuals. Furthermore, in contemporary study security is no longer defined simply as military security but it is also defined as things like environmental, identity and financial security. There are now many issues which challenge our security. Some of these are still related to military security, especially in light of the RMA which is yielding ever more destructive weaponry and means to employ them. But we are also faced with challenges over the maintenance of our energy and food supplies, as well as the preservation of cultural identities. As has been shown by global financial crises, the interdependence and dynamic nature of the global economy has become extremely important to the economic security and well-being of individuals as well as states as a whole. As the human world develops and becomes ever more complex, so do the security challenges we face.

Reflective questions

1 Traditionally, 'security' has been seen as state- and military-centric. Is this still the case in the twenty-first century?
2 Which processes can you identify that have altered perceptions of security since the 1960s?
3 Why should we consider non-state actors when defining and discussing security issues?
4 In your opinion, which are the most significant security challenges in the contemporary world?
5 In what ways do increasing global energy and food demands, and dwindling supplies threaten your security?
6 How does the 2007–2009 global financial crisis demonstrate how economic interdependence can be a security threat?

Suggestions for further reading

Bellamy-Foster, J. and Magdoff, F. (2009) *The Great Financial Crisis: Causes and Consequences*, New York: Monthly Review Press.
Benbow, T. (2004) *The Magic Bullet? Understanding the Revolution in Military Affairs*, London: Chrysalis Books.
Booth, K. (2004) *Critical Security Studies and World Politics*, Boulder: Lynne Rienner Publishers.
Buzan, B., Ware, A. and Hoffmann-Martinot, V. (2007) *People, States & Fear: An Agenda for International Security Studies in the Post-Cold War Period,* 2nd edn, Colchester: ECPR Press.
Castle, S. (2008) *The Age of Migration: International Population Movements in the Modern World*, 4th edn, Basingstoke: Palgrave Macmillan.
Food and Agriculture Organization of the United Nations (2008) Aquastat Global Map: Total actual renewable water resources per inhabitant (http://www.fao.org/nr/water/aquastat/globalmaps/index.stm).
Garrison, N., Homer-Dixon, T. and Wright, R. (2009) *Carbon Shift: How the Twin Crises of Oil Depletion and Climate Change Will Define the Future*, New York: Random House.
Halliday, F. (2001) *Two Hours That Shook the World; September 11th 2001*, London: Saqi Books.
Homer-Dixon, T. (2001) *Environment, Scarcity and Violence*, Princeton: Princeton University Press.
Hough, P. (2007) *Understanding Global Security*, 2nd edn, New York: Routledge.
Ohmae, K. (1999) *The Borderless World: Power and Strategy in the Interlinked Economy*, London: Harper Paperbacks.
UN Department of Economic and Social Affairs: Population Division (2009) *International Migration 2009*.

Concluding thoughts and remarks

This book can be used as an interpretive guide to actual events in the 'real world', but also to differing positions that interpret and describe these events. Of course, there are going to be differing views/perspectives on all issues and phenomena, but having read this book you should now be able to assess these in a more informed and critical manner.

One might assume that theoretical positions are relatively fixed, given their key concepts and assumptions. While this is true to some extent, all theories are constantly open to challenge and critique. As is demonstrated in Chapter 1, on the theoretical foundations of IPE, and Chapter 2, on mainstream contemporary approaches, each school of thought has a particular world view which is increasingly subject to challenge as global systems and structures evolve. Some theorists may interpret these changes as reinforcing their core beliefs. Others may struggle to rationalise their theoretical position in relation to emerging processes and their consequences. The alternative approaches discussed in Chapter 3 are necessarily more in tune with processes of globalisation given their relatively recent evolution. Nevertheless, even some of these approaches can include some quite dogmatic and fixed positions and opinions.

The debate surrounding the extent and significance of processes of globalisation continues. There is no clear consensus on this with actively competing views between the hyperglobalists and the sceptics. Even the transformationalists remain far from being a homogeneous group, with differing protagonists emphasising differing aspects of globalisation as being significant. Regardless of one's position within the globalisation debate, even arch sceptics, it is undeniable that the world is experiencing some significant changes. For example, the national security agenda of the twenty-first century is different to that of the eighteenth, nineteenth or twentieth centuries. Basic principles of sovereignty, citizenship and self-determination may be ongoing concepts but how each of these are understood and promoted has changed. Similarly, the issues covered in the above chapters have also undergone elements of transformation both in terms of the actual phenomena and their relative position on national and international agendas.

The jigsaw analogy referred to at the start of this book can be applied in relation to the various issues under consideration here. However, depending on which approach you are taking you may have a different set of 'jigsaw pieces' compared to someone who favours a differing theoretical approach. For example, classical realists only deal with states and how they relate to each other. They do not have 'pieces' that represent individuals or other species. The liberal approach would be more complex as it would include 'pieces' for numerous non-state actors. At the same time, green theorists would wish to consider the whole spectrum of biological and environmental interactions. Some of these approaches are clearly more complex in their approach than others, yet each is able to construct a world view with its own internal logic and rationale.

All of the issues that have been discussed in this book overlap and interrelate to some extent. Governance, for example, can be seen in relation to international/global finance and trade via the Bretton Woods institutions. Issues of environment and development are closely related to finance and trade, but are generally dealt with in alternative forums. There is, therefore, a certain tension and potential conflict between the actors and agendas in these two discrete but related areas. Cultural issues have not normally been part of traditional security agendas. However, in recent years the security agenda has evolved to include many more non-military issues. This is reflected in the culture, environment, development and technology chapters. As such, it is clear that the division of issue areas in IPE is increasingly difficult to maintain given the close connections between them. Furthermore, some issues which are of importance to IPE such as health and media, while not being addressed in individual chapters in this book are still relevant and have been included in discussions regarding other issues.

As a practical guide this book should have provided you with an insight into the range of issues that form part of the study of IPE. You will have seen differing interpretations and emphasis placed on certain aspects of international political economy. As you continue with your studies you should be able to return to this book and read it afresh in light of your growing understanding of the subject area. In particular you will find the further reading lists in each chapter a useful starting point for extending your awareness and understanding of IPE. The Companion Website will also be a useful tool with contemporary examples and analyses of case studies as well as further reflective questions, learning tasks and resources.

Glossary

absolute advantage   A position developed by Adam Smith representing the ability of one state to produce a good more efficiently and cheaply than other states. When a state has absolute advantage it benefits from trading with others through specialisation in this good(s) and the importation of goods for which the production costs are lower abroad.

alienation   The concept created by Karl Marx denoting the effects of class conflict and materialism on the identities and associations of the individual. Through the competition for material possessions and wealth individuals are separated from each other, and in particular across class boundaries, in an atmosphere of mistrust and belligerency.

anarchy   The absence of a centralised authority which governs the behaviour of actors within any given theatre of relations. At the global level of analysis this equates to the absence of a global government which creates and enforces rules of behaviour for states and multinational/transnational actors.

autarky   The concept of being self-sufficient and self-reliant. An actor possesses this ability if it can survive in its form and function without relying on interactions with other actors such as trade for the import of goods and services or export for raising revenues.

balance of payments   An accounting system used to calculate and record a state's international financial transactions related to the import and export of goods, services and capital. Ideally the inward flow of financial resources should equal the outward flow to ensure a balance.

balance of trade   The net worth of a state's exports and imports of goods and services. Higher exports than imports will result in a trade surplus while higher imports will lead to a trade deficit. The balance of trade often does not remain constant and (short-term) surpluses or deficits are common.

banks   Financial institutions which act as repositories for capital deposits and sources of borrowed capital. Banks take in deposits and lend a large amount of them to other actors as investments for interest returns. In this way they act as mechanisms which direct capital supplies to areas of demand (from depositors to borrowers).

bilateralism   Form of policy making and action which involves interaction between two actors. This type of relationship is largely characterised by communication and coordination between the two actors resulting in agreement on a course of mutual action.

bonds   Credit instruments which are issued by governments or corporations in exchange for capital to cover expenditures which cannot be covered by existing resources. These are usually long-term instruments which can be traded on international markets and have variable values depending on interest rates and the ability of the issuer to generate capital.

Bretton Woods   Post-Second World War global system of political and economic organisation based on liberal ideologies. It is named after the New Hampshire, USA, town which hosted the 1944 conference between the Allied powers that would go on to win the war and create the post-war organisations and regimes which would seek to regulate international relations for much of the twentieth century. The system consisted of the three core organisations and related regimes: the IMF, the World Bank and the GATT/WTO. The system is seen to have ended in its original form with the 1971 end of the dollar–gold conversion mechanism. But the regimes and the structure that it established remain in most ways.

capital   A term which has a number of meanings in different theoretical contexts but which is most commonly used in classical/neo-classical economics to refer to man-made physical resources used to generate goods and services as well as financial resources. In order to generate the former the latter needs to be available and invested where market demands arise. Other traditions see the term as also referring to labour and natural resources which go into productive processes.

capital accounts   Part of the balance of payments between states. This is the existing amount of capital within a state and the amount of capital being exchanged with others. If there are fewer capital resources in one state compared to the demand for capital then imports of capital are required. Where there is a surplus of capital in one state's account then capital may be invested abroad (exported).

capital markets   The sources of excess or under-utilised capital resources which can be accessed by actors or markets with capital shortages. These markets rely on intermediary institutions which act as mechanisms to connect capital supply (savings) with capital demand (borrowers). Largely characterised by high fluidity, these markets are central to the well-being of the contemporary global economy.

capitalism/capitalist production   A system of organising human activity and production which largely relies on competition between actors for the accumulation of productive capabilities, resources, wealth and power. According to liberal triumphalists this is the highest form of human development and the last stage in the movement from the original human condition to its final condition. Market forces determine production and other human activity through supply and demand mechanisms.

civil society   Sub-state collective of individuals into directly or indirectly associated groups with similar motivations and interests. Often seen as acting as a key entity occupying the space between state apparatus and the masses. This can be local/domestic, national, international or even global in scope as well as focused on private or public sector issues.

class   Seen as the main way in which people are grouped together in the capitalist world system. An individual's role in, and relationship to, the means of production and capital formation and movement determines which class one is associated with. For Marxists the labourers that operate in production are seen as the proletariat while the owners of the means of production and those that facilitate the allocation of capital are the bourgeoisie. In the modern/postmodern era the classes are seen as being in conflict due to the maintenance of the position of each by the other.

climate change   The result of a set of environmental processes which are, at of the time of writing, not universally accepted or understood. Characterised by rapid changes in climatic conditions and in particular the raising of global temperatures and changing environmental patterns which seem to be linked to human agency (industrialisation and the burning of fossil fuels). Sea level rises, desertification, drought and decreasing fresh water supplies are linked to climate change and are negatively impacting the human condition for many around the world.

common market   Level of regional integration between states characterised by the establishment of a customs union or its equivalent, as well as the unrestricted movement of capital and labour. Member states will negotiate the deregulation of common borders and markets to ensure a high level of economic integration and the accompanying regime(s). This is classed as the final stage of regional integration.

comparative advantage   David Ricardo's development of the concept of absolute advantage which addresses the limitations of the latter in a global economy. A state has a comparative advantage in the production of a certain good if it produces it at a lower cost than other goods it produces. This is an important neo-liberal assumption which supports arguments for specialisation and free trade.

conditionality   Notion employed by one actor towards another when the former is approached for assistance by the latter. Most commonly used to refer to the terms governing the supply of financial support by the IMF to member states. Here the provider of support will request certain changes in policy or behaviour by the borrowing state in exchange for its support. It can also apply to bilateral and multilateral relations between states.

corporation   A business entity which can be created with various productive functions supplying goods, services or capital to consumer markets. This type of actor has an undetermined lifetime, raises capital through shared ownership with private shareholders but has limited liability and is unlimited in potential size. The 'bottom line' of corporations is to maximise profits and grow in size.

current account   The key element in calculating balance of payments, measuring a state's net flows of imports and exports of goods, services and capital.

debt   The total amount of capital resources an actor has borrowed in the past and owes to another actor (the creditor). Global access to capital markets means that debt is no longer held by one actor to another in the same state/market but can be owed to an actor almost anywhere else in the global system.

debt crisis   The name given to the global phenomenon which emerged in the early 1980s when many states around the world, but primarily in the developing world, defaulted on debt previously taken from other governments and private sector actors. During the oil boom years of the 1970s petrodollars were readily available as capital deposits and were used to lend to states which were seen as being unable to 'go bust'. Variable and very high interest rates coupled with economic stagnation resulted in wide-ranging governmental defaults and the inability to service long-term debts. The problem continues at the start of the twenty-first century.

debt relief   As a result of the debt crisis many states have sought the cancellation or rearranging of debt owed to external actors. Bilateral and multilateral agreements have resulted in some rescheduling and cancelling of some developing states' debts but interest rates and repayments remain unmanageable by many.

decentralisation   A term used to describe the devolution of governance from a central authority to peripheral authorities. This usually relates to the deregulation of human activity by state governments to local governments but can also refer to more widespread deregulation where private sector actors assume the role of (limited) governance.

deficit   The condition which emerges when expenditures exceed the available revenues over a period of time. This is most commonly a term used when discussing governmental budgets over a fiscal year or the budgets of corporations.

deindustrialisation   Term referring to the reduction of productive capacity within an economy. States may pursue this course of action and replace the lost manufactured goods through imports while specialising in knowledge-based sectors. Also a policy suggested by some environmentalists in order to protect the environment.

democratisation   The process of reform of instruments of governance which leads to representative and accountable government. It is often a slow process which relies upon the emergence of a strong middle class and private sector.

dependency theory   Approach largely developed by Andre Gunder Frank which suggests that international relations between states are characterised by asymmetric integration. One state relies upon another to a large extent for essential products and services such as technology, manufactured goods, capital and security. These types of relationships are structural in nature and are fixed. Most commonly used to explain the relationship between rich and poor states and the reason for underdevelopment.

depression   An economic condition characterised by significantly declining levels of income, production, investment and employment. Can be restricted to individual states but in the globalised economic system depressions usually affect many states at any one time.

derivatives   Financial products whose value is derived from that of other products or processes. Using some version or other of mathematic models for calculating the price or expected change in price of a package of investment products, derivatives are established. These emerged in the 1990s as important investment vehicles. By the 2000s, they had taken so many varied forms that it had become impossible to define very accurately what a derivative is or was. Those selling derivatives had to understand both the mathematics and the markets they were dealing with if they were to succeed without simply engaging in a dressed-up gamble.

development   This is a term which can be used in many different settings. In contemporary IPE development usually means economic growth and modern industrialisation measured primarily by GDP and per capita incomes. However, alternative approaches to IPE can view development as being measured in different ways such as the meeting of basic needs for all, access to education and health services, democracy, human security and environmental sustainability, among others.

developmental state   Type of government policy employed over long periods of time by developing states as they pursue greater economic growth and industrialisation. This relies on government support of domestic industries (especially infant and high-value-added industries) and the maintenance of external barriers to imports. Many newly industrialised economies such as the East Asian Tiger Economies adopted this type of policy to develop but the notion of a 'developmental state' is counter to the Washington Consensus and the neo-liberalism of the global economic system.

economies of scale   These can emerge as a result of improvements in the production process of a good. The main characteristic is the reducing of unit production costs as a result of increases in the number of units produced which derives from greater investment and increasing efficiency of production. Of course economies of scale can only emerge when the demand for the good being produced is sufficiently high; states with small domestic markets must access foreign markets to develop economies of scale.

efficiency   The efficient production of a good or service is measured by the combination of the natural resources, labour and capital which are used in the production process as well as its duration. Fewer inputs and shorter time taken to produce a good or service results in higher efficiency.

exchange rate system   The system by which national currencies are exchanged in global markets. This system is founded on certain rules which specify the ways in which appreciation and depreciation of currencies can take place. Fixed exchange rate systems require governments to control the amount of currency movements to limit variations in exchange rates to a narrow rate. In a floating exchange rate system governments can allow currency movements to whatever rate they want.

factor endowment   An actor's (most commonly used to refer to states) endowment of labour, land, capital and natural resources – known as factor endowments.

fair trade   System of international trade which requires a greater level of government and civil society involvement to influence or control the exchange of goods and services. This is a more recent phenomenon in IPE which has been used or desired to help developing states to get a fair price for their products and to get fair access to more developed markets. Regulation in some areas is needed, such as the governmental certification that goods are produced using suitable labour and resources.

false consciousness   One of Karl Marx's core assumptions about modern human society. The masses are burdened with false consciousness as a result of their alienation from each other and the means of production as well as hegemonic forms of knowledge and materialism. This is characterised by the inability to understand the origins of their condition and the ability for change.

fiscal policy   A strategy used by governments to influence domestic demand through tax and spending policies. By expanding government spending and/or reducing taxes governments can help to encourage domestic economic demand and output. By reducing spending and/or raising taxes governments can discourage economic demand and output.

foreign aid   Official or private sector financial support given by one actor to another. This usually is given by developed states to developing states to assist in development projects or to deal with sudden and significant burdens. Foreign aid can come with some conditionality but often only requires some form of guarantee as to where the support is being utilised. Bilateral and multilateral agreements on foreign aid are quite common in the contemporary era but are criticised for not doing enough to help developing societies.

foreign direct investment   The financial and resource investment in one state by an actor in another state. Usually a corporation or group of individuals based in one state builds or purchases productive capabilities in another state in the pursuit of maximising profits.

foreign exchange   The purchasing of an amount of capital in one currency by using an equal amount in value terms of another currency. Exchange rates rarely remain constant unless the relevant governments have pursued a policy of pegging currencies to each other.

free trade   The deregulation of international trade through the removal of governmental barriers to trade, including taxes, tariffs and quotas on imports and exports. The removal of official barriers to trade is seen in neo-classical economics to facilitate international trade and investment, thus encouraging development and integration. Much criticism has been levelled at the notion of free trade by developing states as it removes protection for domestic infant and sensitive industries (which are seen by many as the keys to industrialisation).

free trade agreement   A bilateral or multilateral agreement engaged in by governments to facilitate trade in goods, services and capital between them by removing barriers to trade such as taxes, tariffs and quota limits. Some free trade agreements cover the liberalisation of all trade while others only cover trade in certain products and services. Most will require a number of years for full implementation as barriers are reduced to zero in stages. Free trade agreements are key components of the Washington Consensus.

globalisation   Name given to represent processes of integration between states/markets/peoples at the global level of analysis. Through these processes actors in one part of the world can become interdependent with others in geographically distant places.

gross domestic product (GDP)   The total monetary value of goods and services produced in an economy in one year. In IPE this measure is primarily used to measure the production value of national economies but can also be used to measure the production values of common markets, regional groupings and the global economy as a whole.

hegemonic stability   Most famously developed and articulated by Charles Kindleberger in the early 1970s. It argues that a dominant state is needed to enforce rules of interaction between states in order to avoid the security dilemmas and instability associated with a system that lacks the oversight of such a power.

hierarchy   The ranking of actors in any given arena according to their power, wealth, influence and productive capabilities. For example, if a state's capabilities are greater compared to others, this state will sit atop the hierarchy.

historical materialism   An approach to understanding and explaining human relations by analysing modes of production and the relationship of individuals to these as well as looking at how the changes in production affect society. This is a core Marxist approach which sees the human condition as being determined by the historical drive for greater productive capabilities.

hyperinflation   Rapid inflation within a state over a period of time which results in rapid and catastrophic falls in the value of its currency.

imperialism   The political, economic and in some ways cultural domination by one state over others. The imperial state will use its greater power and productive capabilities to dominate others and alter the patterns of production and economic exchange to its benefit. Imperialism is largely characterised by the monopolisation of international relations by the imperial power while other states are isolated from each other. Imperialism is seen as a thing of the past, most often equated with the European imperialism of the 1600s to mid 1900s.

import substitution   A strategy used by developing states or states pursuing greater levels of self-reliance. This entails governmental support of targeted domestic industries which produce goods or services which would normally be obtained from foreign sources. It is often costly and directs resources to activities which are less efficient than others but raises independence from external actors and can lead to efficiency over time.

Industrial Revolution   The process of economic transformation which began in the UK and north-western Europe in the mid 1700s. This revolution was founded on technological developments which allowed for the use of fossil fuels as sources of power and machinery in production. The result was the rapid increase in productivity and efficiency which led to significantly greater economic wealth and productive capabilities.

inflation   A constant increase in the absolute consumer price of goods and services due to an inability of supply to meet demand; or the constant decline in the purchasing power of money due to an increase in the amount of money circulating in the economy which is not met by a corresponding increase in available goods or services.

intellectual property rights (IPRs)   Legal recognition of the exclusive ownership rights of the creator for new creations or production processes. The tools for ensuring protection of this recognition include patents, trademarks, copyright and trade secrets.

interest rates   The payment made to savers for gaining access to the capital resources they make available. This is usually facilitated by banks and is a tool which encourages savers to make the funds available for investment elsewhere. It is usually determined by a percentage or rate which may or may not be fixed depending on the agreement established at the time capital is made available.

interdependence   Dependence as described by Robert Keohane and Joseph Nye is a state of existence that is determined or affected by external forces. Interdependence, therefore, is quite simply a condition where mutual dependence exists between two or more actors. In a situation of asymmetric interdependence two or more actors are dependent on each other but to varying degrees. In a system of complex interdependence the use of military force or other forms of violent confrontation will be counter-productive and irrational due to the reliance of actors on each other.

invisible hand   Also referred to as the invisible hand of the market: a term used to identify the self-regulating nature of the free market. The term was first coined by Adam Smith and includes the key processes of supply, demand, competition and efficiency as ways in which resources are allocated to further production and development. State regulation or involvement in the market is seen as preventing the work of the invisible hand.

labour   The contribution that individuals collectively make to the production of a good or service.

laissez-faire   A French term meaning 'to let be' or 'to allow'; this idea is synonymous with free trade policies. The *laissez-faire* school of thought holds a pure capitalist or free market view that capitalism is best left to its own devices. The basic idea is that less governmental interference in private economic matters, such as pricing, production and distribution, makes for a better system.

letters of credit   A binding commercial document which is usually issued by a bank or other financial institution which obliges the applicant to make a payment of a fixed amount to a beneficiary at a future date. This tool is normally applied in international trade of substantial value and/or where the applicant and the beneficiary are in separate states.

liquid assets   Things that can be used in a crisis to pay demands for money which include cash reserves, short-term debt and gold and other precious metals.

macroeconomics   The consideration of overall economic processes and characteristics. This area of political economy explores issues at the macro level such as overall production, consumption, supply and demand, GDP, employment levels, debt, trade, fiscal policy and capital accounts.

market   A term with varying meanings but which in contemporary IPE means the way in which the economic activity of societies is organised for production and consumption of goods and services. This is in effect the 'place', albeit in abstract form, and ways in which goods and services are produced and purchased.

Marshall Plan   A broad-ranging foreign policy strategy employed by the Truman Administration in the United States following the Second World War. This policy provided vast amounts of financial and productive aid to Western European states as they sought to rebuild after the war as a means of promoting markets for US goods and services and as a bulwark against the growth of communist movements in Europe.

means of production   In the modern global economic system these are things which are usually owned by private corporations but can be communally owned in some states/systems. These are the actual structures and equipments used in the production of goods and services.

medium of exchange   This is a key function of money but does not exclusively refer to money alone. In order to purchase a certain good or service something needs to be given in return but rather than relying on a system of pure bartering an object of a given value can be used in multiple transactions. This is most commonly now money but can be other things such as metals.

mercantilism   Central concern within realist strands of thought with the security of the state. The security of a state was seen as directly related to its power in relation to other states. This security can be enhanced not just by the creation of a large and well-equipped army but also by the acquisition of wealth. At the domestic level this leads to policies designed to maximise tax revenues and at the international level to pursue an overall trade surplus.

monetary policy   A governmental strategy used to influence the economic activity which takes place in a given economy by controlling the supply of money available. This may take two forms: either expanding the money supply to stimulate economic activity in a depression or restricting it to discourage inflation in an economic upturn.

monopoly   A condition where a single actor dominates the production of a certain good or service in a market and so can control the supply and cost of these commodities.

most-favoured nation status (MFN)   A WTO rule which requires that any preferential treatment between two WTO member states in terms of the framework governing trade between them must be given to all other members and reciprocated. If two states agree to bilaterally lower barriers to trade with each other, they must also give the same treatment to all other WTO member states.

multilateralism   Form of policy making and action which involves interaction between three or more actors. This type of relationship is largely characterised by communication and coordination between the group of actors resulting in agreement on a course of mutual action.

multinational corporation (MNC)   A corporation which has commercial activities, including production of goods and/or services as well as capital investments, in more than one state. In the contemporary global economy such entities tend to be very large and are usually headquartered in one state while having operations in a large number of others.

mutually assured destruction (MAD)   During the Cold War, with the proliferation of nuclear weapons between the United States and the USSR, this term arose to represent the effects of a nuclear conflict. Once each side had reached what they saw as an effective first-strike capability, the need arose to develop a second-strike capability which would allow them to launch a devastating attack even after sustaining a full assault from the other side. Even with their first strikes both states would still be hit with the rival's second-strike capabilities and thus be destroyed.

neo-classical economics   This is the dominant school of economic thought in the capitalist system. Its fundamental focus is on the deregulation of economic activity and the acceptance of purely market forces to determine production, prices, employment and so on. It is based on the belief that unhindered competition in the market will lead to maximum efficiency, productivity and self-regulation. In policy terms neo-classical economics manifests in free trade, open markets and *laissez-faire* economics.

neo-imperialism   The term given to the modern exploitation and domination of poorer societies/states by richer ones. Here, military conquest and direct political control is no longer seen as the requisites for imperialism. Rather, it is structures which promote economic relationships which are similar to those evident in the era of European imperialism and which result in developing states being dependent on the wealthier and more powerful states. Furthermore, these structures are only alterable by the developed states that create them.

neo-liberalism   In the contemporary global system this term represents the marked shift away from the pursuit of governmental involvement in the economy and towards placing greater responsibility for economic processes on the market itself. This type of change is favoured and actively pursued by many governments in the West but also, importantly, by the large international institutions established as part of the Bretton Woods System.

oligopoly   A condition where a small number of actors dominate the production of a certain good or service in a market and so can coordinate with each other to control the supply and cost of these commodities.

open markets   Markets which are fully liberalised, having no barriers to external trade in products, services and capital as well as fewer restrictions on the movement of labour.

per capita income   The amount each person earns if the total national income is divided equally across the population.

power   Most commonly defined as the ability of one actor to make a second behave/not behave in a way which it would not/would normally act. This can be reliant on a number of categories of capability or a combination of them. For example, wealth, military power and political influence.

prisoner's dilemma   Game theory model where two prisoners are held in isolation from each other and the release, or non-release, of each is determined by the action of the other. Crucially, which outcome is arrived at is determined by each prisoner assessing the probability of how the other prisoner responds to questioning. It is commonly used to predict behaviour and policy directions by focusing on the likelihood of cooperation or cheating.

protectionism   Governmental policy which aims to protect domestic industries (usually infant or sensitive industries) from external competition. Tools available include taxes, quotas and other tariffs on imports as well as subsidies on exports.

purchasing power parity (PPP)   An economics method used to determine the relative capabilities of individuals in different states to purchase goods and services. Using per capita GDP methods does not accurately portray the comparative living standards of people in different states because the costs of goods and services may differ from one state to another. By comparing consumer prices of produce and adjusting relative capabilities to purchase, a clearer picture can be established of the comparative wealth of individuals in different states.

real interest rates   When trying to accurately compare interest rates in different states it is essential to take account of differing national inflation rates. Real interest rates are determined by deducting the rate of inflation from the actual or nominal rate of interest.

regimes   These are the combination of procedures, rules/laws, values, ideas, norms and traditions in order to form a way of organising specific forms of international relationships such as trade. States which join such a regime will find their behaviour and expectations influenced accordingly/to some extent. Regimes can be described as collections of non-tangible institutions which are supported by organisations: so the WTO supports the global trading regime.

regionalism   Can operate within a national boundary or, more commonly, within the context of international political economy, across several nation states. Some regions are identified by their geographical location, such as the tropics or temperate regions. Others are known by their economic interactions, such as the North American Free Trade Area. The most advanced form of regionalism to date is the European Union, which has elements of a common currency, integrated military units and a degree of supranationality with some legislation taking precedence over national parliaments.

regulation   A government or intergovernmental policy to control aspects of a 'free' market. This may be on the grounds of common public good, such as health and safety regulations, to avoid monopolies forming or to reduce the risk of market failure.

rentier   Can be an individual whose income is predominantly derived from rents. A rentier state is one where its income comes from the export of its natural resources such as oil or timber. Renting out part of the state's sovereign territory to allow another power to develop military bases there may also generate external income.

savings   An important part of both personal and governmental economic strategies. They are the difference between disposable income and expenditure. There are marked differences between attitudes towards saving for either a specific purchase or as a precaution against unforeseen expenditures and the counter-position of not only avoiding savings but actually exceeding affordable expenditure, funded by taking out secured loans.

scarcity   A fundamental aspect of the international political economy as it drives market demand and pricing of commodities. The more widely a product is available, the greater the opportunity for competition between providers, unless a monopoly of provision applies, and this is likely to drive costs down. The model of supply and demand therefore suggests that as a commodity's scarcity increases, a rise in its value will follow.

securitisation A process by which assets, such as mortgaged property, are treated as commodities which can be bought and sold. If a lender defaults on a repayment that has been 'secured' in relation to property or some other tangible good then the lender can repossess whatever has been offered as security for the loan.

self-interest Refers to any policy or action taken which in the interest of the actor initiating such action, or possibly reaction to the acts of others.

self-regulation A concept that can be applied to a range of activities. In the context of international political economy it is mainly associated with the private sector and the attempts by multinational corporations to monitor and control their actions in the absence of international authority to do so.

socialism A system of social organisation whereby the ownership and control of the means of production and distribution of capital and other goods rests with the community as a whole. In Marxist theory socialism is seen as the stage following capitalism in the transition to a fully communal society.

sovereignty A key element of the modern state system. The concept of there being no higher authority above the sovereign state underpins the majority of international relations. This remains the case despite many processes of globalisation that appear to be making national boundaries more open to external influence. These include growing economic interdependence, trans-boundary pollution and electronic communications that bypass governmental controls.

stocks Stocks and shares are tradable commodities which are the basis of business at various stock exchanges around the world. Investors and speculators will buy stock, or a share, of certain commodities or businesses in the hope that over time the value of this stock will rise, thereby producing a profit should the relevant stocks or shares be sold on. Of course these values can also decline so there can be a lot of volatility in certain markets. Traders try to follow patterns in the fluctuation of stock and share prices in order to judge when to buy or sell in order to maximise profit.

structure Structure can take many forms. This may be in the political, economic or even socio-cultural fields. Structures are not always easily identifiable. Johan Galtungs' theory of 'structural violence' highlights how particular aspects of structures within which they operate can disadvantage certain individuals. For example, women living in a patriarchy are likely to face a range of gender-based disadvantages and discriminations.

surplus value The difference between what a product costs to produce and what it is actually sold for. In other words it is the profit margin. Neo-Marxist and structuralists pay particular attention to this value as it is often closely tied to the role of labour and the way in which this is undervalued under capitalism.

sustainable development A term that has become something of a 'catch all' phrase that is open to many varied interpretations and has, therefore, lost much of its original substance. In essence it refers to a type of development where the needs of the current generation are met without compromising the ability of future generations to meet their own needs. This definition still holds true but is clearly compromised to some extent when there is a lack of consensus on how to define 'development'.

tariffs   Imposed by governments as a form of import duty. In addition to raising revenue for the national exchequer this is also a method by which domestic industries can be 'protected' from cheap imports. Despite the rhetoric of the majority of the world's governments and economists that embrace and promote free market economic policies there remains considerable evidence of the imposition of tariffs and other barriers to trade, particularly in relation to agricultural produce exported from the global South to the global North.

technology   Can often be thought of in terms of 'hi-tech' applications to weaponry, communications, health sciences or a range of other applications. However, it can also be relatively 'low' levels of technological development that can prove to be decisive. The invention of the stirrup, for example, created a cavalry force that proved superior to infantry forces. Similarly, it is low or intermediate technology such as solar cookers or small-scale hydropower projects that is at the forefront of meeting the basic needs of the world's poorest people.

Third World   A term which has its origins in the time of the French Revolution and the so-called 'third estate'. More recently it has come to be associated with the developing countries of the global South. In this scenario the US, Western Europe and similarly 'developed' states were seen as the First World, with the communist bloc states the Second World in the bipolar world order of the Cold War. Third World is less commonly used to describe the developing states as it has gained a rather negative association of backwardness and helplessness. Full consensus has yet to be achieved on a suitable alternative epithet.

trade   The range and diversity of traded goods in the contemporary global economy is immense. This is based on a system of exchange that can be traced back to the earliest human communities and their interactions. The exchange of goods and services may be based on raw materials, manufactured products and a range of services to facilitate this trade.

transaction costs   The costs incurred as a result of a particular exchange of goods or services. These may be in connection to the respective values of what is exchanged in terms of which buyer or seller makes the most profit or loss. Alternatively costs may be of a more abstract nature with regard to issues related to but not directly associated with a particular exchange. Trading with one partner may alienate other potential partners if they disapprove of this transaction. Other costs could include the use of intermediaries or some form of payment made to facilitate a transaction, such as the commission charged when buying or selling different currencies.

unilateralism   A policy or other action that is taken by a single actor, or single representative of a collection of actors, which is not part of an agreement with other actors. An example of this could be a unilateral declaration of independence, rather than a managed and agreed timetable towards independence.

veto   A position taken which effectively prevents the implementation of a proposal or action. For example, on the UN Security Council the five permanent members have the power of veto, which enables any one of them to block resolutions put before the Council.

Washington Consensus   The post-Second World War agreement between the major powers which established the Bretton Woods international financial institutions and agreed the criteria by which the post-war international economic system would be coordinated and managed.

Westphalian system   The Treaty of Westphalia (1648) marked the end of the Thirty-Year War in Europe. It is also often referred to as the start of the modern nation state system. This system places national sovereignty as its central guiding principle. There is no international authority higher than national government, with an ethos of self-help and non-intervention between sovereign states.

world-system theory   A view of the world which takes into account relatively long periods of history with a particular emphasis on the expansion of European empires and resulting patterns of trade. As wealth flowed from the colonies to the centre of power of each empire this maintained and reinforced the 'core/periphery' relationship between the colonisers and their subjugated territories. Importantly, this underlying relationship has continued to impact upon the relative division of power in the international system well beyond the period in formal decolonisation.

zero-sum game   The result of a competition or exchange where there is a finite and balanced amount of profit or loss. For example, an equal division would be a 50/50 split, or there may be a variation of 49/51 or 1/99, but whatever is gained from one actor in a relationship is necessarily lost by another, with the total value of the resources under dispute remaining the same. In contrast, a non-zero-sum game can see both win–win and lose–lose outcomes.

Index